Praise for *RESTful Web APIs*

"This book is the best place to start learning the essential craft of API Design."

—Matt McLarty
Cofounder, API Academy

"The entire time I read this book, I was cursing. I was cursing because as I read each explanation, I was worried that they were so good that it would be hard to find a better one to use in my own writing. You will not find another work that explores the topic so thoroughly yet explains the topic so clearly. Please, take these tools, build something fantastic, and share it with the rest of the world, okay?"

—Steve Klabnik
Author, *Designing Hypermedia APIs*

"Wonderfully thorough treatment of hypermedia formats, REST's least well understood tenet."

—Stefan Tilkov
REST evangelist, author, and consultant

"The best practical guide to hypermedia APIs. A must-have."

— Ruben Verborgh
Semantic hypermedia researcher

RESTful Web APIs

Leonard Richardson and Mike Amundsen
Foreword by Sam Ruby

Beijing · Cambridge · Farnham · Köln · Sebastopol · Tokyo

RESTful Web APIs

by Leonard Richardson and Mike Amundsen with a Foreword by Sam Ruby

Printed in the United States of America.

Published by O'Reilly Media, Inc., 1005 Gravenstein Highway North, Sebastopol, CA 95472.

O'Reilly books may be purchased for educational, business, or sales promotional use. Online editions are also available for most titles (*http://safaribooksonline.com*). For more information, contact our corporate/institutional sales department: 800-998-9938 or *corporate@oreilly.com*.

Editors: Simon St. Laurent and Meghan Blanchette	**Indexer:** Judith McConville
Production Editor: Christopher Hearse	**Cover Designer:** Randy Comer
Copyeditor: Jasmine Kwityn	**Interior Designer:** David Futato
Proofreader: Linley Dolby	**Illustrator:** Rebecca Demarest

September 2013:   First Edition

Revision History for the First Edition:

2013-09-10:   First release

2015-05-22:   Second release

See *http://oreilly.com/catalog/errata.csp?isbn=9781449358068* for release details.

ISBN: 978-1-449-35806-8

[LSI]

For Sienna, Dalton, and Maggie. —Leonard

For Milo "The Supervisor," my constant and patient companion throughout this and so many other projects. Thanks, buddy! —Mike

Table of Contents

Foreword

Progressive Disclosure is a concept in User Interface Design which advocates only presenting to the user the information they need when they need it. In many ways, the book you are reading right now is an example of this principle. In fact, it is quite likely that this book wouldn't have "worked" a mere seven years ago.

For you see, the programming world was quite a different place when *RESTful Web Services*, the predecessor of this book, was written. At that time, the term "REST" was was rarely used. And when it was used it was often misapplied, and widely misunderstood.

This was the case despite the fact that the standards upon which REST is based, namely HTTP and HTML, were developed and became IETF and W3C standards in roughly their current form in the second half of the 1990s. Roy Fielding's thesis paper in which he introduced the term REST and on which this book was based was itself published in 2000.

Leonard Richardson and I set out to correct this injustice. To do this, we focused primarily on the concepts underpinning HTTP, and we provided practical guidance on how to apply those concepts to applications.

I'd like to think that we helped kick a few pebbles loose that started the avalanche of support for REST that came forth since that time. REST rapidly took on a life of its own, and in the process has become a buzzword. In fact it now is pretty much the case that presenting a web interface and calling it REST is practically the default. We've definitely come a long way in a few short years.

Admittedly, REST as a term is often over applied, and not always correctly. But all things considered, I am very pleased that the concepts of resources and URIs have successfully managed to infiltrate their way into application interface design. The web, after all, is a resilient place, and these new interfaces, albeit imperfect, are leaps and bounds better than the ones that they replace.

But we can do better.

Now that those building blocks are in place, it is time to take a step back, survey the territory, and build on top of these concepts. The next logical step is to explore media types in general, and hypermedia formats in specific. While the first book focused almost exclusively on the correct application of HTTP, it is time to delve more deeply into the concepts behind hypertext media types like HTML—media types that aren't tightly bound to a single application or even a single vendor.

HTML remains a prime example of a such a hypermedia format, and it continues to hold a special place in web architecture. In fact, my personal journey of discovery has been to take a deep dive into development of the W3C standard for HTML, now branded as HTML5. And while HTML does have a prominent place in this new book, there is so much more to cover on the topic of hypermedia. So while I have remained in touch, Leonard picked up a capable replacement for my role as coauthor in Mike Amundsen.

It has been a pleasure to watch this book be written, and in reading this book I've learned about a number of media types that I had not been exposed to by any other source. More importantly, this book shows what these types have in common, and how to differentiate them, as each has its own specialty.

Hopefully the pebbles that this book kicks loose will have the same effect as its predecessor did. Who knows, perhaps in another seven years it will be time to do this all over again, and highlight some other facet of Representational State Transfer that continues to be under-appreciated.

—Sam Ruby

Introduction

"Most software systems are created with the implicit assumption that the entire system is under the control of one entity, or at least that all entities participating within a system are acting towards a common goal and not at cross-purposes. Such an assumption cannot be safely made when the system runs openly on the Internet."

> — Roy Fielding
> *Architectural Styles and the Design of Network-based Software Architectures*

"A Discordian Shall Always use the Official Discordian Document Numbering System."

> — Malaclypse the Younger and Lord Omar Khayyam Ravenhurst
> *Principia Discordia*

I'm going to show you a better way to do distributed computing, using the ideas underlying the most successful distributed system in history: the World Wide Web. I hope you'll read this book if you've decided (or your manager has decided) that your company needs to publish a web API. It doesn't matter whether you're planning a public API, a purely internal API, or an API accessible by trusted partners—they can all benefit from the philosophy of REST.

This is not necessarily the book for you if you want to learn how to write API *clients*. That's because most existing API designs are based on assumptions that are several years old, assumptions that I'd like to destroy.

Most of today's APIs have a big problem: once deployed, they can't change. There are big-name APIs that stay static for years at a time, as the industry changes around them, because changing them would be too difficult.

But RESTful architectures are designed for managing change. The World Wide Web is made of millions of websites, running atop thousands of different server implementations, and undergoing periodic redesigns. Websites are accessed by billions of users who are using hundreds of different client implementations on dozens of hardware platforms. Your deployment won't look like this howling mess, but the closer you come to web scale, the more familiar this picture will look.

A very simple system is always easy to change. At small scales, a RESTful system has a larger up-front design cost than a push-button solution. But as your API matures and starts to change, you'll really need some way—like REST—of adapting to change.

- An API that's commercially successful will stay available for years on end. Some APIs have hundreds or even thousands of users. Even if the problem domain only changes occasionally, the cumulative effect on clients can be huge.

- Some APIs change all the time, with new data elements and business rules constantly being added.

- In some APIs, each client can change the workflow to suit its needs. Even if the API itself never changes, each client will experience it differently.

- The people who write the API clients usually don't work on the same team as the people who write the servers. All APIs that are open to the public fall under this category. If you don't know what kind of clients are out there, you need to be very careful about making changes—or you need to have a design that can change without breaking all the clients.

If you copy existing designs for your API, you will probably only repeat the mistakes of the past. Unfortunately, most of the improvements are happening below the surface, in experiments and through slow-moving standards processes. I'll cover dozens of specific technologies in this book, including many that are still under development. But my main goal is to teach you the underlying principles of REST. Learn those, and you'll be able to exploit whichever experiments pan out and whichever standards are approved.

There are two specific problems I'm trying to solve with this book: duplication of effort and avoidance of hypermedia. Let's take a look at them.

Duplication of Effort

An API released today will be named after the company that hosts it. We talk about the "Twitter API," the "Facebook API," and the "Google+ API." These three APIs do similar things. They all have some notion of user accounts and (among other things) they all let users post a little bit of text to their accounts. But each API has a completely different design. Learning one API doesn't help you learn the next one.

Of course, Twitter, Facebook, and Google are big companies that compete with each other. They don't *want* to make it easy for you to learn their competitors' APIs. But small companies and nonprofits do the same thing. They design their APIs as though nobody else had ever had a similar idea. This interferes with their goal of getting people to actually use their APIs.

Let me show you just one example. The website ProgrammableWeb (*http://www.programmableweb.com/*) has a directory of over 8,000 APIs. As I write this, it knows about 57 microblogging APIs—APIs whose main purpose is posting a little bit of text to a user account.[1] It's great that there are 57 companies publishing APIs in this field, but do we really need 57 different *designs*? We're not talking about something complicated here, like insurance policies or regulatory compliance. We're talking about posting a little bit of text to a user account. Do you want to be the one who designs the 58th microblogging API?

The obvious solution would be to create a standard for microblogging APIs. But there already *is* a standard that would work just fine: the Atom Publishing Protocol. It was published in 2005, and almost nobody uses it. There's something about APIs that makes everyone want to design their own from scratch, even when that makes no sense from a business perspective.

I don't think I can single-handledly stop this wasted effort, but I do think I can break down the problem into parts that make sense, and present some ways for a new API to reuse work that's already been done.

Hypermedia Is Hard

Back in 2007, Leonard Richardson and Sam Ruby wrote the predecessor to this book, *RESTful Web Services* (O'Reilly). That book also tried to address two big problems. One of the problems has been solved; the other is nowhere close to being solved.[2]

The first problem: in 2007, the REST school of API design was engaged in a standoff against a rival school that used heavyweight technologies based on SOAP and questioned the very legitimacy of the REST school. *RESTful Web Services* was a salvo in this standoff, a defense of RESTful design principles against the attacks of the SOAP school.

Well, the standoff is over, and REST won. SOAP APIs are still used, but only within the big companies that were backing the SOAP school in the first place. Pretty much all new public-facing APIs pay lip service to RESTful principles.[3]

Which brings me to the second problem: REST isn't just a technical term—it's also a marketing buzzword. For a long time, REST was a slogan that signified nothing beyond opposition to the SOAP school. Any API that didn't use SOAP was marketed as REST, even if its design made no sense or betrayed the technical principles of REST. This was inaccurate, confusing, and it gave REST—i.e., REST as a technical term—a bad name.

---

1. The full list of ProgrammableWeb APIs tagged with microblogging (*http://www.programmableweb.com/apitag/microblogging*) provides information about each of these APIs.

2. *RESTful Web Services* is now freely available as part of O'Reilly's Open Books Project (*http://oreilly.com/openbook/*). You can download a PDF copy of the book from the book's page.

3. If you're wondering, this is why we changed the title. The term "web services" became so tightly coupled with SOAP that when SOAP went down, it took "web services" with it. These days, everyone talks about APIs instead.

This situation has improved a lot since 2007. When I look at new APIs, I see the work of developers who understand the concepts I'll be explaining in the first few chapters of this book. Most developers who fly the REST flag today understand resources and representations, how to name resources with URLs, and how to properly use HTTP methods. The first three chapters of this book don't do much but get new developers up to speed.

But there's one aspect of REST that most developers still don't understand: hypermedia. We all understand hypermedia in the context of the Web. It's just a fancy word for links. Web pages link to each other, and the result is the World Wide Web, driven by hypermedia. But it seems we've got a mental block when it comes to hypermedia in web APIs. This is a big problem, because hypermedia is the feature that makes a web API capable of handling changes gracefully.

Starting in Chapter 4, my overriding goal for *RESTful Web APIs* will be to teach you how hypermedia works. If you've never heard of this term, I'll teach it to you along with the other important REST concepts. If you've heard of hypermedia but the concept intimidates you, I'll do what I can to build up your courage. If you just haven't been able to wrap your head around hypermedia, I'll show it to you in every way I can think of, until you get it.

RESTful Web Services covered hypermedia, but it wasn't central to the book. It was possible to skip the hypermedia parts of the book and still design a functioning API. By contrast, *RESTful Web APIs* is effectively a book about hypermedia.

I did it this way because hypermedia is the single most important aspect of REST, and the least understood. Until we all understand hypermedia, REST will continue to be viewed as a marketing buzzword rather than a serious attempt to handle the complexity of distributed computing.

What's in This Book?

The first four chapters introduce the concepts behind REST, as it applies to web APIs.

Chapter 1, Surfing the Web
> This chapter explains basic terminology using a RESTful system you're already familiar with: a website.

Chapter 2, A Simple API
> This chapter translates the lessons of the Web to a programmable API with identical functionality to the website discussed in Chapter 1.

Chapter 3, Resources and Representations
> Resources are the fundamental concept underlying HTTP, and representations are the fundamental concept underlying REST. This chapter explains how they're related.

Chapter 4, Hypermedia
> Hypermedia is the missing ingredient that ties representations together into a coherent API. This chapter shows what hypermedia is capable of, mostly using a hypermedia data format you're already familiar with: HTML.

The next four chapters describe different strategies for designing a hypermedia API:

Chapter 5, Domain-Specific Designs
> The obvious strategy is to design a completely new standard that deals with your exact problem. I use the Maze+XML standard as an example.

Chapter 6, The Collection Pattern
> One pattern in particular—the collection pattern—shows up over and over again in API design. In this chapter, I show off two different standards that capture this pattern: Collection+JSON and AtomPub.

Chapter 7, Pure-Hypermedia Designs
> When the collection pattern doesn't fit your requirements, you can convey any representation you want using a general-purpose hypermedia format. This chapter shows how it works using three general hypermedia formats (HTML, HAL, and Siren) as examples. This chapter also introduces HTML microformats and microdata, which lead in to the next chapter.

Chapter 8, Profiles
> A profile fills in the gaps between a data format (which can be used by many different APIs) and a specific API implementation. The profile format I recommend is ALPS, but I also cover XMDP and JSON-LD.
>
> In this chapter, my advice begins to outstrip the state of the art at the time this book was written. I had to develop the ALPS format for this book, because nothing else would do the job. If you're already familiar with hypermedia-based designs, you might be able to skip up to Chapter 8, but I don't think you should skip past it.

Chapters 9 through 13 cover practical topics like choosing the right hypermedia format and getting the most out of the HTTP protocol.

Chapter 9, The Design Procedure
> This chapter brings together everything discussed in the book so far, and gives a step-by-step guide to designing a RESTful API.

Chapter 10, The Hypermedia Zoo
> In an attempt to show what hypermedia is capable of, this chapter discusses about 20 standardized hypermedia data formats, most of them not covered elsewhere in the book.

Chapter 11, HTTP for APIs

This chapter gives some best practices for the use of HTTP in API implementations. I also discuss some extensions to HTTP, including the forthcoming HTTP 2.0 protocol.

Chapter 12, Resource Description and Linked Data

Linked Data is the Semantic Web community's approach to REST. JSON-LD is arguably the most important Linked Data standard. It's covered briefly in Chapter 8, and I revisit it here. This chapter also covers the RDF data model, and some RDF-based hypermedia formats that I didn't get to in Chapter 10.

Chapter 13, CoAP: REST for Embedded Systems

This chapter closes out the core body of the book by covering CoAP, a RESTful protocol that doesn't use HTTP at all.

Appendix A, The Status Codex

An extension of Chapter 11, this appendix provides an in-depth look at the 41 standard status codes defined in the HTTP specification, as well as a few useful codes defined as extensions.

Appendix B, The Header Codex

Similar to Appendix A, this appendix is also an extension of Chapter 11. It provides a detailed outline of the 46 request and response headers defined in the HTTP specification, as well as a few extensions.

Appendix C, An API Designer's Guide to the Fielding Dissertation

This appendix includes an in-depth discussion of the foundational document of REST, in terms of what it means for API design.

Glossary

The glossary contains definitions to terms you'll frequently encounter when working with RESTful web APIs. It's a good place to turn for familiarizing yourself with basic concepts or if you need a quick, at-a-glance reminder of a particular concept's definition.

What's Not in This Book

RESTful Web Services was the first book-length treatment of REST, and it had to cover a lot of ground. Fortunately, there are now over a dozen books on various aspects of REST, and that frees up *RESTful Web APIs* to focus on the core concepts.

To keep this book focused, I've removed a few topics that you might have been expecting me to cover. I want to tell you what is not in this book, so that you don't buy it and then feel disappointed:

- Client programming is not covered here. Writing a client to consume a hypermedia-based API is a new kind of challenge. Right now, the closest thing we have to a generic API client is a library that sends HTTP requests. This was true in 2007, and it's still true. The problem is on the server side.

  When you write a client for an existing API, you're at the mercy of the API designer. I can't give you any general advice, because right now there's no consistency across APIs. That's why, in this book, I'm trying to drum up enthusiasm for a little server-side consistency. When APIs become more similar to each other, we'll be able to write more sophisticated client-side tools.

  Chapter 5 contains some sample client implementations and tries to classify different types of clients, but if you want a whole book on API clients, this is not your book. I don't think the book you want exists right now.

- The most widely deployed API client in the world is JavaScript's XMLHttpRequest library. There's a copy in every web browser, and most websites today are built atop APIs designed for consumption by XMLHttpRequest. But that's far too big a field to cover properly in this book. There are whole books written about individual JavaScript libraries.

- I spend quite a bit of time on the mechanics of HTTP (Chapter 11, Appendix A, and Appendix B), but I don't cover any given HTTP topic in a lot of depth, and there are some topics—notably HTTP intermediaries like caches and proxies—which I barely cover at all.

- *RESTful Web Services* focused heavily on breaking down your business requirements into a set of interlinked resources. My experience since 2007 has convinced me that thinking of API design as resource design is a very effective way to avoid thinking about hypermedia. This book takes a different approach, focusing on representations and state transitions rather than resources.

  That said, the resource design approach is certainly valid. For advice on moving in that direction, I recommend *RESTful Web Services Cookbook* by Subbu Allamaraju (O'Reilly).

Administrative Notes

This book has two authors (Leonard and Mike), but for the duration of this book we've merged our identities into a single authorial "I."

Nothing in this book is tied to any particular programming language. All of the code takes the form of messages (usually JSON or XML documents) sent over a network protocol (usually HTTP). I will be assuming that you're familiar with common programming concepts like antipatterns and breadth-first search, and that you have a basic understanding of how the World Wide Web works.

I won't be presenting it, but there is real code behind the servers and clients I talk about in Chapter 1, Chapter 2, and Chapter 5. You can get that code from the *RESTful Web APIs* GitHub repository (*https://github.com/RESTful-Web-APIs*), or from the official website (*http://www.restfulwebapis.org/*), and run it yourself. These clients and servers are written in JavaScript, using the Node library.

I chose Node because it lets me use the same programming language for client and server code. You won't need to mentally switch back and forth between programming languages to understand both sides of a client-server transaction. Node is open source and available on Windows, Mac, and Linux systems. It is easy to install on these operating systems, and you shouldn't have much trouble getting the examples up and running.

I'm hosting the code on GitHub because that will make it easy to update the implementations over time. This also makes it possible for readers to contribute ports of the example clients and servers to other programming languages.

Understanding Standards

The World Wide Web isn't an objective thing that's out there to be studied scientifically. It's a social construct—a set of agreements to do things a certain way. Fortunately, unlike other social constructs (like etiquette), the agreements underlying the Web are generally agreed upon. The core agreements underlying the human web are RFC 2616 (the HTTP standard), the W3C's specification for HTML 4, and ECMA-262 (the standard that underlies JavaScript, also known as ECMAScript). Each standard does a different job, and over the course of this book, I'll discuss dozens of other standards designed specifically for use in APIs.

The great thing about these standards is the solid baseline they give you. You can use them to build a completely new kind of website or API, something that no one has ever tried before. Instead of having to explain your entire system to all your users, you'll only have to explain the part that's new.

The bad news is that these agreements are often borderline unreadable: long walls of ASCII text written in tooth-achingly precise English in which everyday words like "should" have technical meanings and are capitalized "SHOULD."[4] A lot of technical books are bought by people who are hoping to avoid having to read a standards document.

Well, I can't make any guarantees. If one of these standards looks like something you can use in your work, you need to be willing to dive into its spec and really understand it (or buy a book that covers it in more detail). I don't have space to give more than a basic overview of standards like Siren, CoAP, and Hydra. Not to mention that giving a

---

4. The meaning of "SHOULD" is given in RFC 2119.

lot of detail would bore all the readers who *don't* need those particular standards to do their work.

When navigating the forest of standards, it's useful to keep in mind that not all standards have equal force. Some are extremely well established, used by everyone, and if you go against them you're causing a lot of trouble for yourself. Other standards are just one person's opinion, and that opinion might be no better than yours.

I find it helpful to divide standards into four categories: fiat standards, personal standards, corporate standards, and open standards. I'll be using these terms throughout the book, so let me explain each one in a bit more depth before we move on.

Fiat Standards

Fiat standards aren't really standards; they're behaviors. No one agreed to them. They're just a description of the way somebody does things. The behavior may be documented, but the core assumption of a standard—that other people ought to do things the same way—is missing.

Pretty much every API today is a fiat standard, a one-off design associated with a specific company. That's why we talk about the "Twitter API," the "Facebook API," and the "Google+ API." You may need to understand these designs to do your job and you may write your own clients for these designs, but unless you work for the company in question, there's no expectation that you should use this design for *your* API. If you reuse a fiat standard, we don't say your API conforms to a standard; we say it's a clone.

The main problem I'm trying to solve in this book is that hundreds of person-years of design work is locked up in fiat standards where it can't be reused. This needs to stop. Designing a new API today means reinventing a long series of wheels. Once your API is finished, your client developers have to reinvent corresponding wheels on the client side.

Even under ideal circumstances, your API will be a fiat standard, since your business requirements will be slightly different from everyone else's. But ideally a fiat standard would be just a light gloss over a number of other standards.

When I describe a fiat standard, I'll link to its human-readable documentation.

Personal Standards

Personal standards are standards—you're invited to read the documents and implement the standards yourself—but they're just one person's opinion. The Maze+XML standard I describe in Chapter 5 is a good example. There's no expectation that Maze+XML is the standard way to implement a maze game API, but if it works for you, you might as well use it. Someone else has done the design work for you.

Personal standards generally use less formal language than other kinds of standards. Many open standards start off as personal standards—as side projects that are formalized after a lot of experimentation. Siren, which I cover in Chapter 7, is a good example.

When I describe a personal standard, I'll link to its specification.

Corporate Standards

Corporate standards are created by a consortium of companies trying to solve a problem that plagues them all, or by a single company trying to solve a recurring problem on behalf of its customers. Corporate standards tend to be better defined and to use more formal language than personal standards, but they have no more force than personal standards. They're just one company's (or a group of companies') opinion.

Corporate standards include Activity Streams and schema.org's microdata schemas, both of which are covered in Chapter 10. Many industry standards start off as corporate standards. OData (also discussed in Chapter 10) started as a Microsoft project, but it was submitted to OASIS in 2012 and will eventually become an OASIS standard.

When I describe a corporate standard, I'll link to its specification.

Open Standards

An open standard has gone through a process of design by committee, or at least had an open comment period during which a lot of people read the specification, complained about it, and made suggestions for improvement. At the end of this process, the specification was blessed by some kind of recognized standards body.

This process gives an open standard a certain amount of moral force. If there's an open standard that does more or less what you want, you really should use it instead of making up your own fiat standard. The design process and the comment period probably turned up a lot of issues that you won't encounter until it's too late.

In general, open standards come with some kind of agreement that promises you can implement them without getting hit with a patent infringement lawsuit from a company that was involved in the standards process. By contrast, implementing someone else's fiat standard may *incite* them to file a patent infringement lawsuit against you.

A few open standards mentioned in this book came out of the big-name standards bodies: ANSI, ECMA, ISO, OASIS, and especially the W3C. I can't say what it's like to sit on one of these standards bodies, because I've never done it. But the most important standards body[5] is one anyone can contribute to: the IETF, the group that manages the all-important RFCs.

---

5. For the purposes of this book, anyway. If you need standard sizes for screws and bolts, you want ANSI or ISO.

Requests for Comments (RFCs) and Internet-Drafts

Most RFCs are created through a process called the Standards Track. Throughout this book, I'll be referencing documents that are in different places on the Standards Track. I'd like to briefly discuss how the track works, so that you'll know how seriously to take my recommendations.

An RFC begins life as an *Internet-Draft*. This is a document that looks like a standards document, but you're not supposed to build implementations based on it. You're supposed to find problems with the specification and give feedback.

An Internet-Draft has a built-in lifetime of six months. Six months after it is published, a draft must be approved as an RFC or replaced with an updated draft. If neither of those things happens, then the draft expires and should not be used for anything. On the other hand, if the draft is approved, it expires immediately and is replaced by an RFC.

Because of the built-in expiration date, and because an Internet-Draft isn't technically any kind of standard, it's tricky business mentioning them in a book. At the same time, API design is a field that's changing rapidly, and an Internet-Draft is better than nothing. I will be mentioning many Internet-Drafts in this book under the assumption that they'll become RFCs without major changes. That assumption has held up pretty well; several Internet-Drafts that I mention here became RFCs while I was writing the book. If a particular draft doesn't pan out, all I can do is apologize in advance.

RFCs and Internet-Drafts are given code names. When I describe one of these, I *won't* link to its specification. I'll just refer to it by its code and let you look it up. For example, I'll refer to the HTTP/ 1.1 specification as RFC 2616. I'll refer to an Internet-Draft by its name. For example, I'll use "draft-snell-link-method" to refer to the proposal to add LINK and UNLINK methods to HTTP.

Whenever you see one of these code names, you can do a web search and find the latest version of the RFC or Internet-Draft. If an Internet-Draft becomes an RFC after this book is published, the final version of the Internet-Draft will link to the RFC.

When I describe a W3C or OASIS standard, I'll link to the specification, because those standards aren't given code names.

Conventions Used in This Book

The following typographical conventions are used in this book:

Italic
    Indicates new terms, URLs, email addresses, filenames, and file extensions.

Constant width

Used for program listings, as well as within paragraphs to refer to program elements such as variable or function names, databases, data types, environment variables, statements, and keywords.

Constant width bold

Shows commands or other text that should be typed literally by the user.

Constant width italic

Shows text that should be replaced with user-supplied values or by values determined by context.

 This icon signifies a tip, suggestion, or general note.

 This icon indicates a warning or caution.

Using Code Examples

This book is here to help you get your job done. In general, if this book includes code examples, you may use the code in this book in your programs and documentation. You do not need to contact us for permission unless you're reproducing a significant portion of the code. For example, writing a program that uses several chunks of code from this book does not require permission. Selling or distributing a CD-ROM of examples from O'Reilly books does require permission. Answering a question by citing this book and quoting example code does not require permission. Incorporating a significant amount of example code from this book into your product's documentation does require permission.

We appreciate, but do not require, attribution. An attribution usually includes the title, author, publisher, and ISBN. For example: "*RESTful Web APIs* by Leonard Richardson and Mike Amundsen (O'Reilly). Copyright 2013 Leonard Richardson and amundsen.com, Inc., and Sam Ruby. 978-1-449-35806-8."

If you feel your use of code examples falls outside fair use or the permission given here, feel free to contact us at *permissions@oreilly.com*.

Safari® Books Online

 *Safari Books Online* is an on-demand digital library that delivers expert content in both book and video form from the world's leading authors in technology and business.

Technology professionals, software developers, web designers, and business and creative professionals use Safari Books Online as their primary resource for research, problem solving, learning, and certification training.

Safari Books Online offers a range of plans and pricing for enterprise, government, education, and individuals.

Members have access to thousands of books, training videos, and prepublication manuscripts in one fully searchable database from publishers like O'Reilly Media, Prentice Hall Professional, Addison-Wesley Professional, Microsoft Press, Sams, Que, Peachpit Press, Focal Press, Cisco Press, John Wiley & Sons, Syngress, Morgan Kaufmann, IBM Redbooks, Packt, Adobe Press, FT Press, Apress, Manning, New Riders, McGraw-Hill, Jones & Bartlett, Course Technology, and hundreds more. For more information about Safari Books Online, please visit us online.

How to Contact Us

Please address comments and questions concerning this book to the publisher:

O'Reilly Media, Inc.
1005 Gravenstein Highway North
Sebastopol, CA 95472
800-998-9938 (in the United States or Canada)
707-829-0515 (international or local)
707-829-0104 (fax)

We have a web page for this book, where we list errata, examples, and any additional information. You can access this page at *http://oreil.ly/RESTful-Web-APIs*.

To comment or ask technical questions about this book, send email to *bookquestions@oreilly.com*.

For more information about our books, courses, conferences, and news, see our website at *http://www.oreilly.com*.

Find us on Facebook: *http://facebook.com/oreilly*

Follow us on Twitter: *http://twitter.com/oreillymedia*

Watch us on YouTube: *http://www.youtube.com/oreillymedia*

Acknowledgments

We owe a debt of thanks to Glenn Block who spent untold hours listening to ideas and working through real code to test those ideas. To Benjamin Young and all the folks at RESTFest who agreed to be part of our experiments, and who gave great feedback and advice even when we didn't want to hear it. To Mike's colleagues at Layer 7 Technologies, including Dimitri Sirota and Matt McLarty, who supported and encouraged his work on this project. To Sam Ruby and Mike Loukides, who were essential to *RESTful Web Services*, this book's predecessor. To Sumana Harihareswara, Leonard's supportive wife. To the social communities that create an excellent place to collaborate and converse on REST and APIs; especially Yahoo's REST-Discuss, Google Groups' API-Craft, and the Hypermedia group at LibreList.

And finally, to all those who read the early drafts of this manuscript and provided much-needed criticism and support: Carsten Bormann, Todd Brackley, Tom Christie, Timothy Haas, Jamie Hodge, Alex James, David Jones, Markus Lanthaler, Even Maler, Mark Nottingham, Cheryl Phair, Sergey Shishkin, Brian Sletten, Mark Stafford, Stefan Tilkov, Denny Vrandečić, Ruben Verborgh, and Andrew Wahbe.

CHAPTER 1
Surfing the Web

The World Wide Web became popular because ordinary people can use it to do really useful things with minimal training. But behind the scenes, the Web is also a powerful platform for distributed computing.

The principles that make the Web usable by ordinary people also work when the "user" is an automated software agent. A piece of software designed to transfer money between bank accounts (or carry out any other real-world task) can accomplish the task using the same basic technologies a human being would use.

As far as this book is concerned, the Web is based on three technologies: the URL naming convention, the HTTP protocol, and the HTML document format. URL and HTTP are simple, but to apply them to distributed programming you must understand them in more detail than the average web developer does. The first few chapters of this book are dedicated to giving you this understanding.

The story of HTML is a little more complicated. In the world of web APIs, there are dozens of data formats competing to take the place of HTML. An exploration of these formats will take up several chapters of this book, starting in Chapter 5. For now, I want to focus on URL and HTTP, and use HTML solely as an example.

I'm going to start off by telling a simple story about the World Wide Web, as a way of explaining the principles behind its design and the reasons for its success. The story needs to be simple because although you're certainly familiar with the Web, you might not have heard of the concepts that make it work. I want you to have a simple, concrete example to fall back on if you ever get confused about terminology like "hypermedia as the engine of application state."

Let's get started.

Episode 1: The Billboard

One day Alice is walking around town and she sees a billboard (Figure 1-1).

Figure 1-1. The billboard

(By the way, this fictional billboard advertises a real website that I designed for this book. You can try it out yourself.)

Alice is old enough to remember the mid-1990s, so she recalls the public's reaction when URLs started showing up on billboards. At first, people made fun of these weird-looking strings. It wasn't clear what "http://" or "youtypeitwepostit.com" meant. But 20 years later, everyone knows what to do with a URL: you type it into the address bar of your web browser and hit Enter.

And that's what Alice does: she pulls out her mobile phone and puts *http://www.youtypeitwepostit.com/* in her browser's address bar. The first episode of our story ends on a cliffhanger: what's at the other end of that URL?

Resources and Representations

Sorry for interrupting the story, but I need to introduce some basic terminology. Alice's web browser is about to send an HTTP request to a web server—specifically, to the URL *http://www.youtypeitwepostit.com/*. One web server may host many different URLs, and each URL grants access to a different bit of the data on the server.

We say that a URL is the URL of some thing: a product, a user, the home page. The technical term for the thing named by a URL is *resource*.

The URL *http://www.youtypeitwepostit.com/* identifies a resource—probably the home page of the website advertised on the billboard. But you won't know for sure until we resume the story and Alice's web browser sends the HTTP request.

When a web browser sends an HTTP request for a resource, the server sends a document in response (usually an HTML document, but sometimes a binary image or something else). Whatever document the server sends, we call that document a *representation* of the resource.

So each URL identifies a resource. When a client makes an HTTP request to a URL, it gets a representation of the underlying resource. The client never sees a resource directly.

I'll talk a lot more about resources and representations in Chapter 3. Right now I just want to use the terms resource and representation to discuss the principle of addressability, to which I'll now turn.

Addressability

A URL identifies one and only one resource. If a website has two conceptually different things on it, we expect the site to treat them as two resources with different URLs. We get frustrated when a website violates this rule. Websites for restaurants are especially bad about this. Frequently, the whole site is buried inside a Flash interface and there's no URL that points to the menu or to the map that shows where the restaurant is located —things we would like to talk about on their own.

The principle of addressability just says that every resource should have its own URL. If something is important to your application, it should have a unique name, a URL, so that you and your users can refer to it unambiguously.

Episode 2: The Home Page

Back to our story. When Alice enters the URL from the billboard into her browser's address bar, it sends an HTTP request over the Internet to the web server at *http://www.youtypeitwepostit.com/*:

```
GET / HTTP/1.1
Host: www.youtypeitwepostit.com
```

The web server handles this request (neither Alice nor her web browser need to know how) and sends a response:

```
HTTP/1.1 200 OK
Content-type: text/html

<!DOCTYPE html>
<html>
    <head>
        <title>Home</title>
    </head>
    <body>
        <div>
            <h1>You type it, we post it!</h1>
```

```
    <p>Exciting! Amazing!</p>

    <p class="links">
      <a href="/messages">Get started</a>
      <a href="/about">About this site</a>
    </p>
  </div>
</body>
</html>
```

The 200 at the beginning of the response is a *status code*, also called a *response code*. It's a quick way for the server to tell the client approximately what happened to the client's request. There are a lot of HTTP status codes, and I cover them all in Appendix A, but the most common one is the one you see here. 200 (OK) means that the request was fulfilled with no problems.

Alice's web browser decodes the response as an HTML document and displays it graphically (see Figure 1-2).

Figure 1-2. You Type It... home page

Now Alice can read the web page and understand what the billboard was talking about. It was advertising a microblogging site, similar to Twitter. Not as exciting as advertised on the billboard, but good enough as an example.

Alice's first real interaction with the web server reveals a couple more important features of the Web.

Short Sessions

At this point in the story, Alice's web browser is displaying the site's home page. From her perspective, she's "landed" on that page, which is is her current "location" in cyberspace. But as far as the server is concerned, Alice isn't anywhere. The server has already forgotten about her.

HTTP sessions last for one request. The client sends a request, and the server responds. This means Alice could turn her phone off overnight, and when her browser restored the page from its internal cache, she could click on one of the two links on this page and it would still work. (Compare this to an SSH session, which is terminated if you turn your computer off.)

Alice could leave this web page open in her phone for six months, and when she finally clicks on a link, the web server would respond as if she'd only waited a few seconds. The web server isn't sitting up late at night worrying about Alice. When she's not making an HTTP request, the server doesn't know Alice exists.

This principle is sometimes called statelessness. I think this is a confusing term because the client and the server in this system both keep state; they just keep different *kinds* of state. The term "statelessness" is getting at the fact that the *server* doesn't care what state the *client* is in. (I'll talk more about the different kinds of state in the following sections.)

Self-Descriptive Messages

It's clear from looking at the HTML that this site is more than just a home page. The markup for the home page contains two links: one to the relative URL */about* (i.e., to *http://www.youtypeitwepostit.com/about*) and one to */messages* (i.e., *http://www.youty peitwepostit.com/messages*). At first Alice only knew one URL—the URL to the home page—but now she knows three. The server is slowly revealing its structure to her.

We can draw a map of the website so far (Figure 1-3), as revealed to Alice by the server.

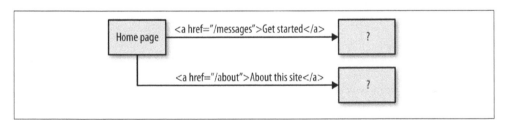

Figure 1-3. A map of the website

What's on the other end of the */messages* and */about* links? The only way to be sure is to follow them and find out. But Alice can look at the HTML markup, or her browser's graphical rendering of the markup, and make an educated guess. The link with the text "About this site" probably goes to a page talking about the site. That's nice, but the link with the text "Get started" is probably the one that gets her closer to actually posting a message.

When you request a web page, the HTML document you receive doesn't just give you the immediate information you asked for. The document also helps you answer the question of what to do next.

Episode 3: The Link

After reading the home page, Alice decides to give this site a try. She clicks the link that says "Get started." Of course, whenever you click a link in your web browser, you're telling your web browser to make an HTTP request.

The code for the link Alice clicked on looks like this:

```
<a href="/messages">Get started</a>
```

So her browser makes this HTTP request to the same server as before:

```
GET /messages HTTP/1.1
Host: www.youtypeitwepostit.com
```

That GET in the request is an *HTTP method*, also known as an *HTTP verb*. The HTTP method is the client's way of telling the server what it wants to do to a resource. "GET" is the most common HTTP method. It means "give me a representation of this resource." For a web browser, GET is the default. When you follow a link or type a URL into the address bar, your browser sends a GET request.

The server handles this particular GET request by sending a representation of */messages*:

```
HTTP/1.1 200 OK
Content-type: text/html
...

<!DOCTYPE html>
<html>
    <head>
        <title>Messages</title>
    </head>
    <body>
      <div>
        <h1>Messages</h1>

        <p>
          Enter your message below:
        </p>

        <form action="http://youtypeitwepostit.com/messages" method="post">
            <input type="text" name="message" value="" required="true"
                   maxlength="6"/>
            <input type="submit" value="Post" />
        </form>

        <div>
```

```
    <p>
      Here are some other messages, too:
    </p>
    <ul>
      <li><a href="/messages/32740753167308867">Later</a></li>
      <li><a href="/messages/7534227794967592">Hello</a></li>
    </ul>
  </div>

  <p class="links">
    <a href="http://youtypeitwepostit.com/">Home</a>
  </p>

      </div>
    </body>
  </html>
```

As before, Alice's browser renders the HTML graphically (Figure 1-4).

Figure 1-4. You Type It... "Get started" page

When Alice looks at the graphical rendering, she sees that this page is a list of messages other people have published on the site. Right at the top there's an inviting text box and a Post button.

Now we've revealed a little more about how the server works. Figure 1-5 shows an updated map of the site, as seen by Alice's browser.

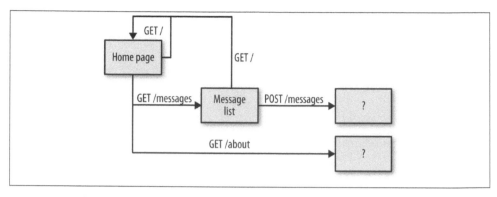

Figure 1-5. The browser's view of You Type It…

Standardized Methods

Both of Alice's HTTP requests used GET as their HTTP method. But there's a bit of HTML in the latest representation that will trigger an HTTP POST request if Alice clicks the Post button:

```
<form action="http://youtypeitwepostit.com/messages" method="post">
    <input type="text" name="message" value="" required="true"
           maxlength="6"/>
    <input type="submit" />
</form>
```

The HTTP standard (RFC 2616) defines eight methods a client can apply to a resource. In this book, I'll focus on five of them: GET, HEAD, POST, PUT, and DELETE. In Chapter 3, I'll cover these methods in detail, along with an extension method, PATCH, designed specifically for use in web APIs. Right now the important thing to keep in mind is that there are a small number of standard methods.

It's not impossible to come up with a new HTTP method (it happened with PATCH), but it's a very big deal. This is not like a programming language, where you can name your methods whatever you want. When I built the simple microblogging website for use in this example, I didn't define new HTTP methods like GETHOMEPAGE and HELLOPLEASESHOWMETHEMESSAGELISTTHANKSBYE. I used GET for both "show the home page" and "show the message list," because in both cases GET ("give me a representation of this resource") was the best match between HTTP's interface and what I wanted to do. I distinguished between the home page and the message list not by defining new methods, but by treating those two documents as separate resources, each with its own URL, each accessible through GET.

Episode 4: The Form and the Redirect

Back to our story. Alice is tempted by the form on the microblogging site. She types in "Test" and clicks the Post button.:

Again, Alice's browser makes an HTTP request:

```
POST /messages HTTP/1.1
Host: www.youtypeitwepostit.com
Content-type: application/x-www-form-urlencoded

message=Test&submit=Post
```

And the server responds with the following:

```
HTTP/1.1 303 See Other
Content-type: text/html
Location: http://www.youtypeitwepostit.com/messages/5266722824890167
```

When Alice's browser made its two GET requests, the server sent the HTTP status code 200 ("OK") and provided an HTML document for Alice's browser to render. There's no HTML document here, but the server did provide a link to another URL, in the Loca tion header—and here, the status code at the beginning of the response is 303 ("See Other"), not 200 ("OK").

Status code 303 tells Alice's browser to *automatically* make a fourth HTTP request, to the URL given in the Location header. Without asking Alice's permission, her browser does just that:

```
GET /messages/5266722824890167 HTTP/1.1
```

This time, the server responds with 200 ("OK") and an HTML document:

```
HTTP/1.1 200 OK
Content-type: text/html

<!DOCTYPE html>
<html>
    <head>
        <title>Message</title>
    </head>
    <body>
        <div>
            <h2>Message</h2>
            <dl>
                <dt>ID</dt><dd>2181852539069950</dd>
                <dt>DATE</dt><dd>2014-03-28T21:51:08Z</dd>
                <dt>MSG</dt><dd>Test</dd>
            </dl>
            <p class="links">
                <a href="http://www.youtypeitwepostit.com/">Home</a>
            </p>
```

```
      </div>
    </body>
  </html>
```

Alice's browser displays this document graphically (Figure 1-6), and, finally, goes back to waiting for Alice's input.

Figure 1-6. You Type It... posted message

 I'm sure you've encountered HTTP redirects before, but HTTP is full of small features like this, and some may be new to you. There are many ways for the server to tell the client to handle a response differently, and ways for the client to attach conditions or extra features to its request. A big part of API design is the proper use of these features. Chapter 11 covers the features of HTTP that are most important to web APIs, and Appendix A and Appendix B provide supplementary information on this topic.

By looking at the graphical rendering, Alice sees that her message ("Test") is now a fully fledged post on YouTypeItWePostIt.com. Our story ends here—Alice has accomplished her goal of trying out the microblogging site. But there's a lot to be learned from these four simple interactions.

Application State

Figure 1-7 is a state diagram that shows Alice's entire adventure from the perspective of her web browser.

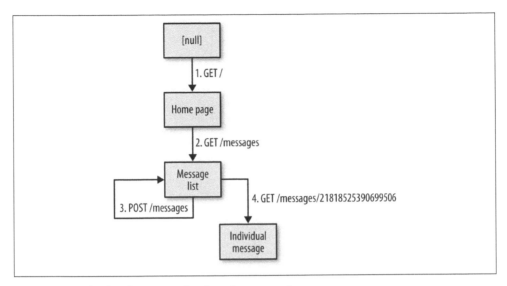

Figure 1-7. Alice's adventure: the client's perspective

When Alice started up the browser on her phone, it didn't have any particular page loaded. It was an empty slate. Then Alice typed in a URL and a GET request took the browser to the site's home page. Alice clicked a link, and a second GET request took the browser to the list of messages. She submitted a form, which caused a third request (a POST request). The response to that was an HTTP redirect, which Alice's browser made automatically. Alice's browser ended up at a web page describing the message Alice had just created.

Every state in this diagram corresponds to a particular page (or to no page at all) being open in Alice's browser window. In REST terms, we call this bit of information—which page are you on?—the *application state*.

When you surf the Web, every transition from one application state to another corresponds to a link you decided to follow or a form you decided to fill out. Not all transitions are available from all states. Alice can't make her POST request directly from the home page, because the home page doesn't feature the form that allows her browser to construct the POST request.

Resource State

Figure 1-8 is a state diagram showing Alice's adventure from the perspective of the web server.

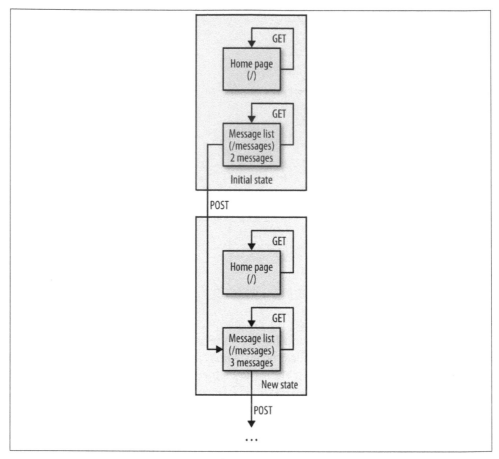

Figure 1-8. Alice's adventure: the server's perspective

The server manages two resources: the home page (served from /) and the message list (served from /messages). (The server also manages a resource for each individual message, and one for the "About this site" page. I've omitted those resources from the diagram for the sake of simplicity.) The state of these resources is called, simply enough, *resource state*.

When the story begins, there are two messages in the message list: "Hello" and "Later." Sending a GET to the home page doesn't change resource state, since the home page is a static document that never changes. Sending a GET to the message list won't change the state either.

But when Alice sends a POST to the message list, it puts the server in a new state. Now the message list contains three messages: "Hello," "Later," and "Test." There's no way back to the old state, but this new state is very similar. As before, sending a GET to the home page or message list won't change anything. But sending another POST to the message list will add a fourth message to the list.

Because HTTP sessions are so short, the server doesn't know anything about a client's application state. The client has no direct control over resource state—all that stuff is kept on the server. And yet, the Web works. It works through REST—representational state transfer.

Application state is kept on the client, but the server can manipulate it by sending representations—HTML documents, in this case—that describe the possible state transitions. Resource state is kept on the server, but the client can manipulate it by sending the server a representation—an HTML form submission, in this case—describing the desired new state.

Connectedness

In the story, Alice made four HTTP requests to YouTypeItWePostIt.com, and she got three HTML documents in return. Although Alice didn't follow every single link in those documents, we can use those links to build a rough map of the website from the client's perspective (Figure 1-9).

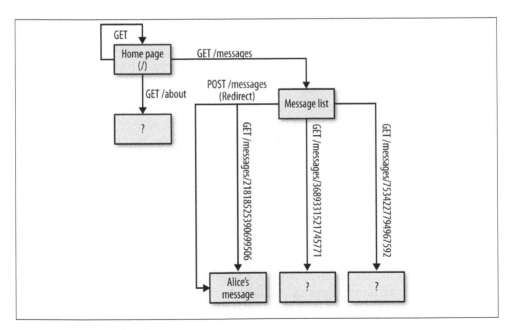

Figure 1-9. What the client saw

This is a web of HTML pages. The strands of the web are the HTML `<a>` tags and `<form>` tags, each describing a GET or POST HTTP request Alice might decide to make. I call this the principle of *connectedness*: each web page tells you how to get to the adjoining pages.

The Web as a whole works on the principle of connectedness, which is better known as "hypermedia as the engine of application state," sometimes abbreviated HATEOAS. I prefer "connectedness" or "the hypermedia constraint," because "hypermedia as the engine of application state" sounds intimidating. But at this point, you should have no reason to find it intimidating. You know what application state is—it's which web page a client is on. *Hypermedia* is the general term for things like HTML links and forms: the techniques a server uses to explain to a client what it can do next.

To say that hypermedia is the engine of application state is to say that we all navigate the Web by filling out forms and following links.

The Web Is Something Special

Alice's story doesn't seem that exciting. because the World Wide Web has been the dominant Internet application for the past 20 years. But back in the 1990s, this was a very exciting story. If you compare the World Wide Web to its early competitors, you'll see the difference.

The Gopher protocol (defined in RFC 1436) looks a lot like HTTP, but it lacks addressability. There is no succinct way to identify a specific document in Gopherspace. At least there wasn't until the World Wide Web took pity on Gopherspace and released the URL standard (first defined in RFC 1738), which provides a *gopher://* URL scheme that works just like *http://*.

FTP, a popular pre-Web protocol for file transfer (defined in RFC 959), also lacks addressability. Until RFC 1738 came along with its *ftp://* URL scheme, there simply was no machine-readable way to point to a file on an FTP server. You had to use English prose to explain where the file was. It took the brainpower of a human being just to locate a file on a server. What a waste!

FTP also featured long-lived sessions. A casual user could log on to an FTP server and tie up one of the server's TCP connections indefinitely. By contrast, even a "persistent" HTTP connection shouldn't tie up a TCP connection for longer than 30 seconds.

The 1990s saw a lot of Internet protocols for searching different kinds of archives and databases—protocols like Archie, Veronica, Jughead, WAIS, and Prospero. But it turns out we don't need all those protocols. We just need to be able to send GET requests to different kinds of websites. All these protocols died out or were replaced by websites. Their complex protocol-specific rules were folded into the uniformity of HTTP GET.

Once the Web took over, it became a lot more difficult to justify creating a new application protocol. Why create a new tool that only techies will understand, when you can put up a website that anyone can use? All successful post-Web protocols do something the Web can't do: peer-to-peer protocols like BitTorrent and real-time protocols like SSH. For most purposes, HTTP is good enough.

The unprecedented flexibility of the Web comes from the principles of REST. In the 1990s, we discovered that the Web works better than its competition. In 2000, Roy T. Fielding's Ph.D dissertation[1] explained why this is, coining the term "REST" in the process.

Web APIs Lag Behind the Web

The Fielding dissertation also explains a lot about the problems of web APIs in the 2010s. The simple website I just walked you through is much more sophisticated than most currently deployed web APIs—even self-proclaimed REST APIs. If you've ever designed a web API, or written a client for one, you've probably encountered some of these problems:

- Web APIs frequently have human-readable documentation that explains how to construct URLs for all the different resources. This is like writing English prose explaining how to find a particular file on an FTP server. If websites did this, no one would bother to use the Web.

  Instead of telling you what URLs to type in, websites embed URLs in <a> tags and <form> tags—hypermedia controls that you can activate by clicking a link or a button.

  In REST terms, putting information about URL construction in separate human-readable documents violates the principles of connectedness and self-descriptive messages.

- Lots of websites have help docs, but when was the last time you used them? Unless there's a serious problem (you bought something and it was never delivered), it's easier to click around and figure out how the site works by exploring the connected, self-descriptive HTML documents it sends you.

  Today's APIs present their resources in a big menu of options instead of an interconnected web. This makes it difficult to see what one resource has to do with another.

- Integrating with a new API inevitably requires writing custom software, or installing a one-off library written by someone else. But you don't need to write custom software to use a new website. You see a URL on a billboard and plug it into your web browser—the same client you use for every other website in the world.

---

1. Fielding, Roy Thomas. *Architectural Styles and the Design of Network-based Software Architectures*. Doctoral dissertation, University of California, Irvine, 2000.

We'll never get to the point where a single API client can understand every API in the world. But today's clients contain a lot of code that really ought to be refactored out into generic libraries. This will only become possible when APIs serve self-descriptive representations.

- When APIs change, custom API clients break and have to be fixed. But when a website undergoes a redesign, the site's users grumble about the redesign and then they adapt. Their browsers don't stop working.

  In REST terms, the website redesign is entirely encapsulated in the self-descriptive HTML documents served by the website. A client that could understand the old HTML documents can understand the new ones.

These are the problems I'm trying to solve with this book. The good news is that it used to be a lot worse. A few years ago, it was common to see RESTful APIs that used safe HTTP methods in unsafe ways, or mixed up application and resource state. This doesn't happen much anymore. Designs have gotten better, and they can get better still.

The Semantic Challenge

Now for the bad news. The story I've told you, the story of Alice's trip through a website, went as smoothly as it did thanks to a very slow and expensive piece of hardware: Alice herself. Every time her browser rendered a web page, Alice, a human being, had to look at the rendered page and decide what to do next. The Web works because human beings make all the decisions about which links to click and which forms to fill out.

The whole point of web APIs is to get things done without making a human sit in front of a web browser all day. How can we program a computer to make the decisions about which links to click? A computer can parse the HTML markup `<a href="/messag es">Get started</a>`, but it can't understand the phrase "Get started." Why bother to design APIs that serve self-descriptive messages if those messages won't be understood by their software consumers?

This is the biggest challenge in web API design: bridging the semantic gap between understanding a document's structure and understanding what it means. As a shorthand, I'm going to call it the *semantic challenge*. Very little progress has been made on the semantic challenge, and we will never solve it completely. The good news is that because so little progress has been made so far, the first bit of progress is really easy. We just have to start working together, instead of duplicating each other's work.

I'll be checking in with the semantic challenge over the next few chapters, as I talk about the technologies of the Web and how you can use them in API designs. By Chapter 8, we'll have the tools necessary to tackle the semantic challenge head-on.

CHAPTER 2

A Simple API

In Chapter 1, I showed off a very simple microblogging website located at *http://www.youtypeitwepostit.com/*. As it happens, I've also designed a programmable API for this website. You can see it live at *http://www.youtypeitwepostit.com/api/*.

The ideal API would have the same characteristics that make the World Wide Web easy to use. As a developer, you would be able to figure out how to use it, starting with nothing but a URL you saw on a billboard.

Let's spin out that fantasy to see how it would work. First, you would have your programmable client make a GET request for the billboard URL—the equivalent to entering that URL into your web browser's address bar. Your client would take over from there, examining the response to see what the available options are. It would follow links (not necessarily HTML links), fill out forms (not necessarily HTML forms), and eventually accomplish the task you set out for it.

This book is not going to get us all the way to that goal. There are problems I can't solve with a book: problems surrounding the absence of standards, problems with the current level of tool support, and the brute fact that computers just aren't as smart as human beings. But we can get a long way toward that goal—a lot further than you may think.

As I said, there is a real microblogging API at *http://www.youtypeitwepostit.com/api/*. If you're feeling adventurous, go ahead and write some code to do something with that API. See how much you can figure out, knowing nothing but that URL. You've done this before with websites: all you knew was the home page URL, and you figured it out. How far can you get with an API?

If you're not feeling adventurous or don't have much experience writing clients for web APIs (or you're reading this book in the far future, and I'm not hosting that website anymore), we'll go through it together. The first step is to get a representation of the API's home page.

HTTP GET: Your Safe Bet

If you have a URL that starts with *http://* or *https://*, and you don't know what's on the other side, the first thing to do is to issue an HTTP GET request. In REST terms, you know the URL to a resource and nothing else. You need to discover your options, and that means getting a representation of the resource. That's what HTTP GET is for.

You can write code in a programming language to make that GET request, but when doing an initial reconnaissance of an API, it's often easier to use a command-line tool like Wget. Here I use the -S option, which prints out the full HTTP response from the server, and the -O - option, which prints out the document instead of saving it to a file:

```
$ wget -S -O - http://www.youtypeitwepostit.com/api/
```

This sends an HTTP request like this to the server:

```
GET /api/ HTTP/1.1
Host: www.youtypeitwepostit.com
```

The HTTP standard says that a GET request is a request for a representation. It's not intended to change any resource state on the server. This means that if you have a URL to a resource and don't know anything more, you can always make a GET request and get a representation in return. Your GET request won't do something disastrous like delete all the data. We say that GET is a *safe* method.

It's OK for the server to change incidental things because of a GET request, like incrementing a hit counter or logging the request to a file, but that's not the *purpose* of the GET request. Nobody makes an HTTP request just to increment the hit counter.

In real life, there's no guarantee that HTTP GET is safe. Some older designs *will* force you to make an HTTP GET request if you want to delete some data. But this misfeature is pretty rare in newer designs. Most API designers now understand that clients frequently GET a URL just to see what's behind it. It's not fair to give that GET request significant side effects.

How to Read an HTTP Response

In response to my GET request, the server sends a big chunk of data that looks like this:

```
HTTP/1.1 200 OK
ETag: "f60e0978bc9c458989815b18ddad6d75"
Last-Modified: Thu, 10 Jan 2013 01:45:22 GMT
Content-Type: application/vnd.collection+json

{ "collection":
  {
    "version" : "1.0",
    "href" : "http://www.youtypeitwepostit.com/api/",
    "items" : [
```

```
    { "href" : "http://www.youtypeitwepostit.com/api/messages/21818525390699506",
      "data": [
      { "name": "text", "value": "Test." },
      { "name": "date_posted", "value": "2013-04-22T05:33:58.930Z" }
      ],
      "links": []
    },

    { "href" : "http://www.youtypeitwepostit.com/api/messages/3689331521745771",
      "data": [
      { "name": "text", "value": "Hello." },
      { "name": "date_posted", "value": "2013-04-20T12:55:59.685Z" }
      ],
      "links": []
    },

    { "href" : "http://www.youtypeitwepostit.com/api/messages/7534227794967592",
      "data": [
      { "name": "text", "value": "Pizza?" },
      { "name": "date_posted", "value": "2013-04-18T03:22:27.485Z" }
      ],
      "links": []
    }
    ]
  },

  "template": {
    "data": [
      {"prompt": "Text of message", "name": "text", "value":""}
    ]
  }
}
```

How much can we learn from this? Well, every HTTP response can be split into three parts:

The status code, sometimes called the response code

This is a three-digit number that summarizes how the request went. The response code is the first thing an API client sees, and it sets the tone for the rest of the response. Here, the status code was 200 (OK). This is the status code a client hopes for—it means that everything went fine.

In Appendix A, I explain all of the standard HTTP response codes, as well as several useful extensions.

The entity-body, sometimes called just the body

This is a document written in some data format, which the client is expected to understand. If you think of a GET request as a request for a representation, you can think of the entity-body as the representation (technically, the entire HTTP response is the 'representation', but the important information is usually in the entity-body).

In this case, the entity-body is the huge document at the end of the response, the one full of curly brackets.

The response headers

These are a series of key-value pairs describing the entity-body and the HTTP response in general. Response headers are sent between the status code and the entity-body. In Appendix B, I explain all the standard HTTP headers and many useful extensions.

The most important HTTP header is `Content-Type`, which tells the HTTP client how to understand the entity-body. It's so important that its value has a special name. We say the value of the `Content-Type` header is the entity-body's *media type*. (It's also called the *MIME type* or the *content type*. Sometimes "media type" is hyphenated: *media-type*.)

On the part of the Web that human beings can see with their web browsers, the most common media types are `text/html` (for HTML) and image types like `image/jpeg`. Here, the media type is one you probably haven't seen before: `application/vnd.collection+json`.

JSON

If you're a web developer, you probably recognize this entity-body as a JSON document. In case you don't, here's a very quick introduction to JSON.

JSON, described in RFC 4627, is a standard for representing simple data structures in plain text. It uses double quotes to describe strings:

```
"this is a string"
```

It uses square brackets to describe lists:

```
[1, 2, 3]
```

It uses curly brackets to describe *objects* (collections of key-value pairs):

```
{"key": "value"}
```

JSON data looks a lot like JavaScript or Python code. The JSON standard puts constraints on plain text. It says that a bare string like `It was the best of times.` is unacceptable, even though a human being can look at it and see what's going on. To be valid JSON, a string has to go inside double quotes: `"It was the best of times."`

Collection+JSON

So, this entity-body document is JSON, right? Not so fast! You can feed this document into a JSON parser without crashing the parser, but that's not what the web server wants you to do. Here's what the server said:

```
Content-Type: application/vnd.collection+json
```

That conflicts with the JSON RFC, which says a JSON document should be served as `application/json`, like this:

```
Content-Type: application/json
```

So what is this `application/vnd.collection+json` stuff? Clearly this format is *based* on JSON, since it looks like JSON and its media type has "json" in the name. But what is it, really?

If you search the web for `application/vnd.collection+json`, you'll discover that it's a media type registered for Collection+JSON.[1] When you make a GET request to *http://www.youtypeitwepostit.com/api/*, you don't get just any JSON document—you get a Collection+JSON document.

In Chapter 6, I'll talk about Collection+JSON in detail, but here's the short version. Collection+JSON is a standard for publishing a searchable list of resources over the Web. JSON puts constraints on plain text, and Collection+JSON puts constraints on JSON. A server can't serve just any JSON document as `application/vnd.collection+json`. It can only serve a JSON object:

```
{}
```

But not just any object. The object has to have a property called `collection`, which maps to another object:

```
{"collection": {}}
```

The "collection" object ought to have a property called `items` that maps to a list:

```
{"collection": {"items": []}}
```

The items in the "items" list need to be objects:

```
{"collection": {"items": [{}, {}, {}]}}
```

And on and on, constraint after constraint. Eventually you get the highly formatted document you just saw, which starts out like this:

```
{ "collection":
  {
    "version" : "1.0",
```

---

1. Collection+JSON is a personal standard defined at this page (*http://amundsen.com/media-types/collection/*).

```
        "href" : "http://www.youtypeitwepostit.com/api/",
        "items" : [

        { "href" : "http://www.youtypeitwepostit.com/api/messages/21818525390699506",
          "data": [
          { "name": "text", "value": "Test." },
          { "name": "date_posted", "value": "2013-04-22T05:33:58.930Z" }
          ],
          "links": []
        },
    ...
    }
```

Look at the document as a whole, and the purpose of all these constraints becomes clear. Collection+JSON is a way of serving lists—not lists of data structures, which you can do with normal JSON, but lists that describe HTTP resources.

The collection object has an href property, and its value is a JSON string. But it's not just any string—it's the URL I just sent a GET request to:

```
{ "collection":
  {
    "href" : "http://www.youtypeitwepostit.com/api/"
  }
}
```

The Collection+JSON standard defines this string as "the address used to retrieve a representation of the document" (in other words, it's the URL of the collection resource). Each object inside the collection's items list has its own href property, and each value is a string containing a URL, like *http://www.youtypeitwepostit.com/api/messages/ 21818525390699506* (in other words, each item in the list represents an HTTP resource with its own URL).

A document that doesn't follow these rules isn't a Collection+JSON document: it's just some JSON. By allowing yourself to be bound by Collection+JSON's constraints, you gain the ability to talk about concepts like resources and URLs. These concepts are not defined in JSON, which can only talk about simple things like strings and lists.

Writing to an API

How would I use the API to publish a message to the microblog? Here's what the Collection+JSON specification has to say:

> To create a new item in the collection, the client first uses the template object to compose a valid item representation and then uses HTTP POST to send that representation to the server for processing.

That's not exactly a step-by-step description, but it points toward the answer. Collection +JSON works along the same lines as HTML. The server provides you with some kind of form (the `template`), which you fill out to create a document. Then you send that document to the server with a POST request.

Again, Chapter 6 covers Collection+JSON in detail, so here's the quick version. Look at the big object I showed you earlier. Its `template` property is the "`template` object" mentioned in the Collection+JSON specification:

```
{
  ...
  "template": {
    "data": [
        {"prompt": "Text of message", "name": "text", "value":""}
    ]
  }
}
```

To fill out the template, I replace the empty string under `value` with the string I want to publish:

```
{ "template":
  {
    "data": [
        {"prompt": "Text of the message", "name": "text", "value": "Squid!"}
    ]
  }
}
```

I then send the filled-out template as part of an HTTP POST request:

```
POST /api/ HTTP/1.1
Host: www.youtypeitwepostit.com
Content-Type: application/vnd.collection+json

{ "template":
 {
  "data": [
    {"prompt": "Text of the message", "name": "text", "value": "Squid!"}
  ]
 }
}
```

(Note that my request's `Content-Type` is `application/vnd.collection+json`. This filled-out template is a valid Collection+JSON document all on its own.)

The server responds:

```
HTTP/1.1 201 Created
Location: http://www.youtypeitwepostit.com/api/47210977342911065
```

The 201 response code (`Created`) is a little more specific than 200 (`OK`); it means that everything is OK *and* that a new resource was created in response to my request. The `Location` header gives the URL to the newborn resource.

In Chapter 1, Alice posted to the microblogging site using the web interface. Now I've successfully done the same thing using the site's web API.

HTTP POST: How Resources Are Born

To add a new item to a collection, you send a POST request to the URL of the collection. This isn't just how Collection+JSON does things. It's a basic fact about HTTP. RFC 2616, the HTTP specification, has this to say about POST:

> POST is designed to allow a uniform method to cover the following functions:
>
> - Annotation of existing resources;
> - Posting a message to a bulletin board, newsgroup, mailing list, or similar group of articles;
> - Providing a block of data, such as the result of submitting a form, to a data-handling process;
> - Extending a database through an append operation.

That second bullet point, "posting a message to a… group of articles," covers the microblog exactly.

The POST request I sent looks a lot like an HTTP *response*. It's got a `Content-Type` header and an entity-body. Although the GET request I showed earlier didn't provide any headers, any HTTP request can have headers, and there are a number of headers (such as `Accept`) that are very important in GET requests. I'll be discussing especially important HTTP headers as they show up, but be sure to consult Appendix B for the complete list of standard HTTP headers.

Let's move on. Once again, here's the response I got to my POST request:

```
201 Created
Location: http://www.youtypeitwepostit.com/api/47210977342911065
```

When you get a 201 response code, the `Location` header tells you where to look for the thing you just created. RFC 2616 specifies the meaning of the 201 response code and the `Location` header, but the Collection+JSON specification mentions this as well, just to be clear.

If I send the following GET request:

```
GET /api/47210977342911065 HTTP/1.1
Host: www.youtypeitwepostit.com
```

I'll see a familiar sight:

```
HTTP/1.1 200 OK
Content-Type: application/vnd.collection+json
```

```
{ "collection":
  {
    "version" : "1.0",
    "href" : "http://www.youtypeitwepostit.com/api/47210977342911065",
    "items" : [

    { "href" : "http://www.youtypeitwepostit.com/api/messages/47210977342911065",
      "data": [
        { "name": "date_posted", "value": "2014-04-20T20:15:32.858Z" },
        { "name": "text", "value": "Squid!" }
      ],
      "links": []
    }
    ]
  }
}
```

This individual microblog post is represented as a full `application/vnd.collection` `+json` document. It's a `collection` with an `items` list that only contains one item. The filled-out template was also a valid `application/vnd.collection+json` document, even though it didn't use the `collection` property at all.

This is a convenience feature of Collection+JSON. Almost everything in the document is optional. It means you don't have to write different parsers to handle different types of documents. Collection+JSON uses the same JSON format to represent lists of items, individual items, filled-out templates, and search results.

Liberated by Constraints

One counterintuitive lesson of RESTful design is that constraints can be liberating. The safety constraint of HTTP's GET method is a good example. Thanks to the safety constraint, you know that if you don't know what to do with a URL, you can always GET it and look at the representation. Even if that doesn't help, nothing terrible will happen just because you made a GET request. That's a liberating promise, and it's only possible because of a very severe constraint on the server side.

If the server sends you a plain text document that says 9, you have no way to know if it's supposed to be the number nine or the string "9". But if you get a JSON document that says 9, you know it's a number. The JSON standard constrains the meaning of the document, and that makes it possible for client and server to have a meaningful conversation.

Over the past few years, hundreds of companies have gone through this general line of thinking:

1. We need an API.

2. We'll use JSON as the document format.

3. We'll use JSON to publish lists of things.

All three of these are good ideas, but they don't say much about what the API should look like. The end result is hundreds of APIs that are superficially similar (they all use JSON to publish lists of things!) but completely incompatible. Learning one API doesn't help a client learn the next one.

This is a sign that more constraints are necessary. The Collection+JSON standard provides some more constraints. If I'd come up with my own custom API design instead of using Collection+JSON, an individual item in my list might have looked like this:

```
{
  "self_link": "http://www.youtypeitwepostit.com/api/messages/47210977342911065",
  "date": "2014-04-20T20:15:32.858Z",
  "text": "Squid!"
}
```

Instead, because I followed the Collection+JSON constraints, an individual item looks like this:

```
{ "href" : "http://www.youtypeitwepostit.com/api/messages/1xe5",
  "data": [
  { "name": "date_posted", "value": "2014-04-20T20:15:32.858Z" },
  { "name": "text", "value": "Squid!" }
  ],
  "links": []
}
```

The custom design is certainly more compact, but that's not very important—JSON compresses very well. In exchange for this less compact representation, I get a number of useful features:

- I don't have to tell all my users that the value of href is a URL, and I don't have to explain what it's the URL of. The Collection+JSON standard says that an item's href contains the URL to the item.

- I don't have to write a separate human-readable document explaining to my users that text is the text of the message. That information goes where it's actually needed —in the template you fill out to post a new message:

```
"template": {
  "data": [
    {"prompt": "Text of the message", "name": "text", "value": null}
  ]
}
```

- Any library that understands application/vnd.collection+json automatically knows how to use my API. If I came up with a custom design, I'd have to write brand new client code based on nothing but a JSON parser and an HTTP library, or ask all my users to write that code themselves.

By submitting to the Collection+JSON constraints, I free myself from having to write a whole lot of documentation and code, and I free my users from having to learn yet another custom API.

Application Semantics Create the Semantic Gap

Of course, the Collection+JSON constraints don't constrain everything. Collection +JSON doesn't specify that the items in a collection should be microblog posts with a date_posted and a text. I made that part up, because I wanted to design a simple microblogging example for this book. If I'd chosen to do a "recipe book" example, I could still use Collection+JSON, but the items would have data fields like ingredients and preparation_time.

I'm going to call these extra bits of design the *application semantics*, because they vary from one application to another. Application semantics are the cause of the semantic gap I mentioned in Chapter 1.

If I were designing a real microblogging API, I'd come up with application semantics more complicated than just text and date_posted. That's fine, on its own. But there are currently dozens of companies designing microblogging APIs, coming up with dozens of designs that feature mutually incompatible application semantics, creating dozens of distinct semantic gaps. All of these companies are doing the same thing in different ways. Their users have to write different software clients to accomplish the same task.

The fact that Collection+JSON doesn't solve this problem doesn't mean there's no point to using Collection+JSON. Compatibility is a matter of degree. We took a big step toward compatibility in the 1990s when we stopped inventing custom Internet protocols and standardized on HTTP. If we all agreed to serve JSON documents, that might not be a good idea technically, but it would narrow the semantic gap. Standardizing on Collection+JSON would narrow it even more.

If the publishers of microblogging APIs got together and agreed to use a common set of application semantics, the semantic gap for microblogging would disappear almost entirely. (This would be a *profile*, and I'll cover this idea in Chapter 8.) The more constraints we share and the more compatible our designs, the smaller the semantic gap and the more our users benefit.

Maybe you don't *want* your API to be interoperable with your competitor's APIs, but there are better ways to differentiate yourself than by artificially widening the semantic gap. My goal for this book is to get you focused on the parts of your API that have something new to offer, in the spots where a semantic gap exists because no one else has ever taken that path.

CHAPTER 3

Resources and Representations

So far I've shown you two examples of REST in action: a website (Chapter 1) and a web API (Chapter 2). I've talked in terms of examples, because there's no RFC for REST the way there is for HTTP or JSON.

REST is not a protocol, a file format, or a development framework. It's a set of design constraints: statelessness, hypermedia as the engine of application state, and so on. Collectively, we call these the *Fielding constraints*, because they were first identified in Roy T. Fielding's 2000 dissertation on software architecture, which gathered them together under the name "REST."

The runaway popularity of the term "REST" is out of proportion to the importance of REST to Fielding's dissertation. Fielding used REST primarily as an example, to tie something you're already familiar with (the Web) into a general design process. REST became popular because the term happens to describe the architecture of one of the most successful technologies in human history.

In this chapter, I'll finish my explanation of the Fielding constraints in terms of the World Wide Web. My "bible," as it were, will not be the Fielding dissertation. (You can see Appendix C for a detailed, API-centric discussion of Fielding.) Instead, I'll be drawing from the W3C's guide to the Web, *The Architecture of the World Wide Web, Volume One (http://www.w3.org/TR/2004/REC-webarch-20041215/)* (there is no Volume Two). The Fielding dissertation explains the decisions behind the design of the Web, but *Architecture* explains the three technologies that came out of those decisions: URL, HTTP, and HTML.

I'm sure you already know about these technologies, but understanding them on a deep level is the key to understanding the Fielding constraints, how those constraints drive the success of the Web, and how you can exploit those constraints in your own APIs.

Underlying the three web technologies are two essential concepts: *resources* and *representations*. I've mentioned them before, but now it's time to take a closer look.

A Resource Can Be Anything

A resource is anything that's important enough to be referenced as a thing in itself. If your users might "want to create a hypertext link to it, make or refute assertions about it, retrieve or cache a representation of it, include all or part of it by reference into another representation, annotate it, or perform other operations on it" (*Architecture*), you should make it a resource.

A resource is usually something that can be stored on a computer: an electronic document, a row in a database, or the result of running an algorithm. *Architecture* calls these "information resources," because their native form is a stream of bits. But a resource can be anything at all: a pomegranate, a human being, the color black, the concept of courage, the relationship between mother and daughter, or the set of all prime numbers. The only restriction is that *every resource must have a URL*.

Do you remember that thing, the thing you had a while ago, but then... do you know what I'm talking about? Of course you don't. I wasn't specific enough. I could have been talking about anything. It's the same on the Web. Clients and servers can only talk about something if they can agree on a name for it. On the Web, we use a URL to give each resource a globally unique address. Giving something a URL turns it into a resource.

From the client's perspective, it doesn't matter what a resource is, because the client never sees a resource. All it ever sees are URLs and representations.

A Representation Describes Resource State

A pomegranate can be an HTTP resource, but you can't transmit a pomegranate over the Internet. A row in a database can be an HTTP resource; in fact, it can be an information resource, because you *can* literally send it over the Internet. But what would the client do with a chunk of binary data, ripped from an unknown database without any context?

When a client issues a GET request for a resource, the server should serve a document that captures the resource in a useful way. That's a representation—a machine-readable explanation of the current state of a resource. The size and ripeness of the pomegranate, the data contained in the database fields.

The server might describe a database row as an XML document, a JSON object, a set of comma-separated values, or as the SQL INSERT statement used to create it. These are all legitimate representations; it depends on what the client asks for.

One application might represent a pomegranate as an item for sale, using a custom XML vocabulary. Another might represent it with a binary image taken by a Pomegranate-Cam. It depends on the application. A representation can be *any* machine-readable document containing *any* information about a resource.

Representations Are Transferred Back and Forth

In Chapter 2, I showed a client using a POST request to create a new microblog entry. The client then sent an HTTP GET request, asking for a representation of the new entry:

```
GET /api/5266722824890167 HTTP/1.1
Host: www.youtypeitwepostit.com
```

The server responded with a representation in `application/vnd.collection+json` format, which looked like this:

```
HTTP/1.1 200 OK
Content-Type: application/vnd.collection+json
...
{
  "collection" :
  {
    "version" : "1.0",
    "href" : "http://localhost:1337/api/",

    "items" :
    [{
      "href": "http://localhost:1337/api/5266722824890167",
      "data": [
        {
          "name": "text",
          "value": "Squid!"
        },
        {
          "name": "date_posted",
          "value": "2013-01-09T15:58:22.674Z"
        }
      ]
    }],

    "template" : {
      "data" : [
        {
          "prompt" : "Text of message",
          "name" : "text",
          "value" : ""
        }
      ]
    }
  }
}
```

But there's another representation of that entry: the one the client sent to the server in the first place, along with the POST request. That was also an `application/vnd.collection+json` document, and it looked like this:

```
{ "template":
 {
  "data": [
   {"prompt": "Text of the message", "name": "text", "value": "Squid!"}
  ]
 }
}
```

The two representations look significantly different. One of them has the essential information in a `template` object, and the other has it in an `items` list. But they're clearly different representations of the same resource: a microblog entry that says, "Squid!"

When a client makes a POST request to create a new resource, it sends a representation: the client's idea of what the new resource should look like. The server's job is to create that resource, or else refuse to create it. The client's representation is just a suggestion. The server may add to, alter, or ignore any part of it. (Here, the server added a `date_posted` value to the data.)

The Web works the same way. Back in Chapter 1, my fictional character Alice created a new entry on a microblogging website by sending a POST request, along with a representation in `application/x-www-form-urlencoded` format:

```
message=Test&submit=Post
```

That doesn't look anything like the complex HTML document Alice got in return, but they were both representations of a microblog post that says, "Test."

We think of representations as something the server sends to the client. That's because when we surf the Web, most of our requests are GET requests. We're asking for representations. But in a POST, PUT, or PATCH request, the client sends a representation to the server. The server's job is then to change the resource state so it reflects the incoming representation.

The server sends a representation describing the state of a resource. The client sends a representation describing the state it would *like* the resource to have. That's representational state transfer.

Resources with Many Representations

A resource can have more than one representation. Government documents are often made available in multiple languages. Some resources have an overview representation that doesn't convey much state, and a detail representation that includes everything. Some APIs serve the same data in JSON and XML-based data formats. When this happens, how is the client supposed to specify which representation it wants?

There are two strategies, and I'll describe them in detail in Chapter 11. The first is content negotiation, in which the client distinguishes between representations based on the value of an HTTP header. The second is to give the resource multiple URLs—one URL for every representation.

Just as one person may be addressed by different names in different contexts,[1] one resource may be identified by many URLs. When this happens, the server that publishes the resource should designate one of those URLs the official or "canonical" URL. I'll cover those details, too, in Chapter 11.

The Protocol Semantics of HTTP

Although a resource can be anything at all, a client can't do whatever it wants to a resource. There are rules. In a RESTful system, clients and servers interact only by sending each other messages that follow a predefined protocol.

In the world of web APIs, that protocol is HTTP. (But see Chapter 13 for a RESTful API architecture that doesn't use HTTP.) API clients can interact with APIs by sending a few different types of HTTP messages.

The HTTP standard defines eight different kinds of messages. These four are the most commonly used:

GET
> Get a representation of this resource.

DELETE
> Destroy this resource.

POST
> Create a new resource underneath this one, based on the given representation.

PUT
> Replace this state of this resource with the one described in the given representation.

These two methods are mostly used as a client explores an API:

HEAD
> Get the headers that would be sent along with a representation of this resource, but not the representation itself.

OPTIONS
> Discover which HTTP methods this resource responds to.

The other two methods defined in the HTTP standard, CONNECT and TRACE, are only used with HTTP proxies. I won't be covering them.

---

1. "Hey, Mike!", "@mamund", "Good evening, Mr. Amundsen."

I recommend that API designers consider a ninth HTTP method, defined not in the HTTP standard but in a supplement, RFC 5789:

PATCH
> Modify *part* of the state of this resource based on the given representation. If some bit of resource state is not mentioned in the given representation, leave it alone. PATCH is like PUT, but allows for fine-grained changes to resource state.

I'd also like you to know about two extension HTTP methods that are currently going through the standards process. They're defined in the Internet-Draft "snell-link-method," and I'll come back to them in Chapter 11, at which point they should make a lot more sense:

LINK
> Connect some other resource to this one.

UNLINK
> Destroy the connection between some other resource and this one.

Collectively, these methods define the *protocol semantics* of HTTP. Just by looking at the method used in an HTTP request, you can understand approximately what the client wants: whether it's trying to get a representation, delete a resource, or connect two resources together.

You can't understand exactly what's going on, because a resource can be anything at all. A GET request sent to a "blog post" resource looks just like the GET request sent to a "stock symbol" resource. Those two requests have identical protocol semantics, but different application semantics. HTTP is HTTP, but a blogging API is not a stock quote API.

We can't meet the semantic challenge just by using HTTP correctly, because the HTTP protocol doesn't define any application semantics. But your application semantics should always be *consistent* with HTTP's protocol semantics. "Get a blog post" and "get a stock quote" both fall under "get a representation of this resource," so both requests should use HTTP GET.

The following sections provide a more detailed look at the protocol semantics of the most popular HTTP methods.

GET

You're surely familiar with this method already. The client sends a GET request to ask for a representation of a resource, identified by a URL. Here, the client asks for a representation of a microblog post, and the server sends it in `application/vnd.collec tion+json` format:

```
GET /api/45ty HTTP/1.1
Host: www.youtypeitwepostit.com
```

```
HTTP/1.1 200 OK
Content-Type: application/vnd.collection+json
...

{
  "collection" :
  {
    "version" : "1.0",
    "href" : "http://localhost:1337/api/",

    "items" :
    [{
      "href": "http://localhost:1337/api/2csl73jr6j5",
      "data": [
        {
          "name": "text",
          "value": "Bird"
        },
        {
          "name": "date_posted",
          "value": "2013-01-24T18:40:42.190Z"
        }
      ]
    }],

    "template" : {
      "data" : [
        {"prompt" : "Text of message", "name" : "text", "value" : ""}
      ]
    }
  }
}
```

I mentioned earlier that GET is defined as a *safe* HTTP method. It's just a request for information. Sending a GET request to the server should have the same effect on resource state as *not* sending a GET request—that is, no effect at all. Incidental side effects like logging and rate limiting are OK, but a client should never make a GET request *hoping* that it will change the resource state.

The most common response code to a GET request is 200 (OK). Redirect codes like 301 (Moved Permanently) are also common.

DELETE

The client sends a DELETE request when it wants a resource to go away. The client wants the server to destroy the resource and never refer to it again. Of course, the server is not obliged to delete something it doesn't want to.

In this HTTP snippet, the client asks to delete a microblog post:

```
DELETE /api/45ty HTTP/1.1
Host: www.youtypeitwepostit.com
```

The server returns the status code 204 (No Content), indicating that it's deleted the post and has nothing more to say about it:

```
HTTP/1.1 204 No Content
```

If a DELETE request succeeds, the possible status codes are 204 (No Content, i.e., "it's deleted, and I don't have anything more to say about it"), 200 (OK, i.e., "it's deleted, and here's a message about that"); and 202 (Accepted, i.e., "I'll delete it later").

If a client tries to GET a resource that has been DELETEd, the server will return an error response code, usually 404 (Not Found) or 410 (Gone):

```
GET /api/45ty HTTP/1.1
Host: www.youtypeitwepostit.com

HTTP/1.1 404 Not Found
```

Idempotence

DELETE is obviously not a safe method. Sending a DELETE request is very different from not sending a DELETE request. But the DELETE method has another useful property: it's *idempotent*.

Once you delete a resource, it's gone. The resource state has permanently changed. You can send another DELETE request, and you might get a 404 error, but the resource state is exactly as it was after the first request. The resource is still gone. That's idempotence. Sending a request twice has the same effect on resource state as sending it once.

Idempotence is a useful feature, because the Internet is not a reliable network. Suppose you send a DELETE request and your connection times out. You never got a response, so you don't know if the DELETE went through. You can just send that DELETE request again, and keep trying until you get a response. Nothing extra will happen if a DELETE goes through twice instead of once.

The notion of idempotence comes from math. Multiplying a number by zero is an idempotent operation. 5×0 is zero, but $5 \times 0 \times 0$ is also zero. Once you multiply a number by zero, you can keep multiplying it by zero indefinitely and get the same result: zero. HTTP DELETE effectively multiplies a resource by zero.

Multiplying by 1 is a safe operation, the way HTTP GET is supposed to be safe. You can multiply a number by 1 all day long, and nothing will change. Every safe operation is also idempotent.

POST-to-Append

POST is the other HTTP method you've surely used before. The POST method has two jobs, which I'll cover separately. The first is *POST-to-append*, in which sending a POST request to a resource creates a new resource underneath it. When a client sends a POST-to-append request, it sends a representation of the resource it wants to create in the request's entity-body.

I used POST-to-append in Chapter 2 to add a new post to the microblog API. Since I deleted that post while demonstrating DELETE, let's create a new one:

```
POST /api/ HTTP/1.1
Content-Type: application/vnd.collection+json

{
  "template" : {
    "data" : [
      {"name" : "text", "value" : "testing"}
    ]
  }
}
```

The most common response code to a POST-to-append request is 201 (`Created`). It lets the client know that a new resource was created. The `Location` header lets the client know the URL to this new resource. Another common response code is 202 (`Accepted`), which means that the server *intends* to create a new resource based on the given representation, but hasn't actually created it yet.

The POST method is neither safe nor idempotent. If I send this POST request five times, I'll probably end up with five new microblog posts, each with the same `text` but a slightly different `date_created`.

That's POST-to-append. But you've probably used POST for all sorts of things other than "create a new resource." That's the other job of POST. That's called *overloaded POST*, and I'll talk about it later in this chapter.

PUT

A PUT request is a request to modify resource state. The client takes the representation it got from a GET request, modifies it, and sends it back as the payload of a PUT request. Here, I'm going to modify the text of a microblog post (I want the value of the `text` field to be the string `tasting`, instead of whatever it was before):

```
PUT /api/q1w2e HTTP/1.1
Content-Type: application/vnd.collection+json

{
  "template" : {
    "data" : [
```

```
        {"name" : "text", "value" : "tasting"}
      ]
    }
  }
```

The server is free to reject a PUT request because the entity-body doesn't make sense, because the entity-body tries to change a bit of resource state the server considers read-only, or really for any reason at all. If the server decides to accept a PUT request, the server changes the resource state to match what the client says in the representation, and usually sends either 200 (OK) or 204 (No Content).

PUT is idempotent, just like DELETE. If you send the same PUT request 10 times, the result is the same as if you'd only sent it once.

The client can also use PUT to *create* a new resource, if it knows the URL where the new resource should live. In the following hypothetical example, I'm creating a new microblog post, and I happen to know the URL of the new post:

```
PUT /api/a1s2d3
Content-Type: application/vnd.collection+json

{
  "template" : {
    "data" : [
      {"name" : "text", "value" : "Created."}
    ]
  }
}
```

How is the client supposed to construct that magical URL? We'll look at some possibilities, Chapter 4. For now, just note that PUT is an idempotent operation even when you use it to create a new resource. If I send that PUT request five times, it won't create five posts with the same text (the way five POST requests might).

PATCH

Representations can get really big. "Modify the representation and PUT it back" is a simple rule, but if you just want to change one little bit of resource state, it can be pretty wasteful. The PUT rule can also lead to unintentional conflicts with other users who are modifying the same document. It would be nice if you could just send the server the parts of the document you want to change.

The PATCH method allows for this. Instead of PUTting a full representation, you can create a special "diff" representation and send it to the server as the payload of a PATCH request. RFC 5261 describes a patch format for XML documents, and RFC 6902 describes a similar format for JSON documents:

```
PATCH /my/data HTTP/1.1
Host: example.org
```

```
Content-Length: 326
Content-Type: application/json-patch+json
If-Match: "abc123"

[
  { "op": "test", "path": "/a/b/c", "value": "foo" },
  { "op": "remove", "path": "/a/b/c" },
  { "op": "add", "path": "/a/b/c", "value": [ "foo", "bar" ] },
  { "op": "replace", "path": "/a/b/c", "value": 42 },
  { "op": "move", "from": "/a/b/c", "path": "/a/b/d" },
  { "op": "copy", "from": "/a/b/d", "path": "/a/b/e" }
]
```

The best response codes for a successful PATCH are the same as for PUT and DELETE: 200 (OK) if the server wants to send data (such as an updated representation of the resource) along with its response, and 204 (No Content) if the server just wants to indicate success.

PATCH is neither safe nor idempotent. A PATCH request might turn out to be idempotent, so that if you accidentally apply the same patch twice to the same document, you get an error the second time. But that's not in the standard. As far as PATCH's protocol semantics are concerned, it's an unsafe operation, like POST.

Remember that PATCH is not defined in the HTTP specification. It's an extension designed specifically for web APIs, and it's relatively recent (RFC 5789 was published in 2010). This means that tool support for PATCH, and for the diff documents it uses, is not as good as the support for PUT.

LINK and UNLINK

LINK and UNLINK manage the hypermedia links between resources. To understand these methods, you must understand hypermedia and link relations, so I'm going to defer a detailed discussion to Chapter 11. I'll just show some simple examples here.

Here's an UNLINK request that removes the link between a story (identified by *http://www.example.com/story*) and its author (identified by *http://www.example.com/~omjennyg*):

```
UNLINK /story HTTP/1.1
Host: www.example.com
Link: <http://www.example.com/~omjennyg>;rel="author"
```

And here's a LINK request that declares some other resource (identified by *http://www.example.com/~drmilk*) to be the author of the story resource:

```
LINK /story HTTP/1.1
Host: www.example.com
Link: <http://www.example.com/~drmilk>;rel="author"
```

LINK and UNLINK are idempotent, but not safe. These methods are defined in an Internet-Draft ("snell-link-method"), and until that draft is approved as an RFC, tool support for them will be even worse than for PATCH.

HEAD

HEAD is a safe method, just like GET. In fact, it's best to think of HEAD as a lightweight version of GET. The server is supposed to treat a HEAD request exactly the same as a GET request, but it's not supposed to send a an entity-body—only the HTTP status code and the headers:

```
HEAD /api/ HTTP/1.1
Accept: application/vnd.collection+json

HTTP/1.1 200 OK
Content-Type: application/vnd.collection+json
ETag: "dd9b7c436ab247a7b69f355f2d57994c"
Last-Modified: Thu, 24 Jan 2013 18:40:42 GMT
Date: Thu, 24 Jan 2013 19:14:23 GMT
Connection: keep-alive
Transfer-Encoding: chunked
```

Using HEAD instead of GET may not save any time (the server still has to generate all the appropriate HTTP headers), but it will definitely save bandwidth.

OPTIONS

OPTIONS is a primitive discovery mechanism for HTTP. The response to an OPTIONS request contains the HTTP Allow header, which lays out which HTTP methods the resource supports. Here's an OPTIONS request to the microblog post I created in the PUT example:

```
OPTIONS /api/a1s2d3 HTTP/1.1
Host: www.youtypeitwepostit.com

200 OK
Allow: GET PUT DELETE HEAD OPTIONS
```

Now I know something about the HTTP requests I can make next. I can GET a representation of this resource, modify it with PUT, or delete it with DELETE. This resource supports HEAD and (of course) OPTIONS, but it doesn't understand the PATCH extension, or LINK or UNLINK.

OPTIONS is a good idea, but almost nobody uses it. Well-designed APIs advertise a resource's capabilities by serving hypermedia documents (see Chapter 4) in response to GET requests. The links and forms in those documents explain what HTTP requests a client can make next. Poorly designed APIs use human-readable documentation to explain which HTTP requests a client can make.

Overloaded POST

Now it's time to reveal the skeleton in the HTTP closet. The HTTP POST method has a dirty secret, one you've certainly encountered if you've ever worked in web development. POST is not solely used to create new resources. On the Web we surf with our browsers, HTTP POST is used to convey *any* kind of change. It's PUT, DELETE, PATCH, LINK, and UNLINK all rolled into one.

Here's an HTML form you might see on the Web. The purpose of the form is to edit a previously published blog post:

```
<form method="POST" action="/blog/entries/123">
 <textarea>
  Original content of the blog post.
 </textarea>
 <input type="submit" class="edit-post" value="Edit this blog post.">
</form>
```

In terms of protocol semantics, this operation—"edit this blog post"—sounds like a PUT request. But an HTML form can't trigger a PUT request. The HTML data format doesn't allow it. So we use POST instead.

This is completely legal. The HTTP specification says that POST can be used for:

> Providing a block of data, such as the result of submitting a form, to a data-handling process

That "data-handling process" can be anything. It's legal to send any data whatsoever as part of a POST request, for any purpose at all. The definition is so vague that a POST request really has *no protocol semantics at all*. POST doesn't really mean "create a new resource"; it means "whatever!"

I call this "whatever!" usage of POST *overloaded POST*. Because an overloaded POST request has no protocol semantics, you can only understand it in terms of its application semantics.

I'll have a lot to say about application semantics in the next few chapters, so for now I'll just point them out in this HTML form. The application semantics in that form are the CSS class attached to the submit button (`edit-post`) and the human-readable label attached to the button ("Edit this blog post.")

Those two strings are not much to work from. Until recently, application semantics were so poorly understood that I recommended not using overloaded POST at all. But if you follow the advice I give in Chapter 8, you can use a profile to reliably communicate application semantics to your clients. It won't be as reliable as the protocol semantics—every HTTP client ever made knows what GET means—but you'll be able to do it.

Since an overloaded POST request can do anything at all, the POST method is neither safe nor idempotent. One particular overloaded POST request may *turn out* to be safe, but as far as HTTP is concerned, POST is unsafe.

Which Methods Should You Use?

A RESTful system is made up of independent components: servers, clients, caches, proxies, caching proxies, and so on. These components were created by different people, they've never heard of each other before they start talking, and they can only communicate by passing documents back and forth over HTTP (or some similar protocol). It's essential that everyone agree on a set of protocol semantics ahead of time, or the components won't understand each other.

The protocol semantics of HTTP are mostly defined by the HTTP methods. But there's a lot of redundancy in these methods. PUT can substitute for PATCH. GET can do the job of HEAD. POST can substitute for anything. Do we really need all these methods?

There's no official set of protocol semantics. We can have a lot of fun arguing over which HTTP methods are the best, but it really comes down to membership in a community. When you choose the HTTP methods you're going to use, you choose a community of clients and other components that understand those methods.

The methods I recommend for use in most web APIs are GET, POST, PUT, DELETE, and PATCH. But I can think of a lot of cases where I'd recommend different methods:

- Before 2008, the PATCH method didn't exist. Back then, the method set I recommended for web APIs was GET, POST, PUT, and DELETE.

- In 1997, the first version of the HTTP 1.1 specification (RFC 2068) defined the HTTP methods LINK and UNLINK. In 1999, these methods were removed from the final specification (RFC 2616), because no one was using them.

  LINK and UNLINK were part of HTTP's official protocol semantics for about two years. Then they went away. Since these methods would be useful in a lot of APIs, the Internet-Draft "snell-link-method" is trying to bring them back.

- The WebDAV standard (specified in RFC 4918, and covered briefly in Chapter 11) defines seven new HTTP methods for use in APIs that treat HTTP resources as though they were files on a filesystem. These methods include COPY, MOVE, and LOCK.

- When we humans surf around on our web browsers, we completely ignore most of the methods defined in the HTTP specification, and get by with just GET and POST. That's because the protocol semantics of HTML documents only allow for GET and POST.

- The CoAP protocol (described in Chapter 13) defines the methods GET, POST, PUT, and DELETE. These methods were named after HTTP methods, but they mean slightly different things, because CoAP is not HTTP.

If you want an API entirely described by HTML documents, then your protocol semantics are limited to GET and POST. If you want to speak to filesystem GUI applications like Microsoft's Web Folders, you'll be using HTTP plus the WebDAV extensions. If you need to talk to a wide variety of HTTP caches and proxies, you should stay away from PATCH and other methods not defined in RFC 2616.

Some communities are bigger than others. When you go off the path and make up your own protocol semantics, you're isolating yourself in a community of one.

CHAPTER 4

Hypermedia

The story so far: URLs identify resources. A client makes HTTP requests to those URLs. A server sends representations in response, and over time the client builds up a picture of the resource state, as seen through the representations. Eventually the client makes that fateful PUT or POST or PATCH request, sending a representation back to the server and modifying resource state.

Look closer, and you'll see a question that hasn't been answered: how does the client know which requests it can make? There are infinitely many URLs. How does a client know which URLs have representations behind them and which ones will give a 404 error? Should the client send an entity-body with its POST request? If so, what should the entity-body look like? HTTP defines a set of protocol semantics, but which subset of those semantics does *this* web server support on *this* URL right now?

The missing piece of the puzzle is *hypermedia*. Hypermedia connects resources to each other, and describes their capabilities in machine-readable ways. Properly used, hypermedia can solve—or at least mitigate—the usability and stability problems found in today's web APIs.

Like REST, hypermedia isn't a single technology described by a standards document somewhere. Hypermedia is a strategy, implemented in different ways by dozens of technologies. I'll cover several hypermedia standards in the next three chapters, and a whole lot more in Chapter 10. It's up to you to choose the technologies that fit your business requirements.

The hypermedia strategy always has the same goal. Hypermedia is a way for the server to tell the client what HTTP requests the client might want to make in the future. It's a menu, provided by the server, from which the client is free to choose. The server knows what *might* happen, but the client decides what *actually* happens.

There's nothing new here. The World Wide Web works this way, and we all take it for granted that it *should* work this way. Anything else would be an unusable throwback to the 1980s. But in the world of APIs, hypermedia is a confusing and controversial topic. That's why today's APIs are terrible at managing change.

In this chapter, I want to dispel the mystery of hypermedia, so you can create APIs that have some of the flexibility of the Web.

HTML as a Hypermedia Format

You're probably already familiar with HTML,[1] so let's start with an HTML example.

Here's an HTML `<a>` tag:

```
<a href="http://www.youtypeitwepostit.com/messages/">
  See the latest messages
</a>
```

This tag is a simple *hypermedia control*. It's a description of an HTTP request your browser might make in the near future. An `<a>` tag is a signal to your browser that it can make an HTTP GET request that would look something like this:

```
GET /messages HTTP/1.1
Host: www.youtypeitwepostit.com
```

The HTML standard says that when the user activates a link, the user "visits" the resource on the other end of the link.[2] In practice, this means fetching a representation of the resource and displaying it in the browser window, replacing the original representation (the one that included the link). Of course, that doesn't happen automatically. Nothing will happen until the user clicks on the link. An `<a>` tag is a promise from the web server that a certain URL names a resource you can visit. If you sent a GET request to a URL you made up, such as *http://www.youtypeitwepostit.com/give-me-the-messages? please=true*, you'd probably just get a 404 error.

Compare the `<a>` tag to another of HTML's hypermedia controls, the `<img>` tag:

```
<img rel="icon" src="http://www.example.com/logo.png" />
```

The `<img>` tag also describes an HTTP request your browser might make in the near future, but there's no implication that you're moving from one document to another. Instead, the representation of the linked resource is supposed to be *embedded* as an image in the current document. When your browser finds an `<img>` tag, it makes the request for the image automatically, without asking you to click on anything. Then it

---

1. There are two HTML specifications you should know about: the HTML 4 spec (*http://www.w3.org/TR/html4*) and the HTML 5 spec (*http://www.w3.org/TR/html5*). Both are open standards produced by the W3C. HTML 4 has been stable for over 10 years; HTML 5 is a work in progress.

2. That's in section 12.1.1 of the HTML 4 specification.

---

incorporates the representation in the document you're viewing, again without asking your permission.

Let's look at a more complex hypermedia control—an HTML form:

```
<form action="http://www.youtypeitwepostit.com/messages" method="post">
  <input type="text" name="message" value="" required="true" />
  <input type="submit" value="Post" />
</form>
```

This form describes a request to the URL *http://www.youtypeitwepostit.com/ messages/*. That's the same URL I used for the <a> tag. But the <a> tag described a GET request, and this form describes a POST request.

This form doesn't just give you the URL and send you off to make a POST request. There are also two controls—a text field and a submit button—which are rendered as GUI elements in a web browser.

When you click the submit button, the value you entered in the text field and the value on the button are transformed into a representation, according to rules set down in the HTML specification. Those rules say the media type of the representation will be ap plication/x-www-form-urlencoded, and it will look something like this:

```
message=Hello%21&submit=Post
```

Putting it all together, that <form> tag tells your browser that it can make a POST request that looks something like this:

```
POST /messages HTTP/1.1
Host: www.youtypeitwepostit.com
Content-Type: application/x-www-form-urlencoded

message=Hello%21&submit=Post
```

As with the <a> tag, the server's guiding you, but its hand is pretty light. If you don't want to fill out this form, you can ignore it. If you do fill out the form, you can put whatever you want in the message field (although the server might reject certain values). The <form> tag is the server telling you that, of all the possible POST requests you might make, there's one type of request that's likely to result in something useful. That's a POST to /messages, which includes a form-encoded entity-body that includes a value for message.

Here's one more <form> tag:

```
<form method="GET" action="http://www.youtypewepostit.com/messages/">
  <input type="text" id="query" name="query"/>
  <input type="submit" name="Search"/>
</form>
```

This form also has a text box you're supposed to fill out, but the form is telling you to make a GET request, and GET requests don't include an entity-body. Instead, the data you type into that text box gets incorporated into the request URL—again, according to rules laid out in the HTML specification.

If you fill out this form, the HTTP request your browser makes will look something like this:

```
GET /messages/?query=rest HTTP/1.1
Host: www.youtypeitwepostit.com
```

To sum up, the familiar HTML controls allow the server to describe four kinds of HTTP requests.

- The `<a>` tag describes a GET request for one specific URL, which is made only if the user triggers the control.
- The `<img>` tag describes a GET request for one specific URL, which happens automatically, in the background.
- The `<form>` tag with `method="POST"` describes a POST request to one specific URL, with a custom entity-body constructed by the client. The request is only made if the user triggers the control.
- The `<form>` tag with `method="GET"` describes a GET request to a custom URL constructed by the client. The request is only made if the user triggers the control.

HTML also defines some more exotic hypermedia controls, and other data formats may define controls that are stranger still. All of them fall under the formal definition of hypermedia given in the Fielding dissertation:

> Hypermedia is defined by the presence of application control information embedded within, or as a layer above, the presentation of information.

The World Wide Web is full of HTML documents, and the documents are full of things people like to read—prices, statistics, personal messages, prose, and poetry. But all of those things fall under *presentation of information*. In terms of presentation of information, the Web isn't much different from a printed book.

It's the application control information that distinguishes an HTML document from a book. I'm talking about the hypermedia controls that people interact with all the time, but rarely examine closely. The `<img>` tags that tell the browser to embed certain images, the `<a>` tags that transport the end user to another part of the Web, and the `<script>` tags that supply JavaScript for the browser to execute.

An HTML document that contains a poem will probably also feature a link to "Other poems by this author," or a form that lets the reader "Rate this poem." This is application control information that couldn't show up in a printed book of poetry. The presence of application control information can certainly reduce the emotional impact of a poem, but an HTML document containing only the text of a poem is not a full participant in the Web. It's just simulating a printed book.

URI Templates

The custom URLs you can create using an HTML <form> tag are limited in form. *http://www.youtypeitwepostit.com/messages/?search=rest* doesn't look very nice. On a technical level, this doesn't matter. URLs don't have to look nice. URLs don't even need to make sense to human eyes. But we humans prefer nice-looking URLs, like *http://www.youtypeitwepostit.com/search/rest*.

HTML's hypermedia controls have no way of telling a browser how to construct a URL like *http://www.youtypeitwepostit.com/search/rest*. But URI Templates, a different hypermedia technology, *can* do this. URI Templates are defined in RFC 6570, and they look like this:

```
http://www.youtypeitwepostit.com/search/{search}
```

That's not a valid URL, because it contains curly brackets. Those brackets identify the string as a URI Template. RFC 6570 tells you how to turn that string into an infinite number of URLs. It says you can replace {search} with any string you want, so long as that string would be valid in a URL:

- *http://www.youtypeitwepostit.com/search/rest*
- *http://www.youtypeitwepostit.com/search/RESTful%20Web%20APIs*

This HTML form:

```
<form method="GET" action="http://www.youtypeitwepostit.com/messages/">
 <input type="text" id="query" name="query"/>
 <input type="submit" name="Search"/>
</form>
```

is exactly equivalent to this URI Template:

```
http://www.youtypeitwepostit.com/messages/?query={query}
```

That's a very common case, so the URI Templates standard defines a shortcut for URLs that include a query string. This URI Template is exactly equivalent to the previous one, and it's also equivalent to the previous HTML form:

```
http://www.youtypeitwepostit.com/messages/{?query}
```

The URI Templates standard is full of examples, but here are a few more sample templates, along with just a few of the URLs you can get from them:

```
If parameter values are set to:
   var   := "title"
   hello := "Hello World!"
   path  := "/foo/bar"

Then these URI templates:
   http://www.example.org/greeting?g={+hello}
```

```
http://www.example.org{+path}/status
http://www.example.org/document#{+var}
```

```
Expand to these URLs:
    http://www.example.org/greeting?g=Hello%20World!
    http://www.example.org/foo/bar/status
    http://www.example.org/document#title
```

Although a URI Template is shorter and more flexible than an HTML GET form, the two technologies aren't much different. URI Templates and HTML forms allow a web server to describe an infinite number of URLs with a short string. The HTTP client can plug in some values, choose one URL from that infinite family, and make a GET request to that specific URL.

URI Templates don't make sense on their own. A URI Template needs to be embedded in a hypermedia format. The idea is that every standard that needs this functionality should just use URI Templates, instead of defining a custom format, which is what was happening before RFC 6570 was published.

URI Versus URL

I've put this off for as long as I can, but now I need to explain the difference between URL (the term I use almost everywhere in this book), and URI (the more general term used in the names of technologies such as URI Templates). Most web APIs deal exclusively with URLs, so for most of this book, the distinction doesn't matter. But when it's important (as it will be in Chapter 12), it's *really* important.

A URL is a short string used to identify a resource. A URI is also a short string used to identify a resource. Every URL is a URI. They're described in the same standard: RFC 3986.

What's the difference? As far as this book is concerned, the difference is this: *there's no guarantee that a URI has a representation*. A URI is nothing but an identifier. A URL is an identifier that can be *dereferenced*. That is, a computer can somehow take a URL and get a representation of the underlying resource.

If you see an `http:` URI, you know how a computer can get a representation: by making an HTTP GET request. If you see an `ftp:` URI, you know how a computer can get a representation: by starting up an FTP client and executing certain FTP commands. These URIs are URLs. They have protocols associated with them: rules for obtaining representations of these resources (very detailed rules that a computer can follow).

Here's a URI that's *not* a URL: `urn:isbn:9781449358063`. It designates a resource: the print edition of this book. Not any particular copy of this book, but the abstract concept of an entire edition. (Remember that a resource can be anything at all.) This URI is not a URL because... what's the protocol? How would a computer get a representation? You can't do it.

Without a URL, you can't get a representation. Without representations, there can be no representational state transfer. A resource that's not identified by a URL cannot fulfill many of the Fielding constraints. It can't fulfill the self-descriptive message constraint, because it can't send any messages. A representation can link to a URI that's not a URL (`<a href="urn:isbn:9781449358063">`), but that won't fulfill the hypermedia constraint, because a client can't follow the link.

Here's a *URL* that identifies the print edition of this book: *http://shop.oreilly.com/prod uct/0636920028468.do*. You can send a GET request to this URL and get a representation of the edition. Not a physical copy of the book, but an HTML document that conveys some of its resource state: the title, the number of pages, and so on. The HTML document also contains hypermedia, like links to the book's authors—not the people themselves, but some information about them. A resource identified by a URL can fulfill all the Fielding constraints.

There are some good reasons to use URIs that aren't URLs, and I'll cover them when I discuss the resource description strategy in Chapter 12. But it's a pretty rare situation. In general, when your web API refers to a resource, it should use a URL with the http or https scheme, and that URL should *work*: it should serve a useful representation in response to a GET request.

The Link Header

Here's a technology that puts hypermedia where you might not expect it: inside the headers of an HTTP request or response. RFC 5988 defines an extension to HTTP, a header called `Link`. This header lets you add simple hypermedia controls to entity-bodies that don't normally support hypermedia at all, like JSON objects and binary image files.

Here's a plain-text representation of a story that's been split into multiple parts with cliffhangers (the entity-body of this HTTP response contains the first part of the story, and the `Link` header points to the second part):

```
HTTP/1.1 200 OK
Content-Type: text/plain
Link: <http://www.example.com/story/part2>;rel="next"

It was a dark and stormy night. Suddenly, a...
(continued in part 2)
```

The `Link` header has approximately the same functionality as an HTML `<a>` tag. I recommend you use real hypermedia formats whenever possible, but when that's not an option, the `Link` header can be very useful.

The LINK and UNLINK extension methods use the `Link` header. This example from Chapter 3 (which assigns an author to the story) should make a little more sense now:

```
LINK /story HTTP/1.1
Host: www.example.com
Link: <http://www.example.com/~drmilk>;rel="author"
```

What Hypermedia Is For

I'll be covering a lot of hypermedia data formats in this book, but at this point telling you about one technology after another won't help very much. We need to take a step back and see what hypermedia is for.

Hypermedia controls have three jobs:

- They tell the client how to construct an HTTP request: what HTTP method to use, what URL to use, what HTTP headers and/or entity-body to send.
- They make promises about the HTTP response, suggesting the status code, the HTTP headers, and/or the data the server is likely to send in response to a request.
- They suggest how the client should integrate the response into its workflow.

HTML GET forms and URI Templates feel similar because they do the same job. They both tell the client how to construct a URL for use in an HTTP GET request.

Guiding the Request

An HTTP request has four parts: the method, the target URL, the HTTP headers, and the entity-body. Hypermedia controls can guide the client into specifying all four of these.

This HTML <a> tag specifies both the target URL and the HTTP method to use:

```
<a href="http://www.example.com/">An outbound link</a>
```

The target URL is defined explicitly, in the href attribute. The HTTP method is defined implicitly: the HTML spec says that an <a> tag becomes a GET request when the end user clicks the link.

This HTML form defines the method, the target URL, and the entity-body of a potential future HTTP request:

```
<form action="/stores" method="post">
  <input type="text" name="storeName" value=""  />
  <input type="text" name="nearbyCity" value="" />
  <input type="submit" value="Add" />
</form>
```

Both the HTTP method and the target URL are defined explicitly. The entity-body is defined in terms of a set of questions for the client. The client needs to figure out what values it wants to provide for the variables storeName and nearbyCity. Then it can construct a form-encoded entity-body that the server will accept. (Who says it needs to be form-encoded? That's defined implicitly, by HTML's rules for processing a `<form>` tag.)

This URI Template specifies the target URL of an HTTP request, and nothing else:

```
http://www.youtypeitwepostit.com/messages/{?search}
```

The target URL is defined in terms of a variable that needs to be filled in, just like the entity-body of an HTML form would be. The client uses an algorithm to turn the URI Template and its desired value for the `search` variable into a real URL: say, for example, *http://www.youtypeitwepostit.com/messages/?search=rest*.

A URI Template defines nothing about the HTTP request except for the target URI. It's not telling you to make a GET request, a POST request, or any kind of request in particular. That's why I said URI Templates don't make sense on their own, why they need to be combined with another hypermedia technology.

Here's an HTML form that tells the client to set a specific value for the HTTP header `Content-Type`:

```
<form action="POST" enctype="text/plain">
  ...
</form>
```

Ordinarily, the entity-body of an HTML POST form is form-encoded, and sent over the network with the `Content-Type` header set to `application/x-www-form-urlencoded`. But specifying the `enctype` attribute of the `<form>` tag overrides this behavior. A form with `enctype="text/plain"` tells the browser to encode its entity-body in a plain text format, and to send it over the network with the `Content-Type` header set to `text/plain`.

This isn't a great example, because the `enctype` attribute only changes the `Content-Type` header as a side effect of changing the entity-body. But it is the best example I can come up with using a popular hypermedia format like HTML.

Hypermedia controls generally leave an HTTP client free to send whatever headers it wants. But this laissez-faire attitude is only a convention. A hypermedia control can describe an HTTP request in great detail. It can instruct the client to send an HTTP request to a specific URL, using a specific HTTP method, providing an entity-body constructed according to specific rules, and providing specific values for specific HTTP headers.

Promises About the Response

Here's another HTML tag:

```
<img src="http://www.example.com/logo.png" />
```

Like an `<a>` tag, an `<img>` tag is a promise that the client can make a GET request to a particular URL. But the `<img>` tag makes another promise: that the server will send some kind of *image* representation in response to GET.

Here's another example—a simple XML hypermedia control from the Atom Publishing Protocol (which I'll discuss in more detail in Chapter 6):

```
<link rel="edit" href="http://example.org/posts/1"/>
```

This looks simple enough; in fact, this `<link>` tag could legally show up in an HTML document. But interpreted according to the AtomPub standard, that `rel="edit"` gives you a lot of information about the resource at *http://example.org/posts/1*.

First, `rel="edit"` says that the resource at *http://example.org/posts/1* supports PUT and DELETE as well as GET. You can GET a representation of this resource, modify the representation, and PUT it back to change the resource's state. That's a perfectly standard use of HTTP, and perhaps not something that needs to be stated explicitly. But given that most HTTP resources *don't* respond to PUT or DELETE, it's worth spelling out.

More important, `rel="edit"` means the client needn't speculate about what kind of representation you'll get if you send a GET request to *http://example.org/posts/1*. You'll get back the kind of document AtomPub calls a Member Entry. (The details aren't important right now—skip to Chapter 6 if you want to learn more about AtomPub.)

The server is making a promise to the client: if you make that GET request, you'll receive an AtomPub Member Entry representation in return. The client doesn't have to make a blind GET and see what the `Content-Type` says. It knows the representation will be of type `application/atom+xml`, and it also knows something about the representation's application semantics.

Workflow Control

The third job of hypermedia is to describe the relationships between resources. This is best explained by an example. Here's an HTML `<a>` tag:

```
<a href="http://www.example.com/">An outbound link</a>
```

If you click this link in your web browser, the browser will move to the web page mentioned in the link's `href` attribute. The old page will become completely irrelevant, except as an item in your browser history. The `<a>` tag is an *outbound link*: a hypermedia control that, when activated, *replaces* the client's application state with a brand new state.

Compare this to the `<img>` tag in HTML:

```
<img src="http://www.example.com/logo.png" />
```

This is a link, but it's not an outbound link; it's an *embedded link*. Embedded links don't replace the client's application state. They augment it. If you visit a web page whose

HTML includes this `<img>` tag, the image is automatically loaded in a separate HTTP request (without you having to click anything), and displayed in the same window as the web page itself. You're still on the same page, but now you have more information.

An HTML document can embed more than images. Here's some HTML markup that downloads and runs some executable code written in JavaScript:

```
<script type="application/javascript" src="/my_javascript_application.js"/>
```

Here's some markup that downloads a CSS stylesheet and applies it to the main document:

```
<link rel="stylesheet" type="text/css" href="/my_stylesheet.css"/>
```

Here's some markup that embeds another full HTML document inside this one:

```
<frameset>
  <iframe src="/another-document.html" />
</frameset>
```

All of these are embedding links. The process of embedding one document in another is also called *transclusion*.

Of course, a client is free to ignore the server's guidance. There are browser extensions that prevent the browser from transcluding the files referenced by `<script>` tags, and options to override the formatting instructions specified by stylesheets for greater readability. The point of these tags, as with the `<form>` tag, is to give the client *hints* as to which HTTP requests are likely to get the client what it wants. The client is always free not to make a request.

Beware of Fake Hypermedia!

There are a lot of existing APIs that were designed by people who understood the benefits of hypermedia, but that don't technically contain any hypermedia. Imagine a bookstore API that serves a JSON representation like this:

```
HTTP/1.1 200 OK
Content-Type: application/json

{
 "title": "Example: A Novel",
 "description": "http://www.example.com/"
}
```

This is a representation of a book. The `description` field happens to look like a URL: *http://www.example.com/*. But is this a *link*? Is `description` supposed to link to a resource that gives the description? Or is it supposed to be a textual description, and some smart aleck typed in some text that happens to be a valid URL?

Formally speaking, `"http://www.example.com/"` is a string. The `application/json` media type doesn't define any hypermedia controls, so even if some part of a representation *really* looks like a hypermedia link, it's not! It's just a string!

If you're trying to consume an API like this, you won't get very far dogmatically denying the existence of links. Instead, you'll read some human-readable documentation written by the API provider. That documentation will explain the conventions the provider used to embed hypermedia links in a format (JSON) that doesn't support hypermedia. Then you'll know how to distinguish between links and strings, and you'll be able to write a client that can detect and follow the hypermedia links.

But your client will only work for *that specific API*. The documentation you read is the documentation for a one-off fiat standard. The next API you use will have a different set of conventions for embedding hypermedia links in JSON, and you'll have to do the work all over again.

That's why API designers shouldn't design APIs that serve plain JSON. You should use a media type that has real support for hypermedia. Your users will thank you. They'll be able to use preexisting libraries written against the media type, rather than writing new ones specifically for your API.

JSON has been the most popular representation format for APIs for quite a while, but as recently as a couple years ago, there were no JSON-based hypermedia formats. As you'll see in the next few chapters, that has changed. Don't worry that you'll have to give up JSON to gain real hypermedia.

The Semantic Challenge: How Are We Doing?

At the end of Chapter 1, I set out a challenge: "How can we program a computer to decide which links to click?" A web browser works by passing the representations it gets to a human, who makes all the decisions. How can we get similar behavior without consulting a human at each step?

Providing the links is a step in the right direction. Out of the infinite set of legal HTTP requests, a hypermedia document explains which requests might be useful *right now*, on this particular site. The client doesn't have to guess.

But that's not enough. Suppose an HTML document contains only two links, A and B. Two possible requests the client might make. How does the client choose? On what basis can it make its decision?

Well, suppose one of those links is represented by an HTML `<img>` tag, and the other is represented by a `<script>` tag. As far as HTTP is concerned, there's no difference between these two links. They have the same protocol semantics. They both trigger a GET request to a predetermined URL. But the two links have different application semantics. The representation at the other end of an `<img>` tag is supposed to be displayed as an image, and the representation at the other end of a `<script>` tag is supposed to be executed as client-side code.

For some clients, that's enough information to make a decision. A client designed to scrape all the images from a web page will follow the link in the `<img>` tag and ignore the link in the `<script>` tag.

This shows that hypermedia controls can bridge the semantic gap. They can tell the client *why* it might want to make a certain HTTP request.

But for most clients, the distinction between `<img>` and `<script>` isn't enough information to make a decision. "Image" and "script" are very generic bits of application semantics. The application described by HTML is the World Wide Web, a very flexible application that's used for all sorts of things.

When I think about application semantics, I usually think on a higher level than that. I think about the concepts that separate a wiki from an online store. They're both websites, they both use embedded images and scripts, but they *mean* very different things.

A hypermedia format doesn't have to be generic like HTML. It can be defined in enough detail to convey the application semantics of a wiki or a store. In the next chapter, I'll talk about hypermedia formats that are designed to represent one specific type of problem. Outside that problem space, they're practically useless. But within their limits, they meet the semantic challenge very well.

Domain-Specific Designs

In this chapter, I'll choose a problem space and implement a web API for representing it. The details of the problem space don't matter. The technique is always the same. So I'm going to choose the most frivolous example I can think of: maze games!

Figure 5-1 shows a simple maze with one entrance and one exit. My server's job will be to invent mazes like this and present them to clients.

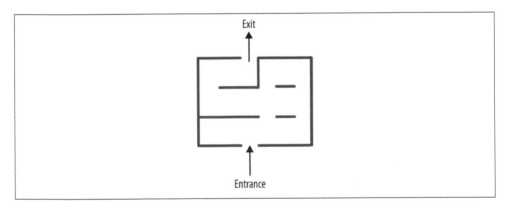

Figure 5-1. The example maze (a view from above)

Although this is a frivolous example, the maze is a good metaphor for hypermedia applications in general. Any complex problem can be represented as a hypermedia maze that the client must navigate. If you've ever been trapped in a phone tree, or searched for products on an online store and then bought something from the search results, you've navigated a hypermedia maze.

I've seen hypermedia APIs for modifying complex insurance policies; for selecting products from a catalog and paying for them; and, yes, for describing phone trees (see

VoiceXML in Chapter 10). All of these APIs have the same shape as the maze games I'm about to show you:

- The problem is too complex to be understood all at once, so it's split up into steps.
- Every client begins the process at the same first step.
- At each step in the process, the server presents the client with a number of possible next steps.
- At each step, the client decides what next step to take.
- The client knows what counts as success and when to stop.

As we go through this book, I'll deal with more specialized problem domains. The documents and the possible next steps will become more complex, but the step-by-step problem-solving algorithm will always work the same way.

Maze+XML: A Domain-Specific Design

Take another look at Figure 5-1. That's a graphical representation of a maze. It makes intuitive sense to a human, but a computer would need to run it through a machine-vision algorithm to understand it. How can we represent the shape of a maze in a format that's easy for a computer to understand?

There are many possible solutions, but instead of designing a solution from scratch, I'm going to reuse some work that's already been done. There's a personal standard called Maze+XML (*http://amundsen.com/media-types/maze/*), for representing mazes in a machine-readable format.

The media type of a Maze+XML document is `application/vnd.amundsen.maze+xml`. If you ever make an HTTP request and see that string used as the `Content-Type` of the response, you'll know that you need the Maze+XML specification to fully understand the entity-body. This is how a domain-specific design meets the semantic challenge: by defining a document format that represents the problem (such as the layout of a maze), and by registering a media type for that format, so that a client knows right away when it's encountered an instance of the problem.

In general, I don't recommend creating new domain-specific media types. It's usually less work to add application semantics to a generic hypermedia format—a technique I'll cover in the next two chapters. If you set out to do a domain-specific design, you'll probably end up with a fiat standard that doesn't take advantage of the work done by your predecessors. You probably won't have the flexibility problems that plague most of today's APIs, but you'll have done more work for no real benefit.

But a domain-specific design is the average developer's first instinct when designing an API. What could be more natural than simply solving the problem at hand? That's why I'm covering domain-specific designs first. It's easy to show how a custom hypermedia format can bridge the semantic gap.

How Maze+XML Works

Instead of looking down on Figure 5-1 from above, imagine being inside the maze. Instead of seeing the whole thing, you'd only see your immediate vicinity. Upon entering the maze, you'd see something like Figure 5-2: a wall in front of you and the entrance behind you. But you'd have two choices: go left or go right. You'd have no way of knowing which direction would take you to the exit.

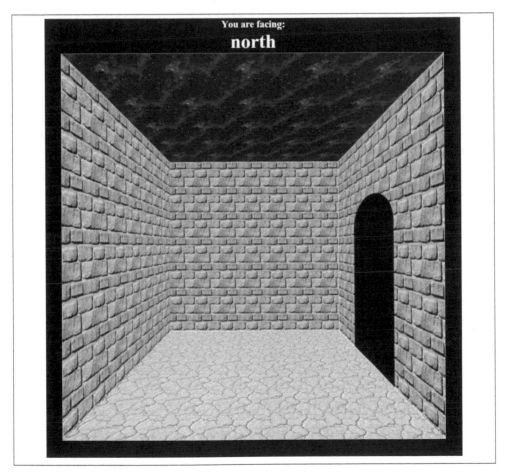

Figure 5-2. Inside the example maze

The Maze+XML format simulates this rat's-eye-view by representing a maze as a network of "cells" that connect to each other. Figure 5-3 shows how the example maze from Figure 5-1 might be represented as a network of cells. I've chopped the maze into a grid and created a cell for each grid square.

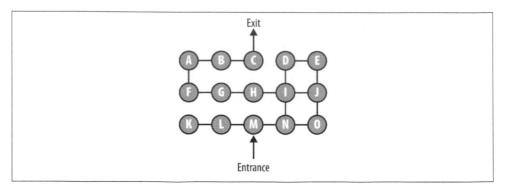

Figure 5-3. The example maze as a network of cells

Maze+XML cells connect to each other in the cardinal directions: north, south, east, and west. Let's say that north points to the top of the page. This means the exit (cell C) is directly north of the entrance (cell M), although you can't just go north to find it—you have to go east and loop around.

Each cell in a Maze+XML maze is an HTTP resource with its own URL. If you send a GET request to the first cell in this maze, you'll get a representation that looks like this:

```
<maze version="1.0">
 <cell href="/cells/M" rel="current">
  <title>The Entrance Hallway</title>
  <link rel="east" href="/cells/N"/>
  <link rel="west" href="/cells/L"/>
 </cell>
</maze>
```

This representation includes a human-readable name of the cell, "The Entrance Hallway," like you'd see in an old, text-based adventure game. But—this is where hypermedia comes in—the representation also includes <link> tags that connect this cell to its neighbors. From cell M, you have a choice of going west to cell L or east to cell N.

Link Relations

This representation shows off a powerful hypermedia tool called the *link relation*. By themselves, rel="east" and rel="west" don't mean anything. A computer doesn't carry around an understanding of the words "east" and "west." But the Maze+XML standard defines meanings for "east" and "west," and developers can program those definitions into their clients. Here are the definitions:

`east`

> Refers to a resource to the east of the current resource. When used in the Maze +XML media type, the associated URI points to a neighboring cell resource to the east in the active maze.

`west`

> Refers to a resource to the west of the current resource. When used in the Maze +XML media type, the associated URI points to a neighboring cell resource to the west in the active maze.

These definitions seem circular. They just say that the link relations `east` and `west` correspond to our everyday geographical notions with the same names. But these definitions serve to bridge the semantic gap, because again, link relations mean nothing by themselves. Without a formal definition, `east` could mean south and `west` could mean underneath.

The Maze+XML standard also defines the link relations `north` and `south`. These definitions let us *expect* directional links to show up in Maze+XML representations, and program a computer to understand this bit of markup if it ever shows up:

```
<link rel="east" href="/cells/N"/>
```

In Maze+XML, following a link marked with the link relation `east` will move your client east through some abstract geographical space. You'll end up in another maze cell. Moving from your current resource to the one to the east is analogous to moving east in real life, or at least to moving your finger east on a map. This is how Maze+XML meets the semantic challenge: by defining link relations that convey its application semantics.

A link relation is a magical string associated with a hypermedia control like Maze+XML's `<link>` tag. It explains the change in application state (for safe requests) or resource state (for unsafe requests) that will happen if the client triggers the control. Link relations are formally defined in RFC 5988, but the idea has been around for a long time, and nearly every hypermedia format supports them.

One of the most important web pages for a RESTful API developer is the registry of link relations managed by the Internet Assigned Numbers Authority (*http://www.iana.org/ assignments/link-relations/*) (IANA). I'll be coming back to this registry throughout the book. It contains about 60 link relations that have been deemed to be generally useful and not tied to a particular data format. The simplest examples are the `next` and `previous` relations, for navigating a list. Maze+XML's `east` and `west` are not on this list; they were deemed not generally useful enough.

RFC 5988 defines two kinds of link relations: registered relation types and extension relation types. Registered link relations look like the ones you see in the IANA registry: short strings like `east` and `previous`. To avoid conflicts, these short strings need to be registered somewhere—not necessarily with the IANA, but in some kind of standard such as the definition of a media type.

Extension relations look like URLs. If you own *mydoma.in*, you can name a link relation `http://mydoma.in/whatever` and define it to mean anything you want. No one can define a link relation that conflicts with yours, since you control the domain. When your users visit *http://mydoma.in/whatever* in their web browsers, they should see a human-readable explanation of the link relation.[1]

Chapter 9 includes a guide explaining when it's OK to use the shorter names of registered relations. Here's a summary:

- You can use extension relations wherever you want.
- You can use IANA-registered link relations whenever you want.
- If a document's media type defines some registered relations, you can use them within the document.
- If a document includes a profile that defines some link relations (see Chapter 8), you can treat them as registered relations within that document.
- Don't give your link relations names that conflict with the names in the IANA registry.

Follow a Link to Change Application State

A client can "go east" from cell M by following the appropriate link (i.e., by sending a GET request to the URL labeled with `rel="east"`). A client that does this will get a second Maze+XML representation, looking something like this:

```
<maze version="1.0">
 <cell href="/cells/N">
  <title>Foyer of Horrors</title>
  <link rel="north" href="/cells/I"/>
  <link rel="west" href="/cells/M"/>
  <link rel="east" href="/cells/O"/>
 </cell>
</maze>
```

This is the Maze+XML representation of cell N on the map. It links back to cell M (using the link relation `west`), as well as to cells I (`north`) and O (`east`).

---

1. If you ever need to format an IANA-registered link relation as an extension relation, you can use the URI Template `http://alps.io/iana/relations#{name}`. The alternate name for the link relation `author` is `http://alps.io/iana/relations#author`. This is a service we're providing as part of the ALPS project described in Chapter 8, not anything official or endorsed by the IANA.

The client's application state has changed. To borrow a term from the HTML standard, the client was "visiting" cell M, and now it's "visiting" cell N. The client has three new options, represented by the links in the representation of cell N.

By following the right links (north, west, west, west, north, east, east, and finally east), a client can make its way from cell N to cell C. That cell includes the exit to the maze, indicated here by a <link> tag with the link relation exit:

```
<maze version="1.0">
 <cell href="/cells/C">
  <title>The End of the Tunnel</title>
  <link rel="west" href="/cells/B"/>
  <link rel="exit" href="/success.txt"/>
 </cell>
</maze>
```

Here's what the Maze+XML standard says about exit:

exit

> Refers to a resource that represents the exit or end of the current client activity or process. When used in the Maze+XML media type, the associated URI points to the final exit resource of the active maze.

Unlike with east and the other directional relations, Maze+XML provides no guidance as to what should appear at the other end of an exit link. It's a "resource," which means it can be anything at all. In this implementation, I've chosen to link to a textual congratulatory message (success.txt).

The Collection of Mazes

Cell C leads out of the maze, because its representation includes a special link with rel="exit". But cell M, the *entrance* to the maze, doesn't include anything to distinguish it from the other fourteen cells. There's no rel="entrance" or anything. Cell M's title is "The Entrance Hallway," but that phrase doesn't mean anything to a computer. How do we bridge the semantic gap? How is the client supposed to know where to start the maze?

The Maze+XML standard solves this problem with a *collection*: a list of mazes. If you send a GET request to the root URL of the maze API, you might get a Maze+XML representation that looks like this:

```
<maze version="1.0">
 <collection>
  <link rel="maze" title="A Beginner's Maze" href="/beginner">
  <link rel="maze" title="For Experts Only" href="/expert-maze/start">
 </collection>
</maze>
```

A collection in Maze+XML is a `<collection>` tag that includes some `<link>` tags with the link relation `maze`. This relation (defined in the Maze+XML specification, just like `east` and `exit`) tells a client that the resource on the other end is the starting cell of a maze. This representation links to two mazes: the beginner's maze I diagrammed, Figure 5-1, and a more complicated maze that I won't show here.

Send a GET request to a URL labeled with the relation `maze` (/beginner, let's say), and you'll get a representation that looks like this:

```
<maze version="1.0">
 <item>
  <title>A Beginner's Maze</title>
  <link rel="start" href="/cells/C"/>
 </item>
</maze>
```

This is a high-level representation of the maze as seen from the outside. It's got a link with the relation `start` which points to cell C.

Here's where Maze+XML represents the fact that /cells/C is the entrance to the maze. It's in the view of the maze from outside. Once you enter the maze, there's no longer anything special about cell C.

The URL to the collection of mazes is the proverbial "URL advertised on the billboard." Starting with no information but this URL, you can do everything it's possible to do with a Maze+XML API:

1. Start off by GETting a representation of the collection of mazes. You know how to parse the representation, because you read the Maze+XML specification and programmed this knowledge into your client.

2. Your client also knows that the link relation `maze` indicates an individual maze. This gives it a URL it can use in a second GET request. Sending that GET request gives you the representation of an individual maze.

3. Your client knows how to parse the representation of an individual maze (because you programmed that knowledge into it), and it knows that the link relation `start` indicates an entrance into the maze. You can make a third GET request to enter the maze.

4. Your client knows how to parse the representation of a maze cell. It knows what `east`, `west`, `north`, and `south` mean, so it can translate movement through an abstract maze into a series of HTTP GET requests.

5. Your client knows what `exit` means, so it knows when it's completed a maze.

There's more to the Maze+XML standard, but you've now seen the basics. A collection links to a maze, which links to a cell. From one cell you can follow links to other cells.

Eventually you'll find a cell with an `exit` link leading out of the maze. That's enough information to start writing clients.

Is Maze+XML an API?

If you've got experience in this field, you may be wondering: where's the API? A maze game isn't a complex application, but even so, you may have expected more than a few XML tag names and link relations. The Maze+XML specification lacks the things you may be accustomed to. It doesn't define any API calls or give any rules for constructing URLs. In fact, it barely mentions HTTP at all! I've shown some URLs in the example representations, but I deliberately made the URL formats internally inconsistent (compare /beginner to /expert-maze/start) so you wouldn't think URL formats were defined by the standard.

The things you're accustomed to are dangerous. In applications intended for use within an organization, a design based on API calls works well and is easy to develop. The API call metaphor assumes away the network boundary and lets a client invoke a method on a remote computer just like it would call the API of a local code library. There are already lots of books and software tools to help you with those designs.

My experience shows that the "API call" metaphor inevitably exposes the server's implementation details to the clients. This introduces coupling between server code and client code. When all the people involved with the API are friends and colleagues, this doesn't matter so much.

But this book focuses on *web* APIs, which is to say, web-scale APIs (i.e., APIs where any member of the public can use a client, or write a client, or, in some cases, write a server). When you allow someone outside your organization to make API calls, you make that person a silent partner in the implementation of your server. It becomes very difficult to change anything on the server side without hurting this unknown customer.

This is why public APIs change so rarely. You *can't* change an API based on API calls without causing huge pain among your users, any more than you can change the API of a local code library without causing pain. At web scale, API call designs become paralyzed.

Designs based on hypermedia have more flexibility. Every time the client makes an HTTP request, the server sends a response explaining which HTTP requests make the most sense as a next step. If the server-side options change, that document changes along with it. This doesn't solve all of our API problems—the semantic gap is a huge problem!—but it solves the one we know how to solve.

Client #1: The Game

The obvious use for the Maze+XML API is a game to be played by a human being. Here's a single-page app that grabs a collection of mazes and lets you choose one to play. Once you enter a maze, you're presented with a rat's-eye view and you navigate the maze by typing in directions. Once you find the exit, you get a score—the number of "turns" you spent in the maze.[2]

We tend to think of an "API client" as an automated client. But human-driven clients like this have a big part to play in the modern API ecosystem. It's very common for a mobile application, driven by a human, to communicate with a server through a web API. Best of all, with a human in the loop, the semantic gap is no problem.

Figure 5-4 shows what the Game client looks like just after I load it in my web browser.

Figure 5-4. The initial state of the Game client

---

2. You'll find the Node source code for the Game client in the *RESTful Web APIs* GitHub repository (look in the *Maze/the-game/* directory).

I type in a billboard URL—the URL to a collection of mazes—and click the Load button. This causes the Game client to make an HTTP GET request to the URL I typed in:

```
GET /mazes/ HTTP/1.1
Host: example.org
Accept: application/vnd.amundsen.maze+xml
```

The server responds with a Maze+XML document:

```
<maze version="1.0">
  <collection href="http://example.org/mazes/">
    <link href="http://example.org/mazes/a-beginner-maze" rel="maze"
      title="A Beginner's Maze" />
    <link href="http://example.org/mazes/for-experts-only" rel="maze"
      title="For Experts Only" />
  </collection>
</maze>
```

The Game client reads this document—a representation of a collection of mazes—and translates it into an HTML interface (Figure 5-5). I'm presented with a choice between two mazes. These correspond to the two links in the Maze+XML document with the link relation "maze."

Figure 5-5. A choice between mazes

I type in "1" to choose a maze, click the Go button, and I'm taken inside the beginners maze. Figure 5-6 shows how the client renders the first room of the maze.

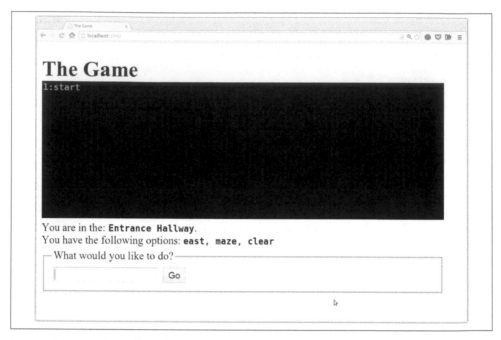

Figure 5-6. The first cell of the beginner's maze

How'd that happen? Through hypermedia. When I typed "1," I told the client to follow the first link with rel="maze", by making an HTTP GET request. The interface was a lot different from clicking on a link, but it had the same effect.

Here's the request:

```
GET /mazes/beginner HTTP/1.1
Host: example.org
Accept: application/vnd.amundsen.maze+xml
```

And here's the Maze+XML document the server sent in response:

```
<maze version="1.0">
  <item href="http://example.org/maze/beginner" title="A Beginner's Maze">
    <link href="http://example.org/mazes/beginner/0" rel="start"/>
  </item>
</maze>
```

Since there's only one link in this document—the link to the start of the maze—the human has no decision to make here. The Game client doesn't even display this representation to me. Instead, it's programmed to automatically follow the link with rel="start". This means another GET request:

```
GET /mazes/beginner/0 HTTP/1.1
Host: example.org
Accept: application/vnd.amundsen.maze+xml
```

Which yields a representation of a cell in the maze:

```
<maze version="1.0">
  <cell href="http://example.org/mazes/beginner/0" rel="current"
        title="Entrance Hallway">
    <link href="http://example.org/mazes/beginner/5" rel="east"/>
    <link href="http://example.org/mazes/beginner/J" rel="south"/>
  </cell>
</maze>
```

That information *is* displayed to the human user, after being translated into HTML.
And that's how I ended up looking at Figure 5-6.

Now I'm inside "A Beginner's Maze." From this point on, I navigate the maze by typing
in compass directions from the provided list: east, north, and so on. Every time I click
the Go button, I tell the client to follow the corresponding link by making an HTTP
GET request. Figure 5-7 shows me in cell G ("The Tool Room"), halfway through the
beginner's maze.

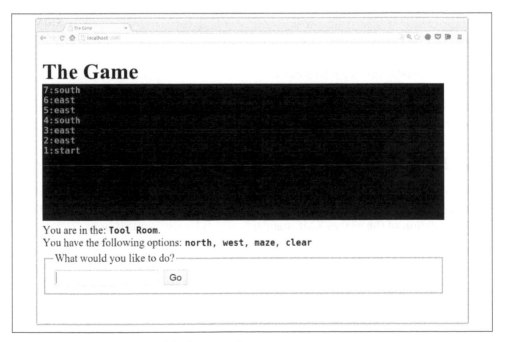

Figure 5-7. In the middle of the beginner's maze.

And Figure 5-8 shows me outside the maze, having just completed it.

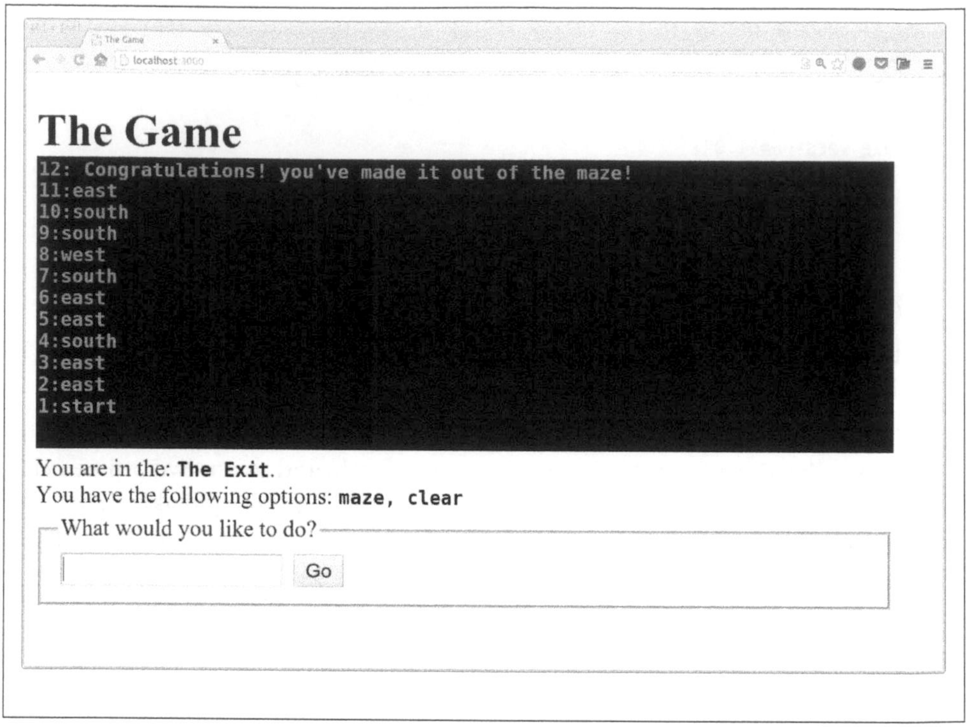

Figure 5-8. Outside the beginner's maze

When I leave the maze, the client shows me the congratulatory message at the other end of the *exit* link (a bit of resource state).

A Maze+XML Server

I'm going to write two more Maze+XML clients, but before I do that, I should talk about the server implementation. All the clients in this chapter run against a very simple server implementation of the Maze+XML standard, which I wrote for this book.[3]

Most of today's APIs are fiat standards, backed by a particular company and only existing at one hostname, but Maze+XML is a personal standard that anyone can implement. This means there can be any number of Maze+XML servers, and any number of server implementations. There's nothing special about my server implementation. In fact, it's quite limited. It can only serve a small subset of Maze+XML mazes: tidy, well-behaved mazes that fit into its JSON-based file format.

---

3. The code for the server is in the *RESTful Web APIs* GitHub repository (look in the *Maze/server*) directory.

My server is by no means the best Maze+XML implementation, but it's very easy to add mazes to it. My server stores maze data in simple JSON documents. Here's the JSON document representing the "beginner" maze I've been using as an example. This is not a representation of the maze in the REST sense, because it will never be sent over HTTP. It's the raw data used to generate the Maze+XML document that *is* sent over HTTP:

```
{
  "_id" : "five-by-five",
  "title" : "A Beginner's Maze",
  "cells" : {
    "cell0":{"title":"Entrance Hallway", "doors":[1,1,1,0]},
    "cell1":{"title":"Hall of Knives", "doors":[1,1,1,0]},
    "cell2":{"title":"Library", "doors":[1,1,0,0]},
    "cell3":{"title":"Trophy Room", "doors":[0,1,0,1]},
    "cell4":{"title":"Pantry", "doors":[0,1,1,0]},
    "cell5":{"title":"Kitchen", "doors":[1,0,1,0]},
    "cell6":{"title":"Cloak Room", "doors":[1,0,0,1]},
    "cell7":{"title":"Master Bedroom", "doors":[0,0,1,0]},
    "cell8":{"title":"Fruit Closet", "doors":[1,1,0,0]},
    "cell9":{"title":"Den of Forks", "doors":[0,0,1,1]},
    "cell10":{"title":"Nursery", "doors":[1,0,0,1]},
    "cell11":{"title":"Laundry Room", "doors":[0,1,1,0]},
    "cell12":{"title":"Smoking Room", "doors":[1,0,1,1]},
    "cell13":{"title":"Dining Room", "doors":[1,0,0,1]},
    "cell14":{"title":"Sitting Room", "doors":[0,1,1,0]},
    "cell15":{"title":"Standing Room", "doors":[1,1,1,0]},
    "cell16":{"title":"Hobby Room", "doors":[1,0,1,0]},
    "cell17":{"title":"Observatory", "doors":[1,1,0,0]},
    "cell18":{"title":"Hot House", "doors":[0,1,0,1]},
    "cell19":{"title":"Guest Room", "doors":[0,0,1,0]},
    "cell20":{"title":"Servant's Quarters", "doors":[1,0,0,1]},
    "cell21":{"title":"Garage", "doors":[0,0,0,1]},
    "cell22":{"title":"Tool Room", "doors":[0,0,1,1]},
    "cell23":{"title":"Banquet Hall", "doors":[1,1,0,1]},
    "cell24":{"title":"Spoon Storage", "doors":[0,0,1,1]}
  }
}
```

Each cell is represented by a name (`"title"`) and a list of binary numbers (`"doors"`) indicating whether or not there's a door to the north, west, south, or east. The cells listed form a two-dimensional 5 × 5 grid, with every cell being the same size. Mazes like this are called *perfect* mazes,[4] and they're rather easy to solve. They are the only mazes my server can understand. But the Maze+XML media type can represent a variety of two-dimensional maze topologies of any size—think of mazes with one-way passages or randomly generated mazes that are infinitely large.

---

4. You'll find lots of information on the topic at Astrolog's Maze Classification page (*http://www.astrolog.org/labyrnth/algrithm.htm*).

Client #2: The Mapmaker

The Game client relied on a human being making the decisions about where to go. But there are algorithms for automatically solving mazes, and there's no reason we can't write an automated client to go along with the manually operated one.

I already wrote a client whose goal was to solve a maze ("Client #1: The Game" on page 68), so to keep things interesting, this client does something a little different. I call it the Mapmaker, and it's a client for *mapping* a maze. (The code for the Mapmaker is in the *RESTful Web APIs* GitHub repository, in the directory *Maze/the-mapmaker*.) This client tries to visit every cell of a maze and construct a map that can be displayed visually. This client isn't trying to leave the maze. It wants to see the whole thing. When it finds the exit, it will mark the exit on its internal representation of the map, and keep moving. It will never follow the "exit" link.

The Game was a web application written in Node that ran in a web browser. The Mapmaker is also written in Node, but it's a command-line application that prints its output to the console. If you give it the billboard URL of a Maze+XML installation, it will map all the mazes on that site. If you give it the URL to an individual maze, it will map that maze. Here's the ASCII-art output of the Mapmaker program when I run it against the beginner's maze.

```
$ node the-mapmaker http://localhost:1337/mazes/tiny
Exploring A Beginner's Maze...
```

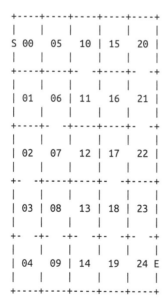

```
Map Key:
S = Start
E = Exit
0:Entrance Hallway
1:Hall of Knives
2:Library
3:Trophy Room
4:Pantry
5:Kitchen
6:Cloak Room
7:Master Bedroom
8:Fruit Closet
9:Den of Forks
10:Nursery
11:Laundry Room
12:Smoking Room
13:Dining Room
14:Sitting Room
15:Standing Room
16:Hobby Room
17:Observatory
18:Hot House
19:Guest Room
20:Servant's Quarters
21:Garage
22:Tool Room
23:Banquet Hall
24:Spoon Storage
```

The server doesn't define mazes in this graphical format; they're stored as JSON documents and served as XML documents. The Mapmaker builds up this graphical view of the maze by automatic exploration.

When the Mapmaker enters a maze, it identifies all the doorways (links) in the first room and "visits" them one at a time, effectively teleporting from room to room without bothering to double back. In each room, the Mapmaker looks at all the exits and builds up a list of rooms it still needs to visit. The Mapmaker effectively does a breadth-first search of the maze.

Once all the cells (and all the links between cells) are accounted for, the Mapmaker uses the data it's collected to generate an ASCII map showing the grid of cells and the connections between them.

The Mapmaker client has a more expansive view of application state than most API clients. The Game client acts like a human walking through the maze. You are always "visiting" one particular cell, and you can only transition to the cells directly adjacent to the one you're visiting. The adjacent cells are your possible next states. When you type in a direction, you choose one of these possible states and leave the others behind. You've moved on. Web browsers work the same way.

The Mapmaker doesn't move on. As far as it's concerned, *every link it has ever seen* is a possible next state. It doesn't walk through the maze like a human. It spreads, like a fungus, until it occupies every cell in the maze.

From the server's perspective, this looks like the Mapmaker teleporting wildly around the maze. This is unusual, but as far as the Maze+XML specification is concerned, it's perfectly legal. The Mapmaker just keeps more application state than the Game does.

Client #3: The Boaster

The Maze+XML standard defines a way of representing mazes and collections of mazes as XML documents. It doesn't say what mazes are *for*. Faced with a maze, the natural inclination of a human being is to walk through it looking for the exit. The Game client recreates that experience. But Maze+XML doesn't require that clients solve the maze the way a human would.

We've already seen this. The Mapmaker client continually teleports around the maze, and it never follows the "exit" link. It jumps around until it's mapped the entire maze, and then it simply stops making HTTP requests. This seems counter to the purpose of a maze, but who's to say?

My third Maze+XML client, the Boaster, takes this logic to an extreme. This client never even enters a maze. It reads a collection of mazes, picks one at random, and simply *claims* to have completed the maze.[5] Here it is in action:

```
$ node the-boaster http://example.org/mazes
Starting the maze called: For Experts Only...
*** DONE and it only took 2 moves! ***
```

Clearly you can't solve the expert's maze in two moves. The Boaster didn't even try. It made one HTTP request, to *http://example.org/mazes*. It read the collection of mazes, chose "For Experts Only," and claimed to have completed it in an unrealistic number of moves.

Is this cheating? In terms of solving mazes, of course it's cheating. But in terms of RESTfulness, or compliance with the Maze+XML standard, it's completely legitimate. The Boaster really does understand what a `vnd.amundsen.application/maze+xml` document means. It knows that links with `rel="maze"` point to mazes. It just doesn't want to be bothered with solving the mazes.

---

5. The code for the Boaster is in the *RESTful Web APIs* GitHub repository (look in the *Maze/the-boaster* directory).

Clients Do the Job They Want to Do

These three clients—the Game, the Mapmaker, and the Boaster—all work from an understanding of the Maze+XML media type. But they have different goals, so they do different things with the same data.

This is fine. The server's job is to describe mazes in a way that the client can engage with. The server's job is *not* to dictate goals to the client. The Maze+XML spec describes a problem space, not a prescribed relationship between client and server. Client and server must share an understanding of the representations they're passing back and forth, but they don't need to have the same idea of what the problem is that needs to be solved.

Extending a Standard

Maze+XML is a contrived example in a frivolous problem domain. But let's imagine that someone really does want to serve hypermedia mazes, either as part of a business or just for fun. That doesn't automatically make Maze+XML the right answer. Even when a standard already exists for your problem domain, it probably won't fit your needs exactly.

Anyone who wants to use Maze+XML for real won't be satisfied with what's in the standard. The standard limits you to two-dimensional mazes using the four cardinal directions: north, south, east, and west. That's not very fun. What if I want to serve three-dimensional mazes?

Creating an entirely new standard from scratch just to support three-dimensional mazes would be silly. The Maze+XML standard is *almost* good enough. I just have to extend it a little to make it support two new directions: up and down.

Fortunately, Maze+XML explicitly allows this sort of extension (see section 5 of the specification). I can add anything I want to a Maze+XML document, so long as I don't redefine something that's already in the specification. To get my three-dimensional mazes, I'll just define two new link relations right here:

up
> Refers to a resource spatially above the current resource.

down
> Refers to a resource spatially below the current resource.

This is a simple extension, but it completely changes what a maze can look like, and how a maze can be stored on the server. My server implementation stores a maze in a two-dimensional array of cells, with each cell having four possible neighbors. To support these two new relations, I need to change the server code to reflect the fact that a maze is a three-dimensional array and each cell now has six possible neighbors.

But the client won't see a big change at all. The client just sees two new link relations in the representations:

```
<maze version="1.0">
 <cell href="/cells/middle-of-ladder">
  <title>The Middle of the Ladder</title>
  <link rel="up" href="/cells/top-of-ladder"/>
  <link rel="down" href="/cells/bottom-of-ladder"/>
 </cell>
</maze>
```

All that extra server-side complexity is hidden from the client by the very thing that makes the Maze+XML standard seem simplistic. The standard just doesn't say much about what a maze "should" look like. Defining two new ways for cells to be connected requires a complete redesign of my server implementation, but the representations are still compliant with the Maze+XML standard, and the clients can still parse them.

But this doesn't mean the clients automatically *understand* these new application semantics. Consider what happens when the Game, the Mapmaker, and the Boaster are served a three-dimensional maze.

Surprisingly, the Game works just fine! That client wasn't hardcoded to know about the four cardinal directions. It was programmed to present every link it finds to the user, and to let the user choose between them. Since I chose the names "up" and "down" for my new link relations, a human being traversing a three-dimensional maze will see a screen like Figure 5-9.

Those options make sense to a human user, and if the user types in "up," the client will follow the link with `rel="up"`. Adding application semantics to Maze+XML doesn't require any changes to the Game client, because there's a human being in the loop.

The Boaster client also fares well in a three-dimensional maze, since it never even enters the maze. In fact, the Boaster should work on any Maze+XML-compatible server, no matter what extensions are made to it.

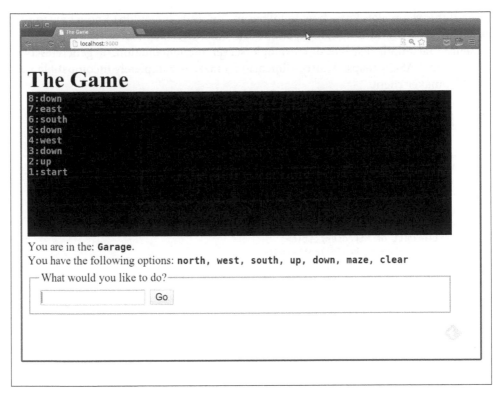

Figure 5-9. The Game client automatically supports "up" and "down".

But the Mapmaker client completely misses the point of a three-dimensional maze. Consider a representation like the following:

```
<maze version="1.0">
 <cell href="/cells/bottom-of-ladder">
  <title>The Bottom of the Ladder</title>
  <link rel="up" href="/cells/middle-of-ladder"/>
  <link rel="east" href="/cells/tunnel"/>
  <link rel="north" href="/cells/underwater-garden"/>
 </cell>
</maze>
```

If the Mapmaker ever gets a representation like this, it will follow the "east" link and the "north" link, but never the "up" link. Set the Mapmaker loose on a three-dimensional maze and it will map *one level* of the maze. It will see only a two-dimensional slice of the maze.

That's understandable. Clients can't be expected to understand link relations they weren't programmed with. But you may not have anticipated that simply telling the Mapmaker about the new link relations won't help!

Even if the Mapmaker knew how to follow an "up" link, it wouldn't know how to represent what it found at the other end of the link. The Mapmaker client has a two-dimensional mind, just like our example server implementation. It generates two-dimensional ASCII maps. A three-dimensional maze is completely incompatible with the Mapmaker client.

The Mapmaker's Flaw

In fact, the Mapmaker can fall down on mazes that don't use any Maze+XML extensions at all. What would happen to the Mapmaker if a server sent it the following representation?

```
<maze version="1.0">
 <cell href="/cells/44">
  <title>Hall of Mirrors</title>
  <link rel="east" href="/cells/45/>
 </cell>
</maze>
```

…and then this one, at the other end of the east link?

```
<maze version="1.0">
 <cell href="/cells/45">
  <title>Mirrored Hall</title>
  <link rel="west" href="/cells/129/>
  <link rel="east" href="/cells/44/>
 </cell>
</maze>
```

These are both legal Maze+XML documents, but they describe a maze that's non-Euclidian. Going east from the Hall of Mirrors takes you to the Mirrored Hall, and going east again takes you back to the Hall of Mirrors. You may recognize this trick from various video games. This is a completely legal maze that uses no Maze+XML extensions, but the Mapmaker will crash trying to map it.

It seems the Mapmaker was designed with a hidden assumption! It assumed that the server would only serve tidy mazes that can be represented on a grid. It's no coincidence that the example server only serves that kind of maze. I designed the Mapmaker client with one specific server in mind. It turns out the client won't work with the full range of mazes allowed by the Maze+XML specification. It only works with the sort of mazes you'll find on that server.

I've found that this rule holds in general. A client written against a specific server implementation can be optimized for that server's quirks, but it will fall down if you try to run it against another implementation of the same standard. This doesn't mean the Mapmaker is a completely useless client; it's just that it can only map certain mazes.

Imagine starting up a web browser that's only ever been tested against one particular website. As soon as you send that browser to a site it wasn't tested on, it's going to crash. That's the situation here. A standard like Maze+XML may have multiple server implementations. Client implementations need to be designed to work against all server implementations, not just one.

The Fix (and the Flaw in the Fix)

Can we fix the Mapmaker? One "fix" is to have the client check whether each newly discovered cell fits into the grid it's trying to build. Rather than crashing when it detects two different cells in the same grid space, it would print an error message and exit gracefully.

But that just gets rid of the crash. We've given the client just enough intelligence to recognize a maze it can't understand. If we want the client to actually understand mazes that aren't perfect, then the "grid" data structure has to go. The correct data structure to use is a directed graph.

We can write a better Mapmaker that builds a directed graph as it traverses the maze, then renders it using an algorithm like force-directed graph drawing. For a maze that more or less fits into a grid, an improved Mapmaker will render a directed graph that looks a lot like the old Mapmaker's ASCII diagrams (Figure 5-10).

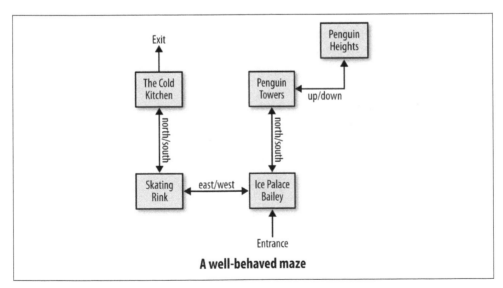

A well-behaved maze

Figure 5-10. A well-behaved maze considered as a directed graph.

Figure 5-10 was generated by a Mapmaker that tries to align "north" with the top of the page. It's not sure what to do about "up" and "down," but it's figured out that they're probably opposites, and it's able to represent them visually.

Now imagine a mischievous maze full of infinite loops and one-way passages. Such a maze would crash the unimproved Mapmaker, but an improved Mapmaker could render a graph like Figure 5-11.

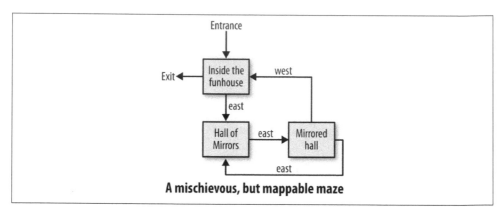
A mischievous, but mappable maze

Figure 5-11. A mischevious maze

Have we perfected the Mapmaker? Unfortunately, no. The improved Mapmaker *still* contains hidden assumptions. Figure 5-12 shows a maze that's infinitely large. It's easy to solve, but impossible to map.

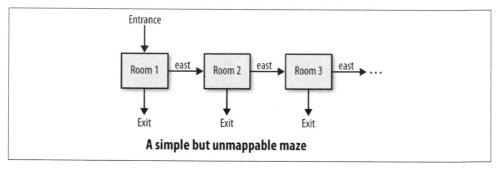
A simple but unmappable maze

Figure 5-12. A simple but unmappable maze

There's no Mapmaker client that can map an infinitely large maze: it'll never get a chance to draw the map. This doesn't mean the Mapmaker is useless. It's just that it can't handle every single maze that the Maze+XML standard allows.

Maze as Metaphor

Take another look at Figures 5-10 through 5-12. Compare them to Figure 1-9, the directed graph I used earlier to capture the structure of a website.

The similarity is no coincidence. As I said at the beginning of this chapter, the maze is a metaphor for hypermedia applications in general. Some "mazes" are tidy and well-behaved. Others are chaotic and infinitely large. Thinking of a state diagram as a maze to be navigated will get you in the right frame of mind to understand hypermedia APIs.

Meeting the Semantic Challenge

For the designer of a domain-specific API, bridging the semantic gap is a two-step process:

1. Write down your application semantics in a human-readable specification (like the Maze+XML standard).

2. Register one or more IANA media types for your design, (like `vnd.amundsen.ap` `plication/maze+xml`. In the registration, associate the media types with the human-readable document you wrote. In Chapter 9, I'll discuss the naming and registration process for media types.

Your client developers can reverse the process to bridge the semantic gap in the other direction:

1. Look up an unknown media type in the IANA registry.

2. Read the human-readable specification to learn how to deal with documents of the unknown media type.

There's no magic shortcut. To get working client code, your users will have to read your human-readable document and do some work. We can't get rid of the semantic gap completely, because computers aren't as smart as humans.

Where Are the Domain-Specific Designs?

When you need to publish an API, the first thing to do is to try to find an existing domain-specific design. There's no point in duplicating someone else's work.

That said, you're not likely to find a complete solution. There are hundreds of domain-specific data formats, but not many of them include hypermedia controls. In Chapter 10, I cover a few exceptions, like VoiceXML and SVG. The domain-specific design you're most likely to use is the problem detail document, a simple JSON-based format for describing error conditions (also covered in Chapter 10).

But just because a data format doesn't include hypermedia controls doesn't mean it's useless. In Chapter 8, I'll show you how JSON-LD can add basic hypermedia capabilities to any JSON format. In Chapter 10, I'll show how XForms and XLink can do the same for XML. These technologies let you graft hypermedia controls onto an existing API that doesn't include them.

The Prize at the End

Hypermedia APIs can also find uses for formats that don't support hypermedia. Consider the JPEG image format. It's well documented, it's got a registered media type (`image/jpeg`), and nothing beats a binary image file for representing a photograph. But you can't use JPEG as the basis for a web API, any more than you could design a website that serves nothing but JPEGs. There's no way for one JPEG to link to another.

A web API for managing photographs will certainly send and receive representations in JPEG format. It would be foolish to make up your own binary image format just because JPEG doesn't have any hypermedia controls. But JPEG will not be the *core* of a hypermedia-based photo API. That honor will go to a format like HTML. HTML can't represent a photograph, but it can embed a photograph in a textual document, pair a photograph with its caption, represent a list of photographs, and present forms for tagging and searching photographs.

An `image/jpeg` representation will be the client's prize for navigating the photo API's hypermedia "maze" and locating one specific photo. The "maze" itself will be described in a document format that supports hypermedia controls. The two formats will work together to form a complete API.

Hypermedia in the Headers

I showed in Chapter 4 how you can use the HTTP header `Link` to add simple hypermedia links and forms to documents that have no hypermedia controls of their own. Using these headers, you *could* conceivably design an API that served nothing but JPEG images, but I don't recommend this.

Steal the Application Semantics

Here's a much different technique. I'd like to introduce the vCard format, defined in RFC 6350 and assigned the media type `text/vcard`. This is a domain-specific plain-text format designed for exchanging the kinds of personal information you find on business cards. Sounds useful, right? Lots of web APIs deal with information about people and businesses.

Here's a simple vCard representation:

```
BEGIN:VCARD
VERSION:4.0
```

```
FN:Jennifer Gallegos
BDAY:19870825
END:VCARD
```

The rules set down in RFC 6350 define the semantics of a `text/vcard` document. You can parse this document according to those rules and build up a picture of a human being who has a name and a date of birth. And… then what?

You're stuck. The application semantics are well defined, but there are no links. This document is a hypermedia dead end.

Of course, the protocol semantics of HTTP still apply. You sent a GET request to get this representation. Maybe the API will let you modify the representation and PUT it back. Maybe you can DELETE the underlying resource. But you can't move from this representation to a related resource, because vCard is not a hypermedia format.

Since vCard is a common format used by phones and software address books, it may make sense to make a vCard representation the prize at the end of a hypermedia maze. The client would locate a "person" resource through hypermedia, and then follow an "export to vCard" link to get a `text/vcard` representation of that "person" resource.

But that's probably not what you want. You don't want basic information about a person to be a "prize." It's probably a major part of the API. You'd like to steal the application semantics of vCard and use them inside a real hypermedia document.

That's what the designers of the hCard microformat (*http://microformats.org/wiki/ hcard*) did. Rather than redoing the work done by the framers of the vCard standard, they made it possible to represent the same information in a hypermedia document format: HTML.

I'll have a lot more to say about hCard in Chapter 7, but here's a preview—an hCard version of the vCard document I showed you earlier:

```
<div class="vcard">
  <span class="fn">Jennifer Gallegos</span>
  <span class="bday">1987-08-25</span>
</div>
```

The hCard microformat lets you combine a vCard-like representation of a human being with the hypermedia links and forms needed to implement a full web API.

This is another reason why it's important to look for domain-specific data formats before you set off to design your API. A standard like vCard represents a lot of time and money spent identifying the application-level semantics for a problem domain. You don't need to start over just because vCard doesn't have hypermedia controls.

Even if you can't directly reuse a domain-specific standard, you may be able to save yourself some time by adapting its application-level semantics into a profile. But that's a topic for Chapter 8.

If You Can't Find a Domain-Specific Design, Don't Make One

If you can't find a domain-specific API for your problem domain, don't panic. People just don't define reusable, domain-specific, hypermedia-aware formats very often. That doesn't mean you have to start from scratch. You should be able to start with a standardized foundation and extend it, reusing work done by other people whenever possible. It'll just take a little work on your part to glue everything together.

In the next two chapters, I'll discuss some of these foundations. In particular, there are a few domain-specific designs that deal with a domain so popular and so general—collections of things—that I don't really consider it a domain at all. It's more like a design pattern.

Kinds of API Clients

Apart from the three Maze+XML client implementations in this chapter, I won't be talking much about API clients in this book. I don't know enough to give a lot of guidance, because right now there aren't many deployed APIs that take full advantage of the Fielding constraints.

A deep understanding of hypermedia won't help you write a client for an API that doesn't serve hypermedia documents. When you're writing a client, you're at the mercy of the server design, and pragmatism always trumps idealism. Right now, pragmatism means adopting a different approach for every individual API.

But I have seen enough deployed hypermedia APIs (including the World Wide Web itself) to say something about the *kinds* of clients people tend to write. I've seen that the client and server must share an understanding of the problem domain, but they don't have to share a goal. This is my first attempt, presented humbly, to classify the clients we write to achieve our goals.

Human-Driven Clients

Human-driven clients can have relatively simple logic because they don't have to make any decisions. They present representations to a human being, and convey the human's decisions back to the server. The differences between human-driven clients come down to how faithful they are in presenting representations to their human users.

A typical web browser is a faithful renderer. Nearly every HTML tag in a web page has some graphical effect on the page displayed on the screen. Every hypermedia link and form in an HTML document appears on screen, unless something else in the document says it should be hidden.

Now consider a web browser that uses text-to-speech to present web pages to a visually impaired user. It will be a little less faithful. Some HTML tags translate well into the medium of speech (`<li>` is a good example), and some don't (like `<div>`). But any web browser must be very faithful when rendering hypermedia controls. Every link and form that a sighted user can trigger should also be available to a visually impaired user.

The Game client is a pretty faithful renderer of Maze+XML documents. Maze+XML documents don't contain layout information, the way HTML documents do, but the Game makes sure to show its human user all the bits of resource state (like the title of a cell) it can find, as well as all the hypermedia links.

A Game client that replaced the directional links with tank controls ("turn left," "turn right," "move forward") would be even a less faithful renderer, even though it sends the same requests to the server as the Game client I showed you. A Game client that refused to show its human users the "exit" link, leaving them trapped in the maze forever, would not be very faithful at all.

A less faithful renderer puts its own editorial vision between what the server sends and what the user experiences. This sounds bad—nobody likes things that are "unfaithful" —but it depends on what the user is trying to do. A store's website may show you a lot of expensive stuff you don't need. You might prefer a less faithful renderer: a client for the store's API that filters out the expensive stuff to help you find bargains.

When the human user selects a maze to play, the Game retrieves a representation of the maze, but it doesn't display that representation. It just scans the representation for a link with `rel="start"`, and automatically follows that link. That's "unfaithful." The Game client believes there's nothing in the representation of the maze that would be of interest to the human user, and that making the human manually click the "start" link would be a waste of time. This is probably true, but it means the Game client is not a completely faithful renderer.

The more devoted a client is to faithfully rendering the representations it receives, and not interposing its own judgment, the less likely it is to break when it encounters a representation it wasn't expecting.

Automated Clients

Automated clients receive representations but don't render them. There's no human to see the rendering. These clients must bridge the semantic gap on their own, by deciding which hypermedia controls to trigger. Of course, most clients don't "decide" anything at all. They carry out simple preprogrammed rulesets that hopefully help them reach some predefined goal.

None of these clients are as smart as human beings, but they do free us from repetitive tasks that don't need our full intelligence. I've seen and created several different types of automated clients.

The crawler

The crawler simulates a very curious but not very picky human. Give it a URL to start with, and it will fetch a representation. Then it will follow all the links it can find to get more representations. It will do this recursively, until there are no more representations to be had.

The Mapmaker client from earlier in this chapter is a kind of crawler for Maze+XML documents. The spiders used by search engines are crawlers for HTML documents.

It's quite difficult to write a crawler for an API that doesn't use hypermedia. But you can write a crawler for a hypermedia-based API without even understanding that API's link relations.

Generally speaking, a crawler will only trigger state transitions that are safe. Otherwise, there's no telling what will happen to resource state. A crawler that sent a DELETE request to every resource it encountered, just to see what happened, would be a terrible client.

The monitor

The monitor is the opposite of the crawler. It simulates a human who's obsessed with one particular web page. Give it a URL to start with, and the monitor will fetch a representation of that URL and process it somehow. But it won't follow any links. Instead, the monitor will wait a while and fetch a new representation of the same resource. Instead of triggering a hypermedia control to change the resource state, the monitor waits for *someone else* to change the resource state, and checks back later to see what happened.

An RSS aggregator is a kind of monitor. A human user points an aggregator at a number of interesting RSS and Atom feeds. The monitor client periodically fetches the feeds and somehow notifies its user of new entries. It never follows the links in those entries.

Suppose that one of those Atom feeds is hooked up to a full-featured API that uses the Atom Publishing Protocol. The aggregator client won't even notice. It just wants to watch the feed. Nothing a user does within an RSS aggregator will change resource state on the sites that publish the feeds.

The script

Most of today's automated API clients are scripts. A script simulates a human with a set routine that never changes. A script happens when a human is tired of this routine and wants to automate it.

The human chooses an API and figures out out which state transitions (for an API that serves hypermedia documents) or API calls (for a hypermedia-ignorant API) are necessary to carry out the routine. Then the human writes an algorithm that automates the process of triggering those state transitions or making those API calls.

The Boaster client from earlier in this chapter is a very simple script. It knows about one bit of information (the title of a maze), and it knows where to find it. It will give a different result every time you run it (because it will choose a different maze every time), but it always accomplishes the same task: pretending to solve a maze.

A client that actually entered a maze and moved east three times would be a more impressive script. If you gave it the right maze, it would even be capable of finding the exit cell! But there's clearly no intelligence in the algorithm. It's a script, playing back a predefined set of state transitions.

A script tends to break when the assumptions underlying it become invalid. A "maze solver" client that always goes east three times can only solve a very small subset of mazes. A screen-scraping script that extracts data from a website will break when the HTML representations are redesigned.

A hypermedia-aware script is less likely to break when something trivial happens, like the URL of a resource changing or new data being added to a representation. This means a hypermedia API has some room to change without breaking the scripts that depend on it. But a script is a playback of a human being's thought process. If it encounters a situation the human didn't originally consider, the script won't be able to fill in the blanks.

The agent

Forget the Boaster. Forget the script that moves east three times and then stops. Imagine a client that *actually* solves a maze on its own, using an algorithm such as wall-following. This client would be able to solve mazes it had never seen before. It would change its behavior on the fly, in response to the representations it got from the server. In short, it would make decisions.[6]

A software agent simulates a human being who is actively engaged with a problem. It's not as smart as a human, and it has no ability to make subjective judgments, but it does what a human would do in the same situation. It looks at a representation, analyzes the situation, and decides which hypermedia control to activate to get closer to its final goal.

The monitor doesn't do this; it never activates hypermedia controls at all. The crawler doesn't do this; it activates every safe hypermedia control it can find. The script doesn't do this; it always activates the next hypermedia control it was programmed with. Human-driven clients don't do this; they delegate the task to the human. A software agent is the only client that can be said to make autonomous "decisions."

---

6. You can see some Maze+XML clients like this at this page (*http://amundsen.com/examples/misc/maze-client.html*).

Software agents can be simple, like maze-solving clients, or they can be driven by complex reasoning engines that synthesize information from many different sources. Right now, software-agent clients tend toward the simple side. But we have a vision of what more sophisticated agents would look like: the personal shoppers and automated news gatherers of science fiction, and the high-frequency trading algorithms used in real-life financial applications.

A software agent is the automated client best positioned to take advantage of the flexibility of a hypermedia API. But it's based on two big underlying assumptions: that its goal makes sense and that the reasoning process it's been programmed with will eventually lead to the goal. An agent will break if those assumptions are violated. If a maze-solving agent encounters a maze where its algorithm doesn't work—say, a maze that contains one-way passages—it will break, just like the script that always moves east three times.

Software agents are programmed by computer programmers, and we know too much about how computers work to leave all important decisions to software. At the moment of truth, an API client may choose to ask a human being to confirm an unsafe state transition ("Do you want me to buy you this shirt?") or make a subjective judgment ("Which of these landscapes is more beautiful?"). In that moment, the agent becomes a human-driven client. This makes mistakes less likely, and reduces their cost when they do happen.

CHAPTER 6

The Collection Pattern

Back in Chapter 2, I showed off a simple microblogging API that served representations with a media type of `application/vnd.collection+json`. The representations looked like this:

```
{ "collection":
  {
    "version" : "1.0",
    "href" : "http://www.youtypeitwepostit.com/api/",

    "items" : [
      { "href" :
        "http://www.youtypeitwepostit.com/api/messages/21818525390699506",
        "data" : [
          { "name" : "text", "value" : "Test." },
          { "name" : "date_posted", "value" : "2013-04-22T05:33:58.930Z" }
        ],
        "links" : []
      },

      { "href" :
        "http://www.youtypeitwepostit.com/api/messages/3689331521745771",
        "data" : [
          { "name" : "text", "value" : "Hello." },
          { "name" : "date_posted", "value" : "2013-04-20T12:55:59.685Z" }
        ],
        "links" : []
      },

      { "href" :
        "http://www.youtypeitwepostit.com/api/messages/7534227794967592",
        "data" : [
          { "name" : "text", "value" : "Pizza?" },
          { "name" : "date_posted", "value" : "2013-04-18T03:22:27.485Z" }
        ],
        "links" : []
```

```
      }
    ],

    "template" : {
      "data" : [
        {"prompt" : "Text of message", "name" : "text", "value" : ""}
      ]
    }
  }
}
```

In this chapter, I'll talk more about Collection+JSON,[1] the standard that defines the structure of this document.

Collection+JSON is one of several standards designed not to represent one specific problem domain (the way Maze+XML does), but to fit a pattern—the collection—that shows up over and over again, in all sorts of domains. This standard makes a good example, because it's a formalized version of the JSON-based APIs that first-time designers tend to come up with. Collection+JSON lets you follow your natural design inclinations without running afoul of the Fielding constraints.

The document just shown represents a collection of microblog posts. A collection of goods in a shopping cart or a collection of readings from a weather sensor would look pretty much the same, and have pretty much the same protocol semantics. My only additions to the Collection+JSON standard are a few bits of application semantics. I decided that a microblog post should have a `date_posted` field and a `text` field. An item in a shopping cart or a reading from a weather sensor would have different fields, reflecting their different application semantics.

If there's no domain-specific standard for your problem domain (and there probably isn't), you may be able to use a collection-based standard instead. Instead of starting from nothing, you'll be able to focus on adapting your application semantics to the collection pattern. Not only will you save time, you'll get access to a preexisting base of client programs and server-side tools.

Although this chapter focuses on Collection+JSON, I'll also cover the Atom Publishing Protocol, or AtomPub. AtomPub is the original standard for collection-based APIs, defined in RFC 5023. It's a relatively old standard, but apart from its use in Google's public APIs, it hasn't caught on—partly because it's an XML-based format in a field now dominated by JSON representations.

In Chapter 10, I'll cover OData, the third major standardization of the collection pattern. OData is an open standard in progress that was originally based on AtomPub. It has the advantages of a JSON representation and backing by Microsoft, which has integrated OData support into its Visual Studio development platform.

---

1. Defined in a personal standard at *http://amundsen.com/media-types/collection/*.

The Hydra standard (Chapter 12) also has support for the collection pattern, although that's not its main purpose. It would be nice if there were a single, agreed-upon standard for collection-based APIs, but four competing standards is better than thousands of one-off designs, which is what we have now.

What's a Collection?

Before going into detail about the standards designed around the collection pattern, let's talk about the pattern itself. It's pretty simple, but I want to spell everything out explicitly so there are no surprises.

A collection is a special kind of resource. Recall from Chapter 3 that a resource is anything important enough to have been given its own URL. A resource can be a piece of data, a physical object, or an abstract concept—anything at all. All that matters is that it has a URL and the representation—the document the client receives when it sends a GET request to the URL.

A collection resource is a little more specific than that. It exists mainly to group other resources together. Its representation focuses on links to other resources, though it may also include snippets from the representations of those other resources. (Or even the full representations!)

A collection is a resource that lists other resources by linking to them.

Collections Link to Items

An individual resource contained within a collection is sometimes called an *item*, an *entry*, or a *member* of the collection. Think about the contact list on your friend's phone. You show up in that list: your name and your phone number. You're an item in the "contact list" collection.

But you're more than an item in a collection: you're a human being. That's not you in your friend's phone. That's a link to you (via your phone number) and some information about you (your name). You have an independent existence; the data in your friend's phone is just a partial representation.

Similarly, a resource that's described in a collection doesn't suddenly become a special thing called an "item." That resource still has its own URL and an independent existence outside the collection. When we talk about an "item" or an "entry" or a "member," we're talking about a standalone resource that happens to be *linked to* from a collection's representation.

Collection+JSON

Now let's get specific, by seeing how Collection+JSON implements the collection pattern. The Collection+JSON standard defines a representation format based on JSON. It also defines the protocol semantics for the HTTP resources that serve that format in response to GET requests.

Here's a Collection+JSON document:

```
{ "collection":
  {
    "version" : "1.0",
    "href" : "http://www.youtypeitwepostit.com/api/",

    "items" : [
      { "href" : "/api/messages/21818525390699506",
        "data" : [
        { "name" : "text", "value" : "Test." },
        { "name" : "date_posted", "value" : "2013-04-22T05:33:58.930Z" }
        ],
        "links" : []
      },

      { "href" : "/api/messages/3689331521745771",
        "data" : [
        { "name" : "text", "value" : "Hello." },
        { "name" : "date_posted", "value" : "2013-04-20T12:55:59.685Z" }
        ],
        "links" : []
      }
    ],

    "links" : [
      {"href" : "/logo.png", "rel" : "icon", "render" : "image"}
    ],

    "queries" : [
      { "href" : "/api/search",
        "rel" : "search",
        "prompt" : "Search the microblog archives",
        "data" : [ {"name" : "query", "value" : ""} ]
      }
    ],

    "template" : {
      "data" : [
        {"prompt" : "Text of message", "name" : "text", "value" : ""}
      ]
    }
  }
}
```

It's basically an object with five special properties, predefined slots for application-specific data:

`href`
> A permanent link to the collection itself.

`items`
> Links to the members of the collection, and partial representations of them.

`links`
> Links to other resources related to the collection.

`queries`
> Hypermedia controls for searching the collection.

`template`
> A hypermedia control for adding a new item to the collection.

There's also an optional `error` section, for error messages, but I won't cover that here.

Representing the Items

Let's zoom in on `items`, the most important field in a Collection+JSON representation:

```
"items" : [
  { "href" : "/api/messages/21818525390699506",
    "data" : [
      { "name" : "text", "value" : "Test." },
      { "name" : "date_posted", "value" : "2013-04-22T05:33:58.930Z" }
    ],
    "links" : []
  },

  { "href" : "/api/messages/3689331521745771",
    "data" : [
      { "name" : "text", "value" : "Hello." },
      { "name" : "date_posted", "value" : "2013-04-20T12:55:59.685Z" }
    ],
    "links" : []
  }
]
```

I say it's the most important field because it makes it clear which items are in the collection. In Collection+JSON, each member is represented as a JSON object. Like the collection itself, each member has a number of predefined slots that can be filled with application-specific data:

The `href` *attribute*
> A permanent link to the item as a standalone resource.

links
> Hypermedia links to other resources related to the item.

data
> Any other information that's an important part of the item's representation.

An item's permanent link

A member's `href` attribute is a link to the resource outside the context of its collection. If you GET the URL mentioned in the `href` attribute, the server will send you a Collection+JSON representation of a single item. It'll look something like this:

```
{ "collection":
  {
    "version" : "1.0",
    "href" : "http://www.youtypeitwepostit.com/api/",

    "items" : [
      { "href" : "/api/messages/21818525390699506",
        "data": [
        { "name" : "text", "value" : "Test." },
        { "name" : "date_posted", "value" : "2013-04-22T05:33:58.930Z" }
        ],
        "links" : []
      }
    ]
  }
}
```

You might be able to modify an item with HTTP PUT to its permanent link, or delete it with HTTP DELETE. These are the item's protocol semantics. They're spelled out as part of Collection+JSON's definition of an "item."

An item's data

At the core of any Collection+JSON application are the application-level semantics you're trying to convey: the bits of data associated with each individual item. Most of this data goes into an item's `data` slot. That slot needs to contain a list of JSON objects, each with the properties `name` and `value`, each describing a single key-value pair. Here's one example from our microblogging API:

```
"data" : [
  {
    "name" : "text",
    "value" : "Test.",
    "prompt" : "The text of the microblog post."
  },
  {
    "name" : "date_posted",
    "value" : "2013-04-22T05:33:58.930Z",
```

```
            "prompt" : "The date the microblog post was added."
        }
    ]
```

The `name` attribute is the key of the key-value pair, the `value` is of course the value, and the (optional) `prompt` is a human-readable description. The Collection+JSON standard says nothing about what keys, values, or prompts you should use. That depends on your needs, and the application-level semantics you've defined for your API.

An item's links

The simplest of Collection+JSON's hypermedia controls is the `href` attribute. I covered this earlier; it's a special link that provides a URL the client should use whenever it wants to refer to one specific item:

```
"href" : "/api/messages/21818525390699506"
```

An item's representation may also contain a list called `links`. This contains any number of other hypermedia links to related resources. Here's a link you might see in the representation of a "book" resource:

```
{
    "name" : "author",
    "rel" : "author",
    "prompt" : "Author of this book",
    "href" : "/authors/441",
    "render" : "link"
}
```

That's approximately equivalent to this snippet of HTML:

```
<a href="/authors/441" id="author" rel="author">Author of this book</a>
```

The `rel` attribute is a slot for a link relation, just like the `rel` attribute in Maze+XML. It's a place for you to put some application semantics. The `prompt` attribute is a place to put a human-readable description, like the link text inside an HTML `<a>` tag.

Here's another link you might see in the representation of a book:

```
{
    "name" : "cover",
    "rel" : "icon",
    "prompt" : "Book cover",
    "href" : "/covers/1093149.jpg",
    "render" : "image"
}
```

That's approximately equivalent to this snippet of HTML:

```
<img src="/covers/1093149.jpg" id="cover" rel="icon" title="Book cover"/>
```

The difference between the `author` link and the `icon` link is the `render` attribute. Setting `render` to `"link"` tells a Collection+JSON client to present the link as an outbound link (see Chapter 4), like an HTML <a> tag. The user can click on the link to move the client's view to another representation. Setting render to "image" tells the client to present the link as an embedded image, like HTML's <img> tag. That link is fetched automatically, and the resulting representation is directly incorporated into the view of the current representation.

The Write Template

Suppose you want to add a new item to a collection. What HTTP request should you make? To answer this question, you need to look at the collection's *write template*.

Here's the write template for our microblogging API:

```
"template": {
 "data": [
   {"prompt" : "Text of message", "name" : "text", "value" : ""}
 ]
}
```

Interpreting this template according to the Collection+JSON standard tells you it's OK to fill in the blanks and submit a document that looks like this:

```
{ "template" :
 {
  "data" : [
   {"prompt" : "Text of the message", "name" : "text", "value" : "Squid!"}
  ]
 }
}
```

Where does that request go? The Collection+JSON standard says you add an item to a collection by sending a POST request to the collection (i.e., to its href attribute):

```
"href" : "http://www.youtypeitwepostit.com/api/",
```

So the POST request will look like this:

```
POST /api/ HTTP/1.1
Host: www.youtypeitwepostit.com
Content-Type: application/vnd.collection+json

{ "template" :
 {
  "data" : [
   {"prompt" : "Text of the message", "name" : "text", "value" : "Squid!"}
  ]
 }
}
```

That means the write template is conceptually equivalent to this HTML form:

```
<form action="http://www.youtypeitwepostit.com/api/" method="post">
 <label for="text">Text of the message</label>
```

```
 <input id="text"/>
 <input type="submit"/>
</form>
```

It's not exactly the same, because filling out the HTML form sends an `application/x-www-form-urlencoded` representation, and filling out a write template sends an `application/vnd.collection+json` representation. But conceptually, those two hypermedia controls are very similar.

Search Templates

If a collection has millions of items, it would be foolish for the server to send representations of all of them to every client that makes a GET request. The server can avoid this by providing search templates—hypermedia forms that the client fills out to filter a Collection+JSON collection.

The search templates for a collection are stored in the `queries` slot. Here's a `queries` slot that includes a simple search template:

```
{
  "queries" :
  [
    {
      "href" : "http://example.org/search",
      "rel" : "search",
      "prompt" : "Search a date range",
      "data" :
      [
        {"name" : "start_date", "prompt": "Start date", "value" : ""},
        {"name" : "end_date", "prompt": "End date", "value" : ""}
      ]
    }
  ]
}
```

That Collection+JSON search template is equivalent to this HTML form:

```
<form action="http://example.org/search" method="get">
  <p>Search a date range</p>
  <label for="start_date">Start date</label>
  <input label="Start date" id="start_date" name="end_date" value=""/>

  <label for="end_date">End date</label>
  <input label="End date" id="end_date" name="end_date" value=""/>
</form>
```

Which is equivalent to this URI Template:

```
http://example.org/search{?start_date,end_date}
```

I say they're equivalent because all three will make the same HTTP GET request given the same inputs. It'll look something like this:

```
GET /search?start_date=2010-01-01&end_date=2010-12-31 HTTP/1.1
Host: example.org
```

How a (Generic) Collection Works

There's not much more to Collection+JSON than what I've just shown. It was designed without any real application semantics, so that it can be used in many different applications. Because it's so general, it does a good job illustrating the common features of the collection pattern.

Before moving on to AtomPub, I'd like to go up a level and lay out the pattern itself as I see it, by describing the behavior of a generic "collection" resource under HTTP. Collection+JSON, AtomPub, OData, and Hydra take different approaches to collections, but they all have more or less the same protocol semantics.

GET

Like most resources, a collection responds to GET by serving a representation. Although the three main collection standards don't say much about what an item should look like within a collection, they go into great detail about what a collection's representation should look like.

The media type of the representation tells you what you can do with the resource. If you get an `application/vnd.collection+json` representation, you know that the rules of the Collection+JSON standard apply. If the representation is `application/atom+xml`, you know that AtomPub rules apply.

If the representation is `application/json`, you're out of luck, because the JSON standard doesn't say anything about collection resources. You're using an API that went off on its own and defined a fiat standard. You'll need to look up the details for the specific API you're using.

POST-to-Append

The defining characteristic of a collection is its behavior under HTTP POST. Unless a collection is read-only (like a collection of search results), a client can create a new item inside it by sending it a POST request.

When you POST a representation to a collection, the server creates a new resource based on your representation. That resource becomes the latest member of the collection. Recall Chapter 2, when a POST sent to the microblog API created a new entry "inside" the microblog.

PUT and PATCH

None of the main collection standards define a collection's response to PUT or PATCH. Some applications implement these methods as a way of modifying several elements at once, or of removing individual elements from a collection.

Collection+JSON, AtomPub, and OData all define an *item's* response to PUT: they say that PUT is how clients should change the state of an item. But these standards are just repeating what the HTTP standard says. They're not putting new restrictions on item resources. PUT is how clients change the state of *any* HTTP resource.

DELETE

None of the three big standards define how a collection should respond to DELETE. Some applications implement DELETE by deleting the collection; others delete the collection and every resource listed as an item in the collection.

The main collection standards all define an *item's* response to DELETE, but again, they're just restating what the HTTP standard says. The DELETE method is for deleting things.

Pagination

A collection may contain millions of items, but again, the server is under no obligation to serve millions of links in a single document. The most common alternative is pagination. A server can choose to serve the first 10 items in the collection, and give the client a link to the rest:

```
<link rel="next" href="/collection/4iz6"/>
```

The `"next"` link relation is registered with the IANA to mean "the next in the series." Follow that link and you'll get the second page of the collection. You'll probably be able to keep following `rel="next"` links indefinitely, until you reach the end of the collection.

There are a number of generic link relations for navigating paginated lists. These include `"next"`, `"previous"`, `"first"`, `"last"`, and `"prev"` (which is a synonym for "previous"). These link relations were originally defined for HTML, but now they're registered with the IANA, so you can use them with any media type.

Some collection-based standards explicitly define a pagination technique. Others simply assume you know about `"next"` and `"previous"`. Collection+JSON falls into the latter category. It has no explicit support for pagination, but you can get that feature by combining its generic hypermedia links with the IANA's generic link relations:

```
"links" : [
  {
    "name" : "next_page",
    "prompt" : "Next",
```

```
      "rel" : "next",
      "href" : "/collection/page/3",
      "render" : "link"
   },
   {
      "name" : "previous_page",
      "prompt" : "Back",
      "rel" : "previous",
      "href" : "/collection/page/1",
      "render" : "link"
   }
]
```

Search Forms

The final common feature of the collection pattern is the hypermedia search form. This also helps with very large collections. Search forms let a client find the interesting parts of a collection without downloading the whole thing.

Collection+JSON and OData explicitly define their own formats for hypermedia search forms. I showed you a Collection+JSON search template earlier in this chapter. Atom-Pub has no native support for search. It assumes you'll plug in another standard, such as OpenSearch, if you need this feature.

The Atom Publishing Protocol (AtomPub)

The Atom file format was developed as an alternative to RSS for syndicating news articles and blog posts. It's defined in RFC 4287, which was finalized in 2005. The Atom Publishing Protocol is a standardized workflow for editing and publishing news articles, using the Atom file format as the representation format. It's defined in RFC 5023, which was finalized in 2007. Those are pretty early dates in the world of REST APIs. In fact, AtomPub was the first standard to describe the collection pattern.

Here's an Atom representation of the same microblog I showed you as a Collection +JSON earlier. AtomPub has the same concepts as Collection+JSON, but uses different terminology. Instead of a "collection" that contains "items," this is a "feed" that contains "entries."

```
<feed xmlns="http://www.w3.org/2005/Atom">

  <title>You Type It, We Post It</title>
  <link href="http://www.youtypeitwepostit.com/api" rel="self" />
  <id>http://www.youtypeitwepostit.com/api</id>
  <updated>2013-04-22T05:33:58.930Z</updated>

  <entry>
    <title>Test.</title>
    <link
      href="http://www.youtypeitwepostit.com/api/messages/21818525390699506" />
```

```
    <link rel="edit"
      href="http://www.youtypeitwepostit.com/api/messages/21818525390699506" />
    <id>http://www.youtypeitwepostit.com/api/messages/21818525390699506</id>
    <updated>2013-04-22T05:33:58.930Z</updated>
    <author><name/></author>
  </entry>

  <entry>
    <title>Hello.</title>
    <link
      href="http://www.youtypeitwepostit.com/api/messages/3689331521745771" />
    <link rel="edit"
      href="http://www.youtypeitwepostit.com/api/messages/3689331521745771" />
    <id>http://www.youtypeitwepostit.com/api/messages/3689331521745771</id>
    <updated>2013-04-20T12:55:59.685Z</updated>
    <author><name/></author>
  </entry>

  <entry>
    <title>Pizza?</title>
    <link
      href="http://www.youtypeitwepostit.com/api/messages/7534227794967592" />
    <link rel="edit"
      href="http://www.youtypeitwepostit.com/api/messages/7534227794967592" />
    <id>http://www.youtypeitwepostit.com/api/messages/7534227794967592</id>
    <updated>2013-04-18T03:22:27.485Z</updated>
    <author><name/></author>
  </entry>

</feed>
```

This document is served with the media type `application/atom+xml`, and an AtomPub client is allowed to make certain assumptions about it. You know you can POST a new Atom entry to the `href` of the collection. An entry's `rel="edit"` link is the URL you send a PUT to if you want to edit the entry, or send a DELETE to if you want to delete the entry.

None of this should come as a surprise. It's similar to what Collection+JSON does, and it mostly restates ideas found in the HTTP standard.

There's one big conceptual difference between Collection+JSON and AtomPub. Collection+JSON defines no particular application semantics for "item." An "item" can look like anything. But since Atom was designed to syndicate news articles, every AtomPub entry looks a bit like a news article. Every entry in an AtomPub feed must have a unique ID (I used the URL of the post), a title (I used the text of the post), and the date and time it was published or last updated. The Atom file format defines little bits of application semantics for news stories: fields like "subtitle" and "author." Collection+JSON doesn't do any of this; it doesn't even require that every member of a collection have a permalink (although you really should have one).

Despite this focus on news and blog posts, AtomPub is a fully general implementation of the collection pattern. Google, the biggest corporate adopter of AtomPub, uses Atom documents to represent videos, calendar events, cells in a spreadsheet, places on a map, and more.

The secret is extensibility. You're allowed to extend Atom's vocabulary with whatever application semantics you care to define. Google defined a common Atom extension called GData for all of its Atom-based APIs, then defined additional extensions for videos, calendars, spreadsheets, and so on.

A few interesting facts about AtomPub with respect to the collection pattern:

- Since news articles are often classified under one or more categories, the Atom file format defines a simple category system, and AtomPub defines a separate media type for a list of categories (`application/atomcat+xml`).

- AtomPub also defines a media type for a *Service Document*—effectively a collection of collections.

- Atom is strictly an XML-based file format. AtomPub installations do not serve JSON representations. This makes it difficult to consume an AtomPub API from an Ajax client. Google recognized this as a problem and added JSON representations of its documents alongside the AtomPub representations. But Google presented this as a fiat standard, not as something everyone is encouraged to reuse.

- Although Atom is an XML file format, clients may POST binary files to an AtomPub API. An uploaded file is represented on the server as two distinct resources: a Media Resource whose representation is the binary data, and an Entry Resource whose representation is metadata in Atom format. This feature lets you use AtomPub to store a collection of photos or audio files, along with Atom documents containing descriptions and related links.

AtomPub Plug-in Standards

Because they're so extensible, Atom and AtomPub are used as the basis for a lot of small plug-in standards that enhance the collection pattern:

- The Atom Threading Extensions (defined in RFC 4685) make it easy to describe structures like the conversations found in email threads and message boards. This extension is nothing big—just a few extra tags and a new link relation called `"replies"`.

- The Atom `deleted-entry` element (defined in RFC 6721) lets the server put up a "tombstone" for an item when it's deleted from a collection, rather than simply removing it. This tells clients they need to purge the deleted entry instead of caching it.

- RFC 5005 ("Feed Paging and Archiving") defines the concept of an "archived feed," a more efficient way of paginating a large feed across multiple resources. It defines the link relations `"next-archive"`, `"prev-archive"`, and `"current"`, to be used instead of `"next"`, `"prev"`, and `"first"`.

- OpenSearch (*http://www.opensearch.org/Specifications/OpenSearch/1.1*) is a consortium standard for an XML-based search protocol. An OpenSearch document is the equivalent of an HTML form, or the "queries" section of a Collection+JSON document. A client that fills out the form can perform a search (through HTTP GET) and get an Atom feed of search results. OpenSearch defines a new link relation, `"search"`, which lets an Atom feed link to an OpenSearch document.

  OpenSearch isn't Atom-specific. Your web browser's search bar also uses OpenSearch. OpenSearch lets you search different websites without actually going to those sites and using their HTML search engines. I'm including OpenSearch here because AtomPub doesn't define a search protocol, and this is the one you should use.

  In Chapter 10, I'll cover OpenSearch in a little more detail.

- PubSubHubbub (*http://code.google.com/p/pubsubhubbub/*) is a corporate standard describing a publish-subscribe protocol that lets clients sign up to receive a notification (via HTTP POST) whenever an Atom feed is updated. It defines a new link relation, "hub".

All the link relations defined by these plug-in standards are registered with the IANA. This means that `"replies"`, `"next-archive"`, `"prev-archive"`, `"current"`, `"search"`, and `"hub"` are generic relations that can also be used *anywhere*, without explanation. The `"search"` link relation was defined for OpenSearch, but `rel="search"` doesn't mean "this is a link to an OpenSearch document." It means "this is a link to some kind of search form."

Even if you're not using AtomPub, you can benefit from the work done by the people who've spent the past several years working on Atom extensions. They've created a standard vocabulary for a lot of common operations; you just have to decide to reuse it.

Why Doesn't Everyone Use AtomPub?

Six years after the RFC was finalized, and despite all the plug-in standards, it's safe to say that AtomPub has not caught on. The standard never got much traction outside of Google, and even Google seems to be phasing it out. What's wrong with AtomPub?

The problem stems from a technical decision made back in 2003: AtomPub representations are XML documents. This seemed like the obviously correct decision in 2003, but over the next 10 years, as in-browser API clients became more and more popular,

JSON gained an overwhelming popularity as a representation format. It's a lot easier to process JSON from in-browser JavaScript code than it is to process XML. Today, the vast majority of APIs either serve JSON representations exclusively, or offer a choice between XML and JSON representations. AtomPub is nowhere to be seen.[2]

So why devote a big section of this book to AtomPub? Partly because there's nothing wrong with the standard. It works fine for what it is. It has historical significance as the first general implementation of the "collection" API pattern. The plug-in standards define generic IANA-registered link relations that can be cleanly reused in other representation formats.

But the AtomPub story also shows that "nothing wrong with the standard" isn't good enough. People won't go through the trouble of learning a standard unless it's directly relevant to their needs. It's easier to reinvent the "collection" pattern using a fiat standard based on JSON, so that's what thousands of developers did—and continue to do.

My main purpose in writing this book is to try to halt this duplication of effort. I don't know whether the answer is Collection+JSON or any of the other hypermedia formats I cover in the next few chapters. There's probably no single answer.

I do know that the "collection" pattern has proven itself dominant. The question is whether we'll collectively allow ourselves to reinvent the same basic ideas over and over again.

The Semantic Challenge: How Are We Doing?

Remember, the semantic challenge is: How can we program a computer to decide which links to click? To answer this question, we must bridge the gap between the protocol semantics of HTTP (generic "resources" identified by URLs and responding to methods like GET and PUT) and the application semantics of your special, unique web API (a microblogging service, a payment processor, or whatever it is you're doing).

A domain-specific design like Maze+XML bridges the gap with a custom-designed hypermedia type, plus link relations defined especially for your problem space. But that's a lot of work, and almost nobody goes that far.

The collection pattern recognizes two different kinds of resources: item-type resources (which tend to respond to GET, PUT, and DELETE) and collection-type resources (which tend to respond to GET and POST-to-append). A collection-type resource *contains* a number of item-type resources. Its representation links to those items and includes partial representations of them.

---

2. Joe Gregorio, a major contributor to both Atom and AtomPub, makes the same case in a blog post (*http://bitworking.org/news/425/atompub-is-a-failure*).

The distinction between collection and item is a small layer of application semantics on top of HTTP's protocol semantics. Collection+JSON, AtomPub, and OData all define the same collection/item distinction. With the distinction in place, a lot of the IANA's generic link relations suddenly make sense: relations for navigating a collection, like "first", "next", and "next_archive"; the "search" relation for searching through a collection; the "item" relation for pointing out an item within a collection, the "edit" relation for editing an item, and the "collection" relation that connects an item to a collection that contains it.

But an "item" still isn't anything in particular. It's almost as vague a term as "resource." In a microblogging API, an "item" will be a bit of text with a timestamp. In a payment processor, an "item" will include a creditor, a debitor, a method of payment, and an amount of money. There's still an enormous gap between the application semantics of the collection pattern and the application semantics of your individual API.

Take another look at this Collection+JSON representation of a microblog post:

```
{ "collection":
  {
    "version" : "1.0",
    "href" : "http://www.youtypeitwepostit.com/api/",

    "items" : [
      {
        "href" :
        "http://www.youtypeitwepostit.com/api/messages/21818525390699506",
        "data" : [
          {
            "name" : "text",
            "value": "Test.",
            "prompt" : "The text of the microblog post."
          },
          {
            "name" : "date_posted",
            "value": "2013-04-22T05:33:58.930Z",
            "prompt" : "The date the microblog post was added."
          }
        ]
      }
    ]
  }
}
```

HTTP tells us how to edit this item: change the representation (somehow) and PUT it back. Collection+JSON tells us what that representation should look like. It should look like a filled-out Collection+JSON "template":

```
PUT /api/messages/21818525390699506 HTTP/1.1
Host: www.youtypeitwepostit.com
Content-Type: application/vnd.collection+json
```

```
"template" : {
  "data" : [
    {"prompt" : "Text of message", "name" : "text", "value" : "The new value"}
  ]
}
```

But Collection+JSON doesn't say what "text" and "date_posted" *mean*. To understand those things a human must read the human-readable explanation in the prompt element. That's how Collection+JSON bridges the semantic gap. Maze+XML bridged the gap by defining its application semantics ahead of time, in the specification of the media type. Collection+JSON puts the application semantics in prompt elements scattered throughout its representations.

If everyone used Collection+JSON for their APIs, we would all share a common definition of "collection". But there'd be 57 different definitions of "item", 57 sets of data elements with differing values for prompt. Some APIs would call the text field "text"; others would call it "content" or "post" or "blogPost", and they'd all describe the same thing in different words. We'd still have 57 different microblogging APIs.

So we're still not there. We still need something more.

CHAPTER 7

Pure-Hypermedia Designs

The collection pattern is powerful, but it's not ubiquitous. The maze game from Chapter 5 could technically be implemented with Collection+JSON representations, but it would look terrible. The whole point of the game is that the client sees one cell at a time. There's nothing to "collect" inside a collection. The application semantics of the maze game don't match what the collection pattern can provide.

Nothing says you have to use the collection pattern, but it is the most popular design pattern for APIs. If you want to implement some other pattern, or if your API design doesn't fit any particular pattern, you can describe an API's semantics using pure hypermedia. You don't have to create an entirely new standard like Maze+XML, with its own media type. You can represent the state of your resources using a generic hypermedia *language*.

In this chapter, I'll discuss APIs that use a generic hypermedia language as their representation format. I'll talk about a number of newfangled representation formats, but the focus of my explanation will be an old format that you're already familiar with: HTML.

Why HTML?

We think of HTML in the context of the World Wide Web: a network of documents intended to be read by human beings. That popularity makes it the obvious choice for any *part* of an API that serves documents intended for human consumption. Even if the rest of your API serves XML- or JSON-based representations, you can use HTML for the parts that will be rendered to a human user. Such is HTML's popularity that every modern operating system ships with a tool for debugging HTML-based web APIs: a web browser.

HTML has distinct advantages even for an API designed to be consumed entirely by machines. HTML imposes more structure on a document than XML or JSON does, but not so much structure as to solve only one specific problem, the way Maze+XML does. HTML sits somewhere in the middle, like Collection+JSON.

Unlike bare XML or JSON, HTML comes packaged with a standardized set of hypermedia controls. But HTML's controls are very general, and not bound to a specific problem space. Collection+JSON defines a special hypermedia control for search queries; HTML defines a hypermedia control (the `<form>` tag) that can be used for any purpose at all.

Finally, there's the popularity argument. HTML is by far the world's most popular hypermedia format. There are lots of tools for parsing and generating HTML, and most developers know how to read an HTML document. Because HTML is so popular, it's the base standard for two enormous, ongoing efforts to bridge the semantic gap: microformats and microdata, which I'll cover later in this chapter.

HTML's Capabilities

HTML was designed to represent the nested structure of a text document. Any HTML tag may contain a mixture of textual content and other tags:

```
<p>
 This 'p' tag contains text
 <a href="http://www.example.com/">and a link</a>.
</p>
```

That document doesn't correspond to any data structure—English sentences rarely do—but HTML documents can include the same basic data structures as you find in JSON. Ordered lists use the `<ol>` tag, and sets of key-value pairs use the `<dl>` tag. (It's called "dl" because HTML calls that data structure a "definition list.")

HTML also supports unordered lists (the `<ul>` tag), two-dimensional arrays (the `<table>` tag), and arbitrary ways of grouping tags together (using the `<div>` and `<span>` tags) without regard to standard data structures.

Hypermedia Controls

More important, HTML has built-in hypermedia controls. I mentioned these controls back in Chapter 4, but just to recap, here are the most important ones:

- The `<link>` tag and `<a>` tag are simple outbound links, like the `<link>` tag in Maze+XML. They tell the client to make a GET request to a specific URL in order to get a representation. That representation becomes the current view.

- The `<img>` tag and `<script>` tags are embedding links. They tell the client to automatically make a GET request to another resource, and to embed the representation of that resource in the current view. The `<img>` tag says to embed the other representation as an image; the `<script>` tag says to execute the representation as code. HTML defines a few other types of embedding links, but these are the main ones.

- When the `<form>` tag has the string `"GET"` as its method attribute (i.e. `<form meth od="GET">`), it acts as a templated outbound link. This works like a URI Template, or the `queries` slot in Collection+JSON. The server provides the client with a base URL and some input fields (HTML `<input>` tags). The client plugs in values for those fields, combines them with the base URL to form a one-of-a-kind destination URL, and makes a GET request to that URL.

- When the `<form>` tag has `"POST"` as its method attribute, it describes an HTTP POST request that can do anything at all. The `<input>` tags are still present, but instead of being used to create the request URL, they're used to create an entity-body with the media type `application/x-www-form-urlencoded`. The request URL is hard-coded in the `action` attribute of the `<form>` tag.

Plug-in Application Semantics

HTML defines application semantics for a very general application: human-readable documents. The HTML standard defines tags for paragraphs, headings, sections, lists, and other structural elements found in news articles and books.

HTML doesn't define tags for mazes or for cells in mazes. That's not its application. But HTML is different from Maze+XML or Collection+JSON in that it's easy to use HTML outside of its application. HTML 4 defines three generic attributes that we can use to add application-level semantics not defined in the HTML standard. (HTML 5 defines a few more, which I'll cover later.)

The rel attribute

HTML's `<a>` and `<link>` tags have an attribute called `rel`, which defines the relationship between the resource being linked to and this one. We've seen `rel` before:

    <link rel="stylesheet" type="text/css" href="/my_stylesheet.css"/>

That bit of HTML says that the resource *my_stylesheet.css* should be retrieved and automatically used to style the current page. In this context, HTML's `<link>` tag serves as an embedding link. With a different value for `rel` (say, `rel="self"`) the `<link>` tag would serve as an outbound link.[1]

---

1. HTML 4 also allows links to have the `rev` attribute, which is the opposite of `rel`. The value of `rev` represents *this* resource's relationship to the *linked* one. In a link to the next page, `rel` would be `next` and `rev` would be `previous`. It turns out the `rev` attribute is not really necessary, and it was removed in HTML 5, which is why I'm only mentioning it in a footnote. Don't confuse `rel` with its opposite.

Although there are standard lists of link relations (like the IANA registry I mentioned in Chapter 5), there's nothing special about the strings "stylesheet" or "self". Someone made them up for HTML. If you're publishing a maze API in HTML, you can adopt the link relations defined in Maze+XML ("north", "south", and so on). Use them in an HTML document. This will give the HTML format some application-level semantics it didn't have before: the semantics of mazes and cells in mazes. You can also make up extension link relations (the ones that look like URLs) to describe the very specific relationships between the resources in your application.

The disadvantage of making up your own link relations is that your users will have no idea what those relationships mean. You'll need to document these bits of application semantics in a profile (see Chapter 8).

The id attribute

Almost any HTML tag[2] can define a value for the id attribute. This attribute uniquely identifies an element within a document:

```
<div id="content">
```

If you happen to be looking for the tag with id="content", well, here it is. An HTML document can't contain two elements with the same ID.

I don't recommend using the id attribute as a hook for your application-level semantics. The requirement that IDs be unique across a document is too limiting. It creates situations where two HTML documents can't be combined into a larger document, because they both define the same id.

The class attribute

Almost any HTML tag[3] can define a value for the class attribute. This is the most flexible of HTML's semantic attributes. On the World Wide Web, class is usually used to apply CSS formatting, but it can also be used to convey something about a tag's application semantics; literally, what "class" it belongs to.:

Here's a simple example of a <div> tag that contains two <span> tags:

```
<div class="vcard">
  <span class="fn">Jennifer Gallegos</span>
```

2. In HTML 4, the tags that can't have an id attribute are base, head, html, meta, script, style, and title. In HTML 5, any tag can have an id attribute. I'm only reprinting this list so you can see this probably won't be a problem for you.

3. In HTML 5, *any* tag can have a class attribute. In HTML 4, the seven tags mentioned in the previous footnote can define neither id nor class. The param tag can define id but it can't define class. Again, this probably won't be a problem for you.

```
<span class="bday">1987-08-25</span>
</div>
```

By itself, the `<div>` tag means nothing—it's just a way to group other tags together. A `<span>` tag also means nothing on its own. But suppose I tell you that the vcard class groups together information about a human being (for the moment, don't worry about *how* I tell you this; I'll cover that later). I tell you that a tag marked with the fn class contains the person's name, and a tag marked with the bday class contains the person's date of birth in ISO 8601 format.

Now the `<div>` tag is a description of a person. Now it *means* something. Now you know that "Jennifer Gallegos" is the name of a human being, not the title of a book. You know that "1987-08-25" is a date in a specific format, not a random string that happens to look like a date. When you understand what certain values for class mean, you understand some application semantics that were not defined by the HTML specification.

Many tags in the same document can have the same class, and a single tag can have multiple values for class, separated by spaces:

```
<ul>
 <li><a class="link external" href="http://www.example.com/>Link 1</a></li>
 <li><a class="link external" href="http://www.example.org/>Link 2</a></li>
 <li><a class="link internal" href="/page2">Link 3</a></li>
</ul>
```

If you're ever tempted to use id for a piece of application semantics, I recommend using class instead. Unlike with id, many tags in a representation can have the same class attribute.

Microformats

I chose some pretty cryptic CSS class names to turn a `<div>` tag and a couple `<span>` tags into a description of a human being: "vcard," fn, and bday. If I'd made up those class names myself, I'd have used more descriptive names like birthday. But I didn't make them up. I took them from an existing standard called hCard (*http://microfor mats.org/wiki/hcard*). If you ever see class="vcard" on an HTML tag, you'll know that everything inside that tag should be interpreted according to the hCard standard.

Like Maze+XML, the hCard standard doesn't have an associated RFC or Internet-Draft. Unlike with Maze+XML, that's not because it's a personal standard. hCard is a *microformat*: a lightweight industry standard defined through informal collaboration on a wiki, rather than through the formal IETF process that results in RFCs.

Consult the hCard standard and you'll find out that the fn class is used to mark up a person's full name, and that the bday class is used to mark up a person's date of birth in ISO 8601 format. Now you know what a document means when it uses those CSS classes. The HTML standard says nothing about names or birthdates, but the hCard standard does deal with those things.

Microformats let you add extra application semantics to HTML. HTML's class attribute, plus the hCard microformat, lets you create an HTML document that's also a description of a human being.

hCard only defines values for the class attribute. The <span> and <div> tags I used mean nothing to hCard; I could have used other tags. Since almost every HTML tag supports the class attribute, I can write unstructured text that's also an hCard document:

```
<p class="vcard">My name is <i class="fn">Jennifer Gallegos</i> and I
was born on <date class="bday">1987-08-25</date>.</p>
```

A human being will read this representation as an English sentence. An hCard processor will ignore all the "extraneous" text and focus on the tags that use hCard's CSS classes.

Although the hCard microformat didn't go through a formal standardization process, it's based on a standard that did: vCard, a heavyweight plain-text format for representing business cards, defined in RFC 6350.

I mentioned vCard in Chapter 5 as an example of a domain-specific standard that lacks hypermedia controls. hCard is just a translation of vCard into HTML. That's why the top-level class value of an hCard document is vcard instead of hcard.

The vCard RFC was the result of a lot of expensive research into, and long arguments about, what kind of information tends to go onto business cards. As I said in Chapter 5, there's no reason to redo that research and rehash those arguments just because vCard has no hypermedia controls. We can steal vCard's semantics and adapt them to a generic hypermedia language: HTML.

The hMaze Microformat

In this section, I'll do to Maze+XML what hCard did for vCard. I'll take a non-HTML standard designed for a specific domain—mazes—and turn it into an HTML microformat. This will let me use HTML to represent the semantics of a domain that the base HTML standard doesn't understand.

I'm calling my new microformat "hMaze," by analogy with "hCard." (The "h" stands for "HTML.") My microformat defines a few special CSS classes:

hmaze
  Indicates the parent tag of an hMaze document. Analogous to hCard's vcard class.

collection
  May appear within hmaze. Describes a collection of mazes.

maze
> May appear within hmaze. Describes an individual maze.

error
> May appear within hmaze. Describes an error message.

cell
> May appear within hmaze. Describes a cell in a maze.

title
> May appear within cell. Contains the name of the cell.

Microformats can also define link relations, and I'll steal all the ones defined by Maze +XML. The relations north, south, east, west, exit, and current have special meaning inside a tag with class="cell" (specifically, the special meaning defined in the Maze +XML standard). The relation maze has special meaning when found inside a tag with class="collection" (it links to a particular maze, just like it does in Maze+XML).

That's it! That's the hMaze microformat, at least the first version of it. If I were going to put this on the Microformat Wiki, I'd spell out a few more CSS classes like the ones that go beneath error, but this is good enough for an example. This microformat can represent any maze Maze+XML can represent, but in HTML.

My microformat only defines values for class and rel. As with hCard, the choice of tags is left to the server. A server can serve a stuffy-looking HTML document that looks more or less like Maze+XML:

```html
<div class="hmaze">
 <div class="cell">
  <div class="title">
   Hall of Pretzels
  </div>
  <div>
   <a href="/cells/143" rel="west"/>
   <a href="/cells/145" rel="east"/>
  </div>
 </div>
</div>
```

Or a server can present the same data in a human-readable way that allows human beings to use their web browsers as API clients:

```html
<div class="hmaze">
 <div class="cell">
  <p><b class="title">Hall of Pretzels</b></p>

  <ul>
   <li><a href="/cells/143" rel="west">Go west</a></li>
   <li><a href="/cells/145" rel="east">Go east</a></li>
  </ul>
```

```
    </div>
  </div>
```

Both of these are valid hMaze documents, and as far as hMaze is concerned, they have identical application semantics. All that matters is that you use the `class` and `rel` attributes the way the hMaze specification says you should. (As far as HTML itself is concerned, the documents have different application-level semantics, because HTML's "application" is human-readable documents.)

Microdata

Microdata is a refinement of the microformat concept for HTML 5. You see, microformats are kind of a hack. HTML's `class` attribute was designed to convey information about visual display (via CSS), not to convey bits of application semantics.

HTML Microdata[4] introduces five new attributes specifically for representing application semantics: `itemprop`, `itemscope`, `itemtype`, `itemid`, and `itemref`. These attributes may appear on any HTML tag.

I'll be focusing on the first three of these attributes. The `itemprop` attribute is used the way a microformat uses the `class` attribute. The `itemscope` attribute is a Boolean attribute, used on a tag to indicate that the tag contains microdata. And the `itemtype` attribute is a hypermedia control that tells the client where it should go to find out what the microdata means.

With a little tweaking, most of the information in a microformat can be presented as microdata. Here's an HTML document that presents a microdata type that's a slight variant of hMaze:

```
<div itemscope itemtype="http://www.example.com/microdata/Maze">
 <div itemprop="cell">
  <div itemprop="title">
   Hall of Pretzels
  </div>
  <div>
   <a href="/cells/143" rel="west"/>
   <a href="/cells/145" rel="east"/>
  </div>
 </div>
</div>
```

With microformats, the client needs to "just know" that if it finds a tag labeled with `class="hMaze"`, everything beneath that tag is an hMaze document. With microdata, the `class="hMaze"` isn't necessary. The `itemscope` property indicates that everything

---

4. An open standard, defined in a W3C specification [currently in draft form] (*http://www.w3.org/TR/micro data/*).

beneath this tag is described according to the rules laid out in some document, and itemtype points to that document.[5]

A microformat does have one advantage over a microdata item. A microdata item cannot define any values for the rel attribute—only for itemprop. This means that rel="east" and rel="west" are not technically part of my hMaze-like microdata item. The document at *http://www.example.com/microdata/Maze* will probably mention that a client can expect to see rel="east" and rel="west" in representations of maze cells. But as far as the microdata standard is concerned, there's no relationship. You can't define link relations in a microdata item.

The main source of microdata items is schema.org, a project of four big search engines (Bing, Google, Yahoo!, and Yandex) to define application semantics for different problem domains. Search engines have an interest in understanding the high-level application semantics of a web page—that is, whatever real-world thing the web page is talking about. Since APIs often deal with the real-world things we talk about on web pages (people, products, events, and so on), we can reuse their work for our APIs.

I'll list the major microdata types near the end of Chapter 10, and from this point on in the book, you'll start seeing examples that refer to schema.org microdata items. To a human being, it should be pretty obvious what they mean. The URL *http://schema.org/Person* points to the schema.org microdata item corresponding to our everyday notion of a "person."

Changing Resource State

I've now gotten hMaze roughly to the point where it can substitute for Maze+XML. But you didn't come here to see me rehash Maze+XML. Let's add a new feature: a mysterious switch that can rearrange the structure of the maze.

I'll add mysterious switches to the hMaze microformat by defining two new CSS classes:

switch
> May appear within cell. Describes a switch that can be set to one of two positions. Each position corresponds to a different configuration of the maze.

position
> May appear within switch. Contains the position of the switch: either up or down.

Here's a representation of a cell in the maze. You've seen it before, but now there's a switch in this cell:

```
<div class="hmaze">
 <div class="cell">
```

---

5. That document is called a *profile*, and in Chapter 8, I'll explore the question of what it should look like.

```
<p>
 <b class="title">
  <a href="/cells/H" rel="current">Hall of Pretzels</a>
 </b>
</p>

<ul>
 <li><a href="/cells/G" rel="west">Go west</a></li>
 <li><a href="/cells/I" rel="east">Go east</a></li>
</ul>

<div class="switch">
 A mysterious switch is mounted on one wall. The
 switch is <span class="position">up</span>.
</div>

</div>
</div>
```

When the player flips the switch, the maze will completely change its configuration. If the maze looked like Figure 7-1 before the client flips the switch, it might look like Figure Figure 7-2 afterward.

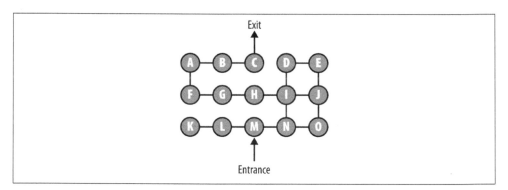

Figure 7-1. Before the switch

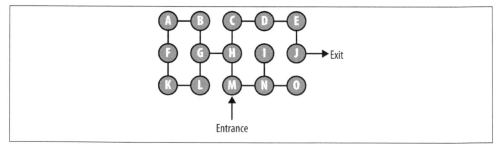

Figure 7-2. After the switch

Flipping the switch again would restore the original maze configuration.

Unfortunately, you'll have to take my word for it, because I haven't explained how a client can actually flip the switch. I assure you, it's possible! I've devised a special HTTP request that a client can make to flip that switch. But I'm not going to tell you what that request looks like. You have to guess.

OK, I'll tell you. But I won't use English—I'll use hypermedia.

Adding Application Semantics to Forms

The hMaze microformat defines values for HTML's `rel` attribute that give new application semantics to HTML links. When you notice that an ordinary-looking HTML link has its `rel` set to `east`, it stops being an ordinary link and becomes a passage through a geographical space.

The `rel` attribute describes the relationship between two resources. It explains a state transition: the change in application state that will happen if the client follows a link.

What I'd really like to do is create a value for `rel` that means "flip this switch." Instead of changing application state (moving the client from one part of the maze to another), a link with `rel="flip"` would change *resource* state. Your application state would be unchanged—you'd still be in the Hall of Pretzels—but the switch would now be in the other state, and the structure of the maze would be different.

There's a big problem with this idea. HTML links only support the GET method, and I can't use GET because "flip a switch" is not a safe operation. It modifies resource state. That's the whole point. The position of the switch used to be `off`, and now it's `on`. The exit to the maze used to be in cell C, and now it's in cell J.

Fortunately, HTML also defines hypermedia forms. An HTML form can tell the client to make a POST request, and a POST request can do anything at all.

There's a smaller problem that's specific to HTML. The buttons that submit HTML forms don't support the `rel` attribute. But they do support `class` and (in HTML 5) `itemprop`. So let's define a bit of application semantics to be applied to the `class` of a form's submit button:

flip
> May appear on a form submission control within `switch`. When activated, the control will have the effect of flipping the switch.

Now it's clear how to flip a switch. You look inside the tag with `class="switch"`, find the form submission control with `class="flip"`, and activate that control. Here's the representation of the Hall of Pretzels again:

```
<div class="hmaze">
 <div class="cell">
```

```
<p>
 <b class="title">
  <a href="/cells/H" rel="current">Hall of Pretzels</a>
 </b>
</p>

<ul>
 <li><a href="/cells/G" rel="east">Go west</a></li>
 <li><a href="/cells/I" rel="west">Go east</a></li>
</ul>

<div class="switch">
 A mysterious switch is mounted on one wall. The
 switch is <span class="position">up</span>.

 <form action="/switches/4" method="post">
  <input class="flip" type="submit" value="Flip it!"/>
 </form>
</div>
</div>
</div>
```

Now it's clear how to flip the switch. Using the hypermedia form as a guide, a client that understands hMaze can send the magical HTTP request I refused to explain earlier. The request looks like this:

```
POST /switches/4 HTTP/1.1
Content-Type: application/x-www-form-urlencoded

submit=Flip%20it%21
```

The response might look like this:

```
303 See Other
Location: /cells/H
```

A client that follows the link in the `Location` header will refresh its representation of its current maze cell:

```
<div class="hmaze">
 <div class="cell">
  <p>
   <b class="title">
    <a href="/cells/H" rel="current">Hall of Pretzels</a>
   </b>
  </p>

  <ul>
   <li><a href="/cells/G" rel="west">Go west</a></li>
   <li><a href="/cells/C" rel="north">Go north</a></li>
   <li><a href="/cells/M" rel="south">Go south</a></li>
  </ul>
```

```
<div class="switch">
 A mysterious switch is mounted on one wall. The
 switch is <span class="position">down</span>.

 <form action="/switches/4" method="post">
  <input class="flip" type="submit" value="Flip it!"/>
 </form>
</div>

</div>
</div>
```

The resource state has changed! The "Go west" link is still there, but the link to the east is missing, and there are two new links to cells that weren't accessible before (rel="north" and rel="south"). The switch is still there, but its position is now down instead of up.

I could add features to this game all day, but I think this shows how I go about defining a set of application semantics that can be used with a general hypermedia format like HTML. Here's the entire hMaze microformat in one place. I define seven CSS classes that can apply to any tag at all:

hmaze
> Indicates the parent tag of an hMaze document. Analogous to hCard's vcard class.

collection
> May appear within hmaze. Contains a collection of mazes.

error
> May appear within hmaze. Indicates an error message.

cell
> May appear within hmaze. Describes a cell in a maze.

title
> May appear within cell. Contains the name of the cell.

switch
> May appear within cell. Describes a switch found in the maze.

position
> May appear within switch. Describes the position of the switch. There are two positions: up and down.

I define eight link relations, which only apply to hypermedia controls: maze, start, north, south, east, west, current, and exit. These relations have the same meaning in hMaze as they do in Maze+XML.

And I define one CSS class that only applies to a submit button within a `<form>` tag (again, I have to use CSS classes for this because HTML's form submit buttons don't support the `rel` attribute):

flip

> May appear on a form submission control within `switch`. When activated, the control will have the effect of flipping the switch.

And that's the API. Specifically, that's the *specification* for an API, a personal standard with the same standing as Maze+XML. There are a couple loose ends, things I didn't define:

- What exactly should the HTML documents look like? I didn't define this because I don't care. Your hMaze implementation can serve full human-readable documents with lots of flavor text, or it can serve very compact documents optimized for automated clients. As long as you use the hMaze CSS classes and link relations correctly, your choice will have no effect on the application semantics of the maze.

- Could a mysterious switch be a first-class resource, with its own representation? The switch in the example appears to have its own URL (*/switches/4*), but a client is never invited to make a GET request to that URL, only a POST request. It's easy to imagine a link to that URL:

```
A <a rel="switch" href="/switches/4">mysterious switch</a>
is mounted on one wall.
```

But I didn't define a link relation called `switch`, so this is not part of my design. I'll come back to this idea in Chapter 9.

The Alternative to Hypermedia Is Media

I think it's useful to contrast the hMaze specification with what passes for API documentation today. In typical API documentation, a bunch of server-side methods are exposed as discrete API calls. Each call is given its own action URL and documented in excruciating detail. You've probably seen this sort of thing before:

> To flip a switch, send a POST request to:
>
> ```
> http://api.example.com/switches/{id}?action=flip
> ```
>
> Where {id} is the switch ID.
>
> You can only flip a switch if you are in the same cell as the switch.

If you find yourself writing up (or generating) documentation like this example, you're using human-readable documentation as a substitute for hypermedia. That's unacceptable. You're creating useless work for yourself and your users.

Certainly the server must provide that information *somehow*. The client needs to know exactly what HTTP request to send, and approximately what will happen if it sends that request. But almost all of this information can be written for its intended audience—a piece of software—and served when needed. You don't need to spell it out in English ahead of time.

By contrast, here's my machine-readable explanation of how to flip the mysterious switch:

```
<div class="switch">
 A mysterious switch is mounted on one wall. The
 switch is <span class="position">down</span>.

 <form action="/switches/4" method="post">
  <input class="flip" type="submit" value="Flip it!"/>
 </form>
</div>
```

Or, stripped down to essentials:

```
<div class="switch">
 <span class="position">down</span>
   <form action="/switches/4" method="post">
    <input class="flip" type="submit"/>
   </form>
  </div>
 </span>
</div>
```

That takes care of the protocol semantics. It explains exactly what HTTP request the client can make to trigger the state transition `flip`. The only human-readable documentation I need to provide is the hMaze spec, which defines the application semantics of `flip`:

flip

> May appear on a form submission control within `switch`. When activated, the control will have the effect of flipping the switch.

I don't have to provide a template for constructing the action URL, or force the client to reckon with my internal concept of a "switch ID," because the `<form>` tag for flipping a switch includes the actual URL the client should use. I don't have to make caveats like "You can only flip a switch if you're in the same cell as the switch," because hypermedia controls are presented only when they can be used. If the submit button isn't there, the state transition isn't available.

I used to think that you should design APIs by identifying the resources and tying them together with hypermedia. This resource-oriented approach is good advice when you're trying to move away from publishing all your internal methods as a huge list of API calls. Thinking in terms of resources will at least group the API calls together in sensible ways.

But in a hypermedia-based design, resources don't matter as much. The designer's job is to identify all the *state transitions*. A resource-oriented design would focus heavily on the mysterious switch as a resource, as a thing in itself. But the switch itself isn't all that important. My design focuses on the state transition, on what you can *do* with the switch.

HTML's Limits

Technically, HTML is a domain-specific standard, not a general hypermedia format. I'm covering it here instead of in Chapter 5 because HTML's "domain" is a very general one: human-readable documents. It's fine to use HTML for other purposes, like maze games played by robots, but you will quickly run into the limits of the data format. On the World Wide Web, no one even notices these limits. But if you design an API that serves HTML, you'll notice very quickly.

- HTML includes a lot of hypermedia controls, but the controls can't describe all of HTTP's protocol semantics. There's no way to tell an HTML client to make a PUT or DELETE request without using JavaScript.

- Forms in HTML 4 can only build entity-bodies in two different formats: either `application/x-www-form-urlencoded` (for basic key-value pairs) or `multipart/form-data` (for key-value pairs plus file uploads).

- Unlike JSON, HTML 4 doesn't distinguish between strings and numbers. Any string within an HTML tag is assumed to be just that—a string. If you want to say that a string should be interpreted in some other way, you'll need to specify that yourself, outside of the HTML document.

- HTML 4 doesn't define a way of representing dates (JSON has the same problem). When the vCard standard defines the `bday` class, it says that any data provided for `bday` should be interpreted as a date in ISO 8601 format. Without that extra information (presented in human-readable form), there's no way to know for sure whether `"1987-08-25"` is a date, or just a string that happens to look like a date.

HTML 5 to the Rescue?

The new HTML 5 standard[6] solves some of HTML 4's problems:

---

6. Open standard (*http://www.w3.org/TR/html5/*) currently under development.

- HTML 5 defines the `time` tag, which can be used to represent a date or timestamp in a specific format.

- There are a few cases where you can use HTML 5's `meter` tag to represent a number, but it doesn't work in general.

- HTML 5 offers a few new hypermedia controls for creating embedded links, including: `<audio>`, `<video>`, `<source>`, and `<embed>`. None of them are terribly useful in APIs, unless part of the API's job is delivering multimedia to human beings.

- HTML 5 defines several new options for validating `input` tags. An `input` tag can specify that it wants a `date`, a `number`, or a `url` as input. An `input` tag can be marked as `required`, meaning that the form can't be submitted without providing a value for the field. An HTML 5 client can use this information to do client-side validation.

  In HTML 4, validation must be done on the server side, or using custom written JavaScript code that runs when the client tries to submit the form.

- I mentioned earlier that HTML 5 will define the microdata properties for representing application semantics. That's a definite improvement over the way microformats reuse the `class` attribute.

Unfortunately, some things haven't changed. HTML 5 forms still can't trigger PUT or DELETE requests. HTML 5 adds one new representation format for its forms, `text/plain`, but it's just a plain-text representation of the same key-value pairs you'd get with `application/x-www-form-urlencoded`.

In summary, HTML 5 offers some useful new features, but it doesn't drastically change HTML *as a hypermedia format*.

The Hypertext Application Language

HTML is old, crufty, and designed for human-readable documents. Several new hypermedia formats have emerged in reaction to HTML, formats designed specifically for use in web APIs. The Hypertext Application Language (HAL) is a new format that takes the fundamental concept of HTML—the hyperlink—and ruthlessly prunes away everything else. I think it prunes too much, but it's a good example of a general hypermedia language that doesn't have HTML's historical baggage. Let's see how it works.

HAL comes in two flavors: one that uses XML (media type: `application/hal+xml`) and one that uses JSON (media type: `application/hal+json`). I'll call them HAL+XML and HAL+JSON for short.[7] The two are formally identical, but I'm going to focus on HAL

---

7. The JSON version of HAL is specified in the Internet-Draft "draft-kelly-json-hal." The XML version is a personal standard (*http://stateless.co/hal_specification.html*). The developer's plan is to publish an RFC for HAL+JSON, and follow it up with a separate RFC for HAL+XML.

+XML, because I think it's easier to look at a HAL+XML document and see what's going on.

Here's a HAL+XML document I made up, a representation from a hypothetical HAL version of the maze game. It represents a maze cell in more or less the same way as hMaze. It includes a number of links to other cells, and a switch that can be flipped:

```
<resource href="/cells/H">
 <title>Hall of Pretzels</title>

 <link href="/cells/G" rel="east"/>
 <link href="/cells/I" rel="west"/>

 <resource href="/switches/4">
  <switch>
   <position>up</position>
   <link href="/switches/4" rel="flip" title="Flip the mysterious switch."/>
  </switch>
 </resource>

</resource>
```

HAL only defines two concepts: resources and links. HAL+XML represents these as `<resource>` and `<link>` tags. All the other tags in that document are application-specific tags I made up, based on hMaze.

The `<resource>` tag just says that the XML inside the tag is a representation of some HTTP resource.

The `<link>` tag is a completely generic hypermedia control. This is the big difference, hypermedia-wise, between HAL and HTML. HTML has different controls for different purposes. The `<a>` tag makes a GET request when activated, and when it gets a document in response, the application's focus moves to that document. The `<img>` tag makes a GET request *automatically* and embeds the resulting representation as an image in the current document, without changing the application's focus. The `<form>` tag can be set up to make either a POST request or a GET request. But there's no HTML tag that can trigger a PUT or DELETE request. If you want to describe an HTTP request using HTML, but the W3C didn't define a tag that does what you want, you're out of luck.

HAL has only one hypermedia control, but that control can do *anything*. It can trigger a GET request, a POST request, or a PUT request with a specific entity-body. It can offer the user a choice between DELETE and UNLINK. The `<link>` tag in a HAL+XML document can trigger *any HTTP request at all* when activated.

Let's take a look at just the links in my HAL+XML document:

```
<link href="/cells/G" rel="east"/>
<link href="/cells/I" rel="west"/>
<link href="/switches/4" rel="flip" title="Flip the mysterious switch."/>
```

This is why I think HAL strips too much away from HTML. How are you supposed to know which of the infinite possibilities are present in a given link? The `<link>` tag with `rel="east"` should trigger a GET request that gives you a representation of the cell to the east. The `<link>` tag with `rel="flip"` should trigger a POST request that flips the switch. One of them is a safe operation that modifies application state; the other is an unsafe, non-idempotent operation that modifies resource state. In HAL, those two links look almost identical. The only real difference is the link relation.

And that's where HAL says to keep the distinguishing information about any state transition: inside the link relation. When I define `rel="flip"`, I'm supposed to mention that the `flip` state transition is triggered with a POST request. This means writing some human-readable documentation like this:

flip

> May appear within `switch`. When activated *with a POST request*, will have the effect of flipping the switch.

Do you see the problem? The API's protocol semantics are creeping out of machine-readable hypermedia and into human-readable text. We know it's possible to tell a computer to make a POST request instead of a GET request. That's what the HTML tag `<form action="post">` does. But HAL has no way of conveying protocol semantics in a machine-readable way. I have to spell it out in the docs, and everyone who implements a maze client has to read my docs and program the protocol semantics into their client.

It's understandable if an API's application semantics are documented in English. It's hard to get a computer to understand that stuff (although I'll take a stab at it in Chapter 8). But it's *not* hard to tell a computer that it should make an HTTP POST request.

The `flip` relation is pretty simple, so this may not seem like a big deal, but keep in mind that a link relation in HAL can represent *any* state transition, or even a set of state transitions. Take a look at the HAL Browser (*http://haltalk.herokuapp.com/*), an example application maintained by the creator of HAL, and you'll see what I mean.

To create an account on the HAL Browser you need to activate the link with the relation `ht:signup`. Figure 7-3 shows the human-readable documentation for that link relation.

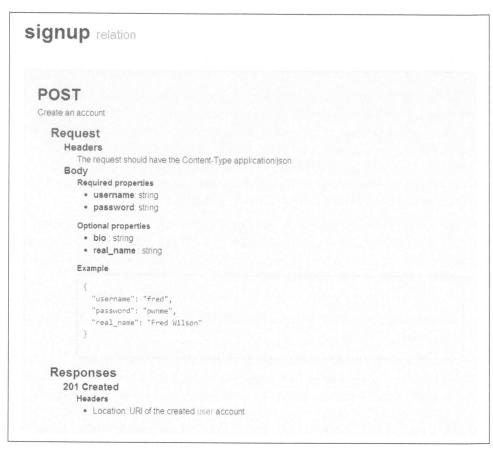

Figure 7-3. All about the ht:signup link relation

This is very clear, well-written documentation, but it's exactly the sort of thing that gives web APIs a bad name. It looks like the "API documentation" I slammed earlier. It spends a lot of time detailing the HTTP request necessary to trigger a state transition, and only mentions in passing that the *purpose* of the state transition is to create a new account. Ideally, the HTTP request and response would be described in machine-readable form, and only the part that a computer can't understand—the point of the whole thing— would be kept in human-readable form.

HAL allows a link relation to trigger any state transition at all, but the only way to describe the state transition is to write a bunch of human-readable prose. That's not a good combination.

If you keep the gap between your application semantics and HTTP's protocol semantics relatively small, this is not a big deal. For a read-only API, where all the state transitions are safe, HAL would work well. But you only have to go as far as the semi-official example application to see HAL's limitations. There's a huge semantic gap between HTTP's POST method and the HAL Browser's `ht:signup` link relation. HTML would do a much better job than HAL of bridging that gap.

Siren

I'll close out this chapter by taking a brief look at another general hypermedia format: Siren.[8] Siren is a newer format than HAL, and although it's based on JSON, it takes a more HTML-like approach to hypermedia than HAL's minimalism.

Here's a sample Siren document—a representation of the maze cell you've already seen in HTML and HAL formats:

```
{
  "class" : ["cell"],
  "properties" : { "title": "Hall of Pretzels" },

  "links" : [
    { "rel" : ["current"], "href" : "/cells/H" },
    { "rel" : ["east"], "href" : "/cells/G" },
    { "rel" : ["west"], "href" : "/cells/I" }
  ],

  "entities" : [
    { "class" : ["switch"],
      "href" : "/switches/4",
      "rel"  : ["item"],
      "properties" : { "position" : ["up"] },
      "actions" : [
        { "name" : "flip",
          "href" : "/switches/4",
          "title" : "Flip the mysterious switch.",
          "method": "POST"
        }
      ]
    }
  ]
}
```

Siren is designed to represent abstract groupings of data it calls *entities*. A Siren "entity" is conceptually similar to HTML's `<div>` tag. It's a convenient way of splitting up your data. An entity may be an HTTP resource with its own URL, but it doesn't have to be.

Like a Collection+JSON item, a Siren entity defines a special slot called `links` for containing links. My cell entity contains three links: a `current` link to itself, and `east` and `west` links to other cells.

---

8. A personal standard, defined at the GitHub Siren page (*https://github.com/kevinswiber/siren*).

This cell entity also contains a subentity: the mysterious switch. The switch defines a resource state transition called flip, a transition we've seen many times in this chapter.

The flip state transition is defined by a Siren *action*, a hypermedia control analogous to an HTML form. (Note the method, just like an HTML form.) The name of the Siren action serves the same purpose as the class of an HTML form, or the rel of a link. It makes it clear which state transition will happen if the client decides to activate the control. The *purpose* of the state transition—to flip the switch—still needs to be described in human-readable text. I put this text in the title attribute.

The only new feature in this representation is that I started using item as a link relation:

```
....
  "entities": [
  { "class" : ["switch"],
    "href" : "/switches/4",
    "rel"  : ["item"],
  ...
```

This link relation describes the relationship between a switch and the cell that contains the switch. The Siren standard requires that every subentity provide a rel describing the relationship between its parent and itself. The item link relation is an IANA-registered relation describing the relationship between a collection (the cell) and the things it contains (such as mysterious switches).

Siren sits somewhere between HTML and Collection+JSON. Its system of nested entities would work well to implement the collection pattern I described in Chapter 6. But where Collection+JSON defines certain kinds of resources and sets out their behavior under HTTP POST, PUT, and DELETE, Siren allows state transitions even more sophisticated than those available through HTML forms.

The upside of this approach is greater flexibility in representing state transitions that don't fit the collection pattern. The downside is that two Siren applications (or two HTML applications) will have less in common, and require more special client-side programming, than two Collection+JSON applications.

The Semantic Challenge: How Are We Doing?

Let's recap the situation as it stands. We have a client-server Internet protocol, HTTP, which assigns very general meanings to different kinds of requests: GET, POST, PUT, and so on.

We have the idea of hypermedia, which allows the server to tell the client which HTTP requests it might want to make next. This frees the client from having to know the shape of the API ahead of time.

We have the idea of application semantics, which extend hypermedia controls with information about *what specifically will happen*, to application or resource state, if the client makes a certain HTTP request.

And we have a whole lot of standards for building APIs.

We have domain-specific standards like Maze+XML, which define the application-level semantics *and* the protocol-level semantics for one tiny problem space (like maze games).

We have standards like Collection+JSON and the Atom Publishing Protocol, which see the world in terms of "collection" and "item" resources. These standards define protocol-level semantics in great detail, but they leave the application-level semantics almost completely undefined. An item-type resource must respond to HTTP PUT in a very specific way, but an item can *mean* absolutely anything.

We have microformats like hCard, and microdata items like schema.org's *http://sche ma.org/Person*. These define a lot of application-level semantics for explaining what a document means, but little or no protocol semantics for explaining how the underlying resource should behave under HTTP.

And we have standards like HTML, HAL, and Siren, languages that give you free rein to define your own protocol semantics *and* your own application-level semantics.

Our challenge is to bridge the semantic gap I defined back in Chapter 1. Given an API, how can a client developer write a computer program that makes decisions based on the API's application semantics?

If the API is described by a domain-specific standard like Maze+XML, bridging the semantic gap is straightforward. All the information you need is in the standard. It explains both the protocol semantics and the application semantics. You read the standard, you decide how your client should respond in any given situation, and you write your client.

But domain-specific hypermedia standards are rare. Most hypermedia APIs use collection standards like AtomPub, or generic hypermedia languages like HTML. These standards define an API's protocol semantics, but they don't say much about the application semantics. A human being must read some other document to understand the meanings encoded in the representations the API is serving.

But where is that document? Does the API use a microformat? Which microformat? How do you find out? Are you just supposed to know about all the microformats?

What if the API doesn't use HTML? Siren has no support for microformats or microdata. What if an API designer wants to put hCard-like data in a Siren document?

At this point, we reach the limits of current technology. There are no well-accepted answers to these questions. The result is that every API designer simply makes up application-level semantics that fit with their preexisting server-side design, and documents those semantics… somewhere.

This is how we ended up with 57 microblogging APIs. We're stuck. API technology can't advance beyond the "hypermedia" state without answering these questions. In the next chapter, I'll present some preliminary answers.

Profiles

Over the past three chapters, I've built up a set of rules for designing a brand new API. There's still some work to do on these rules, but I can now present them in something approaching their complete form:

- Is there a domain-specific standard for your problem? If so, use it. Document any application-specific extensions (Chapter 5).

- Does your problem fit the collection pattern? If so, adopt one of the collection standards. Define an application-specific vocabulary and document it (Chapter 6).

- If neither of those is true, choose a general hypermedia format. Break down your application into its state transitions. Document those state transitions (Chapter 7).

- At this point, you have your protocol semantics nailed down. The application semantics are all that remain. Are there existing microdata items or microformats that cover your problem domain? If so, use them. Otherwise, define an application-specific vocabulary and document it (Chapter 7).

The issue here is not whether to use "hypermedia." Maze+XML, AtomPub, and HAL all use hypermedia to describe state transitions, but they use it in different ways to solve different problems. The issue is choosing a format that lets you represent the state transitions that make up your API.

HAL is great for read-only applications. Maze+XML is great for read-only applications that happen to be maze games. AtomPub is great for read-write applications that work more or less like weblogs. Move outside a format's comfort zone, and you'll find yourself stretching it, defining more and more extensions, and defining fake resources just to conform to the patterns set down by the standard.

Every one of these rules mentions one big thing I haven't covered: documentation. "Document any application-specific extensions." "Define an application-specific vocabulary and document it." What do I mean when I say "document it?"

Experience has made me very suspicious of the stuff that comes to mind when one thinks of API documentation. The social norms in the API community allow a barrage of human-readable documentation to compensate for ignorance of the principles of REST, or for just plain bad design. I'd like to cut down on the human-readable documentation, but I can't get rid of it altogether. At some point, I have to tell you that in my maze game, rel="flip" means to flip a switch, not to flip a coin, or to turn over a card on a blackjack table. The hypermedia formats themselves—HTML, AtomPub, and the rest—are defined in human-readable documents like RFCs.

This chapter is devoted to the question of documentation. If you add one more API to the world, how much new human-readable documentation do you really need to write? What form should the documentation take? How do you avoid being the one who creates the 58th microblogging API?

How Does A Client Find the Documentation?

Before considering what API documentation should look like, let's think about how clients are supposed to find the documentation in the first place. One of the Fielding constraints is "self-describing messages." The server shouldn't have to guess what an HTTP request means, and the client shouldn't have to guess what a response means. It should be spelled out, or at least implied, in the message itself.

HTTP's Content-Type header is the clearest example of this. The value of this header tells you how to parse the entity-body. Some examples:

```
Content-Type: text/html
Content-Type: application/json
Content-Type: application/atom+xml
Content-Type: application/vnd.collection+json
Content-Type: application/vnd.amundsen.maze+xml
```

If the media type is one that defines hypermedia controls (like an HTML document), then parsing a response document lets you know what HTTP requests you can make next. You now understand the document's protocol semantics. If the media type is a domain-specific format (like Maze+XML), then parsing the document also gives you an understanding of a state in the problem space (like a maze cell). You now understand the document's application semantics. Once you understand both the protocol semantics and the application semantics, you're done. You (or your software) can make a decision based on the available information.

Most of the time, you won't get both types of semantics just from the media type. Think about an HTML document that uses the hCard microformat. Parsing the document as text/html gives you the protocol semantics, but not the application semantics. Think about the JSON document you get from Twitter's API. It's served as application/json. Parsing that document doesn't give you the protocol semantics *or* the application semantics. There's some other mystery specification that's missing.

These "missing" specifications aren't really missing. For hCard, the specification is at *http://microformats.org/wiki/hcard*. For Twitter, the specification is at *https://dev.twit ter.com/docs*. I'm going to call these "missing" specifications *profiles*. Documents like these are the main topic of this chapter.

What's a Profile?

Here's the formal definition of a profile, from RFC 6906:

> A profile is defined to not alter the semantics of the resource representation itself, but to allow clients to learn about additional semantics... associated with the resource representation, in addition to those defined by the media type...

The hCard microformat clearly fits this definition. An HTML document that uses hCard is still an HTML document, but it gains some extra application semantics that most HTML documents don't have. The document is now *about* something. It describes a person, not in free-flowing prose, but in a way a computer can be programmed to understand.

The human-readable documentation for the Twitter API is also a profile. You can parse a Twitter representation without the documentation (it's just JSON), but you'll know nothing about what it means. It's just a JSON object. Twitter's API documentation lets you understand the meaning of the JSON objects the API serves ("allow clients to learn about additional semantics"), without contradicting anything in RFC 4627, the JSON specification ("not alter the semantics of the resource representation itself").

Linking to a Profile

What's "missing" from these representations—the HTML document that uses hCard and the JSON document served by Twitter's API—is not the profile, but the *connection* between the profile and the document that uses it. The client is supposed to "just know" which profile(s) to apply to a given document. Well, we know how to solve that problem. We can *link* a document to its profile using hypermedia.

There are three different ways to do this. Let's take a look at each one in turn.

The profile Link Relation

RFC 6906 defines a link relation called `profile`. This relation is registered with the IANA, which means you can use `profile` in any hypermedia control that supports a link relation: the `<a>` tag defined by HTML; the `<link>` tag defined by HTML, HAL, and Maze+XML; a Siren or Collection+JSON `links` object; or the `Link` HTTP header defined by RFC 5988.

If you get an HTTP response that starts like this, you know that this is an HTML document that uses the hCard microformat:

```
HTTP/1.1 200 OK
Content-Type: text/html

<html>
 <head>
  <link href="http://microformats.org/wiki/hcard" rel="profile">
...
```

JSON has no protocol semantics and next to no application semantics, but if you get an HTTP response that starts like this, you'll know that this document contains an extra layer of semantics on top of JSON's:

```
HTTP/1.1 200 OK
Content-Type: application/json
Link: <https://dev.twitter.com/docs>;rel="profile"

...
```

The profile Media Type Parameter

Depending on the media type you're using, you may be able to link to a profile within the Content-Type header by adding a profile parameter to the media type. Here's what the Content-Type header might look like for a Collection+JSON document:

```
application/collection+json;profile="http://www.example.com/profile"
```

That says: "this is a Collection+JSON document, but it has extra semantics described by the profile found at *http://www.example.com/profile.*"

Unfortunately, you can't stick the profile parameter on any random media type. According to section 4.3 of RFC 4288, you can only use a parameter on a media type that explicitly defines it. The JSON spec doesn't mention the profile parameter, so the following is illegal, as useful as it would be:

```
Content-Type: application/json;profile="https://dev.twitter.com/docs"
```

Right now, the only hypermedia types that allow for the profile parameter are Collection+JSON, JSON-LD, HAL, and XHTML (not HTML!). If you want to link to a profile within the HTTP headers, and you're not using one of those media types, I recommend using the Link header instead.

Special-Purpose Hypermedia Controls

In Chapter 7 I showed off HTML microdata. I said that the itemtype property was "a hypermedia control that tells the client where it should go to find out what the microdata means." Here's an example:

```
<div itemscope itemtype="http://schema.org/Person">
```

I didn't say so at the time, but this is clearly a link to a profile. It points to a document that provides application semantics on top of those defined by the HTML 5 specification.

HTML 4 also has a special hypermedia control for linking an entire document to its profile:

```
<HEAD profile="http://schema.org/Person">
  ...
</HEAD>
```

I don't recommend you use this one, but it's interesting for historical reasons. As we'll see in the next section, this is where the term "profile" comes from in the first place.

Profiles Describe Protocol Semantics

When a profile describes an API's protocol semantics, it usually uses freeform English prose. We see this in the documentation for today's popular APIs, which use prose to describe the "API calls" you can invoke by making GET and POST requests. Figure 8-1 shows an example from Twitter's API.:

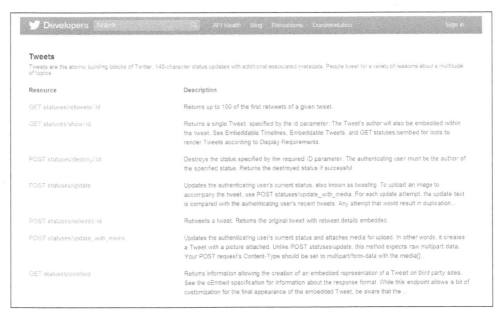

Figure 8-1. A list of API calls

We saw the same thing in Chapter 7, when I showed the human-readable document (we can now call it a profile) that describes a HAL representation:

```
flip
```
> May appear within `switch`. When activated *with a POST request*, will have the effect of flipping the switch.

In both cases, the API provider wrote prose describing an HTTP request the client might make in the future. You could give this information more structure, and even make it understandable by a computer, but then it wouldn't be a profile: it would be hypermedia. A profile only needs to describe protocol semantics when the media type has no hypermedia controls (as with JSON), or when the controls aren't specific enough to explain exactly which HTTP request the client should make (as with HAL).

This is why I recommend you choose a full-featured hypermedia format like HTML or Siren as your representation format. You'll still have to write a profile, but the profile needn't contain a lot of detail about your API's protocol semantics. That stuff will be embedded in the representations themselves.

Profiles Describe Application Semantics

Protocol semantics deal with HTTP requests, but application semantics refer to things in the real world, and computers are terrible at understanding the real world. At some point, we must bridge the semantic gap by writing prose that explains our application semantics. There's nothing analogous to hypermedia that will save us.

But we can exploit a pattern that has shown up over and over again, in the thousands of profiles created over the past few years. An API's application semantics tend to be focused around short, mysterious strings like "fn," "bday," "east," and "flip."

The profile for a microformat is a list of these mysterious strings, with an English explanation of each. The profile for a microdata item is similar. Traditional API documentation spends a lot of time on protocol semantics, but it also spends a lot of time listing and explaining these mysterious strings. They're the keys in JSON objects, they're the names of XML tags, and they're the variables used to expand URI Templates and build query strings.

This is an important discovery. It's a big task to get a computer to understand what it means for a human being to have a name. But it's pretty easy for a computer to understand that "fn" is a magical string that means something special—never mind what—when it's used as a CSS class.

These magical strings will help us simplify our profiles. I've divided them into two categories: link relations and semantic descriptors.

Link Relations

As I said in Chapter 5, a link relation is a magical string attached to a hypermedia control, which describes the state transition that will occur if the client triggers the control. You've now seen many examples of link relations in different media types. Here's a Maze+XML example from Chapter 5:

```
<link rel="east" href="/cells/N"/>
```

Here's an AtomPub example from Chapter 6:

```
<link rel="next" href="/collection/4iz6"/>
```

Here's a Collection+JSON example, also from Chapter 6:

```
{"name" : "cover", "rel" : "icon", "prompt" : "Book cover",
 "href" : "/covers/1093149.jpg", "render" : "image"}
```

Here's an HTML example from Chapter 7:

```
<a href="/rooms/154" rel="east">
```

Here are a few Siren examples from Chapter 7:

```
"links" : [
  { "rel" : ["current"], "href": "/cells/H" },
  { "rel" : ["east"], "href": "/cells/G" },
  { "rel" : ["west"], "href": "/cells/I" }
]
```

A hypermedia control that supports a link relation defines one slot (traditionally called href) for the target URL and a second slot (traditionally called rel) for the link relation.

On their own, the names of link relations are just strings: "east," "next," "icon," "current." Human beings may find these names evocative, but without knowing *exactly* what they mean, there's no way of programming a computer to understand them. That's what profiles are for.

 As the API designer, you are responsible for documenting all of your link relations ahead of time, in a profile document or in the definition of a custom media type. The only exceptions are link relations that you took from the IANA registry (see Chapter 10). You are not excused from this if you think your link relations are self-explanatory, because they never are.

If you use extension link relations (the ones that look like URLs), a human being who puts that URL into a web browser should find an explanation of that link relation.

Unsafe Link Relations

Now, here's a HAL example from Chapter 7:

```
<link href="/switches/4" rel="flip" title="Flip the mysterious switch."/>
```

My other examples described, well, *links*—transitions between one application state and another, to be triggered with GET requests. The HAL example is unusual because its link relation (`flip`) describes a change in *resource* state, to be triggered with a POST request.

The `name` attribute of a Siren action works the same way. It associates a magical string with a potentially unsafe state transition. Here's the Siren equivalent of the HAL example:

```
"actions" : [
  { "name": "flip",
    "href": "/switches/4"
    "title": "Flip the mysterious switch.",
    "method": "POST"
  }
]
```

It's a little odd to call these magical strings "link relations," since we think of a "link" as something that's activated with a GET request. I considered introducing the more general term "transition relation," but given the fact that formats like HAL use "link relation," I think it's best to stick with existing usage, and say "link relation" for a string that describes *any* state transition.

Semantic Descriptors

Now for the second kind of magical string. The hCard microformat defines the CSS class `fn` for marking up a person's full name:

```
<span class="fn">Jenny Gallegos</span>
```

There's a schema.org microdata item called *http://schema.org/Person* which defines the property `name` for the same purpose:

```
<span itemprop="name">Jenny Gallegos</span>
```

The documentation for the Twitter API mentions a key called `name`, which is inserted into certain JSON dictionaries to indicate the name associated with a Twitter account (not necessarily the name of a human being):

```
{ "name": "Jenny Gallegos"}
```

These are three different approaches to the same goal: pointing out which part of a representation is someone's (or something's) name. I'm going to call this kind of thing a *semantic descriptor*.

Let's look at a few more examples. The class of a Siren entity is a semantic descriptor, and so are the names of the entity's properties:

```
"class" : ["person"],
"properties" : { "name" : "Jenny Gallegos" },
```

```
    ...
}
```

The name of a data field in a Collection+JSON item is a semantic descriptor:

```
"data" : [
 { "name" : "family-name", "value" : "Gallegos" }
],
```

In ad hoc JSON—not just in the documents served by the Twitter API—it's customary to use semantic descriptors as object keys:

```
{"name" : "Jenny Gallegos"}
```

(JSON-LD, which I'll cover in an upcoming section, is based on this convention.)

Similarly, in ad hoc XML documents, the tag names often correspond to semantic descriptors:

```
<person>
 <name>Jenny Gallegos</name>
</person>
```

But those last two are only conventions. Clients can't rely on them in general. That's one reason I don't think you should design APIs using ad hoc JSON or XML.

 As the API designer, you are responsible for documenting all of your semantic descriptors ahead of time, in a profile document or in the definition of a custom media type. You are not excused from this if you think your semantic descriptors are self-explanatory, because they never are.

XMDP: The First Machine-Readable Profile Format

What would a profile look like if all you had to describe were these magic strings, the link relations and the semantic descriptors? It would look like a microformat; that's what a microformat does. It's no surprise, then, that the first machine-readable profiles were descriptions of microformats. The format used in these profiles, XMDP, isn't one I recommend using today, but it's so simple that it makes for a good introduction to the concept.

The idea of a profile ultimately stems from the HTML 4 specification, which introduced the concept of a "meta data profile." Unfortunately, the specification didn't define what a meta data profile should look like. It only explained how you'd link to a profile from an HTML document, if you somehow managed to get hold of a profile. The link would look like this one, which I showed you earlier:

```
<HEAD profile="http://example.com/profile">
 ...
</HEAD>
```

This lack of detail in the spec was a recipe for inaction. There was no real-world use case for a meta data profile (this was before web APIs) and no guidance as to what a meta data profile should look like. The `profile` attribute on `<HEAD>` wasn't very good syntax, either. HTML profiles never caught on, and the idea has been dropped from HTML 5.

But one man, Tantek Çelik, kept the dream alive. He collected a few obscure clues from the HTML 4 specification and defined the missing meta data profile standard, a microformat called XMDP. [1] XMDP is a microformat for explaining other microformats.

The best way to explain XMDP is to see how it explains a microformat I've already covered. Here's an edited sample of the XMDP profile for the hCard microformat.[2] The XMDP profile lists all the CSS classes hCard defines, and gives a human-readable description of each. The human-readable descriptions don't really tell you much. They just point you to RFC 2426, which defines the vCard standard on which hCard is based:

```
<dl class="profile">

<dt>class</dt>
 <dd>
  <p>All values are defined according to the semantics defined in the
    <a rel="help start" href="http://microformats.org/wiki/hcard">
    hCard specification</a>
    and thus in
    <a href="http://www.ietf.org/rfc/rfc2426.txt">RFC 2426</a>.</p>
 <dl>

 <dt id="vcard">vcard</dt>
  <dd>A container for the rest of the class names defined in this
   XMDP profile.  See section 1. of RFC 2426.</dd>
 </dt>

 <dt id="fn">fn</dt>
  <dd>See section 3.1.1 of RFC 2426.</dd>

 <dt id="family-name">family-name</dt>
  <dd>See "Family Name" in section 3.1.2 of RFC 2426.</dd>

 <dt id="given-name">given-name</dt>
  <dd>See "Given Name" in section 3.1.2 of RFC 2426.</dd>

 ...

 </dl>
```

1. The XMDP specification is located here (*http://microformats.org/wiki/XMDP*). You can read Çelik's exegesis of the HTML 4 standard at this page (*http://gmpg.org/xmdp/description*).

2. The full XMDP description of hCard is located here (*http://microformats.org/profile/hcard*). You can compare it against hCard's human-readable profile (*http://microformats.org/wiki/hcard*).

```
    </dd>
  </dl>
```

This doesn't seem like much, but it gives us a very useful feature. A computer can compare an HTML document against an XMDP description of hCard and determine which CSS classes are part of hCard, and which are not.

In the following snippet, `bold` is just an ordinary CSS class whose meaning is defined in a stylesheet somewhere. The `family-name` class may be described in a stylesheet, but it also has special meaning to hCard:

```
<div class="family-name bold">Gallegos</div>
```

Without the profile, a computer has no way of knowing that "family-name" is an hCard-specific CSS class. A human being must read the hCard standard ahead of time and turn that knowledge into software. With the XMDP profile, a computer that understands XMDP *in general* will understand that "family-name" has special meaning to this XMDP profile.

This doesn't bring a computer any closer to knowing what a "family-name" is, but it does make it possible to write simple software tools that combine HTML documents with XMDP profiles. Without XMDP, you'd have to write such a tool especially for hCard, and then write an identical tool for hCalendar, hRecipe, XFN, and every other microformat.

To go along with XMDP, Çelik defined a simple microformat called "rel-profile,"[3] which simply defines a link relation called `profile`:

```
<link rel="profile" href="http://example.com/profiles/microformats/hcard"/>
```

This eventually became the `profile` link relation defined in RFC 6906.

ALPS

XMDP is a good start, but we can do better. I've created a standard called ALPS that addresses the major problem I see with XMDP: it's an HTML microformat designed for describing other HTML microformats. You can only use it if your representation format is HTML.

Now, HTML is really, really popular. It's the dominant representation format on the human web. But it's *not* the dominant format for web APIs. That honor belongs to JSON, with XML a runner-up. HTML is a very distant third or fourth.

This means that today's APIs *don't use microformats or microdata*, even when that would make perfect sense. There are no rules for applying these profiles to JSON or XML

---

3. More information on rel-profile is available at this page (*http://microformats.org/wiki/rel-profile*).

documents. I've seen API designers reinvent JSON versions of hCard and the other microformats over and over, slightly differently each time. When you use a JSON-based representation, you have no way of reusing other peoples' application semantics. You must write a profile from scratch. Then you publish your API and your users must *read* your profile and write special code to implement its application semantics.

What if there there were a profile format like XMDP that wasn't limited to describing HTML documents? What if it could express application semantics like those found in microformats and microdata, in a machine-readable way that could be translated to HTML, Collection+JSON, Siren, and the other hypermedia formats I've discussed in this book? I have tried to make ALPS into that format. It won't solve all our problems, but I think it represents progress.

Let's take a look. Here's an excerpt from an ALPS profile that describes the application semantics of hCard. The human-readable text is taken almost verbatim from the XMDP profile, but the document's structure is much different:

```xml
<?xml version="1.0" ?>
<alps>

 <link rel="self" href="http://alps.io/microformats/hcard" />

 <doc>
   hCard is a simple, open format for publishing people, companies,
   and organizations on the web.
 </doc>

 <descriptor id="vcard" type="semantic">
  <doc>
   A container element for an hCard document. See section 1. of RFC 2426.
  </doc>
  <descriptor href="#fn"/>
  <descriptor href="#family-name"/>
  <descriptor href="#given-name"/>
 </descriptor>

 <descriptor id="fn" type="semantic">
  <doc>See section 3.1.1 of RFC 2426.</doc>
 </descriptor>

 <descriptor id="family-name" type="semantic">
  <doc>See "Family Name" in section 3.1.2 of RFC 2426.</doc>
 </descriptor>

 <descriptor id="given-name" type="semantic">
  <doc>See "Given Name" in section 3.1.2 of RFC 2426.</doc>
 </descriptor>

 ...
</alps>
```

This ALPS document contains one `<descriptor>` tag for each semantic descriptor defined by the hCard microformat. The `type` attribute of the `<descriptor>` tag is set to `semantic`, and the `<doc>` tag within the `<descriptor>` contains the human-readable explanation. Apart from the contents of the `<doc>` tags, everything in the document is machine-readable.

Syntactically, the main improvement over XMDP is that an ALPS `<descriptor>` tag can be a hypermedia link from one ALPS element to another. The `<descriptor href="#fn"/>` within the `<descriptor id="vcard">` indicates that clients can expect to see `fn` elements nested inside elements tagged with `vcard`. In XMDP, that information was conveyed in human-readable text. Here, it's machine-readable.

The XMDP profile of hCard explained how to express its application semantics as an HTML microformat. The ALPS version of the same profile allows an approximation of those application semantics to be represented as microdata instead:

```
<div itemscope itemtype="http://alps.io/microformats/hcard#vcard">
 My name is <div itemprop="fn">Jennifer Gallegos</div>.
</div>
```

Or as part of a HAL representation:

```
<vcard>
 <fn>Jennifer Gallegos</fn>
 <family-name>Gallegos</family-name>
</vcard>
```

Or as a Siren entity:

```
{
 "class": ["vcard"],
 "properties": { "fn": "Jennifer Gallegos" }
}
```

Or as ad hoc JSON:

```
{"vcard": {
    "fn": "Jennifer Gallegos",
    "family-name": "Gallegos"
  }
}
```

This is also valid ad hoc JSON:

```
{
 "fn": "Jennifer Gallegos",
 "family-name": "Gallegos"
}
```

One ALPS profile can explain the application semantics of all of these documents. All you have to do is connect the document to the profile using the `profile` link relation.

But we're just getting started. An ALPS profile can represent link relations as well as semantic descriptors. Here's part of an ALPS document that approximates the application semantics of Maze+XML:

```xml
<?xml version="1.0" ?>
<alps>

 <link rel="self" href="http://alps.io/example/maze" />
 <link rel="help" href="http://amundsen.com/media-types/maze/" />

 <doc format="html">
     <h2>Maze+XML Profile</h2>
     <p>Describes a common profile for implementing Maze+XML.</p>
 </doc>

 ...

 <descriptor id="cell" type="semantic">
   <link rel="help"
         href="http://amundsen.com/media-types/maze/format/#cell-element" />
   <doc>Describes a cell in a maze.</doc>
   <descriptor href="#title"/>
   <descriptor href="http://alps.io/iana/relations#current"/>
   <descriptor href="#start"/>
   <descriptor href="#north"/>
   <descriptor href="#south"/>
   <descriptor href="#east"/>
   <descriptor href="#west"/>
   <descriptor href="#exit"/>
 </descriptor>


 <descriptor id="title" type="semantic">
  <doc>The name of the cell.</doc>
 </descriptor>

 <descriptor id="north" type="safe">
   <link rel="help"
         href="http://amundsen.com/media-types/maze/format/#north-rel" />
   <doc>Refers to a resource that is "north" of the current resource.</doc>
 </descriptor>

 <descriptor id="south" type="safe">
   <link rel="help"
         href="http://amundsen.com/media-types/maze/format/#south-rel" />
   <doc>Refers to a resource that is "south" of the current resource.</doc>
 </descriptor>

 ...

</alps>
```

The cell descriptor is a semantic descriptor, just like the vcard element in the ALPS profile of hCard. But the north and south descriptors represent link relations. They have their type set to safe, which means that north and south are safe state transitions that can be triggered with HTTP GET.

If you represented these semantics as HTML microdata, it might look like this:

```
<p itemtype="http://alps.io/example/maze#cell">
You are in the <span itemprop="title">Foyer of Horrors</span>.
Exits: <a href="/cells/I" rel="north">north</a>,
       <a href="/cells/M" rel="west">west</a>,
       <a href="/cells/O" rel="east">east</a>.
</p>
```

If you represented the same semantics as a Siren document, it might look like this:

```
{
 "class": ["cell"],
 "properties": { "title": "Foyer of Horrors" },
 "links": { "north": "/cells/I",
            "west": "/cells/M",
            "east": "/cells/O" }
}
```

ALPS can also describe unsafe state transitions. Here's a snippet from an ALPS document describing the application semantics of hMaze (there's a semantic descriptor for a switch, and an unsafe state transition for flipping the switch):

```
<descriptor id="switch" type="semantic">
 <doc>A mysterious switch found in the maze.</doc>
 <contains href="#flip"/>
</descriptor>

<element id="flip" type="unsafe">
  <description>Flips a switch.</description>
</element>
```

Here, the type is unsafe, indicating that the state transition is neither safe nor idempotent. ALPS also defines the type="idempotent", for describing a transition that is idempotent but not safe.

ALPS doesn't say which HTTP method to use for an unsafe or idempotent state transaction. That's left up to the hypermedia control. ALPS just explains the state transition that will happen when the hypermedia control is triggered. In HTML, the HTTP method would be POST:

```
<form action="/switches/4" method="POST">
 <input type="submit" class="flip" value="Flip it!">
</form>
```

A HAL document wouldn't specify the HTTP method at all:

```
<link href="/switches/4" rel="flip"/>
```

Advantages of ALPS

An HTML document can invoke an ALPS profile by linking to it using the `profile` link relation. Here's an HTML document that uses `profile` to bring in an ALPS profile that approximates the application semantics of hCard:

```
<html>
 <head>
  <link href="http://alps.io/microformats/hcard" rel="profile"/>
 </head>

 <body>

  <p>Some unrelated content.</p>

  <div class="vcard">
   <span class="fn">Jennifer Gallegos</span>
   <date class="bday">1987-08-25</span>
  </div>

  <p>More unrelated content.</p>

 </body>
</html>
```

The body of the page is just HTML plus hCard. However, consider a client that understands HTML and ALPS, but *not* hCard. That client can download the ALPS profile and use it to pinpoint the hCard document within the HTML. The client can locate individual bits of data such as `fn`, and cross-reference that data against a human-readable description of it—despite having no idea what hCard means.

And we're not limited to HTML. You've already seen ALPS profiles used by Siren, HAL, XML, and JSON representations. It also works with Collection+JSON:

```
{
  "collection" :
  {
    "version" : "1.0",
    "href" : "http://www.example.com/jennifer",

    "links" : [
      { "href" : "http://alps.io/microformats/hcard",
        "rel": "profile"
      }
    ],

    "items" : [
      { "_class" : "vcard",
        "fn" : "Jennifer Gallegos",
```

```
        "bday" : "1987-08-25"
      }
    ]
  }
}
```

There's no need to create a special jCard microformat that adapts the application semantics of hCard to JSON.[4] You can just use the ALPS profile of hCard.

One ALPS document brings the application semantics of hCard to many different hypermedia formats, and gives hypermedia capabilities to ad hoc XML and JSON documents. All you have to do is link the representation to the ALPS document using the link relation `profile`.

Now there's no excuse for reinventing microformats and microdata items over and over again. When a new hypermedia format comes on the scene, defining how an ALPS profile applies to the new format makes it possible to apply *every* ALPS profile to documents in the new format.

Even if you stick to HTML (which can use microformats and microdata natively), you can get use out of the ALPS documents. I've set up a searchable repository of ALPS documents here (*http://alps.io/*). I'll talk about the repository a bit more in "The Semantic Zoo" on page 230 in Chapter 10. The repository includes ALPS versions of most of the microformats, of schema.org's microdata items, and of a few other standards.

The ALPS repository makes it easy to find and reuse individual semantic descriptors and link relations that someone else has already defined—even if they defined those elements for use with a representation format you're not using. By uploading your ALPS document to the repository, you make your work available for reuse by other interested parties, without having to go through a formal standards process.

Instead of writing human-readable documentation, you can write an ALPS document and convert to human-readable documentation using a simple XSLT stylesheet. ALPS also allows representations to be integrated with development tools in new ways. Imagine an IDE plug-in that finds all the link relations and semantic descriptors in a document, and provides mouseover explanations of what everything means. Back when every microformat was defined in its own human-readable document, writing that tool would require understanding every individual microformat, and committing to adding new microformats as they were approved. Now, you can write that tool based on nothing but an understanding of ALPS.

I'm not saying that anyone *will* write that tool, but it illustrates the pattern. A tool that understands ALPS doesn't have to add support for profiles one at a time. By supporting

---

4. This may seem like a silly idea, but there's an Internet-Draft (draft-ietf-jcardcal-jcard) that does something very similar. There's also an xCard standard, defined in RFC 6351, which is simply a port of vCard to XML.

ALPS, you support ALPS profiles of all the microformats—and all the schema.org microdata items, and more.

There are a few more features of ALPS that I won't cover here, because I don't want to turn this into a book about my pet standard. I will be using ALPS snippets throughout the rest of the book as a shorthand way of representing application semantics in a machine-readable form. If you're interested in ALPS as a standard, visit the ALPS website (*http://alps.io*). As I write this, I'm working on a specification for ALPS that I plan to submit as an Internet-Draft.

ALPS Doesn't Do Everything

Like XMDP, ALPS doesn't have every feature you could possibly want when writing a machine-readable profile. I omitted a lot of features to keep ALPS simple, flexible, and as generic as possible across media types.

ALPS is a very lenient format. It provides human-readable definitions of an API's magical strings, and a rough guide to where those strings are likely to be found within representations. It doesn't provide a machine-readable way of saying that a semantic descriptor is required, or can only show up once in a certain place.

Suppose you've defined an HTML microformat that says the tag with a certain `id` attribute has special meaning within the document:

```
<div id="a-very-important-tag">
```

In Chapter 7, I recommended against this, but sometimes it happens. There's no way to represent this special `id` in ALPS. I omitted this ability from ALPS because only XML-based representations support a document-wide unique ID. You can use human-readable text to *say* that a given semantic descriptor should only be used once per document, but you can't use ALPS to say that in machine-readable form.

In Chapter 12, I'll cover RDF Schema, a profile language that goes a lot further than ALPS does to make application semantics machine-readable. I came up with ALPS because I saw that RDF Schema is too complicated for most developers to even consider using.

JSON-LD

JSON-LD[5] is another profile language that was invented because people weren't using RDF Schema. JSON-LD lets you combine a machine-readable document called a *context* with an ordinary JSON document. This makes it easy to define a profile for an

---

5. An open standard in progress, defined at this page (*http://json-ld.org/spec/latest/json-ld-syntax/*).

existing API without changing the document format, which would break existing clients.

JSON-LD comes out of the RDF tradition, and I'll be returning to it in Chapter 12, after I discuss RDF. But you don't need to understand anything about RDF to use JSON-LD as a simple profile language.

Here's a bare JSON representation that's pretty typical of what APIs serve today:

```
HTTP/1.1 200 OK
Content-Type: application/json

{ "n": "Jenny Gallegos",
  "photo_link": "http://api.example.com/img/omjennyg" }
```

Looking at this through human eyes, we see one bit of data (a string) that has a semantic descriptor (n), and one hypermedia link whose link relation has the unwieldy name of photo_link. Looking at it through the eyes of an automated client, we see… nothing. Since the application/json media type has no hypermedia controls, the link is just a string that happens to look like a URL. The string "n" isn't a semantic descriptor, it's just a string. The string "photo_link" isn't a link relation, it's just a string.

There are hundreds of APIs like this. In fact, it's the status quo as I write this book. I'm trying to give the designers of new APIs the tools to do better than this, but what about an API that already exists? Can we improve this API without changing the document format?

We can improve the situation a little by having the API link each document it serves to its human-readable profile—its *API documentation*:

```
HTTP/1.1 200 OK
Content-Type: application/json
Link: <http://help.example.com/api/>;rel="profile"


...
```

But that's not much help.

Here's how JSON-LD would do it. Instead of serving a link to a human-readable profile or an ALPS profile, we'll serve a link to a JSON-LD context. The link relation here is more specific than the IANA-registered relation profile. It's an extension relation designed specifically for linking to JSON-LD contexts:

```
HTTP/1.1 200 OK
Content-Type: application/json
Link: <http://api.example.com/person.jsonld>;rel="http://www.w3.org/ns/json-ld↵
#context"

{ "n": "Jenny Gallegos",
  "photo_link": "http://www.example.com/img/omjennyg" }
```

Make a second HTTP GET request to *http://api.example.com/person.jsonld,* and you'll find the context. The HTTP response might look something like this:

```
HTTP/1.1 200 OK
Content-Type: application/ld+json

{
  "@context":
  {
    "n": "http://api.example.org/docs/Person#name",

    "photo_link":
    {
      "@id": "http://api.example.org/docs/Person#photo_link",
      "@type": "@id"
    }
  }
}
```

Any JSON object that defines the property @context can be a JSON-LD context. This particular context explains the application semantics of a JSON representation, in terms of human-readable API documentation.

The value of n is a JSON string, which JSON-LD interprets as a URL. Whatever's behind this URL will explain the application semantics of the n property from the original JSON document.

This says...

```
"n": "http://api.example.org/docs/Person#name"
```

...that if you're confused about how to understand this...

```
"n": "Jenny Gallegos"
```

...you can visit *http://api.example.org/docs/Person#name* and read the explanation. Unlike ALPS profiles, JSON-LD contexts don't usually explain bits of application semantics directly. They use links to point to an explanation somewhere else.

The value of photo_link is a JSON object:

```
"photo_link":
{
  "@id": "http://api.example.org/docs/Person#photo_link",
  "@type": "@id"
}
```

In JSON-LD, @id basically means "hypermedia link." The object's @id property is a link to the explanation of the term's application semantics.

The @type of this term is also @id. This is the magic that turns a JSON document into a hypermedia document. Setting the @type of photo_link to @id says that whenever photo_link occurs in a JSON document, the client can treat it as a hypermedia link, not as a string that happens to look like a URL.

Thanks to JSON-LD, our first HTTP response, which originally looked so hopeless, has become a self-describing message:

```
HTTP/1.1 200 OK
Content-Type: application/json
Link: <http://api.example.com/person.jsonld>;rel=
  "http://www.w3.org/ns/json-ld#context"

{ "n": "Jenny Gallegos",
  "photo_link": "http://www.example.com/img/omjennyg" }
```

A computer can combine this JSON document with the JSON-LD context and pick out the hypermedia links. In this example, that's pretty much all a computer can do. My JSON-LD context contains links to descriptions of the resource type, n and pho to_link, but they're links into the preexisting human-readable API documentation.

But a JSON-LD context can just as easily link to a machine-readable ALPS description of the application semantics:

```
{
  "@context":
  {
    "@type": "http://alps.io/schema.org/Person",
    "n": "http://alps.io/schema.org/Person#name",
    "photo_link":
    {
      "@id": "http://alps.io/schema.org/Person#image",
      "@type": "@id"
    }
  }
}
```

Or, as we'll see in Chapter 12, a JSON-LD context can describe a resource's application semantics in terms of an RDF vocabulary like FOAF:

```
{
  "@context":
  {
    "@type": "http://xmlns.com/foaf/0.1/Person",
    "n": "http://xmlns.com/foaf/0.1/name",
    "photo_link":
    {
      "@id": "http://xmlns.com/foaf/0.1/image",
      "@type": "@id"
    }
  }
}
```

However you do it, the goal is always the same. JSON-LD lets you explain the application semantics of a normal JSON document by adding a context on top of it.

Embedded Documentation

Here's the HTML form for flipping the mysterious switch in the maze game from Chapter 7:

```
<form class="flip" action="/switches/4">
  <input type="submit" value="Flip it!"/>
</form>
```

Here's the HAL version:

```
<link href="/switches/4" rel="flip" title="Flip the mysterious switch."/>
```

Here's the Siren version:

```
"actions" : [
  { "name": "flip",
    "href": "/switches/4"
    "title": "Flip the mysterious switch.",
    "method": "POST"
  }
]
```

The `value` of the HTML button, the `title` of the HAL link, and the `title` of the Siren action are all human-readable text explaining the hypermedia control. HTML's `label` tag and Collection+JSON's `prompt` attribute serve the same purpose for form fields. In all three cases, the documentation of the application semantics—the sort of thing you'd expect to find in a profile—is embedded in the document itself.

Here's the weird thing: this text is redundant. "Flip the mysterious switch." isn't a profile, because nothing technically connects the English text to the link relation `flip`. Either you understand the link relation, in which case the human-readable text is irrelevant; or you don't, in which case the link relation is meaningless. Why should a document contain human-readable and machine-readable representations of the same application semantics?

The two versions of the semantics are aimed at different audiences. This redundancy allows human-driven clients and automated clients to use the same representations. The formal definition of the `flip` relation (as revealed in the profile) is written for client programmers, and the English text (embedded in the document itself) is intended for human consumption.

A human user will ignore the profile. The human reads "Flip the mysterious switch." and decides whether or not to flip the switch. An automated client will ignore the embedded documentation. It sees `class="flip"` (or `rel="flip"` or `"name": "flip"`), connects the hypermedia control to the meaning of `flip` as revealed in the profile, and makes its decision on that basis.

If you're designing an API, and you know that all the decisions about state transitions will be made by human endusers, you don't need a profile at all. Websites don't have profiles. If you know that all the decisions will be made by automated clients, you don't need embedded documentation at all.

But in reality, you don't know any of this. You probably don't know what your users will do with your API, and you certainly don't know what will happen in the future. The best strategy is to define a profile for use when writing automated clients, and to *also* embed natural-language documentation inside your representations, for the benefit of human endusers (assuming the media type supports it, of course).

The markup `title="Flip the mysterious switch."` doesn't *explain* the markup `rel="flip"`. They're two ways of saying the same thing, aimed at different audiences. Embedded documentation can be valuable, but it "solves" the semantic challenge by bringing in an expensive piece of hardware—a human being. It's best saved for when you already know a human being is making the decisions.

In Summary

This chapter covers a lot of ground—I had to define a whole new data format to tell the story I needed to tell—but we're finally at the end of a journey that began in Chapter 5. We can solve the semantic challenge with a combination of a well-chosen media type and a profile that fills in the gaps. Here's the essential information necessary to solve it:

- A *link relation* is a string describing the state transition that will happen if the client triggers a hypermedia control. Example: Maze+XML's `east` relation, which lets you know that a certain link points to something geographically east of the current resource. Traditionally, the state transition is a change in application state (triggered with a GET request), but it can also be a change in resource state (triggered by PUT, POST, DELETE, or PATCH).

- A *semantic descriptor* is a short string that indicates what some part of a representation means. Example: hCard's `fn` descriptor, which is used as a CSS class to mark up a person's name in HTML. Unlike "link relation," this is a term I made up for this book.

- Although link relations and semantic descriptors are meaningless on their own, there's always some document nearby that contains a human-readable explanation. We call this document a *profile*.

- Profiles have traditionally taken the form of tedious "API documentation." But if you chose a good hypermedia format for your representations, your profile will just be a list of link relations and semantic descriptors, with a prose explanation for each. This optimization lets you create a *machine-readable profile* using XMDP, ALPS, or JSON-LD.

- A machine-readable profile allows a client to automatically look up the human-readable definition of a link relation or semantic descriptor. Machine-readable profiles can be searched and remixed. The ALPS Registry (*http://alps.io*) contains a lot of ALPS profiles to work with.

- JSON-LD contexts can take the ad hoc JSON documents served by today's APIs, and describe their application and protocol semantics in a machine-readable way. You can use JSON-LD to retrofit a JSON API with simple hypermedia controls, without breaking the API's existing clients.

- ALPS profiles are representation agnostic. One ALPS profile can be applied to an HTML document, a HAL document, a Collection+JSON document, an ad hoc JSON or XML document, and many others.

- Profiles are not a substitute for human-readable text embedded in hypermedia representations. There are two different use cases here. Profiles allow developers to write smart clients. Text embedded in a representation allows a human being to use an application through a client that faithfully renders representations.

In the next chapter, I'll sum up the past few chapters by presenting a general procedure for designing hypermedia-based APIs.

The Design Procedure

It's taken quite a while, but I'm now in a position to address the basic concern that may have led you to buy this book. You need to design an API: what should it look like? In this chapter, I'll lay out a procedure that begins with business requirements and ends with some software and some human-readable documentation.

Two-Step Design Procedure

In its simplest form, the procedure has two steps:

1. Choose a media type to use in your representations. This puts constraints on your protocol semantics (the behavior of your API under the HTTP protocol) and your application semantics (the real-world things your representations can refer to).

2. Write a profile that covers everything else.

This won't necessarily give you a *good* API. In fact, this version of the procedure describes every API ever designed. If you wanted a really generic design that's hard to learn, you'd blaze through step 1 by choosing `application/json` as your representation format. Since JSON puts no constraints on your protocol or application semantics, you'd spend most of your time in step 2, defining a fiat standard and describing it with human-readable API documentation.

That's what most APIs do today, and that's what I'm trying to stop. A big chunk of the work that goes into creating a fiat standard is unnecessary, and client code based on a fiat standard can't be reused. But doing anything else requires some preparatory thought and a willingness to reuse other people's work when possible.

Seven-Step Design Procedure

So I've expanded the procedure into seven detailed steps. Doing some preparatory work up front will help you choose a representation format and keep your profile as simple as possible.

1. List all the pieces of information a client might want to get out of your API or put into your API. These will become your semantic descriptors.

   Semantic descriptors tend to form hierarchies. A descriptor that refers to a real-world object like a `person` will usually contain a number of more detailed, more abstract descriptors like `givenName`. Group your descriptors together in ways that make intuitive sense.

2. Draw a state diagram for your API. Each box on the diagram represents one kind of representation—a document that groups together some of your semantic descriptors. Use arrows to connect representations in ways you think your clients will find natural. The arrows are your state transitions, triggered by HTTP requests.

   You don't need to assign specific HTTP methods to your state transitions yet, but you should keep track of whether each state transition is safe, unsafe but idempotent, or unsafe and nonidempotent.

   At this point, you may discover that something you put down as a semantic descriptor (the `customer` of a `business`) makes more sense as a link relation (a `business` links to a `person` or another `business` using the link relation `customer`). Iterate steps 1 and 2 until you're satisfied with your semantic descriptors and link relations.

Now you understand your API's protocol semantics (which HTTP requests a client will be making) and its application semantics (which bits of data will be sent back and forth). You've come up with a list of magic strings (semantic descriptors and link relations) that make your API unique, and you know roughly how those magic strings will be incorporated into HTTP requests and responses. You can then move on to the following steps:

3. Try to reconcile your magic strings with strings from existing profiles. I list some places to look in "The Semantic Zoo" on page 230. Think about IANA-registered link relations, semantic descriptors from schema.org or alps.io, names from domain-specific media types, and so on.

   This may change your protocol semantics! In particular, unsafe link relations may switch back and forth between being idempotent and not being idempotent.

   Iterate steps 1 through 3 until you're satisfied with your names and with the layout of your state diagram.

4. You're now ready to choose a media type (or define a new one). The media type must be compatible with your protocol semantics and your application semantics.

   If you're lucky, you may find a domain-specific media type that already covers some of your application semantics. If you define your own media type, you can make it do exactly what you need.

   If you choose a domain-specific media type, you may need to go back to step 3, and reconcile your names for semantic descriptors and link relations with the names defined by that media type.

5. Write a profile that documents your application semantics. The profile should explain all of your magic strings, other than IANA-registered link relations and strings explained by the media type.

   I recommend you write the profile as an ALPS document, but a JSON-LD context or a normal web page will also work. The more semantics you borrowed from other people in step 4, the less work you'll have to do here.

   If you defined your own media type, you may be able to skip this step, depending on how much of this information you put in the media type specification.

6. Now it's time to write some code. Develop an HTTP server that implements the state diagram from step 3. A client that sends a certain HTTP request should trigger the appropriate state transition and get a certain representation in response.

   Each representation will use the media type you chose in step 4, and link to the profile you defined in step 5. Its data payload will convey values for the semantic descriptors you defined in step 1. It will include hypermedia controls to show the client how to trigger the further state transitions you defined in state 2.

7. Publish your billboard URL. If you've done the first five steps correctly, this is the only information your users will need to know to get started with your API. You can write alternate human-readable profiles (API documentation), tutorials, and example clients to help your users get started, but that's not part of the design.

Now let's take a closer look at each step, using the maze game from Chapter 7 as an example.

Step 1: List the Semantic Descriptors

Here are all the pieces of data in play in the maze game:

- A maze
- A maze cell
- A switch
- The position of a switch ("up" or "down")

- The title of a maze cell
- A doorway connecting one maze cell to another
- An exit from a maze
- A list of mazes

When I try to put them into a hierarchy, here's what I come up with:

- A list of mazes
  — A maze
    — A maze cell
      — A title
      — A doorway connecting one maze cell to another
      — An exit from the current maze
      — A switch
        — A position ("up" or "down")

Figure 9-1 shows my first attempt at dividing the data into representations. I took the hierarchical list of semantic descriptors and drew boxes around the chunks of data I think belong together.

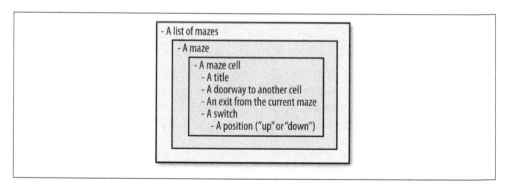

Figure 9-1. Dividing the descriptors into representations

These divisions give me three different representations: the list of mazes, an individual maze, and a cell within a maze (which may or may not contain a switch).

Step 2: Draw a State Diagram

Now the question is this: how are these representations related? What are the links between them? Figure 9-2 shows my first try at a state diagram for the maze game.

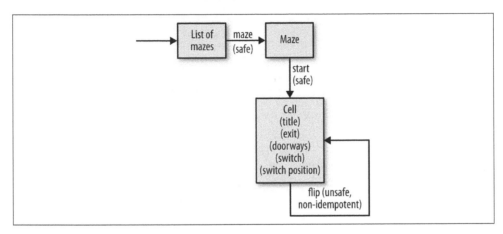

Figure 9-2. A state diagram for a maze game

Some of the links are obvious. In the hierarchical view of Figure 9-1, if one box completely contains another box, those two representations are probably related. Clearly, there should be a link from the list of mazes to an individual maze, and from a maze to the starting cell in the maze. For now, I'll call the link relations for these links maze and start.

Semantic descriptors may become link relations

Once you get a diagram with boxes and arrows, it may become obvious that some of your semantic descriptors are actually the names of safe state transitions. Looking at the diagram in Figure 9-2, it should be clear by now that "a doorway connecting one maze cell to another" isn't a standalone piece of data. It's a link: a relationship between two cells. Similarly, "an exit from the current maze" is not a piece of data. It's a link between a maze cell and something else not on the diagram. This means north and exit shouldn't be semantic descriptors: they should be link relations.

Figure 9-3 shows a revised version of the state diagram, in which exits and doorways are represented as links rather than data.

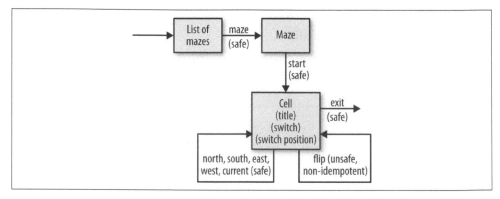

Figure 9-3. A revised state diagram for the maze game

Now the state diagram for the maze game resembles an actual maze—compare it to Figure 5-3. It's not a very interesting maze. All the fun of solving a maze—of going north, then east, then east again—has been abstracted into a single arrow that connects one `cell` representation to another. But the important thing is that every HTTP request a client makes can be represented as a journey along one of those arrows, from one representation to another. You can't say that about Figure 9-2.

I'm going to turn one more semantic descriptor into a link relation. Figure 9-4 shows a slightly different way of dividing representations into resources than Figure 9-1: I've drawn an extra box around the switch. In Figure 9-4, a switch is its own resource, independent of the maze cell that contains it. The string `switch` used to be a semantic descriptor, but now it's a link relation pointing to the switch as a standalone resource. Figure 9-5 shows how that change is reflected in the state diagram.

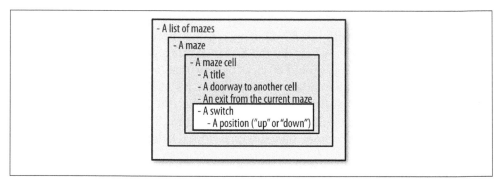

Figure 9-4. Splitting out the switches into standalone resources

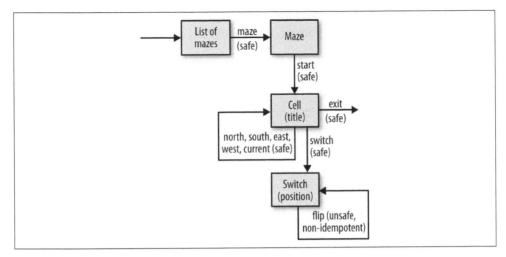

Figure 9-5. The state diagram when switches are standalone resources

I made this change because the switch supports a state transition (`flip`) that the maze cell doesn't support. That says to me that client and server should be able to talk about the switch as a thing in itself. As I said in Chapter 3, anything important enough to be the topic of a client-server conversation should be a resource with its own URL. Making a switch a standalone resource will eliminate any ambiguity about whether an HTTP request is addressing a maze cell or a switch.

If I wanted to, I could go further. I could turn the title of a maze cell into a standalone resource with its own URL (say, */cells/I/title*). At that point, `title` would change from a semantic descriptor to a link relation, the way `switch` just did.

This isn't technically wrong, but I don't see the point. A switch is part of a maze cell, but it supports a state transition (`flip`) that doesn't apply to the cell as a whole. That's why a switch makes sense as a standalone resource. The title of a cell is just a bit of information about the cell. Without a compelling performance reason to serve that information separately, I don't think it should be a standalone resource.

Locating the home page

Your state diagram should include one arrow that comes in out of nowhere. This represents the client's initial GET request to your billboard URL. Every other arrow must originate in one of the representations, and every representation must be accessible from the starting representation, via a state transition.

If there's an obvious top level to the hierarchy you set up in step 1, then you have an obvious candidate for your top-level representation. In this case, the top-level representation is the list of mazes. If there's no obvious top level, you should create one. It doesn't have to be fancy. You just need a list of safe state transitions that link to other important representations and perform searches. You may also want to include some unsafe state transitions that do important things like create new resources.

Step 3: Reconcile Names

Technically, you can skip this step. Your API will have the same design no matter what names you give to your magic strings. But names matter quite a bit to humans. Although computers will be your API's consumers, they'll be working on behalf of human beings, who need to understand what the magic strings mean. That's how we bridge the semantic gap.

Thousands of people have spent hundreds of person-years coming up with profiles for all kinds of problem domains. (Again, see "The Semantic Zoo" on page 230.) There are profiles conveying the application semantics necessary to represent people, groups of people, companies, events, products, payment methods, geographical locations, landmarks, books, TV shows, job listings, medical conditions, blog posts, recipes, and more. Not to mention the online interactions of human beings with all of these—joining groups, leaving groups, RSVPing to events, writing blog posts, "liking" videos, and so on. The most generic, most reusable bits of these profiles are promoted to the hall of fame: the list of IANA-registered link relations.

I suggest you spend some time looking through these profiles for names you can reuse. Reusing existing names when possible will reduce the chance that a human being will misunderstand one of your magic strings. It reduces the amount of documentation you have to write, since you'll be able to reuse the profiles that define those names. It increases the chances that a client developer will be able to reuse an existing library. And it reduces the chances that you'll need to change a name later.

It's true that most existing profiles are tied to a specific media type, and I think it's a terrible idea to choose a media type just so you can use a profile. This is why I came up with ALPS, and why I made such a big deal about it in Chapter 8. ALPS liberates profiles from their media types.

A Siren document can't use schema.org's microdata profile for describing books. But it can use an ALPS profile that's *based on* schema.org's profile. That's a lot less work than coming up with a brand new Siren profile, and it increases the chances that your users will already be familiar with a given set of application semantics.

To take this back to my maze-game API: I called my directional link relations `north`, `south`, `east`, and `west` because those are the names Maze+XML uses. Even if I don't end up choosing Maze+XML as my media type in step 4, it's useful to know that someone already thought about this problem and decided that `north` was a better name than `n`. And thanks to the ALPS profile at alps.io that describes Maze+XML's application semantics, I can reuse some of Maze+XML's application semantics without having to adopt the Maze+XML media type.

Almost any consumer-facing API can reuse some semantics in this way. Most notably, you shouldn't need to come up with your own terms for describing personal information about human beings. Between hCard, schema.org's Person, and FOAF, that domain is pretty well covered.

The coverage is not as good for professional domains like finance, law, or even software development. Terms tend to be defined from the point of view of an average consumer, not a practitioner. And link relations have much worse coverage than semantic descriptors.

For instance, there's a schema.org item called *http://schema.org/Offer*, which describes an offer to sell something. It defines semantic descriptors like `price`, `warranty`, and `deliveryLeadTime`. But it doesn't define the unsafe link relation that would actually let a client buy something. For that, you might use the `purchase` link relation, defined by alps.io and taken from the Activity Streams standard. Or you might make up your own name.

If you think my vision of reusable semantics across APIs is ridiculously unrealistic, or that it's too much work to scavenge for reusable semantic descriptors, you're free to make up your own names for everything. As I said, on a technical level, the names don't matter at all. But I do have two rock-bottom pieces of advice that you should always follow.

First, don't autogenerate the names of your semantic descriptors from the fields in your database schema or object model. That will give your clients a software dependency on your server-side code. When you change that code, you'll break all your clients until you introduce a compatibility layer that presents the old names through your API.

Second, don't come up with link relations that duplicate the functionality of IANA-registered link relations. Those link relations were put in the registry specifically because they're not tied to a media type or an application domain. These are the most generic bits of application semantics around, and they're all listed in one place for easy reuse.

Here are some specific examples:

- Any time you've got a relationship between a list of things and an individual thing in the list, consider using the IANA-registered link relations `collection` and `item`, instead of (or in addition to) something more specific.
- There are two main ways of paginating resource state across multiple representations. The obvious way, which you should be familiar with from websites, uses the link relations `first`, `last`, `next` and `previous` (or `prev`). The archive-based technique described in RFC 5005 uses the link relations `current`, `next-archive`, and `prev-archive`. Unless you've come up with a third pagination technique, there's no reason to make up new names for these relationships.

- You can describe message threads with the `replies` relation, originally defined for Atom by RFC 4685.

- If you keep the history of a resource's state, you can link between different revisions of that state with `latest-version`, `successor-version`, `predecessor-version`, `working-copy`, and `working-copy-of` (defined in RFC 5829).

- The link relations `edit` and `edit-media` are generic enough to cover a lot of unsafe state transitions. If you've got a state transition that does nothing but update some bit of resource state, you might be able to call it `edit` instead of something more specific.

Let me show you `edit` replacement in action. In the maze game, the link relation `flip` relation inverts the position of a switch. If the switch was up, the `flip` transition sets it in the down state, and vice versa if the switch was down. It's not a safe transition, and it's not idempotent. Flipping the switch twice is not the same as flipping it once.

What if instead of `flip`, the link relation was called `edit`? Instead of changing the position of a switch relative to its current position, the client would decide what position it wanted—either up or down—and send that information along when it triggered the `edit` transition. The API's state diagram would look like Figure 9-6.

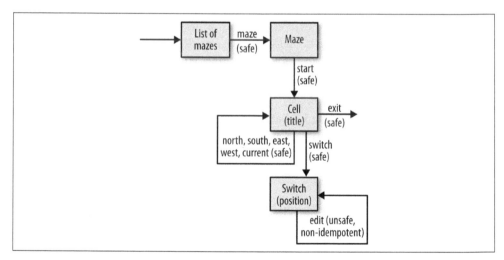

Figure 9-6. The state diagram with "flip" replaced with IANA "edit"

Replacing `flip` with `edit` would have two advantages. Instead of learning a brand new link relation, a client can reuse its existing knowledge of an IANA-registered relation (`edit`). All it has to learn is a custom semantic descriptor (`position`), which it would have had to learn anyway if it wanted to *read* a representation.

Second, the state transition is now idempotent. Setting a switch to down twice is the same as setting it to down once. If a hypermedia document describes the edit transition with a PUT request, the client knows it can retry the request if it doesn't go through.

An HTML hypermedia form for the edit relation might look like this:

```
<form action="/switches/4" method="POST">
 <input type="radio" name="position" value="up" default="default"/>
 <input type="radio" name="position" value="down"/>
 <input type="submit" class="edit" value="Set the switch!"/>
</form>
```

(The method here is POST, not PUT. That's because an HTML form can't use PUT. So a client for this HTML form can't take advantage of the fact that edit is idempotent. But a client is still more likely to understand edit than flip. In a Siren API, the edit state transition could be represented with PUT, and a client would know that the state transition was idempotent.)

If you want the old, nonidempotent behavior of flip, you can simulate it with edit. You'd do this by serving a different hypermedia form that triggers the same state transition, but that doesn't allow the client to change the position away from a preset value:

```
<form action="/switches/4" method="POST">
 <input type="hidden" name="position" value="off"/>
 <input type="submit" class="edit" value="Flip the switch!"/>
</form>
```

A client that activates this control will receive a new representation containing a different control:

```
<form action="/switches/4" method="POST">
 <input type="hidden" name="position" value="on"/>
 <input type="submit" class="edit" value="Flip the switch!"/>
</form>
```

In this design, the edit link relation is always idempotent, but a client that activates every edit control it sees will trigger a nonidempotent *series* of state transitions.

As far as I'm concerned, all of these designs are RESTful. They all use hypermedia to describe state transitions. The only reason to prefer edit over flip is that everyone already agrees on what edit means.

Step 4: Choose a Media Type

Now that you've got some semantics that meet your business requirements, it's time to choose a hypermedia format that can represent them. This will probably be one of the hypermedia types I mention in Chapter 6, Chapter 7, or Chapter 10. You're also free to design a new domain-specific media type, although you shouldn't need to.

Although there's not one media type that's always the best choice, a few common patterns emerge at this point. If your state diagram resembles Figure 9-7, your protocol semantics implement the collection pattern. You should consider Collection+JSON, AtomPub, or OData (see Chapter 10).

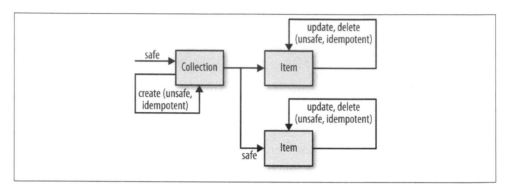

Figure 9-7. Generic state diagram for the collection pattern

If your state diagram looks more like the mess in Figure 9-8, you probably want a generic hypermedia language: HTML, HAL, or Siren.

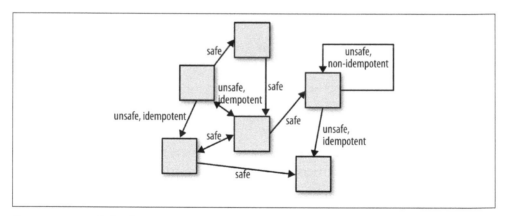

Figure 9-8. A job for hypermedia

If you're thinking of using JSON at this point, I must remind you that *JSON is not a hypermedia format.* The JSON standard defines concepts like numbers, lists, strings, and objects. It does not define the concepts of links or link relations, so it has no hypermedia capabilities. You want something more specific: maybe HAL, Siren, Collection +JSON, or Hydra.

If you're thinking of using XML at this point, well… XML is a hypermedia format, since you can use XLink and XForms (Chapter 10 again) to give HTML-like capabilities to any XML document. But I suspect that's not what you're thinking of. You probably want something a little more specific: HTML, HAL, Siren, or AtomPub.

If you want to serve JSON and XML representations that have the same semantics, you should choose one hypermedia standard that offers both "flavors." Right now that means HAL or OData, although an XML version of Siren is planned.

If your API is read-only—that is, your state diagram doesn't include any unsafe transitions—you've got a lot of good options. I suggest HTML, HAL, or JSON-LD.

If your API does include unsafe transitions, that restricts your choices. JSON-LD can't represent unsafe state transitions on its own; you'll need to add Hydra (see Chapter 12). HAL supports unsafe transitions, but in a way I don't think works very well.

Collection+JSON supports three specific unsafe transitions: adding a new item to a collection, editing an item, and deleting an item. That's it. You can't use any unsafe transitions other than the three defined by the media type.

Step 5: Write a Profile

When your server sends a representation, it will include the Content-Type header, which tells the client how to parse the representation. You'll also include a link to one or more profiles, which will explain the representation's application semantics.

In step 3, you'll probably find some existing profiles that cover some of your application semantics, but you probably won't be able to cover everything. There will be something special about your API. You'll describe the special bits by writing a new profile.

This snippet of markup for Chapter 7's maze game imports two ALPS profiles—a profile from alps.io that brings in the semantics of Maze+XML, and a custom profile that explains the only addition I made to Maze+XML: the mysterious switches.

```
<link rel="profile" href="http://alps.io/example/maze"/>
<link rel="profile" href="/switches.alps"/>
```

Your profile can be an ALPS document, a JSON-LD context, or a web page that uses the XMDP microformat. If none of these choices work for you, you can give up on the idea of a machine-readable profile and write a human-readable profile instead.

A human-readable profile looks like traditional API documentation. It's a web page laying out the meaning of all the link relations and semantic descriptors. You can still reuse link relations and descriptors from alps.io and other profiles—just copy and paste the text, and be sure to link back to the original profile.

Step 6: Implementation

You're going to spend most of your time in this step, and I don't have much advice, because it depends on the framework and programming language you're using. If you have a state diagram and a profile that you're happy with, it won't necessarily be an easy job, but it should at least be straightforward.

Step 7: Publication

If you got lucky and found an existing domain-specific standard that does exactly what you need, with no extensions necessary, you skipped right to step 6 and you're now done. Your API documentation consists of a URL (your API's "billboard URL") and a value for the Content-Type header.

But that almost never happens. Meeting your business requirements inevitably requires that you extend an existing standard, or design something completely new. At this point in the procedure, you've designed the "new" part, and described it using some combination of machine-readable structure (like an ALPS profile) and human-readable text (like the definition of a media type). The only thing left is to publish that information.

This is more complicated than just putting some API documentation up on your website, but it's not *much* more complicated. I'm just laying it all out so you don't accidentally skip a step.

Publish your billboard URL

Back in step 2, I said you should have a box on your state diagram that had an arrow coming into it out of nowhere. This box represents your home page: a hypermedia gateway to all your other resources. Everyone who wants to write a client for your API must know the URL of your home page. The rest is negotiable.

If you got through step 2 without designing a "home page" resource, I recommend you skip back to step 2 and design one. Your billboard URL is the single most important piece of information about your API, because it's the gateway to everything else.

Publish your profile

Your profile document goes on your website, along with the rest of the information about the API. If you've written an ALPS profile, I'd appreciate it if you'd also register it with the ALPS Registry at alps.io. This will help other people find and reuse the link relations and semantic descriptors you defined.

Register new media types

You probably won't need to design a new media type, so I won't take up space here explaining what to do once you're done designing. (Instead, I'll cover it later, in "If You Design a Media Type" on page 183). Suffice to say that once you have an implementation working, you should be confident enough in your design to register your new media type with the IANA.

Register new link relations

If your link relations are URLs (what RFC 5988 calls "extension relation types"), you don't have to do anything special here. No one can define a link relation that conflicts with yours, because you named your relations after domain names you control. If you don't think any other API provider will want to reuse your link relations, you might as well save yourself some trouble and use extension relations.

But throughout this book I've shunned extension link relations. They're too long to use over and over again in print. Instead, I've used link relations that are short strings, like `west` and `flip`. RFC 5988 calls these "registered relation types," and to avoid conflicts they need to be registered somewhere. If you read an HTML document that uses `rel="current"`, it must be unambiguous whether `current` refers to the most recent item in a collection, or to a measurement of electrical current.

RFC 5988 doesn't say exactly how a link relation might be registered, but I'd say there are four ways:

- It might be found in the IANA registry of link relations. Any API provider is allowed to use IANA-registered link relations in its representations without defining them. A useful example is the `replies` relation defined in RFC 4685.

  Section 6.2 of RFC 5988 describes the IANA registration process. Getting a link relation into this registry requires writing an RFC (or equivalent document), and only relations that are generally useful are accepted, so relatively few developers will take this route.

- The link relation might be defined along with a media type, the way Maze+XML defines `west` and `exit`. Some other media type may define the `exit` relation differently, but who cares? A document can only have one media type, so it's always clear which rules to apply.

  If a media type defines a link relation that conflicts with a relation registered with the IANA, the media type's definition takes precedence. Don't do this intentionally! I'm spelling out this rule so that your API's application semantics don't change because its media type uses a link relation that someone just registered with the IANA.

- The link relation might be defined in a machine-readable profile such as an ALPS document. Some other profile may define things differently, but who cares? This document doesn't use that profile.

  If a profile defines a link relation that conflicts with a relation defined by the media type or an IANA-registered relation, the profile's definition takes precedence. Again, don't do this intentionally. This is an "in case of emergency" rule.

- The link relation might be registered with the Microformats wiki.[1] The wiki page is not very exclusive; it attempts to catalog every link relation ever seen or proposed for use in HTML.

  The Microformats wiki makes a good testbed for link relations that might one day enter the IANA registry. If you want other people to use the link relation you invented, putting it on this wiki is a good way to test it out. If not, I recommend using an extension relation instead.

With ALPS, you can split the difference. You can use the full URL to any link relation defined in an ALPS document as an extension link relation (e.g. *http://alps.io/example/maze#exit*), even if you haven't included that ALPS document as a profile. When you do include an ALPS document as a profile, you can treat its link relations as registered link relations (`exit`).

Publish the rest of the documentation

There's plenty more documentation to be published, but it's all human-readable documentation specific to your API: summaries, examples, sample code, instructions on setting up authorization, marketing copy explaining how your API differs from others.

This stuff is important, but you don't need my encouragement to publish it. This is the stuff we think of when we think of API documentation. I've downplayed human-readable documentation throughout this process, because in my experience, it's frequently used as a substitute for hypermedia controls.

Software clients have a limited ability to adapt to changes in hypermedia documents. Software based on human-readable documents have *no* ability to adapt. If an API is described only in prose, then changing the prose means rewriting all the clients. That's a big problem with current APIs, and it's a problem I'm trying to mitigate with this book.

I want to stretch client adaptability as far as possible. This means a design process tightly focused on creating machine-readable documents, with human-readable documents acting only for the convenience of humans.

Well-known URIs

Here's a thought: what if you didn't need to advertise your billboard URL? What if your clients *just knew* how to find the entry point to your API? That's the promise of the IANA's "Well-Known URIs," (*http://www.iana.org/assignments/well-known-uris/*) established in 2010 by RFC 5785.

If a server presents representations in CoRE Link Format (covered in Chapter 13), there's no need to wonder what the billboard URL is. It should always be */.well-known/core*.

---

1. The page is located here (*http://microformats.org/wiki/existing-rel-values*).

That (relative) URL is registered with the IANA. Instead of learning a different billboard URL for every server, a CoRE client can always send a GET request to */.well-known/ core*, and get a list of hypermedia links to other resources hosted on that server. A server that serves a web host metadata document (Chapter 12) should always serve that document from */.well-known/host-meta* or */well-known/host-meta.json*.

This is a pretty minor thing, but it closes the final bit of the semantic gap. Thanks to the Well-Known URI Registry, it's theoretically possible for a client to explore and learn a new API, given only the *hostname*.

The catch is that well-known URIs are generally associated with specific media types. As I write this, if you're not using CoRE Link Format or web host metadata, you can't publish your API at a well-known URI. Those are the only two formats in the Well-Known URI Registry that are useful for APIs.

Example: You Type It, We Post It

It took a while to run Chapter 7's maze game through my design process, because I was explaining each step of the process as I went. Here's another, much shorter example. I'll just show my decisions rather than explaining all the steps. My problem domain will be the "You Type It, We Post It" website from Chapter 1. I'll do the first five steps and end up with a design and a profile, but no implementation.

List the Semantic Descriptors

Looking at the description of the website from Chapter 1, I identified the following semantic descriptors:

- The home page
    - Some kind of "about this site" text
    - The list of messages
        - An individual message
            - The ID of a message
            - The text of a message
            - The publication date of a message

Then I grouped the descriptors in a way I think makes sense. The result is in Figure 9-9. I've got three distinct kinds of representations: the "about this site" text, the list of messages, and an individual message. I decided to use the message list as the "home page," rather than having a separate home page that just links to the message list and "about this site."

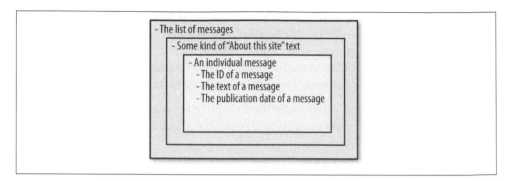

Figure 9-9. The semantic descriptors for You Type It..., grouped into representations

Draw a State Diagram

Figure 9-10 shows the state diagram I came up with.

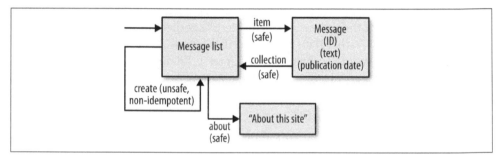

Figure 9-10. Initial state diagram for the You Type It... API

Using the links on the You Type It... website as a guide, I connected the three types of resources with safe state transitions. I also created an unsafe state transition, corresponding to the HTTP POST form on the website that creates a new message.

Reconcile Names

When I was naming the safe state transitions for the state diagram, I made sure to choose IANA-registered names: about, collection, and item. The "about this site" text is a human-readable document, so I won't worry about its semantic descriptors.

There are six things left to name, for which IANA is no help: "list of messages," "message," "create," "ID," "text," and "publication date." A look through "The Semantic Zoo" on page 230 helps with five of them.

There's a schema.org microdata item called BlogPosting (*http://schema.org/BlogPost ing*), which defines semantic descriptors called articleBody and dateCreated. That takes care of "message," "text," and "publication date." A collection of schema.org `Blog Postings` is called a `Blog`. That takes care of "message list."

I'll name my unsafe state transition `post`. I took that name from the Activity Streams standard, where it means "The act of authoring an object and then publishing it online." Nobody ever intended schema.org microdata and Activity Streams verbs to work together, but ALPS lets me combine their application semantics.

That leaves the message ID. I decided I don't really need to provide this information at all. Each message already has a unique ID: its URL. Why should a client care what internal ID the server uses? So I decided to omit it from my API.

Figure 9-11 shows my state diagram after I reconciled names. Note that the `item` link now has two link relations: `item` and `blogPost`. The second link relation comes from the schema.org `Blog` item, which defines `blogPost` as the relationship between a Blog and a `BlogPost`. This is a little redundant with IANA's more generic `item` relation, but there's no reason I can't stick both link relations on a single link. That way, clients that understand schema.org's `Blog` and `BlogPost` won't also need to understand IANA's `item`.

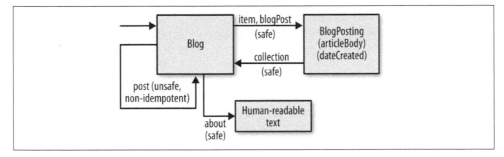

Figure 9-11. State diagram for the You Type It... API, after name reconciliation.

Am I creating the world's 58th microblogging API? In a sense, yes. But I didn't define anything new. I took everything from the IANA, schema.org, and Activity Streams. A client that already understands these semantic descriptors and link relations will understand my API. It's not very likely that such a client exists, but it's a lot more likely that *part* of that client exists than it would be if I'd redesigned these basic concepts for the 58th time.

Choose a Media Type

I can choose from a huge number of media types. My state diagram resembles Figure 9-7, so a media type that implements the collection pattern will help a lot. The actual YouTypeItWePostIt.com API, as shown in Chapter 2, uses Collection+JSON. I can also go the pure hypermedia route: the YouTypeItWePostIt.com website uses

HTML. And I can even choose a domain-specific standard. In Chapter 6, I treated AtomPub as a general "collection pattern" standard, but it was originally defined specifically for publishing standalone bits of text.

My choice may change the vocabulary I use. If I choose Atom as my representation format, I need to stop calling the text of the message `articleBody`, and start calling it `content`, because that's what Atom calls it.

Just for the sake of variety, I'm going to choose HAL. A HAL+XML representation of the message list might look like this:

```
<resource href="/">
 <link rel="profile" href="http://alps.io/schema.org/Blog"/>
 <link rel="profile" href="http://alps.io/schema.org/BlogPost"/>
 <link rel="profile" href="http://alps.io/activitystrea.ms/verbs"/>
 <link rel="about" href="/about-this-site">

 <Blog>
  <link rel="post" href="/messages"/>

  <resource href="/messages/2" rel="item">
   <BlogPost>
    <articleBody>This is message #2.</articleBody>
    <dateCreated>2013-04-24</dateCreated>
   </BlogPost>
  </resource>

  <resource href="/messages/1" rel="item">
   <BlogPost>
    <articleBody>This is message #1.</articleBody>
    <dateCreated>2013-04-22</dateCreated>
   </BlogPost>
  </resource>
 </Blog>
</resource>
```

This conveys all the necessary resource state (descriptions of the two messages in the message list) and includes all the necessary hypermedia links (with the link relations `profile`, `about`, `item`, and `post`).

There's a problem with the `post` link: it's not clear that it's an unsafe state transition that should be triggered with POST, and it's not clear what entity-body the client should send along with the POST request. But that's due to a general shortcoming of HAL. If I don't like that feature of HAL, I can choose a different media type at this point.

Write a Profile

Since I took all my application semantics from existing profiles, I don't technically need to write my own profile. The example representation just links to three existing ALPS profiles:

```
<link rel="profile" href="http://alps.io/schema.org/Blog"/>
<link rel="profile" href="http://alps.io/schema.org/BlogPost"/>
<link rel="profile" href="http://alps.io/activitystrea.ms/verbs"/>
```

That covers everything except the IANA link relations `about` and `item`, which I'm allowed to use without explaining.

Here's a standalone ALPS profile for my "You Type It, We Post It" design (it's a little redundant, but it's a single document containing all the link relations and semantic descriptors my API actually uses):

```
<alps>
 <descriptor id="about" type="semantic"
             href="http://alps.io/iana/relations#about"/>

 <descriptor id="Blog" type="semantic" href="http://alps.io/schema.org/Blog">
  <descriptor id="blogPost" type="semantic"
              href="http://alps.io/schema.org/Blog#blogPost" rt="#BlogPosting"/>
  <descriptor id="item" type="semantic"
              href="http://alps.io/iana/relations#item" rt="#BlogPosting"/>
  <descriptor id="post" type="unsafe"
              href="http://alps.io/activitystrea.ms/verbs#post">
   <descriptor href="#BlogPosting"/>
  </descriptor>
 </descriptor>

 <descriptor id="BlogPosting" type="semantic"
             href="http://alps.io/schema.org/BlogPosting">
  <descriptor id="articleBody" type="semantic"
              href="http://alps.io/schema.org/BlogPosting#articleBody">
  <descriptor id="dateCreated" type="semantic"
              href="http://alps.io/schema.org/BlogPosting#dateCreated">
 </descriptor>
</alps>
```

Instead of having three `profile` links, one of my representations can just link to this profile.

A client that doesn't understand my profile can treat my representations as pure HAL representations. This won't be very useful, because HAL doesn't define any protocol or application semantics on its own. A HAL browser can parse my representations, and distinguish links from data, but it won't know what the links or the data mean.

Some Design Advice

Hopefully by this point you have a good idea of how I go through my design process. Now I'd like to bring up some practical lessons I've learned from developing and applying this process.

Resources Are Implementation Details

Most procedures for designing RESTful web APIs focus on resource design. But there are no resources here. The boxes in the state diagrams aren't resources, they're *representations* of resources—the actual documents sent back and forth between client and server.

This was not an oversight. Resources are primary to HTTP, and they're very important to API implementations, but I've come to realize that they're not very important to REST, per se. My design process focuses on state transitions and semantic descriptors. Once you have those nailed down, you have your resources.

Think of the HTTP back-and-forth between client and server. A resource receives a GET request and serves a representation with a certain media type. The representation contains hypermedia controls, which describe possible state transitions. A client activates a state transition by sending an HTTP request to another resource, which implements the state change and sends another representation. The client never directly interacts with a resource.

If you get to step 6 and you find you need to implement some unanticipated resource, I'm afraid you've skipped a step. The resource you're imagining needs to be linked to from some existing resource. That link is a state transition and it should have shown up on an arrow in your state diagram (step 2). If the resource manages state of its own, it needs a representation. That representation should have shown up as a box on your state diagram (step 2). The representation must have a media type (step 4), and possibly a profile (step 5). The data it conveys to the client should have shown up in the big list you made in step 1. If the resource supports any unsafe state transitions, those transitions should have shown up in step 2. They must be described with a hypermedia control embedded within some representation.

If you haven't decided on a resource's protocol semantics and application semantics, you haven't really designed it. If you have decided on those things, there's not much else to design.

Focusing on resources first won't give you a *bad* design, but it does tend to express a design in terms of the server-side implementation, rather than in terms of the client's experience. It's also easy to use good resource design (backed up by copious human-readable documentation) as an excuse to avoid thinking about hypermedia.

Don't Fall into the Collection Trap

Although the collection pattern is very general and powerful, it contains a trap. I've seen this trap sprung dozens of times over the past few years and my considered advice is not to take the bait. *Don't use your database schema as the basis for your API design.* Draw a state diagram instead.

At first glance, using the database schema seems like a great idea. A SQL database, with its four basic commands (SELECT/INSERT/UPDATE/DELETE) maps naturally onto the CRUD pattern (create/retrieve/update/delete), which maps naturally onto the collection pattern for APIs, which maps naturally onto the four main HTTP methods (GET/POST/PUT/DELETE). There's no technical reason why you can't just skip most of my process and publish your database schema through the collection pattern. What could go wrong?

Thanks to modern tools, this strategy will very quickly get you an API that works, but it has two big problems. The first stems from the fact that your users don't care about your database schema. They care about your application semantics, and the two are only vaguely related. You wouldn't set up a website that was just a raw interface into your database. You should put the same thought into designing an API as you would a website.

On the other hand, you *do* care about your database schema—so much so that you reserve the right to change the schema as your requirements change. That's the second problem. When you publish an API based on a database schema, changes to the schema become basically impossible. You've given a software dependency on your database schema to thousands of people you've never heard of. These people are your clients and supporting them is your responsibility. Changes to the schema, changes that your website users won't even notice, will cause big problems for your API users.

There are all sorts of techniques for dealing with these problems, and I'll discuss them in "When Your API Changes" on page 185. But the best strategy is to avoid getting into this situation in the first place.

That's another reason why my process uses a state diagram. Keeping you out of this trap is a big concern of mine. Thinking about state transitions forces you to consider your application, not the database that contains all the resource state.

I'm not saying to avoid the collection pattern. It's a great pattern. If your state diagram looks like Figure 9-7, go ahead and use it. But draw the state diagram first. Don't confuse the protocol semantics defined by your *application* with the interface defined by your *database*.

Don't Start with the Representation Format

You may be tempted to choose a representation format before starting step 1, so that you can visualize what your documents will look like as you work out the semantics. It's fine to use a general format like HTML for doodling, but I recommend you hold off on a decision until you've gotten, however tentatively, to step 4. That's because representation formats aren't just passive containers for data. They introduce assumptions about protocol and application semantics into every API that uses them. These assumptions may conflict with your business requirements.

To take a silly example, suppose you start off your API design by choosing to use Maze +XML, just because it's the first representation format I discussed in detail. You're probably making a mistake. Maze+XML defines a very specific state diagram that looks similar to the one in Figure 9-6. It defines a set of application semantics in which GET requests mean "enter a maze," "move in a certain direction," or "exit a maze." In short, Maze+XML is for maze games.

You can't choose Maze+XML until you've done the first two steps. You need to decompose your business requirements into a set of protocol semantics and application semantics. If it turns out they fit with the semantics defined by Maze+XML, that's great. But they probably won't.

To take a less silly example, suppose you start off by deciding to use Collection+JSON (or AtomPub, or OData) for your API. That means you've chosen a set of semantics that implement the collection pattern. You're stating up front that your API's state diagram looks something like Figure 9-7.

How can you say that in advance? If it *turns out* your protocol semantics fit the collection pattern (and they often will), then the collection-pattern standards are just what you need. But you can't go on a gut feeling; you need to actually draw the state diagram.

Of course, if the use of a particular representation format *is* one of your business requirements, you might as well make that decision first, and design your API around the mandatory representation format. If your API will be part of a low-power embedded system, you may have to build it around CoRE Link Format (see Chapter 13). If you work for a company that sits on the OData Technical Committee and has already deployed 75 OData APIs (Chapter 10), guess what—you're probably designing number 76.

This doesn't mean your API is doomed. Hypermedia gives you a lot of flexibility. If you had to, you could implement any API you wanted as an extension to Maze+XML. Just think of it as an additional constraint, on top of the Fielding constraints.

URL Design Doesn't Matter

Some API design guides, including the original *RESTful Web Services*, spend a lot of time talking about the URLs you should assign to your resources. Each URL you serve should clearly identify the resource in such a way that a human being looking at the URL can figure out what's on the other end.

If you publish a resource that's a collection of user accounts, it should be called something like */users/*. Subordinate resources should be published *beneath* their parents. So the resource representing Alice's account should be given a URL like */users/alice*.

Well, sort of.

Technically speaking, none of this matters. A URL is just the address of a resource, which a client can use to get a representation. The URL doesn't technically say anything about the resource or its representation. *The Architecture of the World Wide Web, Volume One* puts it this way:

> It is tempting to guess the nature of a resource by inspection of a URI that identifies it. However, the Web is designed so that agents communicate resource information state through representations, not identifiers. In general, one cannot determine the type of a resource representation by inspecting a URI for that resource.

This means it's perfectly legal for the collection of user accounts to have the URL */000000000000a*, and for that collection to link to Alice's user account using the URL */prime-numbers?how_many=200*. The important thing is that the *representation* of a collection of users makes it clear that it's representing a collection of users, and that the *representation* of Alice's user account contains information about the state of that resource.

When you look at a URL and try to make sense of the underlying resource, you're trying to figure out the resource's application-level semantics. That's fine. The advice on URL design given in other books and tutorials is good advice. But I won't rehash that advice in this book, because I don't want your APIs *relying* on URLs to convey their application-level semantics. We have more reliable ways of describing that stuff: media type definitions and machine-readable profiles.

Here's an example. Many of today's APIs have URL construction rules in their human-readable documentation:

> The URL to a user's account looks like this:
>
> /users/{username}

That's basically a URI Template. If you serve a representation format that supports URI Templates, you can replace that documentation with an equivalent hypermedia control. Here's an example in JSON Home Document format (which I'll cover in Chapter 10):

```
"user_lookup": {"href-template": "/users/{username}",
                "href-vars": {
                "username" : "http://alps.io/microformats/hCard#nickname"}
               }
```

Almost all of this is machine-readable to a machine that knows how to parse JSON Home Documents. The only thing that must be explained in human-readable terms is the semantic descriptor `username`. That can go into inline text, or into a machine-readable profile such as the alps.io profile linked to here.

Most formats don't formally support URI Templates, but they include a hypermedia control that does something similar—think of HTML's `<form>` tag with `action="GET"`. You get two big advantages from using these controls instead of human-readable equivalents.

Since hypermedia is machine-readable, your users can use a standard library to manage it. This eliminates the possibility that they'll misunderstand your prose instructions. And since hypermedia is served at runtime, you have a lot of leeway to change this control without breaking your clients—something you couldn't do when the exact same information was kept in your API documentation.

Again, there's nothing wrong with nice-looking URLs. Nice-looking URLs are great! But they're cosmetic. They look nice. They don't *do* anything. Your API clients should continue to work even if all of the nice-looking URLs were suddenly replaced with randomly generated URLs.

Standard Names Are Probably Better Than Your Names

Let's say that your application semantics include "a person's first name." You'd write that down in step 1, you'd try to fit it into a hierarchy, and you'd give it a temporary name based on the corresponding field in your database schema or your data model. Something like `first_name`, `firstname`, `first-name`, `fn`, `first name`, `first`, `fname`, or `giv en_name`. That's fine for step 1. But when you get to step 3 you need to look around, notice that there are lots of existing profiles for describing peoples' first names, and adopt one of them.

You may be attached to the names you chose in step 1. But you're not doing this API for yourself. You're doing this for your users.[2] Over their careers, users will consume lots of different APIs, and they'll benefit from not having to learn 20 slightly different names for the same thing. In the short run, your users will benefit from not having to learn about your internal implementation details. You benefit, too: by adopting standard names for common bits of application semantics, you can change your internal names without changing your API.

But which profile to choose? The hCard standard says that the semantic descriptor for a person's given name is `given-name`. The xCard standard says it's `given`. The FOAF standard says it's `givenName`, but that `firstName` may be used when interpreting legacy data. The schema.org `Person` item only allows for `givenName`. These are well-defined, respected standards that conflict with each other.

That's annoying, but there's no reason to make up *more* names and make the situation worse. Just pick a profile—whichever one has the best overall fit with your API's application semantics—and use the names it defines.

The people responsible for these standards took steps to avoid conceptual pitfalls you probably haven't considered. For instance, "first name" is not an accurate term. It's an artifact of Western culture, in which we put a person's given name first. In some other cultures, the family name comes first. The current president of China is named

---

2. If you are doing this API for yourself, then do whatever you want.

Xi Jinping. His "first name" is Jinping. That's why `givenname` is a better semantic descriptor than `firstname`.[3]

If you're a native English speaker, you probably didn't consider this. And if your internal database schema has a field called `firstname`, it doesn't matter much. But when you start sending your data out to the world, it matters quite a bit how you describe that data.

The designers of hCard, xCard, FOAF, and schema.org's `Person` *did* consider this. Considering tricky issues of naming was part of their job. That's why all those standards use the phrase "given name" as the basis for their semantic descriptors. That's why FOAF says `firstName` should only be used to interpret legacy data. If you care about cultural sensitivity and/or accuracy, you should follow the lead of existing profiles. By adopting them whenever possible, you limit how often you have to do the tricky work of naming.

If You Design a Media Type

The advantage of a new media type is the complete control it gives you over how clients process your documents. You don't have to base your API on XML, JSON, or HTML. You can declare a brand new binary file format and give byte-by-byte instructions for how to handle it. You don't have to scrounge around for profiles that reflect your application semantics. Whatever you say, goes.

Many organizations have XML- or JSON-based file formats that were designed for internal use and never specified formally. It wouldn't take much work to turn those formats into domain-specific hypermedia types, usable by outsiders.[4] The work is the work of writing that formal specification. A media type must come with complete, unambiguous processing instructions.

If you ever find yourself defining 5 or 10 media types for a single API, that's a bad sign. You should use a generic hypermedia type instead, or you should define *one* new media type, plus some rules for applying an ALPS document (or other profile format) to the media type. Those 5 or 10 different bits of semantics can go into 5 or 10 profiles.

Every new media type needs a name, and RFC 6838 explains how to name them. You'll probably end up with a name like `application/vnd.yourcompany.type-name`. A media type based on JSON or XML should be given the +json or +xml suffix, a la `vnd.amundsen.application/maze+xml`.

---

3. The given name used to be called the "Christian name": the name given as part of infant baptism ceremonies. That term is an artifact of Catholic European culture. Not everyone in the world undergoes that ceremony (I never did), so we switched to a more general term. Then we switched again.

4. But it also wouldn't take much work to convert that JSON format to Hydra, a format I cover in Chapter 12.

If you expect people outside your organization to be passing around documents that use your media type, you'll also need to tell the world how to process those documents. This means registering your media type with the IANA.

Registration is a fairly formal procedure, described in sections 4 and 5 of RFC 6838. Basically, you're telling the IANA (and everyone who uses your media type afterward) where to find a description of the media type, and whether it creates any special security concerns. You can register a media type by filling out the form (*http://www.iana.org/form/media-types*).

Here are the main things to consider when filling out that form:

- You must have "a permanent and readily available public specification of the format for the media type." It needs to lay out the format in enough detail that someone can write a parser for your data format, using only the information in the specification.

  You were probably planning on making the media type definition "readily available" as part of your API documentation. But the IANA wants a level of detail that might be more more work than you anticipated. This work is necessary because when you register a media type, people who've never heard of you, who have no connection with your API, will be going to your website, and reading your specification so they can generate their own documents in the format you defined.

- You'll need to mention any security concerns associated with handling documents in your media type. This is especially important if your documents can include executable code.

  RFC 6838 has a basic checklist of things to consider here. If your media type is based on JSON, you should also reference section 6 of RFC 4627, which describes the security concerns related to JSON itself.

- If your media type is based on XML, there are a few special tasks you'll need to do, described in section 7.1 of RFC 3023. These tasks mostly involve adding XML-specific boilerplate to your submission.

- If your media type is not based on XML, you'll need to specify how the data might appear over the wire. The answer will usually be "binary." For media types based on JSON, you can reference the JSON standard, RFC 4627, or just say "binary." If your media type is based on XML, the boilerplate from RFC 3023 takes care of this part.

- You should probably define the `profile` parameter for your media type, so that clients can ask for a specific profile using the `Content-Type` header. (I discussed this trick in Chapter 8.) This is my opinion, not part of RFC 6838. You can just say that your media type takes a `profile` parameter and that its value is the URI of a profile, as per RFC 6906.

If you want to get advice from the community before making your submission, send what you've got as an email message to *media-types@iana.org*. If you want to see a simple example, check out the approved registration for the Maze+XML media type (*http:// www.iana.org/assignments/media-types/application/vnd.amundsen.maze+xml*).

You don't have to register your type with the IANA if you don't want to. If you decide not to register, you'll need to use the `vnd.` prefix (for a commercial project—this is the prefix you were probably using anyway) or the `prs.` prefix (for a personal project or experimental work). But if your media type becomes generally popular, you really should register it. Hundreds of vendor-specific media types, like `application/vnd.ms-powerpoint`, are registered with the IANA.

When Your API Changes

One of today's most hotly debated topics in the API community is versioning. It's an enormous problem. Most companies that put out an API *never change that API after its initial release*. They can't do it.

To be blunt, they can't do it because they ignored the hypermedia constraint. Most APIs put their protocol and application semantics into human-readable documentation. The users of those APIs then write a bunch of client software based on that documentation. Now the API providers are stuck. They can change the documentation, but doing so won't automatically change the behavior of all those clients. They've given their users veto power over any change in their design.

But a change to a hypermedia document *does* change the behavior of every client that receives it. That's why a website can undergo a total redesign without breaking everyone's web browsers. A website is entirely contained in the representations it serves. There's nothing extra hidden away in human-readable documentation.

This is the point at which a lot of the suggestions I made in this book—suggestions which may have initially seemed pedantic and nitpicky—really start to pay off. One of my main goals has been to reduce the amount of human-readable documentation that accompanies your API. That's not just because human-readable documentation is liable to misinterpretation. It's because *changing* a piece of human-readable documentation requires a corresponding change in every piece of code based on that documentation.

Moving your API's semantics out of human-readable documentation and into hypermedia documents makes your API more resilient in the face of change. Choose a good hypermedia format, and you can add new resources and state transitions to your API without affecting existing clients. You'll also have quite a bit of room to change your protocol semantics.

Ideally it would be as easy to redesign an API as it is to redesign a website. We'll probably never get there, for the same reason we'll never fully bridge the semantic gap. If you add a new required field to a state transition, you can add a new semantic descriptor to your machine-readable profile, but the *explanation* of that semantic descriptor will still need to be interpreted by a human. A fully automated client might be able to understand the error message it suddenly starts getting—"You didn't provide a value for `re quired_field`."—but it won't know what value it should send for `required_field`.

There are also changes to which an ideal client would adapt, but that might break real clients, such as changing a hypermedia control to use PUT instead of POST. But overall, you'll have more success changing a bit of semantics if it's described in machine-readable terms.

If you change a resource and your clients can't automatically adapt to the change, you'll need to spend some period of time effectively publishing two different resources—the old one and the new one—with different application or protocol semantics. There are three common strategies for doing this.

Partitioning the URL space

In the most common versioning technique, the entire API is split into two disjoint APIs. Sometimes the two APIs have different billboard URLs, like *http://api-v1.example. com/* and *http://api-v2.example.com/*.

Sometimes there's only one billboard URL, but the billboard representation uses hypermedia to offer the client a choice between versions:

```
<ul>
<li><a class="v1" href="/v1/">Version 1</a></li>
<li><a class="v2" href="/v2/">Version 2</a></li>
</ul>
```

Here, the version number is a semantic descriptor. A client that doesn't know what v2 means won't follow the link.

Partitioning works because representations found beneath /v1 only link to resources found beneath /v1. Both versions of the API probably use the same underlying code, but they can have completely different application semantics, because any given client will use one or the other exclusively.

Versioning the media type

If you defined a domain-specific media type for your application, you can give it a `version` parameter. Clients can then use content negotiation (see Chapter 10) to ask for one version or the other:

```
Accept: application/vnd.myapi.document?version=2
```

I don't think you should define a domain-specific media type in the first place, but even if you do, this is a bad idea. Your media type is not your API. Here's a thought experiment: could another company use your media type in their own, unrelated API? Would they get any benefits from doing that, other than compatibility with your fiat standard? If there's no compelling reason for someone else to adopt your media type, then you've put too much of your API into your media type definition.

Does your media type define every aspect of an API's protocol and application semantics, the way Maze+XML does? If so, then adding a `version` parameter will work. By definition, a change to the semantics means a change in the media type. But if you keep a profile, or any human-readable documentation other than the media type definition, you'll probably end up changing the API without changing the media type definition. Then you'll have a problem: what does the `version` property really apply to? Is it the media type, or the API?

Standardized media types don't do this. HTML 5 is very different from HTML 4, but they're both served as `text/html`, and HTML 5 is roughly backward compatible with HTML 4.[5]

Versioning the profile

I recommended that you base your API around a standardized media type, and obviously you can't go in and declare a new version of someone else's media type. But I also recommended that you define your application semantics in a machine-readable profile, and you *can* declare a new version of a profile.

Your profile neatly isolates the parts of the application that will break clients when they change (because they're described by human-readable text) from the parts that clients should be able to adapt to (because they're described by hypermedia). Keeping two profiles lets you keep two sets of application semantics. A client can use the `Link` header to request one profile or the other. Or, if the media type supports the `profile` parameter, a client can use the `Content-Type` header and do normal content negotiation.

Versoning isn't special

API versioning gets a lot of attention because the problem is a lot worse for an API that ignores the hypermedia constraint. But it's just one example of the general problem addressed by hypermedia. How does the client know which resource has the representation it wants? Once the client gets a representation, how is it supposed to know what the representation means? The techniques I gave earlier are the techniques a server uses *in general* when giving the client a choice between representations.

A server can give out links to two different URLs, and the client can choose which link to follow based on an understanding of the application semantics. It's the same whether

---

5. Version 3.0 of HTML, back in 1995, actually did what APIs are doing now. It introduced a `version` parameter and suggested that HTML documents be served as `text/html;version=3.0`. This was dropped in HTML 4. Backward compatibility works better.

the two URLs point to completely different resources, or to the v1 and v2 versions of a single underlying resource.

A single resource may have representations in different media types. The client can select the representation it wants using content negotiation (with the Accept header; see Chapter 11) or hypermedia. It's the same whether the media types are completely different (Collection+JSON and HTML), or whether they differ only by a version parameter. I think the version parameter is a bad idea, but if you use it, it'll work the same way as if you used two completely different media types.

A single resource may be described by many different profiles, and the client can use content negotiation or hypermedia to select the one it wants. It's the same whether the profiles are different approaches to the same idea (hCard versus schema.org's Person) or whether they're the "v1" and "v2" profiles of a single API.

Have an end-of-life plan

Ultimately, then, versioning is not a technical issue. It's an aspect of your relationship with your users. You don't want a minor change to break everyone's client software, so you describe as many changes as possible using machine-readable hypermedia rather than human-readable docs. When you must change a resource's semantics in a way that breaks backward compatibility, you create a second version of that resource for use by new clients. The second version can be identified by a different URL, a different media type, or whatever. Unmodified clients can still use the old version.

Eventually you'd like to get rid of the old version. After all, if you liked the old functionality, you wouldn't have changed it. Again, there's no technical solution here. The issue is your relationship with your users. You need to set expectations for when one version of your API will be deprecated, and how long a client can expect to keep using a deprecated API.

When you publish your API, include some level of assurance on how long it will be valid. You can give a lifetime assurance ("We'll continue to support this API for 5 years.") or you can give a notification assurance ("We'll give you a one-year warning before we stop supporting this API.") Also set up a communication channel specifically for communication about this: a web page or a mailing list.

When you want to make a change to your API that breaks backward compatibility, here's a procedure that's worked well for me in the past:

1. Declare the current version "deprecated." It will still work, but it is no longer the current version. Announce this on the communication channel you set up for this purpose. Update your documentation and tutorials so that new developers start on the current version, not the deprecated one.

2. After a while, use the communications channel to announce that you no longer will fix bugs on the "deprecated" API, and remind your users of the new version.

3. After some no-bug-fix period, announce a deadline after which the "deprecated" API will be shut off.

4. You'll probably need a grace period after the deadline, but at some point after the deadline, shut off the old API. Requests should result in the HTTP status code 410 (Gone), along with an HTML entity-body that explains this is a dead API and links to the current version.

How quickly you can move through these steps depends on the size of your user base and the average speed at which your community can change. Changing a banking API will take a long time; changing a microblogging API will go faster.

Doesn't sound like much fun, does it? Yeah, it's horrible! But this is how you deploy new server software without breaking all those deployed clients you have no control over. That's why hypermedia is so important. The more of your protocol and application semantics you can put into machine-readable form, the more ability you have to change your API without going through this slow, cumbersome process.

Don't Keep All the Hypermedia in One Place

One of the defining features of old-style, non-RESTful APIs was the *service description document*. This was a large document (usually in WSDL format) that gave a complete description of the API's protocol and application semantics. The file was usually generated by a push-button tool that understood the API based on its server-side implementation.

Users could download a service description document and use it to automatically generate a corresponding client implementation. They could use the client to make remote API calls as though they were local programming-language calls. There was no need to understand anything about hypermedia, representation formats, or HTTP. And then something would change in the server-side implementation, and the whole thing would fall apart.

The problem with this design is that it creates tight coupling between the server-side implementation of the API, its machine-readable description, and the client generated from that machine-readable description. When the server-side implementation changes, the change won't be reflected in the generated client, and the client will break.

Now, you're probably not thinking about generating a WSDL description of your API. But traditional API documentation is effectively a human-readable service description document. It's one big file explaining the API's application and protocol semantics. Human-readable documentation is easier for a human to understand than a WSDL file, but it has the same problem. A change to the server-side implementation results in a change to the "service document," but that change isn't propagated to the already deployed clients. The clients break.

A hypermedia-based API has a limited ability to express server-side changes without breaking clients. But you don't get this ability automatically; you have to work for it. It's quite possible to write a machine-readable "service description document" in HTML. On the Web, we'd call that a site map. A site map is a complete description of a website's protocol semantics, all in one document. You can automatically generate an API client based on an HTML site map. And when the server-side implementation changes, your client will break, because it's based on an out-of-date map.

A client for a hypermedia API can't expect to know about all the possible state transitions ahead of time. It needs to be designed like a maze solver, capable of making a decision based on the possible next steps presented by the server at runtime. That's why I recommend splitting up your hypermedia controls so that each representation, as it's served, contains the controls that are relevant to the current application and resource state. This will force client developers to reckon with hypermedia, instead of pretending they can ignore it.

I bring this up because there are push-button tools that will inspect your server implementation and generate an API for you, an API described by a hypermedia-based service document. There's nothing technically wrong with this—hypermedia in a service document is still hypermedia—but it will encourage your users to put their faith in the idea that the service document won't change. Everything will seem fine at first, but as your API evolves, you'll start running into problems. You will have checked a feature box labeled "hypermedia," but you won't actually get the benefits that come from adopting hypermedia.

Any hypermedia format might be used to write a service document, but there are three in particular that especially lend themselves to this antipattern. They are OData and WADL (which I'll cover in Chapter 10) and Hydra (which I'll cover in Chapter 12). As I cover them, I'll remind you of this forewarning.

Adding Hypermedia to an Existing API

Suppose you already have an API designed and deployed. It's an API typical of today's designs, a fiat standard serving ad hoc JSON or XML representations, with no hypermedia:

```
{
  "name": "Jennifer Gallegos",
  "bday": "1987-08-25"
}
```

You should be able to get your API up to the level of quality I advocate in this book, without breaking your existing clients. Here's a modified version of the seven-step process I laid out earlier, for fixing up a JSON-based API:

1. Document all your existing representations. Each one will contain a number of semantic descriptors. You can't change these, but you should be able to add new ones.

2. Draw a state diagram for your API. The boxes on the diagram are your existing representations. You probably won't have any state transitions, because most existing APIs don't have any hypermedia links. Now's the time to add some. Use arrows to connect representations in ways that make sense. The names of the arrows are your link relations.

   At this point it may turn out that some of your semantic descriptors are actually link relations:

   ```
   { "homepage": "http://example.com" }
   ```

   You can convert them to link relations at this point, but be sure not to rename them when you get to the next step.

3. You can't change the name of anything you wrote down in step 1, because that would break your existing clients. But you can go through the link relations you created in step 2, and make sure their names come from the IANA and other well-known sources whenever possible.

4. You can't change your media type, because that would break your clients. It'll have to stay `application/json` (or whatever it is now).

5. Since you can't change the media type, all your application semantics and protocol semantics must be defined somewhere else. You've got two choices: an ALPS profile or a JSON-LD context.

   If you wrote down any unsafe link relations in step 2, your best choice is JSON-LD with Hydra (see Chapter 12). You should be able to take your human-readable descriptions of API calls and convert them into machine-readable Hydra operations.

6. You've already got most of the code written. You'll just need to extend each representation by serving appropriate links.

7. Your billboard URL will be the same as before. If you didn't have one before, because your API was a group of discrete API calls, you can create a new resource to act as your home page, and know that only hypermedia-aware clients will access it.

Fixing Up an XML-Based API

The procedure is similar for an API that serves XML representations. You can use XLink and XForm (see Chapter 12) to add hypermedia controls to any XML documents.

In step 2, when you discover that one of your semantic descriptors would make more sense as a link relation, like homepage here…

```
<homepage>http://example.com/</homepage>
```

…you can't just convert it to a link relation. That would break your existing clients. You'll need to add redundancy. This example uses XLink to use homepage as both a link relation (xlink:arcrole) and a semantic descriptor:

```
<homepage xlink:href="http://example.com" xlink:arcrole="homepage">
 http://example.com/
</homepage>
```

You may also have some trouble in step 5. You can't use JSON-LD on an XML document, but you might be able to write an ALPS profile. If all else fails, you can fall back to a human-readable profile based on your existing API documentation.

Is It Worth It?

Although it's technically possible to turn a hypermedia-ignorant API into a full hypermedia API, the only profit you gain from the exercise may be a glowing sense of satisfaction. The problem is, your old API already has clients. That's why you couldn't just scrap it and design a new API from scratch. Because the existing clients don't have the flexibility that comes from a knowledge of hypermedia, it's going to be very tough to migrate them to the new API. And why should your users bother to learn the new API? They've already got scripts that work.

If you were planning on changing your API anyway, it makes sense to retrofit it with profiles and hypermedia controls, so that future changes will be easier. But adding hypermedia to an existing API won't solve any problems on its own.

Alice's Second Adventure

In Chapter 1, I talked about a website that used a billboard to advertise the URL to its home page. I told a story about Alice, a fictional character who typed that URL into her web browser and gradually discovered the site's capabilities.

The story was pretty dull, because it just showed the World Wide Web working the way it's supposed to. But now I can tell the same sort of story about an API that has nothing in common with the Web except the HTTP protocol.

Like my earlier story, this one starts with a URL—the billboard URL for an API:

```
https://www.example.com/
```

(As you can tell from the hostname, unlike the website in Chapter 1 and the API in Chapter 2, this API is purely imaginary.)

Episode 1: The Nonsense Representation

It's a dark and stormy night. An HTTP client makes a GET request:

```
GET / HTTP/1.1
Host: www.example.com
```

Someone is driving this client. It's Alice, the fictional character from Chapter 1. But this time she's not using a web browser. She's using a programmable HTTP client to probe the capabilities of a new API. With no web browser to display the representations graphically, Alice may have a hard time understanding what this API does, but she will be able to figure it out.

The server sends back a representation, and Alice examines it:

```
200 OK HTTP/1.1
Content-Type: application/vnd.myapi.qbit

===1 wkmje
<{data} {name:"qbe"} 1005>
<{link} {tab:"profile"} "https://www.example.com/The-Metric-System-And-You">
<{link} {tab:"search"} "https://www.example.com/sosuy{?ebddt}">
===2 qmdk
<{link} {tab:"gyth"} "https://www.example.com/click%20here%20for%20prizes">
<{data} {name:"ebddt"} "Zerde">
<{data} {name:"gioi"} "Snup">
```

"What the heck is this?" says Alice. "It's not quite XML and it's not quite JSON. It's full of nonsensical strings like qbe and URLs that seem to lead to educational filmstrips from the 1970s."

Alice's only clue is the Content-Type header, which identifies the data format as something called application/vnd.myapi.qbit. With nowhere else to go, Alice looks up application/vnd.myapi.qbit in the IANA registry of media types. This points her to a corporate website that describes the not-quite-XML, not-quite-JSON data format she's looking at. That website also features some code libraries for parsing the file format. Using these tools, she's able to extend her programmable HTTP client so it can turn the stream of gibberish into a useful data structure.

Now Alice knows a few things. She knows that the document is in two sections, one called wkmje and one called qmdk. She knows that the document contains three semantic descriptors (gioi, ebddt, and qbe), and three hypermedia controls (two links and a URI Template). For some strange reason, this media type refers to a link relation as a "tab", which means that the three hypermedia controls have the link relations `profile`, `search`, and `gyth`.

But Alice doesn't know what `wkmje` or `qmdk` means. They're nonsense words that are not defined along with the media type. One of the hypermedia controls points to *https://www.example.com/click%20here%20for%20prizes*, but Alice has no idea what's at the other end, because the URL looks like spam and the link relation (`gyth`) is not registered with the IANA.

Alice knows that the `search` control is a URI Template that defines a variable called `ebddt`, but she doesn't know what `ebddt` means. The link relation `search` *is* registered with the IANA, and reading the definition gives Alice confidence that this is some kind of search form. This means `ebddt` is probably a search term. It probably has something to do with the semantic descriptor called `ebddt`, but what does `ebddt` mean?

Episode 2: The Profile

The answer to all these questions sits behind the document's first link:

```
<{link} {tab:"profile"} "https://www.example.com/The-Metric-System-And-You">
```

By this point, Alice has read Chapter 8 of this book. She knows that the link relation `profile` is registered with the IANA, and that it indicates a link to a profile document. She makes her second request, hoping to get a profile document that will make sense of all this `ebddt` and `gyth` stuff:

```
GET /The-Metric-System-And-You HTTP/1.1
Host: www.example.com
```

When Alice read the definition of `application/vnd.myapi.qbit`, she noticed that it included rules for applying an ALPS profile to a representation, so Alice is hoping for an ALPS profile. But even a human-readable web page would be useful.

As it happens, the server sends Alice an ALPS document:

```
HTTP/1.1 200 OK
Content-Type: application/vnd.amundsen.alps+xml

<alps version="1.0">
  <doc>
    A searchable database of recipes.
  </doc>

  <descriptor id="wkmje" type="semantic">
    Information about the recipe database as a whole.
    <descriptor href="#qbe">
  </descriptor>

  <descriptor id="qmdk" type="semantic">
    Information about the currently featured recipe.
```

```
    <descriptor href="#gyth">
    <descriptor href="#ebddt">
    <descriptor href="#gioi">
</descriptor>

<descriptor id="qbe" type="semantic">
  Indicates the total number of recipes in a list.
</descriptor>

<descriptor id="gyth" type="safe">
  A link to a recipe.
</descriptor>

<descriptor id="ebddt" type="semantic">
  The name of a recipe.
</descriptor>

<descriptor id="gioi" type="semantic">
  Whether the recipe meets various dietary restrictions. The value
  "Snup" indicates a vegetarian recipe. The value "5a" indicates a
  recipe that includes meat. Other values are allowed (for gluten
  free, kosher, etc.), but any other value must start with the
  extension prefix "paq-". If two or more values are given, they must
  be separated by the character SNOWMAN, e.g. "Snup☃paq-vegan"
</descriptor>
  ...
</alps>
```

Alice combines the ALPS profile with the vnd.myapi.qbit document, either mentally or using an automated tool. Now it all makes sense. This API is a recipe database. The first section of the representation describes the database as a whole. It includes a way to search by recipe name (ebddt), and a total number of recipes (qbe). The second section is a link to a featured recipe (gyth). It mentions the recipe's name (ebddt="Zerde") and the fact that it's a vegetarian recipe (gioi="Snup").

Combining the vnd.myapi.qbit document with the ALPS profile in a program that understands both media types might yield a GUI that looks like Figure 9-12.

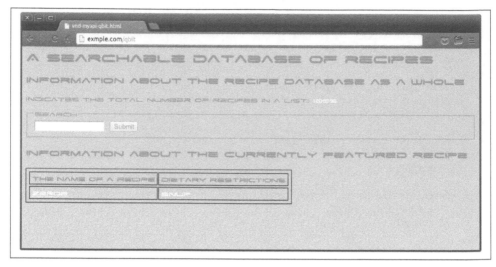

Figure 9-12. Possible rendering of the qbit GUI using the ALPS Profile

This isn't perfect—the human-readable explanations weren't written to be used in a GUI, so the GUI reads awkwardly—but it's a whole lot better than the incomprehensible `vnd.myapi.qbit` document is on its own.

As a programmer, Alice could use the ALPS profile to implement any of the client types I described in Figure 5-3. Here are some examples:

- A human-driven client for searching the recipe database.
- A crawler that downloads all the recipes it can find.
- A monitor that periodically runs a search for new vegetarian recipes.
- An agent that takes a list of ingredients on hand and plans a meal. The agent uses the recipe API to find recipes that use already available ingredients. It also integrates with a grocery store's pricing API to look up the cost of missing ingredients. Its output is a list of recipes that use most of the ingredients on hand and have minimal additional cost.

But as it happens, Alice doesn't care about cooking at all. Once she understands the meaning of the document she was originally served, she stops using this bizarre API and never comes back.

Alice Figured It Out

When I designed this API, I took every step I could to obscure its purpose. I made up a confusing media type, `application/vnd.myapi.qbit`. I used the nonsensical term `tab` to label link relations, instead of the standard term `rel`. I served URLs with mis-

---

leading names. I used random strings of letters to name the semantic descriptors and link relations. I invented ridiculous, arbitrary rules for saying whether a recipe meets different dietary restrictions. The only useful human-readable text in the `vnd.mya pi.qbit` document is "Zerde", the name of the featured recipe.[6] And there was no API documentation as it's commonly understood: just a billboard URL.

Despite all this, Alice was able to figure out how the API works, because even in my sadism I played by the rules I've set down in this book. I served a `Content-Type` header that contained the media type of the confusing representation format. Alice was able to look it up in the IANA registry and read a formal explanation of the format. Within the `vnd.myapi.qbit` document, I used a IANA-registered link relation (`search`) to describe a search form, and another (`profile`) to link to a profile document. The profile document was machine-readable, but it also contained the essential human-readable information about what the representation *means*. Once she found that information and read it, Alice understood the application semantics, and knew she didn't want to use the API.

Obviously you shouldn't set out to make things difficult for your users. You shouldn't serve meaningless URLs, or randomly generate the names of your link relations.[7] The point of this story is *that's not what matters on a technical level*. You need to make sure that your API's protocol and application semantics are documented, through a combination of profiles and media type definitions. You need to treat your documentation not as a separate product, but as a first-class part of your API, as a representation linked to from other representations using a hypermedia control and a link relation.

Within your API's representations, human-readable link relations and URLs are helpful hints—shorthands that keep client developers from having to constantly look up `ebddt` in your documentation. They are not themselves the documentation. The documentation is embedded in your API. That's what allows your API to change over time.

---

6. Zerde is a Turkish dessert, a kind of rice pudding. I chose it thinking that not many of my readers would recognize the word.

7. Unless you want to make absolutely sure they write hypermedia-aware clients.

The Hypermedia Zoo

There are a lot of hypermedia document formats in active use. Some are designed for very specialized purposes—the people who use them may not even think of them as hypermedia formats. Other hypermedia formats are in such common usage that people don't really think about them at all. In this chapter, I'll take you on an educational tour of a "zoo" containing the most popular and most interesting hypermedia formats.

I won't be going into a lot of technical detail. Any one of these formats probably isn't the one you want to use, and I've covered many of them earlier in the book. Many of the formats are still under active development, and their details might change. If you're interested in one of the zoo's specimens, the next step is to read its formal specification.

My goal is to give you a sense of the many forms hypermedia can take, and to show how many times we've tackled the basic problems of representing it. The hypermedia zoo is so full that you probably don't need to define a brand new media type for your API. You should be able to pick an existing media type and write a profile for it.

I've organized the hypermedia zoo along the lines of my introduction to hypermedia. There's a section for domain-specific formats (a la Chapter 5), a section for formats whose primary purpose is to implement the collection pattern (a la Chapter 6), and a section for general hypermedia formats (a la Chapter 7).

For formats like Collection+JSON, which I've already covered in some depth, I'll briefly summarize the format and point you to the earlier discussion. There are a few hypermedia formats that I won't discuss in this chapter, because they take different approaches to REST than the one I've advocated so far in this book. I'll cover RDF and its descendants in Chapter 12, and CoRE Link Format in Chapter 13.

Domain-Specific Formats

These media types are designed to represent problems in one particular domain. Each defines some very specific application semantics, and although you might be able to use them to convey different semantics, it's probably a bad idea.

Maze+XML

- **Media type:** application/vnd.amundsen.maze+xml
- **Defined in:** personal standard (*http://amundsen.com/media-types/maze/*)
- **Medium:** XML
- **Protocol semantics:** navigation using GET links
- **Application semantics:** maze games
- **Covered in:** Chapter 5

Maze+XML defines XML tags and link relations relating to mazes, cells in mazes, and the connections between cells. Figure 10-1 gives the state diagram of its protocol semantics.

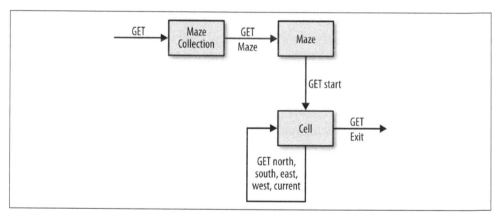

Figure 10-1. The protocol semantics of Maze+XML

Maze+XML defines a <link> tag that takes a link relation and defines a safe state transition; that is, it allows the client to make a GET request. You can extend Maze+XML by bringing in custom link relations, or by defining extra XML tags. Since it's an XML format, you could also use XForms (q.v.) to represent unsafe state transitions.

I don't seriously recommend using Maze+XML, even if you happen to be making a maze game. It's just an example, and I'm putting it first to serve as an example of how I judge hypermedia formats.

OpenSearch

- **Media type:** `application/opensearchdescription+xml` (pending registration)
- **Defined in:** consortium standard (*http://www.opensearch.org/Specifications/Open Search/1.1*)
- **Medium:** XML
- **Protocol semantics:** searching using GET
- **Application semantics:** search queries
- **Covered in:** Chapter 6

OpenSearch is a standard for representing search forms. It can be used standalone, or incorporated into another API using the `search` link relation. Its state diagram looks like this:

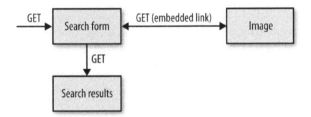

Here's a simple OpenSearch representation. The destination of an OpenSearch form (the `template` attribute of its `<Url>` tag) is a string similar to a URI Template (RFC 6570), though it doesn't have all of URI Template's features:

```
<?xml version="1.0" encoding="UTF-8"?>
<OpenSearchDescription xmlns="http://a9.com/-/spec/opensearch/1.1/">
 <ShortName>Name search</ShortName>
 <Description>Search the database by name</Description>
 <Url type="application/atom+xml" rel="results"
   template="http://example.com/search?q={searchTerms}"/>
</OpenSearchDescription>
```

OpenSearch does not define a way to represent the *results* of a search. You should use whatever list format fits in with your main representation format.

Problem Detail Documents

- **Media type:** `application/api-problem+json`
- **Described in:** Internet-Draft "draft-nottingham-http-problem"
- **Medium:** JSON (with rules for automatically converting to XML)
- **Protocol semantics:** navigation with GET

- **Application semantics:** error reports

A problem detail document describes an error condition. It uses structured, human-readable text to add custom semantics to HTTP's status codes. It's a simple JSON format designed to replace whatever one-off format you were thinking of designing to convey your error messages.

Like most JSON-based hypermedia documents, a problem detail takes the form of a JSON object. Here's a document that might be served along with an HTTP status code of 503 (`Service Unavailable`):

```
{
  "describedBy": "http://example.com/scheduled-maintenance",
  "supportId": "http://example.com/maintenance/outages/20130533",
  "httpStatus" : 503
  "title": "The API is down for scheduled maintenance.",
  "detail": "This outage will last from 02:00 until 04:30 UTC."
}
```

Two of these properties are defined as hypermedia links. The `describedBy` property is a link to a human-readable explanation of the representation.[1]

The `supportId` property is a URL representing *this particular instance* of the problem. There's no expectation that the end user will find anything at the other end of this URL. It might be an internal URL for use by the API support staff, or it might be a URI, a unique ID that doesn't point to anything in particular.

The `describedBy` and `title` properties are required; the rest are optional. You can also add extra properties specific to your API.

SVG

- **Media type:** `image/svg+xml`
- **Medium:** XML
- **Protocol semantics:** the same as XLink
- **Application semantics:** vector graphics

SVG is an image format. Unlike a JPEG, which represents an image on the pixel level, an SVG image is made up of shapes. SVG includes a hypermedia control that lets different parts of an image link to different resources.

---

1. `describedBy` is an IANA-registered link relation that's a more general version of `profile`. A resource is `describedBy` any resource that sheds *any* light on its interpretation.

That hypermedia control is an <a> tag that has the same function as HTML's <a> tag. Here's a simple SVG representation of a cell in Chapter 5's maze:

```
<svg version="1.1" xmlns="http://www.w3.org/2000/svg"
     xmlns:xlink="http://www.w3.org/1999/xlink">

  <rect x="100" y="80" width="100" height="50" stroke="black" fill="white"/>
  <text x="105" y="105" font-size="10">Foyer of Horrors</text>

  <a xlink:href="/cells/I" xlink:arcrole="http://alps.io/example/maze#north">
   <line x1="150" y1="80" x2="150" y2="40" stroke="black"/>
   <text x="130" y="38" font-size="10">Go North!</text>
  </a>

  <a xlink:href="/cells/O" xlink:arcrole="http://alps.io/example/maze#east">
   <line x1="200" y1="105" x2="240" y2="105" stroke="black"/>
   <text x="240" y="107" font-size="10">Go East!</text>
  </a>

  <a xlink:href="/cells/M" xlink:arcrole="http://alps.io/example/maze#west">
   <line x1="100" y1="105" x2="60" y2="105" stroke="black"/>
   <text x="18" y="107" font-size="10">Go West!</text>
  </a>

</svg>
```

Figure 10-2 shows how a client might render this document.

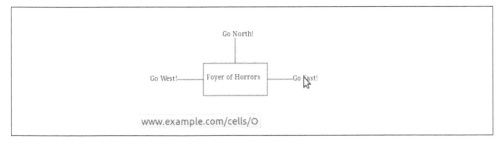

Figure 10-2. The SVG representation of a maze cell

SVG makes a good alternative to HTML for building mobile applications. SVG can also be combined with HTML 5: just stick an <svg> tag into HTML markup to get an inline SVG image.

SVG's <a> tag doesn't actually define any hypermedia capabilities. It's just a placeholder tag for XLink's role and href attributes (q.v.). Since SVG is an XML format, you can also add XForms forms (q.v.) to SVG, and get protocol semantics comparable to HTML's. This is not as useful as embedding SVG into HTML, since it requires a client that understands both SVG and XForms.

VoiceXML

- **Media type:** `application/voicexml+xml`
- **Defined in:** W3C open standard (*http://www.w3.org/TR/voicexml20/*), with extensions (*http://www.w3.org/TR/voicexml21/*)
- **Medium:** XML
- **Protocol semantics:** GET for navigation; arbitrary state transitions through forms: GET for safe transitions, POST for unsafe transitions
- **Application semantics:** spoken conversation

In Chapter 5, I made an analogy between an HTTP client navigating a hypermedia API and a human being navigating a phone tree. Well, a lot of those phone trees are actually implemented on the backend as hypermedia APIs. The representation format they use is VoiceXML.

Here's one possible VoiceXML representation of a cell in Chapter 5's maze game:

```xml
<?xml version="1.0" encoding="UTF-8"?>
<vxml xmlns="http://www.w3.org/2001/vxml"
  xmlns:xsi="http://www.w3.org/2001/XMLSchema-instance"
  xsi:schemaLocation="http://www.w3.org/2001/vxml
   http://www.w3.org/TR/voicexml20/vxml.xsd"
   version="2.1">
 <menu>
  <prompt>
   You are in the Foyer of Horrors. Exits are: <enumerate/>
  </prompt>

  <choice next="/cells/I">
   North
  </choice>

  <choice next="/cells/M">
   East
  </choice>

  <choice next="/cells/O">
   West
  </choice>

  <noinput>Please say one of <enumerate/></noinput>
  <nomatch>You can't go that way. Exits are: <enumerate/></nomatch>
 </menu>
</vxml>
```

If you're playing the maze game over the phone, you'll never see this representation directly. The VoiceXML "browser" lives on the other end of the phone line. When it receives this representation, it handles the document by reading the <prompt> aloud to you: "You are in the Foyer of Horrors. Exits are: north, east, west."

Each <choice> tag is a hypermedia link. The browser waits for you to activate a link by saying something. It uses speech recognition to figure out which link you're activating. There's a validation step: if you say nothing, or you say something that doesn't map onto one of the links, the browser reads you an error message (either <noinput> or <no match>) and waits for input again.

Once you manage to activate a link, the browser makes a GET request to the URL mentioned in the corresponding next attribute. The server responds with a new VoiceXML representation, and the browser processes the representation and tells you which maze cell you're in now.

The <menu> tag is only the simplest of VoiceXML's hypermedia controls. There's also a <form> tag that uses a speech recognition grammar to drive a GET or POST request based on what you tell it. Here's a VoiceXML form for flipping the mysterious switches I defined in Chapter 7:

```
<form id="switches">
 <grammar src="command.grxml" type="application/srgs+xml"/>

 <initial name="start">
  <prompt>
   There is a red switch and a blue switch here. The red switch is
   up and the blue switch is down.

   What would you like to do?
  </prompt>
 </initial>

 <field name="command">
  <prompt>
   Would you like to flip the red switch, flip the blue switch, or
   forget about it?
  </prompt>
 </field>

 <field name="switch">
  <prompt>
   Say the name of a switch.
  </prompt>
 </field>

 <filled>
  <submit next="/cells/I" method="POST" namelist="command switch"/>
 </filled>
</form>
```

The `<grammar>` tag is an inline link analogous to an HTML `<img>` or `<script>` tag. It automatically imports a document written in a format set down by the W3C's Speech Recognition Grammar Specification.[2] I won't show the SRGS file here, because SRGS is not a hypermedia format. Suffice to say that when you say the words "flip the red switch," or "forget about it," the SRGS grammar is what allows the VoiceXML browser to transform those words into a set of key-value pairs that match the form fields `command` and `switch`:

```
command=flip
switch=red switch
```

Once the fields are filled in with values obtained through speech recognition, the `<submit>` tag tells the VoiceXML browser how to format an HTTP POST request. It looks just like an HTML form submission:

```
POST /cells/I HTTP/1.1
Content-Type: application/x-www-form-urlencoded

command=flip&switch=red%20switch
```

A VoiceXML document resembles nothing so much as programming language code. VoiceXML uses idioms from programming to represent the flow of conversation through a dialog tree: `<goto>` to jump from one part of the dialog to another, `<if>` to represent a conditional, and even `<var>` to assign a value to a variable.

Collection Pattern Formats

The three standards in this section have similar application and protocol semantics, because they all implement the collection pattern I laid out in Chapter 6. In the collection pattern, certain resources are designated "item" resources. An item usually responds to GET, PUT, and DELETE, and its representation focuses on representing structured bits of data. Other resources are designated "collection" resources. A collection usually responds to GET and POST-to-append, and its representation focuses on linking to item resources.

These three standards take different approaches to the collection pattern; they may not use the terms "collection" or "item," but they all do pretty much the same thing.

Collection+JSON

- **Media type:** `application/vnd.amundsen.collection+json`
- **Defined in:** personal standard (*http://amundsen.com/media-types/collection/*)

---

2. Defined here (*http://www.w3.org/TR/speech-grammar/*).

- **Medium:** JSON
- **Protocol semantics:** collection pattern (GET/POST/PUT/DELETE), plus searching (using GET)
- **Application semantics:** collection pattern ("collection" and "item")
- **Covered in:** Chapter 6

Collection+JSON was designed as a simple JSON-based alternative to the Atom Publishing Protocol (q.v.). It's a formalized, hypermedia-aware version of the API developers tend to design their first time through the process. Figure 10-3 shows its protocol semantics.

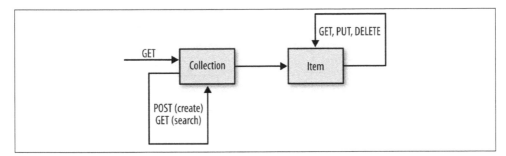

Figure 10-3. The protocol semantics of Collection+JSON

The Atom Publishing Protocol

- **Media types:** `application/atom+xml`, `application/atomsvc+xml`, and `application/atomcat+xml`
- **Defined in:** RFC 5023 and RFC 4287
- **Medium:** XML
- **Protocol semantics:** collection pattern (GET/POST/PUT/DELETE); well-defined extensions add searching and other forms of navigation, all using GET links or forms
- **Application semantics:** collection pattern (`feed` and `entry`); entries have the semantics of blog posts (`author`, `title`, `category`, etc.); an entry that is not an Atom document (e.g., a binary graphic) is split into a binary `Media Entry` and an Atom `Entry` that contains metadata
- **Covered in:** Chapter 6

The original API standard, AtomPub pioneered the collection pattern and the RESTful approach to APIs in general. As an XML-based standard in a field now dominated by JSON representations, AtomPub now looks somewhat old-fashioned, but it inspired several other standards and link relations that can be used with other hypermedia formats. Figure 10-4 shows its protocol semantics.

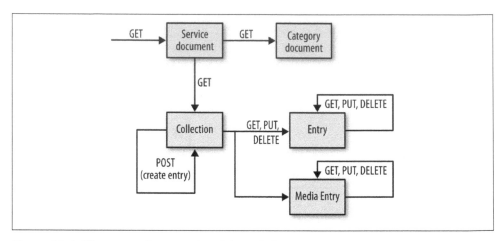

Figure 10-4. The protocol semantics of AtomPub

Although Atom's application semantics imply that it should be used only for news-feed applications like blogging and content management APIs, the standard is very extensible. Perhaps the most notable extension is the Google Data Protocol, the foundation of Google's API platform. Google adds domain-specific tags to AtomPub to describe the application semantics of each of its sites. An Atom feed becomes a collection of videos (the YouTube API) or a collection of spreadsheet cells (Google Spreadsheets).

If you think your application semantics won't fit into the collection pattern, a look at Google's API directory (*https://developers.google.com/gdata/docs/directory*) may convince you otherwise. The Google Data Protocol also defines a JSON equivalent to AtomPub's XML representations, though this is a fiat standard, not something you're invited to reuse.

Several open standards define AtomPub extensions, including the Atom Threading Extensions and the `deleted-entry` element. I covered these in Chapter 6.

OData

- **Media type:** `application/json;odata=fullmetadata`
- **Defined in:** open standard in progress (*http://www.odata.org/docs*)
- **Medium:** JSON for some parts, XML for others

- **Protocol semantics:** modified collection pattern (GET/POST/PUT/DELETE) with PATCH for partial updates and GET for queries; arbitrary state transitions with forms (GET for safe transitions, and POST for unsafe transitions)
- **Application semantics:** collection pattern (`feed` and `entry`)

The semantics of OData are heavily inspired by the Atom Publishing Protocol. In fact, an OData API can serve Atom representations, and a client can treat an OData API as an AtomPub API with a whole lot of extensions. But I'll be considering OData as an API that serves mostly JSON representations.

Figure 10-5 shows a view of OData's protocol semantics, simplified to show only the parts of OData I'll be covering here. And here's an OData representation of a collection from a microblogging API, similar to Chapter 2's You Type It, We Post It:

```
{
  "odata.metadata":
    "http://api.example.com/YouTypeItWePostIt.svc/$metadata#Posts",
  "value": [
    {
      "Content": "This is the second post.",
      "Id": 2,
      "PostedAt": "2013-04-30T03:34:12.0992416-05:00",
      "PostedAt@odata.type": "Edm.DateTimeOffset",
      "PostedBy@odata.navigationLinkUrl": "Posts(2)/PostedBy",
      "odata.editLink": "Posts(2)",
      "odata.id": "http://api.example.com/YouTypeItWePostIt.svc/Posts(2)",
      "odata.type": "YouTypeItWePostIt.Post"
    },
    {
      "Content": "This is the first post",
      "Id": 1,
      "PostedAt": "2013-04-30T04:14:53.0992416-05:00",
      "PostedAt@odata.type": "Edm.DateTimeOffset",
      "PostedBy@odata.navigationLinkUrl": "Posts(1)/PostedBy",
      "odata.editLink": "Posts(1)",
      "odata.id": "http://api.example.com/YouTypeItWePostIt.svc/Posts(1)",
      "odata.type": "YouTypeItWePostIt.Post"
    },
    "#Posts.RandomPostForDate": {
      "title": "Get a random post for the given date",
      "target": "Posts/RandomPostForDate"
    }
}
```

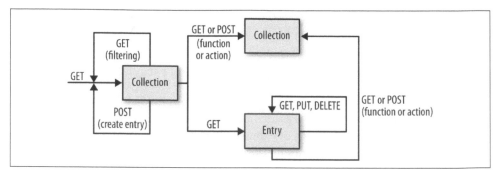

Figure 10-5. The protocol semantics of OData (simplified)

Like the other JSON-based formats we've seen, OData representations are JSON objects whose properties are named with short, mysterious strings. A property like `Content` or `PostedAt` is ordinary JSON data, and its name acts as a semantic descriptor. A property whose name includes the `odata.` prefix is a hypermedia control or some other bit of OData-specific metadata. Some examples from this document:

- The property `odata.id` contains a unique ID—that is, a URI—for one specific entry-type resource.

- The property `PostedAt@odata.type` contains semantic type information for the value of the `PostedAt` property. The type, `Edm.DateTimeOffset`, refers to OData's schema format: the Entity Data Model.

- The property `odata.editLink` acts like an AtomPub link with `rel="edit"`. If you want to modify or delete one of the example posts, you can send a PUT, PATCH, or DELETE request to the relative URL `Posts(2)` or `Posts(1)`.

- The property `PostedBy@odata.navigationLinkUrl` contains a hypermedia link to another resource. The application-specific part of the property name, `PostedBy`, serves as a link relation. In human terms, this is a link to the user who published this particular post.

The protocol semantics of OData resources repeat what you've already seen in Collection+JSON and AtomPub. A collection resource supports GET (to get a representation) and POST (to append a new entry to the collection). Entry-type resources support GET, as well as (via their `odata.editLink`) PUT, DELETE, and PATCH.

Filtering

OData also defines a set of implicit protocol semantics for filtering and sorting a collection, using a query language similar to SQL. If you know you have the URL to an OData collection, you can manipulate that URL in a wide variety of ways. Sending GET to the resulting URLs will yield representations that filter and paginate the collection in different ways.

I say these protocol semantics are implicit because you don't have to look for a hypermedia form that tells you how to make the HTTP request that carries out a particular search. You can construct that request based on rules found in the OData spec.

Let's look at a few examples. Suppose the (relative) base URL of the microblog collection is */Posts*. You don't need a hypermedia form to tell you how to search for blog posts that include the string "second" in their Content property. You can build the URL yourself[3]:

```
/Posts$filter=substringof('second', Content)
```

You can search for posts that include "second" in their Content and were PostedBy a resource whose Username property is "alice":

```
/Posts$filter=substringof('second', Content)+ and +PostedBy/Username eq 'alice')
```

You can pick up only the last five posts that were published in the year 2012:

```
/Posts$filter=year(PostedAt) eq 2012&$top=5
```

Want to get the second page of that list? You don't need to look for a link with the relation next in the representation. The URL you should use is defined by the OData spec:

```
/Posts$filter=year(PostedAt) eq 2012&$top=5&skip=5
```

By default, the microblog collection presents entries in reverse chronological order based on the value of the PostedAt property. If you want to use chronological order instead, the OData spec explains what URL you should use:

```
/Posts$orderBy=PostedAt asc
```

In the other collection-pattern standards, the server must serve a hypermedia control to explicitly describe each allowable family of searches. Collection+JSON serves search templates, AtomPub serves OpenSearch forms. An OData collection doesn't need to provide this information because every OData collection implicitly supports the entire OData query protocol. A client doesn't need a hypermedia form to know it's OK to send GET requests to certain URLs. The OData format itself puts additional constraints on the server that guarantee that certain URLs will work.

OData defines a few more bits of implicit protocol semantics, mostly pertaining to the relationships between resources. I won't be covering them here.

Functions and the metadata document

In addition to the impressive set of state transitions implicitly defined by OData's query protocol, an OData representation may include explicit hypermedia controls describing

---

3. All of these URLs need to be URL-encoded, obviously. I've left them unencoded for the sake of clarity.

any state transition at all. These controls have protocol semantics similar to HTML forms. Safe transitions are called "functions," and they use HTTP GET. Unsafe transitions are called "actions," and they use HTTP POST. I'll be focusing on functions, but actions work the same way.

Here's a simple OData form that takes a date as input. It triggers a state transition where the server looks at all of a microblog's entries from the given date, picks one at random, and serves a representation of it.

```
"#Posts.RandomPostForDate": {
    "title": "Get a random post for the given date",
    "target": "Posts/RandomPostForDate"
},
```

If this was a simple query like "all the microblog entries from a given date," the form wouldn't be necessary. The state transition would be implicitly described by OData's query protocol. But that protocol can't express the concept of "random selection," so this state transition must be described explicitly, using a hypermedia form. Now, here's a question: can you look at this form and figure out which HTTP request to make?

It's a trick question. You can't figure it out, because I didn't show you the whole form. The part of the form gives you the base URL to use (*Posts/RandomPostforDate*), but it doesn't explain how to format your contribution—the date for which you want a random post. It's equivalent to this HTML form:

```
<form action="Posts/RandomPostForDate" method="GET">
 <input class="RandomPostForDate" type="submit"
  value="Get a random post for the given date."/>
</form>
```

That's obviously incomplete. It's missing a formal description for "the given date." What format should "the given date" take? What's its semantic descriptor? Do you trigger the state transition by sending GET to *Posts/RandomPostforDate?Date=9/13/2009*, or to *Posts/RandomPostForDate?the_date_to_use=13%20August%202009*, or to *Posts/RandomPostForDate?when=yesterday*? You just don't have that information.

In the HTML example, the missing information should go into a second <input> tag within the <form> tag. But with OData, that information is kept in a different document —a "metadata document" written not in JSON but in XML, using a vocabulary called the Comma Schema Definition Language (CSDL).[4]

An OData representation links to its metadata document using the odata.metadata property

---

4. For more information on CSDL, go to the OData website (*http://www.odata.org/documentation/odata-v3-documentation/common-schema-definition-language-csdl/*).

```
{
  "odata.metadata":
    "http://api.example.com/YouTypeItWePostIt.svc/$metadata#Posts",
  ...
}
```

Here's the part of the metadata document that completes the definition of the `Random PostForDate` state transition:

```
<FunctionImport Name="RandomPostforDate" EntitySet="Posts"
                IsBindable="true" m:IsAlwaysBindable="false"
                ReturnType="Post" IsSideEffecting="false">
 <Parameter Name="date" Type="Edm.DateTime" Mode="In" />
</FunctionImport>
```

Now you know the whole story. You trigger the state transition `RandomForDate` by formatting a date as a string, in a format defined by OData's Entity Data Model.[5] You know that this state transition is safe, because its CSDL description has the `IsSideEffecting` attribute set to `false`. That means you should trigger the state transition with a GET request rather than with POST.

Combine the metadata document with the OData representation, and you have all the information necessary to trigger the state transition `RandomPostForDate`. You send an HTTP request that looks something like this:

```
GET /YouTypeItWePostIt.svc/Posts/RandomPostForDate?date=datetime'2009-08-13T12:↵
00' HTTP/1.1
Host: api.example.com
```

Although `RandomPostForDate` is a simple transition, OData state transitions can get very complicated. The metadata document stores the messy details that explain exactly how to trigger whatever state transitions you might find mentioned in an OData document. This saves the server from having to include a complete description of a complex state transition in every representation that supports it. A client that's interested in a given state transition can look up a complete description of it.

Metadata documents as service description documents

I've presented OData in a way that makes it look like Collection+JSON or Siren. A microblog post is represented as a JSON object containing data fields like `DatePublish ed`, along with hypermedia controls and other "metadata" explaining the possible next steps.

That's the version of OData I recommend, and it has the media type `application/ json;odata=fullmetadata`. But there's another way to write down an OData document:

---

5. The EDM is defined in the same document as CSDL.

a way that keeps *all* the hypermedia controls, not just the complicated ones, in the metadata document.

The media type of such a document is `application/json;odata=minimalmetadata`. Here's what a representation of the microblog would look like in this format:

```
{
  "odata.metadata":
    "http://api.example.com/YouTypeItWePostIt.svc/$metadata#Posts",
  "value": [
    {
      "Content": "This is the first post.",
      "Id": 1,
      "PostedAt": "2013-04-30T01:42:57.0901805-05:00"
    },
    {
      "Content": "This is the second post.",
      "Id": 2,
      "PostedAt": "2013-04-30T01:45:03.0901805-05:00"
    },
  ]
}
```

That's a lot smaller, but in the world of REST, smaller isn't necessarily better. Where'd the metadata go? What happened to `PostedBy@odata.navigationLinkUrl` and `#Posts.RandomPostForDate`? How are you supposed to decide which HTTP request to make next?

All of that information went into the CSDL document at the other end of the `oda ta.metadata` link. I showed you part of the CSDL document earlier when I was discussing `RandomPostForDate`, but here's a bit more of it (this excerpt shows what happened to `PostedBy` and `RandomPostForDate`):

```
<edmx:Edmx Version="1.0"
 xmlns:edmx="http://schemas.microsoft.com/ado/2007/06/edmx">
 <edmx:DataServices
  xmlns:m="http://schemas.microsoft.com/ado/2007/08/dataservices/metadata"
  m:DataServiceVersion="3.0" m:MaxDataServiceVersion="3.0">

  <Schema Namespace="YouTypeItWePostIt">
   <EntityType Name="Post">
    <Key><PropertyRef Name="Id"/></Key>
    <Property Name="Id" Type="Edm.Int32" Nullable="false"/>
    <Property Name="Content" Type="Edm.String"/>
    <Property Name="PostedAt" Type="Edm.DateTimeOffset" Nullable="false"/>
    <NavigationProperty Name="PostedBy"
     Relationship="YouTypeItWePostIt.Post_PostedBy"
     ToRole="PostedBy" FromRole="Post"/>
   </EntityType>

   ...
```

```
<EntityContainer Name="YouTypeItWePostItContext"
 m:IsDefaultEntityContainer="true">

<EntitySet Name="Posts" EntityType="YouTypeItWePostIt.Post"/>

<FunctionImport Name="RandomPostforDate" EntitySet="Posts"
                IsBindable="true" m:IsAlwaysBindable="false"
                ReturnType="Post" IsSideEffecting="false">
  <Parameter Name="date" Type="Edm.DateTime" Mode="In" />
</FunctionImport>

<EntitySet Name="Users" EntityType="YouTypeItWePostIt.User"/>

</EntityContainer>

...

</Schema>
</edmx:DataServices>
</edmx:Edmx>
```

There's nothing wrong with keeping extra information about a resource outside of that resource's representation. After all, that's what a profile or a JSON-LD context does. The problem here is that the CSDL document can be seen as a service description document: an overview of the API as a whole that makes it look like a relational database.

As I mentioned in Chapter 9, users who see a document like this have a tendency to automatically generate client code based on it. Doing this creates a tight coupling between the generated client and this specific edition of the service description. If the server implementation changes, the CSDL document will change along with it, but the clients won't change to match. They'll just break.

Fortunately, no one is making you use OData this way. If you use the media type `application/json;odata=fullmetadata`, your OData representations will contain their own hypermedia controls. A client will only need to consult the CSDL metadata document when it needs to trigger a complicated state transition—a function or action—that can't be completely described with OData.

Pure Hypermedia Formats

These media types have very generic application semantics, or else they have no application semantics at all. They focus on representing the protocol semantics of HTTP. You provide your own application semantics, by plugging link relations and semantic descriptors into predefined slots.

HTML

- **Media types:** `text/html` and `application/xhtml+xml`
- **Defined in:** open standards for HTML 4 (*http://www.w3.org/TR/html401/*), for XHTML (*http://www.w3.org/TR/xhtml11/*), and for HTML 5 (*http://www.w3.org/TR/html5/*)
- **Medium:** XML-like
- **Protocol semantics:** navigation through GET links; arbitrary state transitions through forms (GET for safe transitions, POST for unsafe transitions)
- **Application semantics:** human-readable documents ("paragraph," "list," "table," "section," etc.)
- **Covered in:** Chapter 7

The original hypermedia format, and a highly underrated choice for an API. HTML can make direct use of microformats and microdata, instead of using an approximation such as an ALPS profile. HTML's `<script>` tag lets you embed executable code to be run on the client, a feature of RESTful architectures ("code on demand"; see Appendix C) not supported by any other hypermedia format. And HTML documents can be graphically displayed to human beings—invaluable for APIs designed to be consumed by an Ajax or mobile client, and useful when debugging any kind of API.

Here's HTML's state diagram:

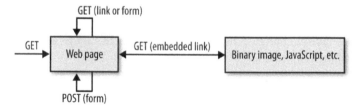

HTML comes in three flavors. HTML 4 has been the stable standard since 1997. HTML 5, its replacement, is still under development. There's also XHTML, an HTML-like format that happens to be valid XML.

As far as this book is concerned, the only important differences between these three standards are HTML 5's new rules for client-side input validation, and the fact that HTML 5 will eventually support microdata.

HAL

- **Media types:** `application/hal+json` and `application/hal+xml`

- **Defined in:** the JSON version is defined in the Internet-Draft "draft-kelly-json-hal"; the XML version is defined in a [personal standard here]
- **Medium:** Either XML or JSON
- **Protocol semantics:** arbitrary state transitions through links that may use any HTTP method; links do not mention the HTTP method to be used—that's kept in human-readable documentation
- **Application semantics:** none to speak of
- **Covered in:** Chapter 7

HAL is a minimalist format. Its state diagram is so generic it looks like something out of the HTTP specification:

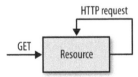

HAL relies on custom link relations (and their human-readable explanations in profiles) to do the heavy lifting.

Siren

- **Media types:** `application/vnd.siren+json`
- **Defined in:** personal standard (*https://github.com/kevinswiber/siren*)
- **Medium:** JSON (an XML version is planned)
- **Protocol semantics:** navigation through GET links; arbitrary state transitions through "actions" (GET for safe actions, POST/PUT/DELETE for unsafe actions)
- **Application semantics:** very generic

A Siren document describes an "entity," a JSON object that has approximately the same semantics as HTML's `<div>` tag. An entity may have a "class" and a list of "properties." It may contain a list of "links," which work like HTML `<a>` tags (with a `rel` and an `href`). It may also contain a list of `actions`, which work like HTML `<form>` tags (with a `name`, an `href`, a `method`, and a number of `fields`).

An entity may also have some number of subentities, similar to how one `<div>` tag may contain another. You can implement the collection pattern this way.

Siren's state diagram looks like a cross between HAL's and HTML's:

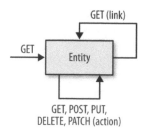

The Link Header

- **Media type:** n/a
- **Described in:** RFC 5988
- **Medium:** HTTP header
- **Protocol semantics:** navigation through GET links
- **Application semantics:** none
- **Covered in:** Chapter 4

The `Link` header is not a document format, but I'm putting it in the zoo because it lets you add simple GET links to representations that lack hypermedia controls, like binary images or JSON documents. The header's `rel` parameter is a slot for the link relation:

```
Link: <http://www.example.com/story/part2>;rel="next"
```

RFC 5988 defines some other useful parameters for the `Link` header, including `type` (which gives a hint as to the media type at the other end of the link) and `title` (which contains a human-readable title for the link).

As far as I'm concerned, the most important use of the `Link` header is to connect a JSON document with a profile. JSON is incredibly popular despite having no hypermedia controls, and the `application/json` media type doesn't support the `profile` parameter, so `Link` is the only reliable way to point to the profile that explains what a JSON document means.

```
Content-Type: application/json
Link: <http://www.example.com/profiles/hydraulics>;rel="profile"
```

The Location and Content-Location Headers

- **Media type:** n/a
- **Described in:** RFC 2616
- **Medium:** HTTP header
- **Protocol semantics:** depends on the HTTP response code

- **Application semantics:** none
- **Covered in:** Chapter 1, Chapter 2, Chapter 3, Appendix B

Here are two simple hypermedia controls defined in the HTTP standard itself. I've mentioned `Location` in passing, but I'll give both detailed coverage in Appendix B.

The `Content-Location` header points to the canonical location of the current resource. It's equivalent to a link that uses the IANA-registered link relation `canonical`.

The `Location` header is used as an all-purpose link whenever the protocol semantics of an HTTP response demand a link. The exact behavior depends on the HTTP status code. When the response code is 201 (`Created`), the `Location` header points to a newly created resource. But when the response code is 301 (`Moved Permanently`), the `Location` header points to the new URL of a resource that moved. Again, the details are in Appendix B.

URL Lists

- **Media type:** `text/uri-list`
- **Medium:** none
- **Described in:** RFC 2483
- **Protocol semantics:** none
- **Application semantics:** none

A `text/uri-list` document is just a list of URLs:

```
http://example.org/
https://www.example.com/
...
```

This is probably the most basic hypermedia type ever devised. It doesn't support link relations, so there's no way to express the relationship between these URLs and the resource that served the list. There are no explicit hypermedia controls, so the client has no way of knowing what kind of requests it's allowed to send to these URLs. The best you can do is send a GET request to each and see what kind of representations you get.

JSON Home Documents

- **Media type:** `application/json-home`
- **Described in:** Internet-Draft "draft-nottingham-json-home"
- **Medium:** JSON
- **Protocol semantics:** completely generic

- **Application semantics:** none

JSON Home Documents are a more sophisticated version of URL lists. The format is intended for use as the "home page" of an API, listing all the resources provided and their behavior under the HTTP protocol.

A JSON Home Document is a JSON object. The keys are link relations, and the values are JSON objects known as "Resource Objects." Here's an example from the world of the maze game:

```
{
 "east": { "href": "/cells/N" },
 "west": { "href": "/cells/L" }
}
```

A Resource Object is a hypermedia control that describes the protocol semantics of a resource, or a group of related resources. Here's a search form, described by a URI Template:

```
{
  "search": {"href-template": "/search{?query}",
             "href-vars": {
                "query" : "http://alps.io/opensearch#searchTerms"
              }
}
```

A Resource Object may include "resource hints" that describe its protocol semantics in more detail. The most common hint is `allow`, which explains which HTTP methods the resource will respond to. Here's a JSON Home Document that uses the `flip` link relation I defined for my extension of the maze game:

```
{
  "flip": { "href": "/switches/4",
            "hints": { "allow": ["POST"] }
          }
}
```

A JSON Home Document says nothing about the application semantics of the resources it links to. That information is kept in the representations on the other side of the links.

By combining a JSON Home Document (which describes an API's protocol semantics) with an ALPS document (which describes its application semantics), you can take an existing API—even one that doesn't use hypermedia—and move most of its human-readable documentation into a structured, machine-readable format.

The Link-Template Header

- **Media type:** n/a

- **Described in:** Internet-Draft "draft-nottingham-link-template" (see also RFC 6570)
- **Medium:** HTTP header
- **Protocol semantics:** navigation through GET
- **Application semantics:** none

The `Link-Template` header works exactly the same way as the `Link` header, except its value is interpreted as a URI Template (RFC 6570) instead of as a URL. Here's a search form in an HTTP header:

```
Link-Template: </search{?family-name}>; rel="search"
```

The `Link-Template` header has a special variable called `var-base`, which allows you to specify a profile for the variables in the URI Template. In the example, the variable name `family-name` is suggestive of what kind of value you should plug into the variable, but it doesn't technically mean anything. It might as well be called `put-something-here`. Add a `var-base`, and suddenly there's a link to a formal definition of `family-name`.

```
Link-Template: </search{?family-name}>; rel="search";↵
var-base="http://alps.io/microformats/hCard#"
```

Now the variable `family-name` expands to the URL *http://alps.io/microformats/hCard#family-name*. The ALPS document at the other end of that URL explains the application semantics of the `family-name` variable.

Here's another example that uses schema.org's application semantics instead of ALPS:

```
Link-Template: </search{?familyName}>; rel="search"; var-base="http://schema.org/"
```

Here, the variable `familyName` expands to the URL *http://schema.org/familyName*, which means basically the same thing as *http://alps.io/microformats/hCard#family-name*.

As of this writing, the Internet-Draft defining the `Link-Template` header has expired. The author of the draft, Mark Nottingham, told me to go ahead and put it in the book anyway. He said he'll revive the Internet-Draft if more people become interested in `Link-Template`.

WADL

- **Media type:** `application/vnd.sun.wadl+xml`
- **Defined in:** open standard (*http://www.w3.org/Submission/wadl/*)
- **Medium:** XML
- **Protocol semantics:** completely generic

- **Application semantics:** none, minimal support for extensions

WADL was the first hypermedia format to support a complete set of protocol semantics. A WADL <request> tag (analogous to an HTML form) can describe an HTTP request that uses any method, provides values for any specified HTTP request headers, and includes an entity-body of any media type. Like AtomPub, this doesn't sound very special now, but it was groundbreaking at the time. WADL can describe the protocol semantics of *any* web API, even one that's poorly designed and violates the HTTP standard.

Here's a snippet of WADL that explains how to flip a switch in Chapter 7's version of the maze game:

```
<method id="flip" name="POST" href="/switches/4">
 <doc>Flip the switch</doc>
</method>
```

WADL can also describe the *content* of XML representations. A WADL document can point out which parts of a representation are interesting—notably, which parts are links to other resources. A WADL document can bring in an XML Schema document to explain the data types of the XML data it describes. This is useful when an XML representation has no associated schema of its own.

WADL's <doc> tag makes it a basic profile format, capable of describing the application semantics of an HTTP request or the inside of an XML representation. But WADL can't describe the inside of a JSON representation at all.[6]

WADL is not in widespread use, but there are some Java JAX-RS implementations that generate WADL descriptions of APIs. Therein lies the problem. An automatically generated description of an API is likely to be tightly coupled to the server-side implementation. What's more, an API that uses WADL typically serves one enormous WADL document describing the protocol semantics of the entire API.

This is a service description document, and as I mentioned in Chapter 9, it encourages users to create automatically generated clients, based on the assumption that they've obtained a complete and unchanging overview of the API's semantics.

But APIs change. When that happens, the WADL description of the API will also change, but the automatically generated clients will not. The clients will break.

XLink

- **Media type:** n/a
- **Defined in:** W3C standard (*http://www.w3.org/TR/xlink11/*)

---

6. The JSON Pointer standard, defined in the Internet-Draft appsawg-json-pointer, may fix this.

- **Medium:** XML documents
- **Protocol semantics:** navigation and transclusion with GET
- **Application semantics:** none

XLink is a plug-in standard that lets you add hypermedia links to any XML document. Unlike HTML and Maze+XML, XLink doesn't define special XML tags that represent hypermedia links. XLink defines a family of attributes that can be applied to *any* XML tag to turn that tag into a link.

Here's an ad hoc XML representation of a cell in the maze game. The <root> and <direction> tags are tag names I made up for demonstration purposes—they have no hypermedia capabilities of their own, but I can turn them into links by adding XLink attributes.

```
<?xml version="1.0"?>
<root xmlns:xlink="http://www.w3.org/1999/xlink">
  <direction
    xlink:href="http://maze-server.com/maze/cell/N"
    xlink:title="Go east!"
    xlink:arcrole="http://alps.io/example/maze/#east"
    xlink:show="replace"
  />

<link
    xlink:href="http://maze-server.com/maze/cell/L"
    xlink:title="Go west!"
    xlink:arcrole="http://alps.io/example/maze/#west"
    xlink:show="replace"
  />
</root>
```

The href and title attributes should look familiar. The link relation goes into the optional arcrole attribute. There's a slight twist here: the arcrole attribute only supports extension link relations—the ones that look like URLs. Your link relation can't look like author or east; it has to look like http://alps.io/maze/#west.

The show attribute lets you switch between a navigation link that works like HTML's <a> tag (show="replace", the default) and an embedding link that works like HTML's <img> tag (show="embed"). The HTTP method used is always GET.

With XLink, I can give an ad hoc XML vocabulary approximately the same hypermedia capabilities that were designed into Maze+XML. There are a few advanced features of XLink I haven't covered: notably, the extended link type, which lets you connect more than two resources using a single link, and the role attribute, which I'll show off in Chapter 12.

XForms

- **Media type:** n/a
- **Medium:** XML documents.
- **Protocol semantics:** arbitrary state transitions through forms (GET for safe transitions, POST/PUT/DELETE for unsafe transitions)
- **Application semantics:** none

XForms does for hypermedia forms what XLink does for links. It's a plug-in standard that adds HTML-like forms to any XML document. Unlike XLink, though, it does define its own tags. Here's how XForms might represent a simple search form:

```
<xforms:model>
 <xforms:submission action="http://example.com/search" method="get"
                    id="submit-button"/>
 <xforms:instance>
  <query/>
 </xforms:instance>
<xforms:model>
```

The `<model>` tag is a container, like HTML's `<form>` tag. The `<submission>` tag explains what HTTP request to make: in this case, a GET request to *http://example.com/search*. The children of the `<instance>` tag explain how to construct the query string (for a GET request) or the entity-body (for a POST or PUT request).

The `<query>` tag is one I made up for this example; it represents a form field called query. The meaning of this tag—e.g., whether it's a text field or a checkbox—is defined separately, in an XForms `<input>` tag:

```
<xforms:input ref="query">
 <xforms:label>Search terms</xforms>
</xforms:input>

<xforms:submit submission="submit-button">
 <label>Search!</label>
</xforms:submit>
```

The `<input>` tag with `ref="query"` says that the query field is a text input with a human-readable `<label>`. The `<submit>` tag gives a `<label>` to the submit button. Together, the `<model>` tag and the two `<input>` tags approximate the functionality of this HTML form:

```
<form action="http://example.com/search" method="GET">
 <input type="text" name="query"/>
 <label for="query">Search terms</label>
 <submit value="Search!">
</form>
```

This is a very basic example; there are many advanced features of XForms that I won't be covering. The W3C's tutorial "XForms for XHTML Authors"[7] uses HTML forms to explain XForms in some detail, going beyond the capabilities of pure HTML into some of the advanced features of XForms.

GeoJSON: A Troubled Type

We've seen the healthy specimens in the hypermedia zoo. Now I'd like to take a look at GeoJSON, a domain-specific document format with some design flaws that hurt its usability in APIs.[8] I'm not doing this to pick on GeoJSON; I've made exactly the same mistakes myself. They're common mistakes, so even if GeoJSON doesn't sound like something you need to learn about right now, stick around.

GeoJSON is a standard based on JSON, designed for representing geographic features like points on a map. Here are its stats:

- **Media type:** `application/json`
- **Defined in:** corporate standard defined here (*http://www.geojson.org/geojson-spec.html*)
- **Medium:** JSON
- **Protocol semantics:** GET for transclusion of coordinate systems
- **Application semantics:** geographic features and collections of features

Like almost all JSON-based documents used in APIs, a GeoJSON document is a JSON object that must contain certain properties. Here's a GeoJSON document that pinpoints the location of an ancient monument on Earth:

```
{
 "type": "FeatureCollection",
 "features":
 [
  {
   "type": "Feature",

   "geometry":
   {
    "type": "Point",
    "coordinates": [12.484281,41.895797]
   },
```

---

7. The tutorial is available at this w3.org page (*http://www.w3.org/MarkUp/Forms/2003/xforms-for-html-authors.html*).

8. These flaws don't hurt GeoJSON so much that no one uses it. It's pretty popular—just not as good as it could be.

```
  "properties":
  {
   "type": null,
   "title": "Column of Trajan",
   "awmc_id": "91644",
   "awmc_link": "http://awmc.unc.edu/api/omnia/91644",
   "pid": "423025",
   "pleiades_link": "http://pleiades.stoa.org/places/423025",
   "description": "Monument to the emperor Marcus Ulpius Traianus"}
  }
 ]
}
```

I adapted this representation slightly from the real-world API provided by UNC's Ancient World Mapping Center (*http://awmc.unc.edu/*). GeoJSON's application semantics are simple, and it should be fairly easy for a human to understand the document. It represents a collection called a `FeatureCollection`. The collection only contains one item: a `Feature`, which has a `geometry` (a single `Point` on the map) and a bunch of miscellaneous `properties` like the human-readable `description`.

A quick look at the GeoJSON standard reveals that instead of a `Point`, the `geometry` could have been a `LineString` (representing a border or a road) or a `Polygon` (representing the area of a city or country).

GeoJSON Has No Generic Hypermedia Controls

Unfortunately, GeoJSON's protocol semantics are anything but straightforward. Do you see `awmc_link` and `pleiades_link` in that representation? They look like hypermedia links, but they're not. According to the GeoJSON standard, those are just strings that happen to look like URLs. When the Ancient World Mapping Center designed their GeoJSON API, they had to stuff all their links into the `properties` list, because GeoJSON doesn't define hypermedia controls for them. This means a generic GeoJSON client can't follow the `pleiades_link`, or even recognize it as a link. To follow that link, you'll need to write a client specifically for the Ancient World Mapping Center's API.

If GeoJSON didn't define any hypermedia controls, this would be understandable. Not every data format has to be a hypermedia format. I simply wouldn't mention GeoJSON in this book. The odd thing is that GeoJSON *does* define a hypermedia control, but it can only be used for one specific thing: changing the coordinate system in use.

By default, the coordinates in a GeoJSON representation (`[12.484281,41.895797]`) are measured in degrees of longitude and latitude—a system we're all familiar with. Since the planet Earth is not a perfect sphere, these measurements are interpreted according to a standard called WGS84,[9] which lays down things like the approximate shape of Earth, the location of the prime meridian, and what "sea level" means.

If you're not a map geek, you can assume Earth is a sphere and be done with it. But for map geeks, WGS84 is just a default. There are many other coordinate systems you could use. British readers may be familiar with the Ordnance Survey National Grid, a coordinate system that uses "easting" and "northing" instead of latitude and longitude, and that can only represent points within a specific 700-by-1300-kilometer area that covers the British Isles. There are *infinitely many* coordinate systems, since you can define a system that puts Earth's prime meridian wherever you want.

And now our story comes back to hypermedia, because this is what GeoJSON's sole hypermedia control is for. GeoJSON lets you link to a description of the coordinate system you're using.

Here's a GeoJSON document containing a genuine hypermedia link that any GeoJSON client will recognize as such:

```
{
 "type":"Feature",
 "geometry":
 {
  "type":"Point",
  "coordinates":[60000,70000]
 },

 "crs": {
  "type": "link",
  "properties": {
    "href": "http://example.org/mygrid.wkt",
    "type": "esriwkt"
    }
  }
}
```

The coordinates [60000,70000] are not valid measurements of longitude and latitude, but that's fine, because we're not using longitude and latitude. We're using a custom coordinate reference system (crs) described by the resource at *http://example.org/ mygrid.wkt*. This is exactly the sort of thing hypermedia is good for. The problem with GeoJSON is that the *only* place it allows a link is within the definition of a coordinate reference system.

This state diagram describes GeoJSON's protocol semantics:

---

9. An industry standard, but from a different industry than the rest of the standards mentioned in this book. You can get a PDF version of the standard at this page (*http://earth-info.nga.mil/GandG/publications/ tr8350.2/tr8350_2.html*).

That's not very useful! Most GeoJSON APIs don't use custom coordinate systems—we're all used to ordinary longitude and latitude. But the GeoJSON standard allows for them, because they are an essential aspect of the problem domain. On the other hand, pretty much any API needs to serve miscellaneous links between its resources, but the GeoJSON standard lacks that capability, presumably because it's *not* directly related to the problem domain. The underlying data format is no help, since JSON defines no hypermedia controls at all. That's why API implementers must resort to hacks like `awmc_link`.

Enough complaining; what would I do differently? A design more focused on hypermedia would allow a list of `links`, each of which could specify a link relation. GeoJSON would look a lot more like Collection+JSON or Siren. Then the Ancient World Mapping Center wouldn't need to smuggle `awmc_link` and `pleiades_link` into the `properties` object.

To link to a coordinate system, you'd use the same kind of link you'd use for anything else. GeoJSON's `crs` would become a link relation, useful in any mapping application, even one that doesn't use GeoJSON.

It's OK to have application-specific hypermedia controls. HTML's `<img>` tag is an application-specific hypermedia control. But you also need to make available a simple, generic link control.

GeoJSON Has No Media Type

There's another problem with GeoJSON: it has no registered media type. A GeoJSON document is served as `application/json`, just like any other JSON document. How is a client supposed to distinguish between GeoJSON and plain old JSON?

The best solution is for the server to treat GeoJSON as a profile of JSON. This means serving a link to the GeoJSON standard with `rel="profile"`. Since JSON on its own has no hypermedia controls, you'll need to use the `Link` header:

```
Link: <http://www.geojson.org/geojson-spec.html>;rel="profile"
```

You could also write an ALPS profile or JSON-LD context for GeoJSON, and serve a link to that using the `Link` header:

```
Link: <http://example.com/geojson.jsonld>;↵
rel="http://www.w3.org/ns/json-ld#context"
```

As far as I know, there's no GeoJSON implementation that does either of these. GeoJSON is served as `application/json` and the client is simply expected to know ahead of time which resources serve GeoJSON representations and which serve ordinary JSON. A

---

client that wants to understand different profiles of JSON must run heuristics against every incoming JSON representation, trying to figure out which profile the server is giving it.

Does it sound unrealistic that one client would need to handle different profiles of JSON? Well, consider this. The ArcGIS platform includes an API that presents the same kind of information as GeoJSON. It serves JSON representations that superficially resemble GeoJSON's representations, and it serves them as `application/json`, with no profile information.

I don't think it's a ludicrous fantasy to imagine a client that can handle both GeoJSON and ArcGIS JSON. If GeoJSON was served as `application/geo+json` and ArcGIS JSON was served as `application/vnd.arcgis.api+json`, a client developer could split up the client code based on the value of the `Content-Type` header, and reunite the code paths once the incoming data was parsed. If GeoJSON and ArcGIS JSON were consistently served as different profiles, a developer could split up the code based on the value of the `Link` header. If they were served with different JSON-LD contexts, a developer could split up the code based on that.

But both formats are served as though they meant the same thing. A unified client must try to distinguish between the two formats using poorly defined heuristics. Or, more likely, the idea of a unified client never occurs to anyone. Like two ships passing in the night, one developer writes a GeoJSON client for GeoJSON APIs, while another duplicates much of the first developer's work, writing an ArcGIS client to run against ArcGIS installations.

No one is to blame for this. The GeoJSON standard was finalized in 2008. Back then, our understanding of hypermedia APIs was pretty poor. The GeoJSON designers didn't forget to register a media type; they considered it and then tabled the issue.

But it's not 2008 anymore. We now have standards that add real hypermedia controls to JSON. We can use profiles to add application-level semantics to generic hypermedia types. We've seen hundreds of one-off, mutually incompatible data formats served as `application/json`, and we know we can do better.

Learning from GeoJSON

When a GeoJSON object is included in a hypermedia-capable JSON document (such as an OData document, which has explicit support for embedded GeoJSON), both of these problems go away. It doesn't matter that GeoJSON has no general hypermedia controls, because it's embedded in a document that can take care of that stuff. It doesn't matter that GeoJSON has no special media type, because it inherits the media type of the parent document. At this point, GeoJSON becomes a plug-in standard, similar to OpenSearch.

If you design a domain-specific format that's not clearly a plug-in for some other format, you should give it a unique media type. It helps if you also register the media type with the IANA, but if you use the vnd. prefix, you don't have to register anything.

Also make sure your format features some kind of general hypermedia control, like Maze+XML's <link> tag. You might think it's not your job to provide a generic hypermedia control, since that has nothing to do with your problem domain. But if you don't provide a hypermedia control, every one of your users will come up with their own one-off design, a la *awmc_link*. You may be able to borrow a simple clip-on hypermedia control by adopting XLink for XML documents, or JSON-LD for JSON documents.

All in all, it may be better to forget the domain-specific media type, and design a domain-specific set of application semantics—a profile. Those semantics can then be plugged in to a general hypermedia type like Siren, or a collection-pattern media type like Collection+JSON.

The Semantic Zoo

I've shown you the wonders of the hypermedia zoo to demonstrate the diversity and flexibility of hypermedia-based designs. Now I'm going to take you on a (much quicker) tour of a different zoo: a series of butterfly gardens full of application semantics for different problem domains. My goal here is more concrete: to help you save time by reusing work other people have already done.

In Chapter 9, I played up the benefits of reusing existing application semantics. The profiles listed here are the result of smart people carefully considering a problem domain and navigating tricky naming issues. There's no reason you should have to duplicate that work. Reusing existing semantics whenever possible also removes the temptation to expose your server's implementation details, leaving you free to change those details without hurting your clients.

Most important of all, when different APIs share the same application semantics, it becomes possible to write interoperable clients, or general semantics-processing libraries, instead of a custom client for each individual API. This is more of a hope than a reality right now, but at least the immediate path forward is clear.

Rather than show you a lot of individual profiles in the semantic zoo, I'll focus mainly on the registries that house the profiles.

The IANA Registry of Link Relations

- **Media types:** any
- **Site:** this IANA page (*http://www.iana.org/assignments/link-relations/*)

- **Semantics:** general navigation

I've talked about the IANA registry of link relations for practically the entire book. It's a global registry containing about 60 link relations. You're allowed to use any IANA-registered relation in any representation, and to assume that your clients know what you're talking about.

Link relations only make it into the IANA registry if they are defined in an open standard such as an RFC or W3C Recommendation, and are generic enough to be useful for any media type. Each link relation is given a short human-readable description and a link to the standard that originally defined it.

In step 3 of Chapter 9's design procedure, I mention several IANA-registered link relations that are especially useful for API design.

The Microformats Wiki

- **Media types:** HTML (ALPS versions are available for some microformats)
- **Site:** this microformats page (*http://microformats.org/wiki/*)
- **Semantics:** the kind of things a human being might want to search for online

The Microformats project was the first successful attempt at defining profiles for application semantics. Microformats are defined collaboratively, on a wiki and mailing list. Of the stable microformats, these are the ones you're most likely to be interested in:

hCalendar
Describes events in time. Based on the plain-text iCalendar format defined in RFC 2445.

hCard
describes people and organizations. Based on the plain-text vCard format (defined in RFC 2426), and covered in Chapter 7.

XFN
A set of link relations describing relationships between people, ranging from `friend` to `colleague` to `sweetheart`.

XOXO
Describes outlines. This microformat is interesting because it doesn't add anything to HTML at all. It just suggests best practices for using HTML's existing application semantics.

These microformat specifications are technically drafts, but most of them haven't changed in several years, so I'd say they're pretty stable:

adr

Physical addresses. This is a subformat of hCard, including only the parts that represent addresses. The idea is that if you don't need all of hCard, you can just use adr.

geo

Latitude and longitude. (Using the WGS84 standard, naturally!) Another subformat of hCard.

hAtom

Blog posts. Based on the Atom feed format (RFC 4287). This is an interesting example of one hypermedia format (HTML) adopting the application semantics of another (Atom).

hListing

Listings of services for hire, personal ads, and so on. This microformat mostly reuses semantics from related microformats: hReview, hCard, and hCalendar.

hMedia

Basic metadata about image, video, and audio files.

hNews

An extension of hAtom that adds a few extra descriptors specific to news articles, like dateline.

hProduct

Product listings.

hRecipe

Recipes.

hResume

Resumes/CVs.

hReview

Describes a review (of anything), with a rating.

There are several interesting microformats I haven't mentioned because they were effectively adopted by HTML 5, and are now IANA-registered link relations: author, nofollow, tag, and license. The rel-payment microformat also became the IANA-registered link relation payment.

I've created ALPS documents that capture the essential application semantics of most of the microformats listed here. They are available from the ALPS registry (*http://alps.io*).

Link Relations from the Microformats Wiki

- **Media types:** HTML
- **Site:** this microformats page (*http://microformats.org/wiki/existing-rel-values*)
- **Semantics:** very, very miscellaneous

The Microformats wiki also has a huge list of link relations defined in standards or seen in real usage, but not registered with the IANA. This wiki page is the official registry for link relations used in HTML 5, but it's also an unofficial registry of *all* link relations that aspire to be useful outside a single application. Maze+XML's link relations would never cut it with the IANA—they're too application-specific—but they're mentioned on the Microformats wiki.

In Chapter 8, I mentioned this wiki page and gave some examples of the relations defined there. I don't recommend simply picking up link relations from this wiki page and using them. Your clients will have no idea what you're talking about. The real advantage of this page is as a way of finding standards you didn't know about before.

If you were planning on making your own maze game API, and you searched this page for `maze` or `north`, you'd discover Maze+XML. You wouldn't necessarily end up *using* Maze+XML, but you'd have a glimpse into how someone else had solved a similar problem.

schema.org

- **Medium:** HTML5, and RDFa (ALPS versions are available)
- **Site:** schema home page (*http://schema.org/*)
- **Semantics:** the kind of things a human being might want to search for online

As I mentioned in Chapter 8, the main source for microdata items is a clearinghouse called schema.org. This site takes the application semantics of standards like rNews (for news) and GoodRelations (for online stores) and ports them to microdata items. In turn, I've automatically generated ALPS documents for schema.org's microdata items and made them available from alps.io.

There are hundreds of microdata items described on schema.org, and more are on the way as the schema.org maintainers work with the creators of other standards to represent those standards in microdata. Rather than talk about all of the microdata items, I'll list the current top-level items and mention some of their notable subclasses:

- CreativeWork (including Article, Blog, Book, Comment, MusicRecording, SoftwareApplication, TVSeries, and WebPage)
- Event (including BusinessEvent, Festival, and UserInteraction)

- Intangible is sort of a catch-all category, which notably includes Audience, Brand, GeoCoordinates, JobPosting, Language, Offer, and Quantity
- MedicalEntity (including MedicalCondition, MedicalTest, and AnatomicalStructure)
- Organization (including Corporation, NGO, and SportsTeam)
- Person
- Place (including City, Mountain, and TouristAttraction)
- Product (including ProductModel)

As you can see, there's a lot of overlap between schema.org microdata items and the microformats. The Person item covers the same ground as the hCard microformat. The Event item is similar to hEvent, Article to hAtom, NewsArticle to hNews, Recipe to hRecipe, GeoCoordinates to geo, and so on.

A word of caution: the schema.org microdata items are very consumer-focused. A Product is something the client can buy, not a project the client is working on. The semantics of the Restaurant item have a lot to do with eating at a restaurant, and almost nothing to do with running one or inspecting one. There's a SoftwareApplication item, but nothing for a bug, a unit test, a version control repository, a release milestone, or any of the other things we deal with when we *develop* software. To my eyes, the only item described in enough detail to be useful to a practitioner is MedicalEntity, and a doctor would probably disagree with me on that.

In short, the schema.org project has a definite point of view. It's not encyclopedic, and even if it defines an item that overlaps with your API's domain, the application semantics it defines may have nothing to do with how you look at things.

Dublin Core

- **Medium:** HTML, XML, RDF, or plain text
- **Site:** Dublin Core home page (*http://dublincore.org/*)
- **Semantics:** published works

The Dublin Core is the original standard for defining application semantics, dating all the way back to 1995. It defines 15 bits of semantics for information about published works: `title`, `creator`, `description`, and so on. These bits of semantics can be used either as semantic descriptors or as link relations.

The Dublin Core Metadata Initiative has also defined a more complete profile, the DCMI Metadata Terms. This profile includes semantic descriptors like `dateCopyrighted`, as well as link relations like `isPartOf` and `replaces`.

Activity Streams

- **Medium:** Atom, JSON
- **Site:** Activity Streams home page (*http://activitystrea.ms/*)
- **Families:** things human beings do online

Activity Streams is a corporate standard for representing our online lives as a sequence of discrete "activities." Each activity has an actor (usually a human being who's using a computer), a verb (something the actor is doing), and an object (the thing to which the actor is doing the verb).

When you watch a video online, that's an activity. You are the actor, the video is the object, and the verb (according to Activity Streams) is the literal string "play." Some activities have a target as well as an object. When I publish a new entry to my blog, I am the actor, the blog entry is the object, the verb is "post," and the target is my blog.

I've put Activity Streams in this section, even though it's a data format, because the data format doesn't define any hypermedia controls. But there are a lot of really useful semantics in here. Activity Streams defines names and semantic descriptors for a lot of the things we interact with online (`Article`, `Event`, `Group`, `Person`). More important, it defines a lot of useful names for verbs (`join`, `rsvp-yes`, `follow`, `cancel`), which make sense as the names of unsafe state transitions.

The Activity Streams standard explains how to represent a sequence of activities as an Atom feed. Use this and Activity Streams will be a real hypermedia format, an extension to Atom.

There's also a standalone JSON-based version of Activity Streams. It has the same problems as GeoJSON: there are no hypermedia controls, and no way to distinguish Activity Streams documents from plain JSON documents.[10] To add hypermedia controls to a JSON Activity Streams document, you'll need to use JSON-LD or Hydra (Chapter 12).

There's a lot of overlap between Activity Streams' semantics and schema.org's microdata items. There are microdata items called Article, Event, Group, and Person. The User-Checkins microdata item is like Activity Streams' "checkin" verb, UserLikes is like "like," and UserPlays is like "play." (For the record, Activity Streams predates schema.org.)

The ALPS Registry

I've set up a registry of ALPS profiles at this page (*http://alps.io/*) for general reuse. As part of my work to liberate application semantics from their media types, I've created

---

10. The Internet-Draft "draft-snell-activity-streams-type" will solve the second problem. It registers the media type `application/stream+json` for Activity Streams documents.

ALPS versions of the schema.org metadata items, several microformats, and the Dublin Core. That's just a start; hopefully by the time you read this I'll have made ALPS profiles that convey the application semantics of other standards as well.

If you want to use an ALPS profile to define your API's application semantics, you can search alps.io to find a profile that works for you, or assemble a new profile out of bits of existing profiles.

If you decide to use an ALPS profile in your API, feel free to reference bits of the profiles in the ALPS Registry. Once you're done, I'd appreciate it if you'd upload the profile to the ALPS Registry (as well as hosting it locally as part of your API). That way other people can find and reuse your application semantics.

HTTP for APIs

Think of the World Wide Web (and of any other RESTful API) as a technology stack. URLs are on the bottom; they identify resources. The HTTP protocol sits on top of those resources, providing read access to their representations and write access to the underlying resource state. Hypermedia sits on top of HTTP, describing the protocol semantics of one particular website or API.

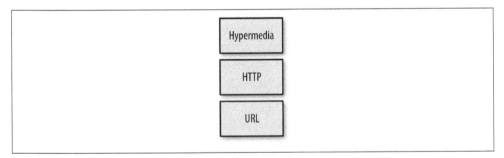

Figure 11-1. The technology stack that forms the World Wide Web

The bottom layer answers the question "Where is the resource?" The middle layer answers the question "How do I communicate with the resource?" The top layer answers the question "What next?"

So far, this book has focused on the top layer of the stack—"What next?" That's because the top layer is the tricky one. Most of today's APIs use URLs and HTTP correctly, but don't even bother with hypermedia.

In this chapter, I take a break from hypermedia, and go down a level to explain the advanced protocol semantics of HTTP. I don't want to explain the HTTP protocol in detail; for that, I recommend *HTTP: The Definitive Guide*, by David Gourley and Brian

Totty (O'Reilly). I'll focus on features of HTTP that are especially useful in APIs, and features that new API developers may not be aware of.

The New HTTP/1.1 Specification

Throughout this book I've used "RFC 2616" as a shorthand for the HTTP 1.1 specification. But Roy Fielding (of Fielding dissertation fame) and an IETF working group are working on a series of replacement RFCs that will render RFC 2616 obsolete.

Nothing about the HTTP protocol will change; the point is to improve the documentation. The new RFCs clarify HTTP's protocol semantics, and consolidate some add-ons that were defined after RFC 2616 was published, such as the definition of the *https://* URI scheme.

Hopefully the new RFCs have been published by the time you read this. But if they're still works in progress, you can read the drafts by going to the working group's document list (*http://datatracker.ietf.org/wg/httpbis/*). It's an easier way to understand some arcane part of the HTTP protocol than poring over RFC 2616.

Response Codes

RFC 2616 defines 41 HTTP response codes. Some of them are useless for our purposes, but collectively, they represent a basic set of semantics, defined in the most fundamental of all API standards. There's no excuse for ignoring this gift. If you reinvent 404 (Not Found) or 409 (Conflict) for your API, you're just creating more work for everybody. *Use your response codes.*

If a client sends some bad data to your API, you should send the response code 400 (Bad Request) and an entity-body explaining what the problem is. *Don't* send 200 (OK) with an error message. You're lying to the client. You'll have to write extra documentation explaining that in your API, OK sometimes doesn't mean "OK."

In Appendix A, I talk about all of the response codes defined in the HTTP standard, and a few more useful codes defined in supplementary RFCs.

Headers

RFC 2616 defines 47 HTTP request and response headers. As with response codes, some are nearly useless, but collectively they define a basic set of semantics that *every* API can benefit from. *Use them.*

A few headers correspond to features of HTTP that are important to APIs: notably, content negotiation and conditional requests. I've given these features their own sections in this chapter. In Appendix B, I talk about *all* the headers defined by the HTTP standard.

I also cover a number of useful extensions: notably, the Link header, which you've seen already.

Choosing Between Representations

A single resource may have many representations. Usually the representations are in different data formats: many web APIs serve XML and JSON "flavors" of all their resources. Sometimes the representations contain prose that's been translated into different human languages. Sometimes the different representations represent different bits of resource state: a resource may have an "overview representation" and a "detail representation.":

When a server offers multiple representations for one resource, how is the client supposed to distinguish between them? How does a client signal whether it wants English or Spanish, XML or JSON, overview or detail? There are two main strategies.

Content Negotiation

The client can use special HTTP request headers to tell the server which representations it wants. This process is called *content negotiation*, and the HTTP standard defines five request headers for it. They're collectively called the Accept-* headers. I'll cover all five in Appendix B, but here I want to highlight the two most important: Accept and Accept-Language.

Most web API clients only understand a single media type. When they make a request, they send a simple Accept header, asking for that media type:

```
Accept: application/vnd.collection+json
```

The client tells the server that it only understands Collection+JSON. If the server has the option of serving Atom or Collection+JSON, it should serve Collection+JSON.

When I make an HTTP request from my web browser, it sends a much more complicated Accept header:

```
Accept: text/html,application/xhtml+xml,application/xml;q=0.9,*/*;q=0.8
```

RFC 2616 gives the complex details of what can go into an Accept-* header, but this real-life example serves as a good indicator of what's possible. The main job of a web browser is to display web pages, so my browser gives top priority to HTML representations (the text/html media type) and XHTML representations (application/xhtml). My browser can also display raw XML (application/xml), but since that doesn't look as nice, XML is given a lower priority than HTML (q=0.9). If neither HTML nor XML representations are available (maybe because the resource is a binary image), my browser will accept any media type at all (*/*). But that's a last-ditch option, and it's given the lowest priority of all (q=0.8).

My web browser also has a setting for language preferences: which languages I'd prefer to get web pages in. With every HTTP request I make, my browser transforms my language preferences into a value for the Accept-Language header:

```
Accept-Language: en-us,en;q=0.5
```

This says I would prefer American English, but I'll accept any dialect of English as a second-best substitute. (I'm actually not this picky about it, but that's what I told my web browser.)

If the server can't fulfill a request due to Accept-* restrictions, it can send the response code 406 (Not Acceptable).

Negotiating a profile

In Chapter 8, I kind of dismissed the profile media type parameter, because not many media types support it, but it has a big advantage in content negotiation. When a media type supports the profile parameter, you can use content negotiation to ask for a specific profile. Here's a client that wants an XHTML representation that uses the hCard microformat:

```
Accept: application/xml+xhtml;profile="http://microformats.org/wiki/hcard"
```

This client wants the same data format (XHTML), but wants the data presented as schema.org microdata:

```
Accept: application/xml+xhtml;profile="http://schema.org/Person"
```

You can't do that if the profile is conveyed through the Link header. And, of course, you can't do it if the media type doesn't support the profile parameter.

Hypermedia Menus

That's content negotiation. But consider how a client finds the representation it wants *in general*. There's no "resource negotiation" process. Instead, the client makes a GET request to an API's billboard URL, and the server serves a home page representation that includes hypermedia links to other resources. The client chooses which link it wants to follow, and makes another GET request for another representation. The client finds the resource it's looking for by making choices, one after another.

This strategy works just as well when the choices are choices between data formats. HTTP's content negotiation features merely optimize for a few common cases. Instead of using them, you can give each representation its own URL, effectively making it an independent resource.

A server offers a choice between these resources by sending the response code 300 (Multiple Choices). The entity-body should contain a hypermedia document that links to the different choices. If you do it this way, you'll need to use a hypermedia format capable of explaining what sort of thing is on the other end of a link. Otherwise, your clients will have no way of deciding which link to click.

HTML's `<a>` and `<link>` tags have good support for this, with the `type` attribute:

```
<a href="/resource/siren" type="application/vnd.siren+json" rel="alternate">
 The Siren version.
</a>

<a href="/resource/html" type="text/html" rel="alternate">
 The HTML version.
</a>
```

The `hreflang` attribute is a hint as to the language at the other end of the link:

```
<a href="/resource.es" hreflang="es">
 Para la versión en español, haga clic aquí.
</a>
```

Since most hypermedia formats don't have these features, I generally recommend header-based content negotiation for this.

The Canonical URL

Whenever a resource has more than one URL, you should identify one of them as the official or canonical URL: the one clients should use when *talking about* the resource rather than sending HTTP requests to it.

There are two ways of doing this. First, you can use the standard HTTP header `Content-Location` as a hypermedia control that points to the current resource's canonical URL. There's also the IANA-registered link relation `canonical`, which serves the same purpose. You can use `canonical` within a representation or in the `Link` header.

HTTP Performance

HTTP clients are allowed to make whatever HTTP requests they want, whenever they want. But some requests turn out to be pointless wastes of time. HTTP defines several optimizations for discouraging requests that are likely to be pointless (caching), for reducing the cost of a request that turns out to be pointless (conditional requests), and for reducing the cost of a request in general (compression).

Caching

Caching is one of the most complex parts of HTTP. RFC 2616 contains detailed rules for cache invalidation, and there are many issues involving HTTP intermediaries like caching proxies. I'm going to focus on the simplest way to add caching to web APIs, using the HTTP header `Cache-Control`. In Appendix B, I'll also discuss the `Expires` header, which is useful in another common scenario. For anything more complex, I'll refer you to HTTP: The Definitive Guide, and to the Internet-Draft "draft-ietf-httpbis-p6-cache," which is part of the current effort to replace RFC 2616.

Here's the `Cache-Control` header in action, as part of a response to an HTTP GET request:

```
HTTP/1.1 200 OK
Content-Type: text/html
Cache-Control: max-age=3600
...
```

The `max-age` directive says how long the client should wait before making this HTTP request again. If a client gets this response and half an hour later, it wants to send the request again, it should hold off. The server said to check back in an hour (3,600 seconds), and not before.

A caching directive applies to the entire HTTP response, including the headers and the response code, not just to the entity-body. The idea is that if the client really needs to look at an HTTP response, it should look at the cached response instead of making the request again.

Another common use of `Cache-Control` is for the server to tell the client *not* to cache a response, even if it would otherwise:

```
HTTP/1.1 200 OK
Content-Type: text/html
Cache-Control: no-cache
...
```

This indicates that the resource state is so volatile that the representation probably become obsolete during the time it took to send it.

Setting `Cache-Control` when you serve a representation requires that you make a judgment call on how often a representation will change. If you get this wrong, it can lead to your users having data that's out of date.

For representations that consist entirely of hypermedia controls, representations that only change when you upgrade your API implementation, it makes sense to set `max-age` pretty high. Or you can use…

Conditional GET

Sometimes you just don't know when a resource's state will change. (Collection-type resources are the worst for this.) It might change all the time, or it might change so rarely that you can't estimate how often a change happens. Either way, you can't decide on a value for `max-age`, so you can't tell the client to stop making requests for that resource for a while. Instead, you can let the client make its request whenever it wants, and eliminate the server's *response* if nothing has changed.

This client-side feature is called a *conditional request*, and to support it, you'll need to serve the Last-Modified or ETag header with your representations (better yet, serve both). The Last-Modified header tells the client when the state of this resource last changed. Here it is in an example HTTP response:

```
HTTP/1.1 200 OK
Content-Length: 41123
Content-type: text/html
Last-Modified: Mon, 21 Jan 2013 09:35:19 GMT

<html>
...
```

The client makes a note of the Last-Modified value, and the next time it makes a request, it puts that value in the HTTP header If-Modified-Since:

```
GET /some-resource HTTP/1.1
If-Modified-Since: Mon, 21 Jan 2013 09:35:19 GMT
```

If the resource state has changed since the date given in If-Modified-Since, then nothing special happens. The server sends the status code 200, an updated Last-Modified, and a full representation:

```
HTTP/1.1 200 OK
Content-Length: 44181
Content-type: text/html
Last-Modified: Mon, 27 Jan 2013 07:57:10 GMT

<html>
...
```

But if the representation hasn't changed since the last request, the server sends the status code 304 (Not Modified), and *no entity-body*:

```
HTTP/1.1 304 Not Modified
Content-Length: 0
Last-Modified: Mon, 27 Jan 2013 07:57:10 GMT
```

This saves both parties time and bandwidth. The server doesn't have to send the representation and the client doesn't have to receive it. If the representation was one that gets dynamically generated from the resource state, a conditional request also saves the server the effort of generating the representation.

Of course, this means some extra work for you. You'll need to track the last-modified date of all your resources. And remember that the value for Last-Modified is the date the *representation* changed. If you have a collection resource whose representation includes bits of other representations, that resource's Last-Modified represents the last time *any* of that stuff changed.

There's another strategy that is easier to implement than `Last-Modified`, and that avoids some race conditions. The `ETag` header (it stands for "entity tag") contains a nonsensical string that must change whenever the corresponding representation changes.

Here's an example HTTP response that includes `ETag`:

```
HTTP/1.1 200 OK
Content-Length: 44181
Content-type: text/html
ETag: "7359b7-a37c-45b333d7"

<html>
...
```

When the client makes a second request for the same resource, it sets the `If-None-Match` header to the ETag it got in the original response:

```
GET /some-resource HTTP/1.1
If-None-Match: "7359b7-a37c-45b333d7"
```

If the ETag in `If-None-Match` is the same as the representation's current ETag, the server sends 304 (`Not Modified`) and an empty entity-body. If the representation has changed, the server sends 200 (`OK`), a full entity-body, and an updated `ETag`.

Serving `Last-Modified` requires that you keep track of a lot of timestamps, but you can generate ETags for representations without tracking any extra data at all. A transformation like the MD5 hash can turn any string of bytes into a short string that's reliably unique.

The problem is, by the time you can run one of those transformations, you've already created the representation as a string of bytes. You may end up saving bandwidth by not sending the representation over the wire, but you've already done the work necessary to build it. Using `ETag` to save time, as opposed to bandwidth, requires that you cache a representation's ETag and invalidate the cache when the representation changes.

Either `Last-Modified` or `ETag` will give you support for conditional requests, but serving both would be ideal, and `ETag` is more reliable than `Last-Modified`.

Look-Before-You-Leap Requests

Conditional GET is designed to save the server from sending enormous representations to a client that already has them. Another feature of HTTP, less often used, can save the *client* from fruitlessly sending enormous (or sensitive) representations to the *server*. There's no official name for this kind of request, so the original *RESTful Web Services* introduced a silly name—look-before-you-leap requests—which seems to have stuck.

To make a LBYL request, a client sends an unsafe request such as a PUT, omitting the entity-body. The client sets the `Expect` request header to the literal string `100-continue`. Here's a sample LBYL request:

```
PUT /filestore/myfile.txt HTTP/1.1
Host: example.com
Content-length: 524288000
Expect: 100-continue
```

This is not a real PUT request: it's a question about a possible future PUT request. The client is asking the server: "would you allow me to PUT a new representation to *filestore/myfile.txt*? The server makes its decision based on the current state of that resource, and the HTTP headers provided by the client. In this case, the server would examine `Content-Length` and decide whether it's willing to accept a 500 MB file.

If the answer is yes, the server sends a status code of 100 (`Continue`). Then the client is expected to resend the PUT request, omitting the `Expect` and including the 500 MB representation in the entity-body. The server has agreed to accept that representation.

If the answer is no, the server sends a status code of 417 (`Expectation Failed`). The answer might be no because the resource at */filestore/myfile.txt* is write-protected, because the client didn't provide the proper authentication credentials, or because 500 MB is just too big. Whatever the reason, the initial look-before-you-leap request has saved the client from sending 500 MB of data only to have that data rejected. Both client and server are better off.

Of course, a client with a bad representation can lie about it in the headers just to get a status code of 100, but it won't do any good. The server won't accept a bad representation on the second request, any more than it would have on the first request. The client's massive upload will probably be interrupted by response code 413 (`Request Entity Too Large`).

Compression

Textual representations like JSON and XML documents can be compressed to a fraction of their original size. An HTTP client library can request a compressed version of a representation and then transparently decompress it for its user.

Here's how it works. When a client sends a request, it includes an `Accept-Encoding` header that says which compression algorithms the client understands. The IANA keeps a registry of acceptable values at this IANA page (*http://www.iana.org/assignments/http-parameters/http-parameters.xml*) (it's the list of "content-codings"), but the value you want to use is `gzip`:

```
GET /resource.html HTTP/1.1
Host: www.example.com
Accept-Encoding: gzip
```

If the server understands one of the compression algorithms mentioned in `Accept-Encoding`, it can use that algorithm to compress the representation before serving it. The server sends the same `Content-Type` it would send if the representation wasn't compressed. But it also sends the `Content-Encoding` header, so the client knows the document has been compressed:

```
HTTP/1.1 200 OK
Content-Type: text/html
Content-Encoding: gzip

[Binary representation goes here.]
```

The client decompresses the data using the algorithm given in `Content-Encoding`, and then treats it as the media type given as `Content-Type`. In this case, the client would use the `gzip` algorithm to decompress the binary data back into an HTML document. As far as the client is concerned, it asked for HTML and it got HTML. This technique can save a lot of bandwidth, with very little cost in additional complexity.

Partial GET

HTTP partial GET allows a client to fetch only a subset of a representation. It's usually used to resume interrupted downloads. Most web servers support partial GET for static content. If your API serves big static files, it's worth the effort to support partial GET on them.

A resource that supports partial GET advertises this fact in response to a normal GET, by setting the `Accept-Ranges` response header to the literal string `bytes`. Here's the response to a successful GET request for a very large video file:

```
HTTP/1.1 200 OK
Content-Length: 1271174395
Accept-Ranges: bytes
Content-Type: video/mpeg

[Binary representation goes here.]
```

If the download is interrupted, a client that supports partial GET can resume the download from the point of interruption, rather than starting over. Here's a request for just the last kilobyte of that video file:

```
GET /large-video-file
Range: 1271173371-
```

The response would look like this:

```
206 Partial Content
content-Type: video/mpeg
Content-Range: 1271173371-1271174395
Content-Length: 1024
```

```
[Binary representation goes here.]
```

In theory, partial GET can be used to slice up a representation not into chunks of bytes, but into *logical* parts. In this fantasy world, the `Accept-Range` header would have a value other than `bytes`, and the `Range` header would be used to retrieve, let's say, items 2 through 5 of a collection.

This is a nice idea, but there are no standards in this area, and I'm generally opposed to making up your own protocol semantics. If you want to split up a collection so that it takes several HTTP requests to get the whole thing, you should create several "page" resources and link their representations together using IANA-registered link relations like `next` and `previous`.

Pipelining

Pipelining reduces latency by allowing the client to send several HTTP requests at once. The server sends back responses from the server in the order it received the requests. Pipelining depends on, but is different from, persistent connections, a feature of HTTP that lets a client send several requests over a single TCP connection.

A client may pipeline any series of idempotent HTTP requests, so long as *the series as a whole* is also idempotent. If the connection is interrupted, you must be able to play back the entire series and get the same result.

Here's a simple example. I'm going to send two requests over a pipeline. First I'll retrieve a representation of a resource, and then I'll delete the resource:

```
GET /resource
DELETE /resource
```

GET and DELETE are idempotent, but their combination is not. If there's a network problem after I send these requests, and I don't get the first response out of the pipeline, I won't be able to send the requests again and get the same result. The resource won't be there anymore. Due to this complication, I only recommend pipelining for strings of GET requests.

On top of that complication, pipelining frequently doesn't help performance. Pipelining only pays off if the client makes a long series of HTTP requests to the same domain, and most websites include elements from different domains.

Non-browser API clients tend to make long series of requests to a single domain, but pipelining isn't terribly useful for hypermedia-based APIs, either, because a hypermedia API generally requires that a client examine the response to one request before making another. Maybe that's why most programmable HTTP client libraries don't support pipelining, either.

Basically, this feature is kind of a bust. The HTTP 2.0 protocol (covered in the final section of this chapter) should implement HTTP pipelining in a more useful way. As it is, pipelining could be useful for a client like Chapter 5's mapmaker, or a client that runs on a high-latency mobile device. It's not a must-have like conditional GET, but when you're thinking of performance improvements, pipelining is worth considering. That's the highest recommendation I can give it, though.

Avoiding the Lost Update Problem

I introduced `ETag` and `Last-Modified` as a way of saving time and bandwidth when making GET requests. But conditional requests are also useful as a way of avoiding data loss when using unsafe HTTP methods like PUT and PATCH.

Suppose Alice and Bob are using different API clients to edit a grocery list. They start by making identical HTTP requests:

```
GET /groceries HTTP/1.1
Host: www.example.com
```

And retrieving identical representations:

```
HTTP/1.1 200 OK
Content-Type: text/plain
ETag: "7359b7-a37c-45b333d7"
Last-Modified: Mon, 27 Jan 2013 07:57:10 GMT

Pastrami
Sauerkraut
Bagels
```

Alice adds an item to the list and PUTs back the new representation:

```
PUT /groceries HTTP/1.1
Host: www.example.com
Content-Type: text/plain

Pastrami
Sauerkraut
Bagels
Eggs
```

She gets a response of 200 (OK).

Bob, unaware of what Alice is doing, adds an item to the list and PUTs back *his* new representation:

```
PUT /groceries HTTP/1.1
Host: www.example.com
Content-Type: text/plain

Pastrami
```

```
Sauerkraut
Bagels
Milk
```

Bob also gets a response of 200 (OK). But Alice's version of the list—the version that included "Eggs"—has been lost. Bob never even knew about that version.

This sort of tragedy can be avoided by making unsafe requests conditional. With conditional GET, we wanted the request to go through only if the representation had changed. Here, Bob wants his PUT request to go through only if the representation has *not* changed. The technique is the same, but the conditional is reversed. Instead of If-Match, the client uses the opposite header, If-None-Match. Instead of If-Modified-Since, the client uses If-Unmodified-Since.

Suppose Bob had made his PUT request conditional:

```
PUT /groceries HTTP/1.1
Host: www.example.com
Content-Type: text/plain
If-Match: "7359b7-a37c-45b333d7"
If-Unmodified-Since: Mon, 27 Jan 2013 07:57:10 GMT

Pastrami
Sauerkraut
Bagels
Milk
```

Instead of 200 (OK), the server would have sent the status code 412 (Precondition Failed). Bob's client would then know that someone else had modified the grocery list. Instead of overwriting the current representation, Bob's client could send a GET request for the new representation, and try to merge it with Bob's version. Or it could escalate the issue and ask Bob to deal with it himself. It depends on the media type and the application.

In my opinion, your API implementations should *require* clients to make conditional PUT and PATCH requests. If a client tries to make an unconditional PUT or PATCH, you should send the status code 428 (Precondition Required).

Authentication

For simplicity's sake, the examples I've presented throughout this book don't require any kind of authentication. You make an HTTP request, and you get a response. There are plenty of real APIs like this, but most APIs require authentication.

There are two steps to authentication. Step 1 is a one-time step in which a user sets up her credentials with the service provider. Usually this means a human being using her web browser to create an account on the API server, or tying in some existing user account on a website with the API server.

Step 2 is the automated presentation of the user credentials along with each request to the API.

Why present the user credentials along with *every* HTTP request? Because of the statelessness constraint, which allows the server to completely forget about a client between requests. There are no sessions in a RESTful server implementation.[1]

Some authentication techniques also include a "step zero" called *registration*. Here, a developer uses her web browser to set up credentials for a software client she is writing. If a thousand people end up using that client, each will have to set up her own personal user credentials (step 1), but they will all share a set of client credentials. When an API adopts this technique, a client that wants to make an HTTP request must present both its client credentials and a set of user credentials.

The WWW-Authenticate and Authorization Headers

I'm about to cover three popular authentication techniques. First I'll talk about what all three have in common: HTTP's authentication headers.

Our story begins, as it did in Chapter 1, with our heroine Alice making a simple request for a representation:

```
GET / HTTP/1.1
Host: api.example.com
```

But this time, the server *refuses* to serve the requested representation. Instead, it serves an error:

```
401 Unauthorized HTTP/1.1
WWW-Authenticate: Basic realm="My API"
```

The 401 response code is a demand for authorization. The WWW-Authenticate header explains what sort of authorization the server will accept. In this case, the server wants the client to use HTTP Basic authentication.

Alice needs to get some credentials… somehow. The details depend on the authentication mechanism in use. Once she's got her credentials she can make the HTTP request again, sending her credentials in the Authorization request header:

```
GET / HTTP/1.1
Host: api.example.com
Authorization: Basic YWxpY2U6cGFzc3dvcmQ=

This time, the server will hopefully give Alice the representation she asked for.
```

---

1. If you ignore this advice and implement sessions in your API, the session ID becomes a kind of temporary credential, presented with every request. All you've done is add another layer of complexity on top of the existing credential system.

Basic Auth

HTTP Basic authentication is described in RFC 2617. It's a simple username/password scheme. The user of an API is supposed to set up a username and password ahead of time—probably by registering an account on an affiliated website, or by sending an email requesting an API account. There's no standard for how to request a username and password for a given site.

However it happens, once Alice has her username and password, she can make that original HTTP request again. This time she uses her username and password to generate a value for the request header `Authorization`, as seen in the previous section.

The server authenticates her, accepts the request and serves a representation instead of a 401 error:

```
HTTP/1.1 200 OK
Content-Type: application/xhtml+xml
...
```

Basic Auth is simple, but it has two big problems. The first is that it's not secure. `YWx pY2U6cGFzc3dvcmQ=` looks like encrypted gibberish, but it's actually the string `alice:password` run through a simple, reversible transform called Base64.[2] This means that anyone spying on Alice's Internet connection now knows her password. They can impersonate Alice by sending HTTP requests that include `Authorization: Basic YWx pY2U6cGFzc3dvcmQ=`.

This problem goes away if the API uses HTTPS instead of plain HTTP. Someone spying on Alice's Internet connection will see her open a connection, but the request and response will be encrypted by the SSL layer.

RFC 2617 defines a second authentication method called Digest, which avoids this problem even when HTTPS is not in use. I'm not covering Digest in this book because Digest and Basic share a *second* problem, which is not a big deal on the World Wide Web, but is very serious in the world of APIs: the people who use an API generally *can't trust their clients*.

To make the problem obvious, imagine a very popular API such as the Twitter API. This API is so popular that Alice is using *10 different clients* for this one API. There are a few on her mobile phone, a few on her desktop computer, and she's given permission to several different websites to use this API on her behalf. (This happens all the time.)

Ten different clients. What happens when one of the clients goes rogue and starts posting spam to Alice's account? (This also happens frequently.)

---

2. Base64 is defined in section 6.8 of RFC 2045. Most programming languages have a Base64 implementation in their standard libraries.

In the wake of the attack, Alice must change her password. She must do this so that the rogue client no longer has valid credentials. But she's given all 10 clients the same password. Nine of the clients are still trustworthy, but changing the password breaks all 10. After changing her password, Alice must go through her nine good clients and tell them the new password. If one of the nine goes rogue, she has to change her password again and go through the eight good clients, telling each one again about her new password.

This wouldn't have been a problem if Alice had been able to give each client a different set of credentials in the first place. That's where OAuth comes in.

OAuth 1.0

Under OAuth, Alice gives each client an individual set of credentials. If she decides she doesn't like one of the clients, she revokes its credentials, and the other nine clients are unaffected. If a client goes rogue and starts posting spam under the names of its users, the service provider can step in and revoke the credentials for *every instance* of that client—Alice's and everyone else's.

There are two versions of OAuth. OAuth 1.0 (defined in RFC 5849) works well for allowing the developers of consumer-facing websites to integrate with your API. It starts falling apart when you want to allow the integration of desktop, mobile, or in-browser applications with your API. OAuth 2.0 is very similar to 1.0, but it defines ways to handle these scenarios.

I'm going to briefly describe the concepts behind OAuth using OAuth 1.0, and point you to Ryan Boyd's Getting Started with OAuth 2.0 (O'Reilly) for a readable, detailed explanation of OAuth 2.0.

Here's what a 401 response code looks like when the server wants a client to provide a set of OAuth credentials:

```
HTTP/1.1 401 Unauthorized
WWW-Authorization: OAuth realm="My API"
```

Obtaining those credentials is an elaborate process. Let's suppose Alice is using a website, *YouTypeItWePostIt.com*. She sees a hypermedia control that tells her she can integrate her account on *Example.net* with her account on *YouTypeItWePostIt.com*. She can do this without telling *YouTypeItWePostIt.com* her password on *Example.net* (see Figure 11-2).

Figure 11-2. YouTypeItWePostIt.com with prompt to login via Example.net

This seems like a good idea to Alice, so she clicks the button to activate the hypermedia control. What happens next?

1. The *YouTypeItWePostIt.com* server secretly requests a set of *temporary credentials* from the API provider, *api.example.net*. This step does not require Alice's involvement at all.

2. The *YouTypeItWePostIt.com* server sends an HTTP redirect to Alice's browser. Alice leaves the website she was using, and ends up on a web page served by the API provider, *Example.net*.

   If Alice is not already logged in on *Example.net*, she needs to log in or create a user account. This means entering her password—but note that she's giving her *Example.net* password to *api.example.net*, not to *YouTypeItWePostIt.com*.

3. After logging in, Alice sees a web page that is tied to the temporary credentials obtained in step 1. The human-readable text of the page explains to Alice what's going on, and asks her if she wants to authorize a set of *api.example.net* token credentials for *YouTypeItWePostIt.com* (see Figure 11-3).

4. Alice makes her decision and her browser is redirected back to *YouTypeItWePostIt.com*, the site she was using originally.

5. a) If Alice said "no" in step 4, the client is out of luck. It won't be getting any `api.example.net` token credentials from Alice.

   b) If Alice said "yes" in step 4, the client is allowed to *exchange* the temporary credentials obtained in step 1, for a set of real *token credentials*. These credentials can be used to cryptographically sign HTTP requests, generating `Authorization` headers like the one in this request:

```
GET / HTTP/1.1
Host: api.example.net
Authorization: OAuth realm="Example API",
    oauth_consumer_key="rQLd1PciL0sc3wZ",
    oauth_signature_method="HMAC-SHA1",
    oauth_timestamp="1363723000",
    oauth_nonce="JFI8Bq",
    oauth_signature="4HBjJvupgIYbeEy4kEOLS%Ydn6qyV%UY"
```

At that point, the client can use the API normally, as though it were Alice.

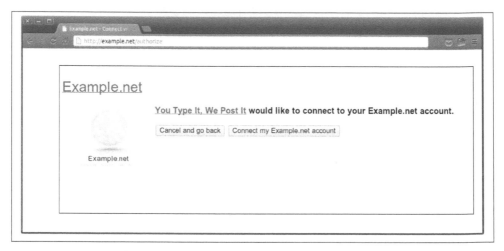

Figure 11-3. Example.net requesting Alice's credentials on behalf of YouTypeItWePostIt.com

Depending on the API, the token credentials may be permanent, or they may automatically expire after a time. (Once they expire, the client will need to send Alice through this process again if it wants to keep using the API.) The token credentials might give the client access to everything Alice can do with the API, or they might allow only a subset of what Alice can do. (One common restriction is read-only access to the API.) These are just a few of the things that are not specified in the OAuth standard, and must be defined by the API provider.

You can see that OAuth is a lot more complicated than HTTP Basic Auth, but—I can't stress this enough—it keeps Alice from having to give her password to 10 different pieces of software she doesn't trust. The complexities of OAuth yield up several other useful features:

- If Alice doesn't like what a client is doing on her behalf, she can revoke its token credentials.

- If the API provider sees that a piece of client software has gone rogue, the provider can revoke its *client credentials*. (That's the `oauth_consumer_key`.) This means the API stops serving *all* copies of that client.

- Unlike HTTP Basic (but like HTTP Digest), OAuth 1.0 can be used over insecure HTTP without revealing Alice's credentials. The token credentials are necessary to create the `oauth_signature` part of the `Authorization` header, but *the credentials don't actually appear anywhere in that header*. The server (which also knows Alice's credentials) can verify that a request was signed by Alice's credentials, but someone spying on the request won't be able to figure out what her credentials are.

- The `oauth_timestamp` and `oauth_nonce` values in the `Authorization` header prevent "replay attacks," in which an attacker spies on Alice's requests, then makes the same requests to impersonate her. (HTTP Digest auth also has this feature.)

Where OAuth 1.0 Falls Short

OAuth 1.0 works great when all the action happens inside Alice's web browser. What if Alice is using a desktop application?

In that case, Alice needs to *switch* to her web browser temporarily. In step 2, instead of redirecting Alice to the page on *api.example.net*, the desktop application opens a new browser window set to that page. Once Alice makes her decision in step 4, there's nowhere for *api.example.net* to redirect her back to. In the background, the desktop application needs to be continually asking *api.example.net* whether Alice has authorized (or denied) the temporary credentials.

That's OAuth 1.0's answer for integrating an API into a desktop application without requiring a username/password entry. It's a little disruptive to have a web browser window suddenly pop up when you're using a desktop application, but it's doable. Unfortunately, there are several other scenarios where the five-step process I described previously is inefficient or doesn't work at all:

- What if Alice is using an app on a mobile phone, or playing a game on a game console? It's a *lot* more disruptive to suddenly pop up a browser window on these devices. It may not even be possible. Some devices don't *have* web browsers.

- What if Alice is the author of her own software client for *api.example.net*? Does it really make sense to make her get temporary credentials and ask her if she wants to authorize her own client?

- What if Alice is using a desktop application that happens to run inside her web browser? Are the temporary credentials really necessary? In step 5, can't *api.example.net* just serve a page that contains the real access token, and let the in-browser application read it using JavaScript code?

OAuth 2.0 was designed to accommodate these use cases.

OAuth 2.0

OAuth 2.0 is defined in RFC 6749. It specifies four different processes for getting an OAuth access token (again, I won't go into a lot of detail; see Getting Started with OAuth 2.0 to learn more):

- By providing an "authorization code" (section 1.3.1 of RFC 6749). This is the system I described for OAuth 1.0. The "resource owner" (Alice) authenticates with an "authorization server" (logs in to *Example.net*), which redirects her to the "client" (*api.example.net*), which gives out the access token.

- Through an "implicit grant" (section 1.3.2 of RFC 6749). This is a good choice for an application that runs inside Alice's web browser. After Alice logs in to *Example.net*, she's redirected to *api.example.net*, which redirects her to a URL containing the access token. There's no need to get temporary credentials; the in-browser application can just read the access token out of the browser's address bar.

- Through "resource owner password credentials" (section 1.3.3 of RFC 6749). That is, Alice provides her *Example.net* username and password to the client, which exchanges them for an OAuth access token.

  This is exactly what OAuth is trying to avoid: Alice giving up her password to an untrusted client. But on a mobile device or a game console, there's no good alternative.

  At this point, a malicious client can steal Alice's password. But a legitimate client will forget Alice's password as soon as it gets an OAuth access token. This means that a legitimate client won't break if Alice changes her password for other reasons.

- Through "client credentials" (section 1.3.4 of RFC 6749). This saves a lot of aggravation when Alice is the author of her own client. When Alice registers her client with *api.example.net*, she's automatically given a set of credentials that will give her client free access to her own *example.net* account.

As an API provider, you don't have to implement all four of these application flows. If you're writing an API to serve as a backend for a mobile application, you can just implement the "resource owner password credentials" flow. But if you want third parties to integrate clients with your API, you'll need to implement the application flows your clients want to use.

When to Give Up on OAuth

Given the complexity of the OAuth standards and their various application flows, it's tempting to just give up and protect your API using HTTP Basic or HTTP Digest authentication. I recommend sticking it out and learning how OAuth works. If you need to, study and copy the implementation of a big-name OAuth provider like Facebook.

OAuth's fundamental advantage—the separation of Alice's *Example.net* username and password from her *api.example.net* credentials—is a *really* important feature. In my opinion, there are only two scenarios where you can do without it:

- Your API is a frivolous piece of entertainment. If a malicious client steals Alice's credentials, it can't cause any real damage.
- *Every* user of your API will be writing her own client. Then there is no security benefit in separating Alice the client developer from Alice the end user. This means that when Alice changes her password on the website, she'll also need to change her password in all her API clients. This shouldn't be a big problem.

If you understand the security issues, but you just don't think your API will ever become popular enough for malicious clients to be a problem, you should go with OAuth anyway. Once you start using HTTP Basic, it's *very* difficult to switch all your clients to OAuth. Don't lock yourself out of success.[3]

Extensions to HTTP

Pretty much by definition, web APIs are based on the HTTP protocol. But the underlying concepts of REST don't require HTTP, any more than the hypermedia constraint requires that you serve HTML representations.

There are two extensions to HTTP that define new methods specifically for use in APIs, and three major protocols that take HTTP as their starting point. One of those protocols, CoAP, is so unusual that I'm dedicating an entire chapter (Chapter 13) to it. WebDAV and HTTP 2.0 are closely based on HTTP, so I'm covering them here, along with a few extension HTTP methods.

The PATCH Method

- **Defined in:** RFC 5789 and others
- **Protocol semantics:** neither safe nor idempotent

I covered this method in Chapter 3 as part of my suggested toolkit for API developers. The PATCH method solves a performance problem with HTTP PUT. PUT replaces a resource's entire representation with a new one, which means the client must resend the

---

3. When the Twitter API switched from Basic Auth to OAuth in 2010, developers dubbed the event the "OAuth-pocalypse."

entire representation even if it's only making a small change. The PATCH method lets the client send only the change it wants to make.

The downside of the PATCH method is that client and server must agree on a new media type for patch documents. Fortunately, you don't have to come up with this format yourself. RFC 6902 defines a standard patch format for JSON, and registers the media type `application/json-patch` for documents in that format. RFC 5261 defines a patch format for XML documents, and the Internet-Draft "draft-wilde-xml-patch" registers the media type `application/xml-patch+xml` for documents in that format.

The LINK and UNLINK Methods

- **Defined in:** Internet-Draft "snell-link-method"
- **Protocol semantics:** idempotent but not safe

The LINK method creates a connection between two resources. Presumably, when resource A is linked to resource B, a hypermedia link to B will start showing up in the representations of A.

But how is the link created? How can one HTTP request refer to two different resources? By including hypermedia, of course. The LINK or UNLINK request is sent to the URL of resource A, and resource B is mentioned in the `Link` header. The link relation associated with the `Link` header describes the desired relationship between A and B.

Here's a request that adds an existing item to a collection (that's a common use case for the collection pattern, but it's not defined in AtomPub or Collection+JSON):

```
LINK /collections/a6o HTTP/1.1
Host: www.example.com
Link: <http://www.example.com/items/4180>;rel="item"
```

Here's a request that removes the second resource from a chain of resources:

```
UNLINK /story/part1 HTTP/1.1
Host: www.example.com
Link: <http://www.example.com/story/part2>;rel="next"
```

After this request goes through, the resources at */story/part1* and */story/part2* still exist. It's just that there's no longer a link between them whose link relation is "next." Perhaps */story/part1* now has a link to */story/part3* with `rel="next"`.

These methods aren't technically necessary. You can duplicate their functionality with PUT. But they simplify things. They split out a common operation—manipulation of the hypermedia links between resources—and give it its own protocol semantics.

In Chapter 3, I mentioned that between 1997 and 1999, these methods were a standard part of HTTP. RFC 2616 removed them because it wasn't clear why or how they should be used. With the rise of web APIs, and the introduction of the Link header, it's a lot clearer.

The only thing stopping me from recommending the use of LINK and UNLINK is the fact that the Internet-Draft describing them is not approved as an RFC yet.

WebDAV

- **Defined in:** RFC 4918 and others
- **Protocol semantics:** Filesystem operations

The goal of WebDAV is to make it easy to publish HTTP resources for files and directories on a remote filesystem. WebDAV defines so many new HTTP methods and other extensions that it can almost be considered a different protocol.

The highest profile uses of WebDAV are Microsoft's Sharepoint and the Subversion version control system. We don't really think of those as APIs, and most APIs that act like remote filesystems (Amazon's S3, the Dropbox API, and so on) don't use WebDAV. They're fiat standards that use standard HTTP methods like PUT, and serve metadata using ad hoc XML or JSON representations. In other words, they look like today's other APIs.

Like AtomPub, WebDAV is an open standard that's widely ignored because it doesn't fit with modern ideas about what an API ought to look like. But it's still useful to understand WebDAV, since it was an early pioneer in the API field. Here are some of WebDAV's more interesting features.

- WebDAV implements the collection pattern (Chapter 6) by defining "collection" resources that act like the directories on a local filesystem. These resources respond to GET and DELETE. WebDAV also defines a brand new HTTP method, MKCOL, which creates a new collection.

  A client uploads a file by sending a PUT request to whatever URL it chooses for the new resource. RFC 5995 is an extension that allows the client to upload new files using POST-to-append instead. In that case, the server chooses the URL of the newborn resource, not the client.

- A file on your local filesystem contains data, but it also has associated metadata: a filename, the date the file was created, and so on. WebDAV resources represent this metadata as "properties" like displayname and creationdate.

  WebDAV defines the HTTP method PROPPATCH for modifying a resource's properties, and the PROPFIND method for searching a collection to turn up resources with certain properties.

- WebDAV allows a client to explicitly lock a resource (using the new HTTP methods LOCK and UNLOCK) so that other clients can't access it. This can be used with the techniques I described earlier in this chapter to avoid the lost update problem.

- WebDAV defines the new HTTP methods MOVE and COPY. They work like the equivalent filesystem operations. MOVE changes the URL of a resource, and COPY puts up a copy of the resource's current representation at some other URL.

  WebDAV also defines a new hypermedia control for these methods: the `Destination` request header. This header contains the new URL of the resource, or the URL to use for the copy. Compare the `Link` request header, as used with the LINK and UNLINK methods.

- WebDAV defines five new HTTP status codes, including some that may look tempting even if you're not using WebDAV, like 423 (`Locked`) and 507 (`Insufficient Storage`). But I don't recommend using WebDAV features outside of Web-DAV. Fall back to a standard status code instead. You can use 409 (`Conflict`) instead of 423 (`Locked`), and provide the extra context in a problem detail document.

HTTP 2.0

- **Defined in:** Internet-Draft "draft-ietf-httpbis-http2"
- **Protocol semantics:** Identical to HTTP 1.1

HTTP 2.0 is the successor to the current version of HTTP defined in RFC 2616 and its replacement RFCs. HTTP 2.0 is based on SPDY, a corporate standard defined by Google that adds a performance layer on top of HTTP. Most web browsers now support SPDY, and many large sites serve data using SPDY if the client supports it.

The goal of HTTP 2.0 is to improve HTTP's performance while preserving its protocol semantics. Despite its imposing name, HTTP 2.0 won't bring in new features that shake the foundations of API design. Whether you're developing an API, an API client, or a website, you should be able to pretend you're using HTTP 1.1, and let a compatibility layer automatically convert between HTTP 1.1 and 2.0.

As I write this, it's too early in the development process to say exactly how HTTP 2.0 will work. It may end up looking nothing like SPDY. But it needs to solve the problems SPDY solves, which means it will probably have these two features:

- HTTP 2.0 will save bandwidth by compressing HTTP headers, something that's not legal under HTTP 1.0.

- An HTTP 2.0 client will be able to send multiple simultaneous requests ("streams") to a server over a single TCP connection. This is similar to the pipelining feature of HTTP 1.1, but as I mentioned earlier, pipelining doesn't help performance very much. HTTP 2.0 needs to include a pipelining-like feature that actually works.

These technical improvements will have a big, positive effect on API design. They'll eliminate the need for a common set of API design patterns that improve performance by bundling requests together.[4] These patterns allow a client to fetch (or update) representations of many resources using a single HTTP request. There's no standard way to package these "virtual requests" together, but doing so saves a lot of time, because every HTTP 1.1 request has a large setup cost.

HTTP 2.0 will eliminate that setup cost. Making 20 HTTP requests, and getting 20 responses, will be almost as fast as making one big request and getting one big response. There will no longer be any need for an API to have special batch features.

4. For a good explanation of these patterns, see Chapter 11 of *RESTful Web Services Cookbook* (O'Reilly).

Resource Description and Linked Data

The data formats I've covered in this book are used primarily to allow resources to talk about themselves. That is, a client sends a GET request to the URL of a resource and receives a representation of that very resource. I'm calling this the *representation strategy*.

But a representation of resource A may also have something to say about resource B. This simple Collection+JSON document is a representation of one resource (a collection) but it has something to say about two other resources (the items in the collection):

```
{ "collection":
  {
    "version" : "1.0",
    "href" : "http://www.youtypeitwepostit.com/api/",

    "items" : [

      { "href" : "/api/messages/21818525390699506",
        "data": [
          { "name": "text", "value": "Test." }
        ]
      },

      { "href" : "/api/messages/3689331521745771",
        "data": [
          { "name": "text", "value": "Hello." }
        ]
      }
    ]
  }
}
```

I'm calling this the *description strategy*. With the description strategy, a representation spends most of its time talking about resources other than the resource it's a representation of.

All hypermedia formats mix the representation and description strategies to some extent, but there's a family of formats that focuses heavily on the description strategy: formats inspired by the Resource Description Framework (RDF) data model and associated with the Semantic Web movement.

I didn't cover these formats in Chapter 10 because, from a REST point of view, they're weird. A pure description strategy violates the Fielding constraints. RDF documents frequently describe resources that, from a REST perspective, "don't exist." To understand what these documents are talking about, you must adopt a different way of thinking.

Fortunately, a second-wave Semantic Web movement called Linked Data aims to refocus RDF on the representation strategy. This is great news, because there are several useful data formats derived from RDF, and a very powerful language for creating machine-readable profiles: RDF Schema.

But before I get to Linked Data, you need to understand RDF. Everything in this chapter is based on, inspired by, or designed in reaction to the RDF data model. You need to understand what RDF documents look like, what they mean, and why the Linked Data movement was necessary in the first place.

RDF

- **Media types:** `application/rdf+xml`, `text/turtle`, etc.
- **Defined in:** W3C open standards, defined here (*http://www.w3.org/standards/techs/rdf*) and notably here (*http://www.w3.org/TR/turtle/*)
- **Medium:** plain text, XML, HTML, etc.
- **Protocol semantics:** navigation with GET
- **Application semantics:** none

Here's an RDF description of a cell in a Maze+XML maze:

```
<rdf:RDF xmlns:rdf="http://www.w3.org/1999/02/22-rdf-syntax-ns#"
         xmlns:maze="http://alps.io/example/maze#">
<rdf:Description about="http://example.com/cells/M">
 <maze:title>The Entrance Hallway</maze:title>
 <maze:east resource="http://example.com/cells/N">
 <maze:west resource="http://example.com/cells/L">
</rdf:Description>
</rdf:RDF>
```

There are many ways of writing down RDF, including an HTML version called RDFa, and a plain-text version called Turtle. You just saw the XML version, called RDF+XML. Here's a Turtle description of the maze cell that means exactly the same thing:

```
<http://example.com/cells/M> <http://alps.io/example/maze#title> ↵
"The Entrance Hallway" .
```

```
<http://example.com/cells/M> <http://alps.io/example/maze#east> ↵
<http://example.com/cells/N> .
<http://example.com/cells/M>↵ <http://alps.io/example/maze#west> ↵
<http://example.com/cells/L> .
```

Set up a few Turtle shortcuts, and you can represent the same information in a more compact way:

```
@prefix maze: <http://alps.io/example/maze#> .
<http://example.com/cells/M> maze:title "The Entrance Hallway" ;
                             maze:east <http://example.com/cells/N> ;
                             maze:west <http://example.com/cells/L> .
```

All three of these documents are describing the same resource: the one with the URI *http://example.com/cells/M*. In RDF+XML, the URI being described goes into the about attribute of a `<Description>` tag. In Turtle, that URI goes at the beginning of a line, in angle brackets. (Sort of like the way the HTTP `Link` header puts its destination URL in angle brackets.)

Each of these documents makes the same assertions about the resource it's describing. Each says that the resource has a property called *http://alps.io/example/maze#title*, with the value of this property being the literal string `The Entrance Hallway`.

Each document also says that the resource has two properties called `http://alps.io/example/maze#east` and `http://alps.io/example/maze#west`. These properties act sort of like extension link relations. Their values are URIs (such as *http://example.com/cells/L*). They explain the relationship between the resource on the right side of the property and the resource on the left side:

```
<http://example.com/cells/M> <http://alps.io/example/maze#west> ↵
<http://example.com/cells/L> .
```

To translate into human terms, that line of Turtle says "cell L is west of cell M."

RDF gives you a framework for talking about a resource's application semantics. You can talk about the link relations that connect one resource to others, and the semantic descriptors that bind it to its own resource state. But unlike other formats, RDF properties can't be short strings like "title" and "east." They can only be URIs, like *http://alps.io/example/maze#title* and *http://alps.io/example/maze#east*. You can use Turtle prefixes and XML namespaces to shorten the URIs to `maze:title` and `maze:east`, but behind the scenes, they're still URIs.

RDF Treats URLs as URIs

So, an RDF document describes a maze cell using a number of properties such as `http://alps.io/example/maze#title`. What do these properties *mean*?

In the world of REST, this question has an obvious answer. An *http:* URL identifies a resource on the Web, and if you send a GET request to that URL, you'll get a representation that captures the state of the resource.

If you send a GET request to *http://alps.io/example/maze*, you'll get an ALPS document. Look up "east" and "title" in that document, and you'll get human-readable explanations. This isn't enough to bridge the semantic gap on its own, but if your automated client gets stuck because it doesn't understand something, you, the developer, know where to go to fix the problem.

But RDF doesn't treat URLs as URLs. It treats them as URIs, a term I haven't mentioned much since Chapter 4. A URI identifies a resource, just like a URL, but there's no guarantee that you can use a computer to get a representation of the resource. This is why I've been downplaying the importance of URIs throughout this book. As I said in Chapter 4, identifying your resources with URIs makes it impossible to fulfill many of the Fielding constraints.

But I used *http:* URIs in my RDF document. Those are URLs. So I'm safe, right? Actually, no, I'm not safe. As far as RDF is concerned, even *http:* URLs are nothing but URIs. The URI *http://example.com/cells/N* may look tempting, but from an RDF perspective there's no guarantee that making a GET request to that URI will give you a representation. An RDF client can try it and see what happens, but is not allowed to assume that anything will happen.

If you sent an HTTP GET request to *http://example.com/cells/M* and got one of these RDF documents in return, we'd say you had a "representation" of the resource at *http://example.com/cells/M*. But in real life, if you send that GET request, you'll get a 404 error. *http://example.com/cells/M* is a fantasy, an example URI I made up for purposes of this book. So we can't say that these RDF documents are "representations" of that resource. They're *descriptions* of a resource that, from a REST perspective, doesn't exist.

As far as RDF is concerned, this is completely legitimate. It's OK to write a description of a resource that has no representation. RDF documents frequently mention *http:* URIs that don't point to anything in particular.

With other data formats, if you see a link, you know that the document is trying to tell you about an HTTP request you could make. To quote Fielding's definition of hypermedia, the link is "application control information" explaining what your HTTP client can do next.

But as far as the RDF standard is concerned, there's no "application" to be "controlled." Links do nothing but name the abstract connections between equally abstract resources. You're supposed to reason about those connections, not follow them to see what's on the other side.

When to Use the Description Strategy

From a REST perspective, this seems pretty crazy, but there are a few good reasons to use the resource description strategy.

First, resource description lets you talk about a resource when you don't control the representation. This might be because the resource is controlled by another server (like the OpenID resource that identifies one of your users), or because the representation format is fixed in stone. You can use the description strategy to have your say about someone else's resource.

Second, many existing APIs serve representations that contain no hypermedia controls. Adding hypermedia to those documents might break existing clients or violate a standard. But with a resource description format, you can add an "exoskeleton" of hypermedia annotations on top of a hypermedia-ignorant document. JSON-LD, which I covered in Chapter 8 and will return to in an upcoming section, was designed for just this purpose.

Finally, you can use the description strategy to talk about a resource that has no representation because it's not on the Web. I mentioned in Chapter 4 that the print edition of this book is a resource with a well-known URI, *urn:isbn:9781449358063*. You can't GET a representation of that resource, but you can GET an RDF document describing it.

Let's say you send a GET request to *http://www.example.com/book-lookup/9781449358063* and receive the following response:

```
HTTP/1.1 200 OK
Content-Type: text/turtle

@prefix schema: <http://schema.org/> .
<urn:isbn:9781449358063> a schema:Book ;
                    schema:name "RESTful Web APIs" ;
                    schema:inLanguage "en" ;
                    schema:isbn "9781449358063" ;
                    schema:author _:mike ;
                    schema:author _:leonard .

_:mike a schema:Person ;
      schema:name "Mike Amundsen" .

_:leonard a schema:Person ;
        schema:name "Leonard Richardson" .
```

The entity-body describes a resource: "the print edition of *RESTful Web APIs*," identified by the URI *urn:isbn:9781449358063*. This URI has a big problem: you can't use it to get a representation of the resource. That's why, when we design web APIs, we don't use URIs. We make up *http:* or *https:* URLs based on domain names we control. We declare that those URLs correspond to things in the real world, and we serve representations that capture the state of those real-world things.

That's not what I've done here. I've created a second resource, "the output of a book lookup function," identified by the URL *http://www.example.com/book-lookup/ 9781449358063*. This resource *describes* the resource state of the real-world thing identified by *urn:isbn:9781449358063*, rather than trying to *represent* that resource directly. Its representation makes a number of assertions about a real-world thing. It says the real-world thing is a book (a `schema:Book`). The book's title is "RESTful Web APIs," it's written in English, and it has two authors, who are people (`_mike a schema:Person`), each with a name. (`schema:name`)..

There's a really good idea here. If 10 different organizations define 10 web APIs that deal with books, we'll end up with 10 different URLs for any given ISBN. It will take extra work to establish that the representation of *http://example.com/books/ 9781449358063* and the representation of *http://api.example.org/work? isbn=9781449358063* are talking about the same book. But if all those URLs serve RDF documents that describe *urn:isbn:9781449358063*, it will be obvious that all the representations are talking about the same underlying thing.

As I say, this is a great idea… for print books. It doesn't work as well for resources that lack a unique identifier. Take human beings. You can use RDF and the schema.org vocabulary to make all kinds of assertions about a human being:

```
HTTP/1.1 200 OK
Content-Type: text/turtle

@prefix rdf: <http://www.w3.org/1999/02/22-rdf-syntax-ns#> .
@prefix schema: <http://schema.org/> .
_:jennifer a schema:Person ;
           schema:name "Jennifer Gallegos" ;
           schema:birthdate "1987-08-25" .
```

This RDF/Turtle document describes a resource. It says that the resource is a person with a certain name and birthdate. But there's no agreed-upon URI scheme for people,[1] so the resource in question has no URI. It just has an internal identifier, "jennifer."

This document is a set of assertions about an *anonymous resource*. There's no agreed-upon way to identify which human being we're talking about. If 10 APIs serve RDF descriptions of the same person, there's no obvious way to discover they're all talking about the same person.

At this point, you might as well make up an *http:* URL for your `person` resource. Then you can serve a representation of the resource when someone makes a GET request to

---

1. The `acct:` URI scheme, defined in the Internet-Draft "draft-ietf-appsawg-acct-uri," can't identify a human being, but it can identify a user account. For many APIs, that's close enough.

its URL. And once you decide to use the representation strategy instead of the description strategy, you probably want to use a data format with better hypermedia controls than RDF/XML or RDF/Turtle.

Resource Types

One of the Semantic Web's most useful ideas is that a resource can be classified under one or more *resource types* (also called *abstract semantic types* or just *semantic types*). These aren't like data types in a programming language. They're classifications, like genres of books or species of animals.

RDF's `type` property assigns a type to a resource. Like everything else in RDF, resource types are identified by URIs. Here's a description of a resource (*http://example.com/~omjennyg*) that is classified as the resource type `http://schema.org/Person`:

```
@prefix rdf: <http://www.w3.org/1999/02/22-rdf-syntax-ns#> .
<http://example.com/~omjennyg> <rdf:type> <http://schema.org/Person> ;
                        <http://schema.org/birthDate> "1987-08-25" .
```

Turtle defines `a` as a shortcut for RDF's `type` property so you don't have to bring the RDF vocabulary into every single Turtle document just to talk about resource types:

```
<http://example.com/~omjennyg> a <http://schema.org/Person> ;
                        <http://schema.org/birthDate> "1987-08-25" .
```

Occasionally the concept of "resource type" bleeds out of the Semantic Web world and into the wider world of web APIs. In the XLink format (Chapter 10), a link may have a `role` attribute, which gives the type of the resource on the other end of the link:

```
<a xlink:href="http://example.com/~omjennyg"
   xlink:arcrole="http://alps.io/iana/relations#author"
   xlink:role="http://schema.org/Person">
```

In CoRE Link Format, which I'll cover in the next chapter, a link's `rt` attribute conveys the type of the resource on the other end (the "rt" stands for "resource type"):

```
<http://example.com/~omjennyg>;rel="author";rt="http://schema.org/Person"
```

A link relation and a resource type are two different things. A resource type (`http://schema.org/Person`) is a statement about the resource on the other end of a link. A link relation (`author` or `http://alps.io/iana/relations#author`) is a statement about the link itself—about the relationship between the two resources.

Speaking of link relations, there's an IANA-registered link relation called `type` that lets a representation make claims about its *own* resource type:

```
HTTP/1.1 200 OK
Content-Type: text/plain
Link: <http://schema.org/birthDate>;rel="type"
```

The role and rt attributes are very useful. They let a client look ahead to see what sort of resource is on the other end of a link. If the client likes what it sees, it can go ahead and follow the link.

But how is the client supposed to know whether it likes what it sees? The concept of "resource type" comes from RDF, and in RDF, *http://schema.org/Person*, isn't a URL. It's a URI, a meaningless identifier. The client is *not* invited to make a GET request to that URI. If you want to know what *http://schema.org/Person* and *http://schema.org/birth-Date* mean, you need to find an RDF document somewhere that describes those resources.

Without the hypermedia constraint, there are no rules for finding the description document. You're just supposed to poke around until you find it. But that document is really important! It's the only way to bridge the semantic gap. Without it, *http://schema.org/birthDate* is just a short, meaningless string.

RDF Schema

Disregard, for the moment, the question of finding that magical document. What would the document look like once you found it? The document would *explain* those short meaningless strings. It would say that the URIs *http://schema.org/Person* and *http://schema.org/birthDate* correspond roughly to our everyday notions of "person" and "date of birth." It would act as a profile, no different in principle from an ALPS or XMDP profile.

An RDF profile is sometimes called a *vocabulary* or an *ontology*. It's written using a kind of metavocabulary called RDF Schema. RDF Schema lets you use RDF to make statements about resource types, not just individual resources.

Here's an RDF Schema document that explains what a *http://schema.org/Person* is:[2]

```
@prefix rdf: <http://www.w3.org/1999/02/22-rdf-syntax-ns#> .
@prefix rdfs: <http://www.w3.org/2000/01/rdf-schema#> .
<http://schema.org/Person> a rdfs:Class ;
                rdfs:label "Person" ;
                rdfs:comment "A person (alive, dead, undead, or fictional)." ;
                rdfs:subClassOf <http://schema.org/Thing> .
```

---

2. The official RDF ontology for schema.org is located here (*http://schema.org/docs/schema_org_rdfa.html*). I wish I could quote directly from that document in my examples, but it uses RDFa, the HTML version of RDF, and I don't have space to explain RDFa here. So I've converted bits of that document into the text-based Turtle format I use throughout this chapter.

The third line says that the resource type of *http://schema.org/Person* is `rdfs:Class`. That means *http://schema.org/Person* doesn't stand in for one specific real-world thing (an individual person). It stands in for a concept (the concept of "person").

The `rdfs:label` and `rdfs:comment` properties point to some human-readable information about this mysterious concept. A human being who reads this document learns that the resource *http://schema.org/Person* corresponds to our everyday notion of a "person." So if the type of some *other* resource is `http://schema.org/Person`, it means that resource corresponds to an individual person.

But there's also a machine-readable element to this RDF Schema profile: the `rdfs:sub ClassOf` property. This says that every resource that's a *http://schema.org/Person* is also a *http://schema.org/Thing*. Are you curious what a *http://schema.org/Thing* is? You can satisfy your curiosity by taking a look at the RDF description of *that* URI, conveniently located in the same file as the description of *http://schema.org/Person*:

```
...
<http://schema.org/Thing> a rdfs:Class
                      rdfs:label "Thing"
                      rdfs:comment "The most generic type of item."
```

It turns out a *http://schema.org/Thing* is... nothing in particular. Kind of an anticlimax. But at least now you know that *http://schema.org/Thing* does not refer to the 1982 John Carpenter film *The Thing*, its 2011 remake, or the Marvel superhero named The Thing.

What about *http://schema.org/birthDate*? What does that mean? Well, here's an RDF description of *that* resource, adapted from the same vocabulary document as the two other descriptions I just showed you:

```
<http://schema.org/birthDate> a <rdf:Property> ;
                      rdfs:label "birthDate" ;
                      rdfs:comment "Date of birth." ;
                      rdfs:domain <http://schema.org/Person> ;
                      rdfs:range <http://schema.org/Date> .
```

The human-readable parts of this description merely confirm what you already suspected: that *http://schema.org/birthDate* is a resource corresponding to the real-world concept of "date of birth." The real interest here is in the machine-readable parts of the description—the `domain` and the `range`:

```
                      rdfs:domain <http://schema.org/Person> ;
                      rdfs:range <http://schema.org/Date> .
```

These two lines of RDF/Turtle say that a `birthDate` is a relationship between a `Per son` and a `Date`. Think of `birthDate` as a function. You put in a person, and you get out a date—the person's date of birth. The `domain` is the input and the `range` is the output.

These two machine-readable assertions are tiny ropes thrown across the semantic gap. Nearly everything in schema.org's RDF vocabulary is blindingly obvious to a human being. But to program a computer to understand just the parts of that vocabulary I've shown you, you have to teach the computer four different concepts: Person, Thing, birthDate, and Date. The schema.org vocabulary contains almost a thousand concepts, with more being added all the time. Nobody's going to program a computer to understand all of them.

That's why the machine-readable parts of an RDF Schema vocabulary—properties like subclassOf, domain, and range—are important. They give a computer a low-level understanding of the application semantics, without the need for human tutoring. An RDF client that doesn't know what a birthDate is can muddle through with the knowledge (derived from domain and range properties) that it's some kind of Date associated with a Person.

ALPS and XMDP profiles rely heavily on human-readable descriptions of application semantics. This means they rely on human labor to turn those descriptions into working client code. RDF Schema profiles put more of an API's application semantics into machine-readable form. An extension to RDF Schema called OWL (which I won't be covering) lets you take this idea even further. The dream is that instead of teaching your computer a million specific concepts, you can teach it a few hundred basic concepts, and let it figure out the rest on its own.

The cost is that the explanations become very complex. You could use RDF Schema and OWL to describe "date of birth" in terms of very basic concepts. It would come out something like "the date of the event in which a person changed state from nonexistence to existence."[3] For most applications, it's easier for the client authors to just write some code that handles birthdates the way they want.

The Linked Data Movement

RDF is great for expressing application semantics in machine-readable terms. But you can't build a RESTful API on top of RDF alone, because RDF uses URIs instead of URLs. There's no guarantee a client can get a representation of any of the resources it sees described. This renders most of the Fielding constraints irrelevant.

Of course, as an API designer, you could just ignore that rule. You could *declare* that all your URIs are URLs, and that all your resources have representations. Your resources could serve RDF documents that focus on describing *themselves*, rather than describing other resources that might or might not have representations. At that point, you'd get the Fielding constraints back. All the URIs in your RDF representations would become hypermedia links, and your clients could feel good about following them.

---

3. The BIO vocabulary (*http://vocab.org/bio/*) doesn't go that far, but it does describe a "birth event" resource, *http://purl.org/vocab/bio/0.1/Birth*, which brings together the person who was born, their parents, a date and a place.

This school of thought is called Linked Data. The term comes from a 2006 essay (*http://www.w3.org/DesignIssues/LinkedData*) by Tim Berners-Lee, in which he identifies four principles for putting machine-readable data on the Web. From a REST perspective, these principles relax RDF's URI constraint—they say it's OK to treat a URI as a URL—to take advantage of the Fielding constraints. They move the Semantic Web philosophy closer to the REST philosophy. Here are Berners-Lee's four principles of Linked Data:

1. Use URIs as names for things.

In REST terms, this says that a URI identifies a resource. In Chapter 1, I called this the principle of addressability.

2. Use HTTP URIs so that people can look up those names.

This has two parts. First, you shouldn't identify your resources with URIs like *urn:isbn:9781449358063*. You should use URLs like *http://example.com/books/9781449358063*. It's true that *urn:isbn:9781449358063* is a much more general way to refer to the resource, but because it's so general, a client can't *do* anything with the reference.

Second, resources should have representations. A client that sends a GET request to a URL should get some useful data in return. A URL like *http://vocab.org/vnd/mamund.com/2013/numbers/primes* looks good, right up to the point when you send a GET request to it and get a 404 error. Then you find out that the URL was actually a URI. It has no representation. There may be a magical document somewhere that *describes* that URI, but good luck finding it.

3. When someone looks up a URI, provide useful information, using the standards (RDF*, SPARQL).

Again, resources have representations. A client that sends a GET request to a resource's URL should receive a document capturing the current state of the resource.

The exact standards don't matter (I'm not even covering SPARQL in this book). What matters is that you use *some* standard, instead of making up a custom data format. That way, a client that understands your standard automatically knows how to handle the data you provide—at least on a basic level. This is a theme I've been hitting throughout this book: you should use an existing hypermedia format instead of defining your own.

4. Include links to other URIs. so that they can discover more things.

And finally, the big payoff: the hypermedia constraint. A URI is now a URL, a link, which a client can follow to get a representation. That representation will contain other links, and the client can follow them to get closer to fulfilling whatever desire it was programmed with.

If you want to write a Linked Data API, I suggest you use JSON-LD as your representation format instead of RDF/XML or RDF/Turtle. JSON-LD is a new serialization of RDF designed specifically for making APIs that resemble today's other hypermedia APIs.

JSON-LD

- **Media type:** `application/ld+json`
- **Described in:** open standard in progress, defined at *http://www.w3.org/TR/json-ld/*
- **Medium:** JSON
- **Protocol semantics:** navigation through GET links
- **Application semantics:** very flexible, but each document must define its own

In Chapter 8, I covered JSON-LD as a profile format. I showed how a bare JSON representation...

```
HTTP/1.1 200 OK
Content-Type: application/json

{ "n": "Jenny Gallegos",
  "photo_link": "http://api.example.com/img/omjennyg" }
```

...could be transformed into a hypermedia document by the addition of a JSON-LD "context":

```
HTTP/1.1 200 OK
Content-Type: application/ld+json

{
  "@context":
  {
    "n": "http://alps.io/schema.org/Person#name",
    "photo_link":
    {
      "@id": "http://alps.io/schema.org/Person#image",
      "@type": "@id"
    }
  }
}
```

This JSON-LD context explains the link relation `photo_link` and the semantic descriptor n by linking to explanations. I showed different versions of this context: one that linked to an ALPS profile, one that linked to human-readable documentation, and one that used URIs described by an RDF vocabulary. Here's another example that uses the schema.org vocabulary:

```
{
  "@context":
  {
    "n": "http://schema.org/name",
    "photo_link":
    {
      "@id": "http://schema.org/image",
      "@type": "@id"
    }
  }
}
```

JSON-LD as a Representation Format

So far, I've presented JSON-LD as a sort of profile format: an add-on to a plain JSON document that explains its application semantics. You use the `Link` header to connect the JSON document to its JSON-LD context:

```
Link: <http://api.example.com/profile.person.jsonld>;↵
rel="http://www.w3.org/ns/json-ld#context"
```

It's not quite accurate to say that JSON-LD is a profile format. Knowing that a JSON document has a JSON-LD context doesn't just give a client some extra information about its application semantics. It completely changes how a client should process the document. Parse a JSON document without looking at the context, and you use JSON rules and end up with a nested data structure. Parse the same document along with its context, and you use RDF rules and end up with a set of RDF assertions.

And JSON-LD isn't limited to this add-on role. *Any* JSON object becomes a JSON-LD document if you add a `@context` property and serve it as `application/ld+json`. This means you can combine the JSON-LD context with the data you're serving, and serve the whole thing at once:

```
HTTP/1.1 200 OK
Content-Type: application/ld+json

{
 "n": "Jenny Gallegos",
 "picture_link": "http://www.example.com/img/omjennyg",
"@type": "http://schema.org/Person",
  "@context":
  {
    "n": "http://schema.org/name",

    "photo_link":
    {
      "@id": "http://schema.org/image",
      "@type": "@id"
    }
  }
}
```

At this point, JSON-LD becomes a traditional hypermedia format. The `Link` header is no longer necessary, because there's only one document. It's still clear that `pho to_link` is a hypermedia link. In fact, it's clearer than it was before, because all the information is in one place.

But as representation formats go, JSON-LD isn't very capable. Thanks to its RDF heritage, JSON-LD can describe application semantics in great detail, but its protocol semantics are very limited. A Linked Data client can do nothing but follow links from one bit of data to another. A client can't *change* the data, because JSON-LD has no hypermedia controls for triggering unsafe HTTP requests.

If you want to use JSON-LD in your API, I recommend you also use an extension called Hydra.

Hydra

- **Media type:** `application/ld+json`
- **Described in:** personal standard in progress at *http://www.markus-lanthaler.com/hydra/*
- **Medium:** JSON
- **Protocol semantics:** completely generic
- **Application semantics:** derived from JSON-LD; implements the collection pattern ("collection" and "resource"), but collections have no special protocol semantics

Hydra is a JSON-LD context that adds a lot of protocol semantics to JSON-LD. By itself, JSON-LD only lets you specify links (using `"@type"`: `"@id"`), to be triggered with GET requests. Add Hydra to the mix, and you can specify almost any HTTP request.

Here's a Hydra document that describes the application and protocol semantics of a blogging API along the lines of *YouTypeItWePostIt.com* (let's suppose this document is served from *http://example.com/youtypeit.jsonld*).

```
{
  "@context": "http://purl.org/hydra/core/context.jsonld",
  "@type": "ApiDocumentation",
  "title": "Microblogging API",
  "description": "You type it, we post it.",
  "entrypoint": "http://example.com/api/",
  "supportedClasses": [
    {
      "@id": "#BlogDirectory",
      "title": "A directory of blogs",
      "description": "Links to all blogs.",
      "supportedProperties": [
        {
```

```
          "@id": "#blogs",
          "@type": "link",
          "title": "Blogs",
          "description": "The available blogs.",
          "domain": "#BlogDirectory",
          "range": "#Blog"
        }
      ]
    },

    {
      "@id": "#Blog",
      "@type": "Class",
      "subClassOf": "Collection",
      "title": "Blog",
      "description": "A collection of posts.",
      "supportedOperations": [
        {
          "@type": "CreateResourceOperation",
          "method": "POST",
          "expects": "#BlogPost"
        }
      ]
    },

    {
      "@id": "#BlogPost",
      "@type": "Class",
      "title": "Post",
      "description": "A single blog post.",
      "supportedProperties": [
        {
          "@id": "#content",
          "@type": "rdfs:Property",
          "title": "Content",
          "description": "The content of a blog post.",
          "domain": "#BlogPost",
          "range": "xsd:string"
        }
      ]
    }
  ]
}
```

A client that understands JSON-LD and RDF Schema can get a lot of information out of this document. It can learn about three resource types (*http://example.com/youty-peit.jsonld#BlogDirectory, http://example.com/youtypeit.jsonld#Blog,* and *http://example.com/youtypeit.jsonld#BlogPost*), each of which has a human-readable description.

Even if a client knows nothing about Hydra, that's enough to make sense of a representation. Here's a JSON-LD representation of an API home page, served from *http://example.com/api/*:

```
HTTP/1.1 200 OK
Content-Type: application/ld+json

{
  "@context": {
    "blogs": "http://example.com/youtypeit.jsonld#blogs",
    "Blog": "http://example.com/youtypeit.jsonld#Blog"
  },
  "@id":"http://example.com/api/",
  "blogs": [
    { "@id": "/api/blogs/1", "@type": "Blog" },
    { "@id": "/api/blogs/2", "@type": "Blog" }
  ]
}
```

Maybe you're wondering what that `blogs` property means? Well, the `@context` says that its application semantics are defined at *http://example.com/youtypeit.jsonld#blogs*. Here it is:

```
{
  "@id": "#blogs",
  "@type": "link",
  "title": "Blogs",
  "description": "The available blogs.",
  "domain": "#BlogDirectory",
  "range": "#Blog"
}
```

It's a list of blogs. More formally, it's a function whose possible outputs (`range`) all have the resource type *http://example.com/youtypeit.jsonld#Blog*. That means this bit of JSON is a description of two different blog-type resources:

```
"blogs": [
  { "@id": "/api/blogs/1", "@type": "Blog" },
  { "@id": "/api/blogs/2", "@type": "Blog" }
]
```

Of course, that's not much of a description. You know nothing about these resources except their URIs and their semantic type. In a traditional RDF document, the story would end here. You'd never learn anything else about these resources unless you found a better description of them lying around somewhere.

But this is a JSON-LD document, so you know it obeys the hypermedia constraint. You're encouraged to make a GET request to */api/blogs/1* or */api/blogs/2*. You know that if you make that GET request, you can expect a representation that fulfills the application semantics of a `Blog`.

Getting to this point has required no knowledge of Hydra at all. A JSON-LD client can make a GET request for the API home page, understand the context, and make a second GET request to */api/blogs/2*. It can compare the representation it gets against the description of the Blog resource type, and gain an understanding of the application semantics of this particular "Blog."

But a client that knows about Hydra has a big advantage here. It understands a special property called supportedOperations. In this context, supportedOperations says that a Blog—type resource supports HTTP POST as well as GET. Take another look at this section:

```
{
  "@id": "#Blog",
  ...
  "supportedOperations": [
    {
      "@type": "CreateResourceOperation",
      "method": "POST",
      "expects": "#BlogPost"
    }
  ]
}
```

That says that a client can create a new resource (of type BlogPost) by making an HTTP POST request to a resource of type Blog. The entity-body of the request should be a JSON-LD representation that fulfils the application semantics of a BlogPost.

What are the application semantics of a BlogPost? Well, the original context says that a BlogPost has a single property, called content, which is a string (xsd:string):

```
{
  "@id": "#BlogPost",
  ...
  "supportedProperties": [
    {
      "@id": "#content",
      "@type": "rdfs:Property",
      "title": "Content",
      "description": "The content of a blog post.",
      "domain": "#BlogPost",
      "range": "xsd:string"
    }
  ]
}
```

Put it all together, and a Hydra client knows that it can send a POST request that looks something like this:

```
POST /api/blogs/2 HTTP/1.1
Host: www.example.com
Content-Type: application/ld+json

{
  "@context": {
    "content": http://www.example.com/youtypeit.jsonld#content"
```

```
    },
    "content": "This is my first post."
}
```

JSON-LD gives an API provider a way to explain the application semantics of a seemingly ordinary JSON document. A JSON-LD context also can explain the protocol semantics of that document, by giving clients blanket permission to make an HTTP GET request to any URI they find. But that's as far as it goes. On its own, JSON-LD can only describe safe state transitions.

Hydra goes further. A JSON-LD context that includes the special Hydra properties can tell a client that it's allowed to make any kind of HTTP request, not just a GET. Hydra makes it possible to describe unsafe state transitions in great detail.

Overall, I'd compare Hydra contexts to WADL documents and OData metadata documents, both of which I covered in Chapter 10. These documents tend to be used to define types of resources (`Blog`, `BlogPost`) up front, rather than representing the behavior of individual resources at runtime. There's nothing inherently wrong with this. Almost any API will have distinct resource types, and all the resources of a given type will have similar application and protocol semantics.

But there's a strong temptation to confuse "the abstract semantic type of a resource" with "the implementation details of a class in my data model." Hydra contexts, OData metadata documents, and WADL documents tempt server-side API developers into automatically generating one-off vocabularies based on their internal data models, instead of reusing standard vocabularies.

And there's a bigger problem, which I mentioned back in Chapter 9. Since these documents don't change very often, client-side API developers are tempted to treat them as service description documents, capable of providing a complete overview of an API's application semantics. Users will be tempted to generate client code based on a Hydra context—client code that breaks when the context does change.

As I write this, the Hydra standard is still a work in progress, but it's a much better choice for JSON-based hypermedia APIs than plain JSON-LD, because it can describe unsafe state transitions. Just be sure you don't use it in a way that negates the benefits of REST's hypermedia constraint.

The XRD Family

I recommend JSON-LD because it adopts a principle that's fundamental to both Linked Data and REST. URIs should be URLs, and they should have useful representations behind them. URIs like *urn:isbn:9781449358063* are more trouble than they're worth.

What if you refused to make this compromise? How far could you get with an API that used a pure description strategy? That's what I want to explore with my coverage of the

XRD format, and two standards that build on it: web host metadata documents and WebFinger.

XRD is the description strategy's answer to the ad hoc XML and JSON formats used by today's APIs. Web host metadata documents make it possible to build a hypermedia API around resources you don't control, resources that may have no representations at all. This may seem like a pointless party trick, but WebFinger shows us a real use case.

XRD and JRD

- **Media type:** `application/xrd+xml` or `application/jrd+json`
- **Defined in:** RFC 6415 (JRD), open standard (*http://docs.oasis-open.org/xri/xrd/v1.0/xrd-1.0.html*) (XRD)
- **Medium:** XML or JSON
- **Protocol semantics:** navigation using GET links
- **Application semantics:** none

XRD is a traditional XML-based document format designed for describing resources from the outside. Unlike RDF, XRD distinguishes between semantic descriptors, which go into `<Property>` tags, and link relations, which go into `<Link>` tags.

It's pretty straightforward once you understand the description strategy. Here's an XRD description of a cell in a Maze+XML maze:

```
<XRD xmlns="http://docs.oasis-open.org/ns/xri/xrd-1.0">
 <Subject>http://example.com/cells/M</Subject>

 <Property type="http://alps.io/example/maze#title">
  The Entrance Hallway
 </Property>

 <Link rel="http://alps.io/example/maze#east"
       href="http://example.com/cells/N" />
 <Link rel="http://alps.io/example/maze#west"
       href="http://example.com/cells/L" />
</XRD>
```

Again, it doesn't matter whether or not the resource identified by *http://example.com/cells/M* "exists" (that is, has a representation). This is just a document with a few things to say about that resource.

RFC 6415 defines a simple way to translate an XRD document into a JSON object. The result is called JRD, and it's served as `application/jrd+json`:

```
{
 "subject": "http://example.com/cells/M",
 "properties": {
```

```
  "http://alps.io/example/maze#title": "The Entrance Hallway"
},
"links": [
 { "rel": "http://alps.io/example/maze#east",
   "href": "http://example.com/cells/N" },
 { "rel": "http://alps.io/example/maze#west",
   "href": "http://example.com/cells/L" }
]
}
```

Web Host Metadata Documents

- **Media type:** `application/xrd+xml` or `application/jrd+json`
- **Defined in:** RFC 6415
- **Medium:** XML or JSON
- **Protocol semantics:** navigation with GET; limited lookup capability with GET
- **Application semantics:** none

A web host metadata document is an XRD document containing a top-level description of an API as a whole. It's sort of like the description found in a JSON Home Document (see Chapter 10). The XRD version of a web host metadata document is supposed to go under the Well-Known URI */.well-known/host-meta*. (See Chapter 9 for an introduction to Well-Known URIs.) If there's a JRD version of that document, it's supposed to go under the Well-Known URI */.well-known/host-meta.json*.

Like any XRD document, a web host metadata document may include properties and links. The properties are properties of the API as a whole, such as the current version of the server implementation. The links are links to especially important resources in the API, such as top-level collections.

An XRD link may have a `template` attribute instead of a `href` attribute. This turns the link into a directory lookup service for URIs. Here's a simple example that shows how useful a lookup service can be in the high-level description of an API:

```
<Link rel="copyright" template="http://example.com/copyright?resource={uri}" />
```

This `<Link>` tag says that if the client wants to find the copyright statement for any resource, whether it's identified by an *http:* URI or a *urn:isbn:* URI, it should send a GET request and pass the URI into the template that has `rel="copyright"`. That GET request will trigger the `copyright` state transition for the URI that was passed in. This way, a client can trigger a state transition for a URI that has no representation! The URI *urn:isbn:9781449358063* has no representation, but if you send a GET request to *http://example.com/copyright?resource=urn:isbn:9781449358063*, you can get the representation of a related resource: the copyright information for the book.

The value of the `template` attribute resembles a URI Template, but it's not a URI Template, because the only variable you're allowed to use is {uri}. A web host metadata document can use the `<Link>` to link to one specific other resource (using the `href` attribute), and it can link to a URI-based lookup service (using the `template` attribute with the {uri} variable), but that's it. You can't put a general search form into a web host metadata document.

Here's the example the authors of RFC 6415 clearly had in mind:

```
<Link rel="lrdd" href="http://example.com/lookup?resource={uri}" />
```

This tells the client that if he ever wants an XRD description of a resource, he can plug its URI into the template and send a GET request to the resulting URL. The `lrdd` link relation is an IANA-registered link to an XRD description. (It's called `lrdd` for reasons too convoluted and dull to go into here.)

The web host metadata document is now an XRD document that tells you how to look up other XRD documents. You may never be able to get a representation of a URI, but a web host metadata document can help you find a wide variety of descriptions of that URI.

WebFinger

- **Media type:** `application/jrd+json`
- **Defined in:** Internet-Draft "draft-ietf-appsawg-webfinger"
- **Medium:** JRD
- **Protocol semantics:** the same as JRD
- **Application semantics:** user accounts

The WebFinger protocol is just a name for the use of JRD documents to look up information about user accounts. An account may be identified by email address, using the `acct:` URI scheme:[4]

```
acct:jenny@example.com
```

Or an account may be identified with an *http:* URL, probably a URL managed by an OpenID provider:

```
http://openid.example.com/users/omjennyg
```

A client makes a WebFinger request by sending a GET request to the passing in the URI to the account it wants to look up:

```
GET /.well-known/webfinger?resource=acct%3Ajenny%40example.com HTTP/1.1
```

---

4. Defined in the Internet-Draft "draft-ietf-appsawg-acct-uri," as I mentioned before.

The server should respond with a JRD description of the user account. This description is supposed to include an extra JSON property called `subject`, which gives the URI of the resource being described:

```
HTTP/1.1 200 OK
Content-Type: application/jrd+json

{
 "subject": "acct:jenny@example.com",
 "properties": {
  "http://schema.org/name": "Jenny Gallegos",
  "http://schema.org/email": "jenny@example.com"
 }
}
```

That's it, really. The JRD file format does most of the work, and the `acct:` URI scheme does almost everything else. The only things unique to WebFinger are the `subject` property and the Well-Known URI template, */.well-known/webfinger?resource={uri}.*

This is a perfect example of a situation where resource description works better than resource representation. When a person signs up for an account on your website, you probably identify her by her email address or OpenID URL. An OpenID URL has a representation, but you probably don't control the OpenID server, so you can't *change* its representation. An email address has no representation at all! Nonetheless, WebFinger lets you publish *descriptions* of your users' accounts. You can say whatever you want to say about those accounts by annotating the corresponding `acct:` URIs.

The Ontology Zoo

This is a follow-up to Chapter 10's "The Semantic Zoo" on page 230, listing some RDF Schema vocabularies of interest. There are a lot of RDF Schema vocabularies, but they're scattered all over the Internet. I'm just going to mention two popular vocabularies, and one site that collects vocabularies.

I've focused on vocabularies that are likely to be useful in consumer-facing APIs. Most of the really heavy-duty vocabularies are used in scientific or medical applications, not to describe the semantics of documents served over the Web. Check out the SWEET ontologies (*http://sweet.jpl.nasa.gov/*) for a very large vocabulary designed for scientific use.

schema.org RDF

- **Site:** Schema home page (*http://schema.org/*)
- **Vocabulary document:** located here (*http://schema.org/docs/schema_org_rdfa.html*)

- **Semantics:** the kinds of things a human being might want to search for online

Earlier in this book, I presented the concepts defined by schema.org—Person, Creati veWork, and so on—as HTML microdata items. That's how they're presented on the schema.org website. But behind the scenes, those concepts are defined by a machine-readable RDF vocabulary. That's the vocabulary I've been referencing throughout this chapter, using URIs like *http://schema.org/Person* and *http://schema.org/birthDate*. I used that same RDF vocabulary to generate ALPS versions of all the schema.org microdata items for my alps.io site.

If you're using RDF or JSON-LD, you can reference the schema.org RDF vocabulary when you describe resources. This lets you talk about all the things schema.org talks about, using the description strategy instead of the representation strategy.

Compare the use of schema.org microdata in the HTML representation of a resource…

```
<div itemscope itemtype="http://schema.org/Person">
 <span itemprop="birthDate">1987-08-25</span>
</div>
```

…with the use of schema.org's RDF vocabulary to describe a resource that has no representation:

```
@prefix schema: <http://schema.org/>
<acct:omjennyg@example.com> a schema:Person ;
                    schema:birthDate "1987-08-25" .
```

Of course, you're not limited to describing people. You can use any of the nearly 1,000 concepts described by schema.org's RDF vocabulary—so long as schema.org sees those concepts the same way you do.

FOAF

- **Site:** FOAF Vocabulary Specification page (*http://xmlns.com/foaf/spec/*)
- **Vocabulary document:** Download index.rdf here (*http://xmlns.com/foaf/spec/index.rdf*)
- **Semantics:** people and organizations

FOAF is the most famous RDF Schema ontology. It's an informal industry standard for describing people, organizations, and the relationships between them.

Here's how to represent a person's name and birthday[5] in RDF/Turtle, using the FOAF vocabulary:

---

5. Not date of birth! That's more complicated.

```
@prefix foaf: <http://xmlns.com/foaf/0.1/>
<acct:omjennyg@example.com> a foaf:Person ;
                            foaf:name "Jennifer Gallegos" ;
                            foaf:birthday "08-25" .
```

vocab.org

- **Site:** located here (*http://purl.org/vocab/*)
- **Vocabulary document:** various
- **Semantics:** miscellaneous

This is a site that hosts RDF Schema documents, maintained by Ian Davis. It's sort of like my own alps.io registry for ALPS documents. The collection is eclectic, and includes the BIO vocabulary I mentioned in a footnote earlier, as well as a vocabulary for describing varieties of whiskey.

As a matter of policy, vocab.org also allows anyone to claim namespace URIs that start with *http://vocab.org/vnd/*. This means I can publish an RDF document that describes a resource with the URI *http://vocab.org/vnd/mamund.com/2013/my-wonderful-resource*. I don't control vocab.org, and I'm not allowed to upload files to it, so that resource will never have a representation. But I own that URI and I can describe it however I want.

Conclusion: The Description Strategy Lives!

To a mind accustomed to REST, RDF documents look strange. This is partly because there are many different ways of writing down an "RDF document," but mostly because RDF documents commonly ignore the Fielding constraints. There are real RDF documents, which real people use to do their jobs, containing URLs that give you 404 errors in response to HTTP GET. From a REST perspective, devoted to the representation strategy, these URLs "don't exist" and the documents that include them are broken. Understand the description strategy, and things will make a little more sense.

This chapter, and life in general, would be simpler if it were possible to ignore the description strategy. Thanks to Linked Data, you sort of can! The Linked Data movement says it's better to use RDF in a way that fulfills the Fielding constraints. Just publish your RDF Schema vocabulary on the Web, and make sure you only use it to describe resources that also exist on the Web.

The upside of Linked Data is pretty big. RDF Schema and OWL are much more powerful than ALPS when it comes to describing application semantics in machine-readable ways. And you don't have to give up the Fielding constraints to take advantage of these technologies.

But I can't pretend that Linked Data is the whole story. The Semantic Web is much older than Linked Data, and even now, not everyone is on the Linked Data bandwagon. When you use Semantic Web technologies, you'll encounter a lot of documents whose URLs turn out to be URIs. I don't think you should create *more* of these documents, but to deal with the ones that already exist, you need to understand what they mean. They're descriptions of resources that have no representations.

CoAP: REST for Embedded Systems

The Constrained Application Protocol[1] is a protocol designed for use in low-power embedded environments like home automation systems. CoAP is inspired by HTTP and can be used to publish hypermedia-driven RESTful APIs, but it's a *very* different protocol from HTTP. CoAP brings a web-like architecture to a highly constrained environment: an "Internet of Things" in which a lot of small, cheap computers communicate over a low-capacity network.

CoAP is designed to live with severe limitations on electricity consumption, network bandwidth, and processing power. Its world resembles the ARPAnet of the 1970s rather than the network people enjoy today. CoAP requests and responses are *very* small. On a network that runs over home power lines, a CoAP message shouldn't be larger than about 1,024 bytes. On a low-power wireless network, you probably don't want to go above 80 bytes.

But in terms of network layout, these environments look a lot like the World Wide Web. There's no single "API provider" that serves a lot of similar clients. Instead, devices from many different manufacturers are placed into the same room, seemingly at random. Some of them have data to provide. Some have the ability to make things happen in the real world. Very rarely, one of these devices might get a human's attention long enough to answer a yes-or-no question.

These devices must locate each other over the network, learn each other's capabilities, and figure out how to work together, all with little or no guidance from the human who installed the equipment. It's utter chaos. In this radically decentralized environment, as on the Web, a strategy based on hypermedia is the only one with a chance of working.

---

1. An open standard under development as the Internet-Draft "draft-ietf-core-coap."

A CoAP Request

You know how a typical HTTP request works. The client opens a TCP connection to the server, sends the request, and awaits a response over the same connection. CoAP was designed to operate over UDP, a sister protocol to TCP that doesn't support connections at all. A CoAP client sends a request message to a server, and then goes about its business. The client has no idea when the response message, if any, will arrive.

Here's an example request message taken from the CoAP standard:

```
CON [0xbc90]
GET /temperature
(Token 0x71)
```

 I need to make it clear that this is *not* the actual CoAP message. This is a human-readable version of the message, which I formatted to look as much like HTTP as possible. The message actually sent over UDP is packed into a binary format that is pretty much unintelligible to humans: CON becomes the 2-bit integer 00, GET becomes 0001, and so on.

What does the request message mean? GET /temperature should make sense to you from HTTP. CoAP defines the four basic HTTP methods (GET, POST, PUT, and DELETE), though their semantics are slightly different than in HTTP.

CON stands for "Confirmable", which means that this message requires an acknowledgment message from the server (I'll talk more about this in the following section).

The hexadecimal number 0xbc90 is a "message ID," which will be used in that acknowledgment message. Without the message ID, a client that makes two GET requests and gets two responses won't know which response goes with which request.

The hexadecimal number 0x71 is a "token." A single CoAP request may trigger several responses, and the token is used in *every* response, not just the initial acknowledgment. Responses sent after the acknowledgment will have new message IDs, but they'll be tied to the original request by the token.

A CoAP Response

So, the client sends its request, and then goes about its business. But its message was a CON message, which requires an acknowledgment. Eventually the original server will send that acknowledgment, in the form of an acknowledgment (ACK) message.

Here's a human-readable version of an acknowledgment message.

```
ACK [0xbc90]
2.05 Content
```

```
(Token: 0x71)
Content-Format: text/plain;charset=utf-8
22.5 C
```

 Again, I formatted this message to resemble HTTP. It doesn't really look like this. A real CoAP message is packed into a tight binary format. For instance, the media type `application/json` is represented by the eight-bit bitstring 00110010.

- "ACK" means that this message is acknowledging receipt of an earlier message (the CON message I showed you earlier, with Message ID 0xbc90 and Token 0x71).

- The line `2.05 Content` is a status code, equivalent to HTTP's `200 OK`.

- `Content-Format` is a CoAP *option*, which serves the same purpose as an HTTP header. The `Content-Format` option does the job of HTTP's `Content-Type` header.

- The string `22.5 C` is the payload, what HTTP calls the "entity-body".

The request and the response are completely different messages. They don't share a TCP connection the way an HTTP request and response do. They're connected by data found in the messages themselves: by the message ID (0xbc90) and the token (0x71).

Kinds of Messages

Each CoAP request has an associated method. CoAP defines four methods, each named after an HTTP method: GET, POST, PUT, and DELETE. CoAP methods are not exactly the same as the corresponding HTTP methods, but they have the same basic properties: GET is safe, PUT is idempotent, and so on.

CoAP defines one additional bit of protocol semantics—the message type—to deal with the fact that CoAP requests and responses are carried in separate messages. Every message is one of these four types:

- A *confirmable* message (CON) requires an *Acknowledgment* message (ACK). A client will keep resending a CON message until it receives an ACK message with the same message ID.

- A *nonconfirmable* (NON) message does not require an acknowledgment message (ACK). Only safe requests (that is, GET requests) should be made nonconfirmable.

- An *acknowledgment* message (ACK) acknowledges that an earlier message was received *and processed*.

- That's in contrast to a *reset* message (RST), which acknowledges an earlier message, but says that the recipient couldn't process it. The recipient may have rebooted and lost the necessary context, or it may have temporarily dropped off the network and missed an earlier message.

These message types basically recreate the request-response structure of HTTP. A CON message plus an ACK message is equivalent to an HTTP request and response. A client that sends a CON message and gets no acknowledgment is supposed to resend the CON message, just as an HTTP client that sends a GET request and gets no response is supposed to resend the request.

But there are two interesting features of CoAP that are not found in HTTP at all. One (delayed response) relies on the fact that one CoAP request can trigger several responses. The other (multicast messages) takes advantage of a feature that HTTP can't use, because TCP doesn't support it.

Delayed Response

Suppose a client sends a CON message that will take a very long time to process. The server can immediately respond with an ACK message. This tells the client that the message has been received, and that the client can stop resending the CON message. The client can expect a *second* message later, containing the actual response.

This second response is *not* an ACK message. It's either a CON message or a NON message. The server is turning the tables on the client. The third message has a different message ID from the initial CON message, but it reuses the token, so the original client knows that it's a response to the original CON message.

The situation is analogous to buying a book from an online bookstore. You send a CON message, and the store immediately sends you an email receipt (an ACK message), confirming your purchase. But the book itself won't arrive for a few days. You might have to sign for delivery (respond to the server's CON message with an ACK message), or the mail carrier might just leave the book on your front porch (the book would be a NON message). Either way, you'll receive your book, along with a receipt (the token) that ties the book to your original order (your original CON message).

HTTP defines a response code (202, `Accepted`) that works sort of like this, but HTTP defines no way for the server to get back in touch with the client once it's finished processing the message that was "accepted." By the time that happens, the TCP connection has been closed. There are ways to get around this (I'll cover them when I talk about `Accepted` in Appendix B), but there's no one well-defined solution. With CoAP, the solution is built into the protocol.

Multicast Messages

A CoAP client can use UDP multicast to broadcast a message to every machine on the local network. TCP does not support multicast, so you can't really do this with HTTP.

The stereotypical use case for CoAP multicast (and for CoAP in general) is home automation. In this scenario, your thermostat, refrigerator, television, light switches, and other home appliances have cheap embedded processors that communicate over a local low-power network. When you plug in a new appliance, it detects other computers on the network, discovers their capabilities through the exchange of hypermedia documents, and starts collaborating with them.

This lets your appliances coordinate their behavior without direct input from you. When you turn the oven on, the climate control system can notice this event and turn down the heat in the kitchen. You can pull out your mobile phone, get a list of all the lights in your current room, and dim the lights through your phone, without having to go over to the light switch.

The home automation use case has been around for over 50 years, and I personally think it's a cheesy pipe dream, but there are other scenarios where multicast discovery is a lot less cheesy. Multicast can let one mobile phone talk to all the other phones in the room. It can allow a group of scientific instruments to share readings, or connect low-bandwidth wireless peripherals to a desktop computer.

Any time there are a lot of small computers in the same place, CoAP and UDP multicast lets them discover each other and figure out how they can cooperate. The principles at work are statelessness, addressability, and self-descriptive messages: core principles of REST.

The CoRE Link Format

- **Media type:** `application/link-format`
- **Defined in:** RFC 6690
- **Medium:** plain text
- **Protocol semantics:** navigation and searches with GET
- **Application semantics:** none!

Of course, REST is a lot more than just the transport protocol. REST works through the exchange of hypermedia representations, and hypermedia representations tend to be pretty large. You can't send HTML or Collection+JSON representations when your entire response has to fit in 80 or a 1024 bytes.[2]

HTTP can compress representations to save bandwidth, but compression won't help here. A light sensor may not have enough processing power to decompress a representation in a reasonable time, much less parse the decompressed document. It may not have enough memory to *store* the whole document. That's why the developers of CoAP designed a new hypermedia format specifically for embedded applications: the CoRE Link Format.

Here's a CoRE Link Format representation of a cell from Chapter 5's maze game.

```
</cells/M>;rel="current";rt="http://alps.io/example/maze#cell",
</cells/N>;rel="east";rt="http://alps.io/example/maze#cell",
</cells/L>;rel="west";rt="http://alps.io/example/maze#cell",
<http://alps.io/example/maze>;rel="profile"
```

There are four links, each with a `rel` attribute. Three of the links (`current`, `west`, and `east`) point to cells in the maze (`cell`). The third link (`profile`) points to some kind of profile that explains what `current`, `east`, `west`, and `cell` mean.

Unlike CoAP messages, documents in CoRE Link Format are human-readable. It's not a binary format. The only change I made to this representation was to add a newline after every link, so it would fit on the page. CoRE Link Format can fit a lot of hypermedia into a kilobyte, without utterly sacrificing human-readability.

CoRE Link Format describes a link using the same syntax as the `Link` HTTP header. RFC 6690 defines some extension parameters, notably `rt` which contains a URI indicating the abstract semantic type (see Chapter 12) of the resource on the other end of the link:

```
</cells/N>;rel="east";rt="http://alps.io/example/maze#cell"
```

RFC 6690 also proposes some optional techniques for sending search queries to CoAP resources and getting back responses in CoRE Link Format. This gives the `application/link-format` media type some features similar to those found in Collection+JSON, OData, or any other implementation of the collection pattern.

But there's no space for data in a CoRE Link Format document. CoRE Link Format is hypermedia in its purest form. It can *only* represent state transitions. Real data—e.g., instrument readings, statistics, and human-readable messages—must be served in some other data format, such as JSON.

---

2. The Internet-Draft "draft-ietf-core-block" will allow a large representation to be split across several CoAP messages. This will help a lot, but building a traditional web-style API around this feature would be very inefficient.

Conclusion: REST Without HTTP

CoAP is very different from HTTP, but its architecture is RESTful. A CoAP system obeys the statelessness constraint. In fact, it's more stateless than HTTP, since a request and its responses are not tied together by a TCP connection. CoAP defines protocol semantics that are similar to (but not identical to) HTTP's. CoRE Link Format can't represent data, but it's a real hypermedia format with more hypermedia controls than HAL.

A CoAP device can connect to a network, send out a UDP multicast message to see who else is around, and start exploring what the other devices have to offer—all without any human interaction. This flexibility is made possible by REST's hypermedia constraint, and it's the only realistic solution for a longstanding pipe dream like home automation. A refrigerator that wants to talk to your microwave can't afford to be picky about what kind of microwave you have installed.

To my mind, this situation looks like the world of APIs as a whole. We live in a house (the Internet) full of thousands of useful but obscure programmable appliances (APIs). REST is about making those appliances work together with minimal human involvement.

Success means agreeing on application semantics. Appliances and APIs should use the same words when talking about the same things. It also means *advertising* our protocol semantics. Every "appliance" must explain what it does, not in a dusty manual kept in a folder, but online, in terms another "appliance" can understand. This may seem like a crazy pipe dream, but it's the only way to manage the complexity of all these things we've created.

The Status Codex

An HTTP status code is a three-digit number attached to an HTTP response. It's a bit of protocol semantics that lets the client know, on the most basic level, what happened when the server tried to handle the request. The 41 HTTP response codes defined in the HTTP specification form a set of basic protocol semantics that any API can use.

Apart from HTTP redirects, and the famous "404 Not Found" error page notwithstanding, we don't really use status codes on the World Wide Web. A human learns what happened to a request by reading the entity-body served as part of the response, not by looking up a numeric code in the HTTP standard. When you fill out a form on a website, but you forget to fill in one of the required fields, the server sends back an error message, but the response code associated with the error message is 200 (OK).

That's fine. You don't even see the response code. You read the error message and correct the problem. But an API that behaved that way would be lying to its client! Computer programs are very good at looking up numeric codes, and very bad at understanding prose. When you serve the 200 status code on an error condition, you must write extra documentation explaining that in your API, OK doesn't necessarily mean OK. That extra documentation means more work for your users.

In the world of APIs, then, HTTP response codes become very important. They tell a client how to regard the document in the entity-body—whether it's a representation or an error message—or what to do if the client can't understand the entity-body. A client (or an intermediary between server and client, like a proxy or firewall) can figure out how an HTTP request went, just by looking at the first few bytes of the response.

That said, some of the HTTP status codes are completely useless. Some are useful only in very limited situations, and some are only distinguishable from one another by careful hairsplitting. To someone used to the World Wide Web (that's all of us), the variety of status codes can be bewildering.

In this appendix, I give a brief explanation of each status code, with tips on when to use it in your APIs, and my personal opinion as to how important it is to API design. If a client must do something specific to get a certain response code, I explain what that is. I also list which HTTP response headers, and what kind of entity-body, the server ought to send along with a response code. This is an appendix for the API developer, but it's also for the client author, who's received a strange response code and doesn't know what it means.

As with link relations and media types, the IANA keeps an official registry of HTTP status codes (*http://www.iana.org/assignments/http-status-codes/*). Here, "official" basically means "defined in an RFC." In this appendix, I'll cover all 41 codes mentioned in RFC 2616, even though some of them (mainly the ones to do with proxies) are a little beyond the scope of this book. I'll also cover a few status codes defined in other RFCs, notably RFC 6585, the aptly named "Additional HTTP Status Codes."

I won't be covering CoAP's HTTP-inspired status codes (4.04 Not Found), or the HTTP status codes defined by extensions like WebDAV. Nor do I cover status codes introduced by web server implementations but not formally defined anywhere. These include 509 (Bandwidth Limit Exceeded), and nginx's many internal error-reporting codes, like 499 (Client Closed Request).

Problem Detail Documents

In Chapter 10, I mentioned problem detail documents—short hypermedia documents that give a human-readable explanation of an HTTP status code. Don't forget about these! You can use them to add API-specific details to a generic status code like 400 (Bad Request). There's no need to invent a new representation format (or, worse, a new status code) for conveying detailed error information. If your representation format has a slot for error reporting, the way Collection+JSON does, you probably don't need problem detail documents.

Remember, detailed error reporting is not an excuse for serving 200 (OK) when something's not OK. The meaning of your representation must always be *consistent* with your HTTP status code.

Families of Status Codes

The first digit of an HTTP status code is a very general indication of how the request went. The HTTP specification defines five families of status codes using the initial digits 1 through 5. I'll be covering each of these in a separate section:

1xx: Informational
    These response codes are used only in negotiations between an HTTP client and server.

2xx: Successful

Whatever state transition the client asked for has happened.

3xx: Redirection

The state transition the client asked for has not happened. But if the client is willing to make a slightly different HTTP request, *that* request should do what the client is asking for.

4xx: Client Error

The state transition the client has asked for has not happened, due to a problem with the HTTP request. The request was malformed, incoherent, self-contradictory, or one that the server cannot accept.

5xx: Server Error

The state transition the client has asked for has not happened, due to a problem on the server side. There's probably nothing the client can do but wait for the problem to be fixed.

Four Status Codes: The Bare Minimum

Before going through the big list of status codes, I want to list just four that I consider the bare minimum for APIs. There's one code from each family (apart from 1xx, which you can more or less ignore):

200 (OK)

Everything's fine. The document in the entity-body, if any, is a representation of some resource.

301 (Moved Permanently)

Sent when the client triggers a state transition that moves a resource from one URL to another. After the move, requests to the old URL will also result in a 301 status code.

400 (Bad Request)

There's a problem on the client side. The document in the entity-body, if any, is an error message. Hopefully the client can understand the error message and use it to fix the problem.

500 (Internal Server Error)

There's a problem on the server side. The document in the entity-body, if any, is an error message. The error message probably won't do much good, since the client can't fix a server problem.

If I could add just two more, they would be different kinds of client errors: 404 (Not Found) and 409 (Conflict). When you need to give more detail, you can adopt another status code from the big list, or provide a problem detail document.

And now, the big list. Unless otherwise noted, all these status codes are formally defined in RFC 2616.

1xx: Informational

The 1xx response codes are used only in negotiations between an HTTP client and server.

100 (Continue)

Importance: low to medium.

This is one of the possible responses to an HTTP look-before-you-leap (LBYL) request, which I described in Chapter 11. This status code indicates that the client should resend its initial request, including the (possibly large or sensitive) representation that was omitted the first time. The client no longer need worry about sending a representation only to have it rejected. The other possible response to a look-before-you-leap request is 417 (Expectation Failed).

Request headers: To make a LBYL request, the client must set the Expect header to the literal value "100-continue." The client must also set any other headers the server will need when determining whether to respond with 100 or 417.

101 (Switching Protocols)

Importance: Very low, potentially medium.

A client will only get this response code when its request uses the Upgrade header to inform the server that the client would prefer to use some protocol other than HTTP. A response of 101 means "All right, now I'm speaking another protocol." Ordinarily, an HTTP client would close the TCP connection once it read the response from the server. But a response code of 101 means it's time for the client to leave the connection open, but stop being an HTTP client and start being some other kind of client.

The Upgrade header is hardly ever used, though it could be used to trade up from HTTP to HTTPS, or from version 1.1 of HTTP to the eventually forthcoming version 2.0. It could also be used to switch from HTTP to a totally different protocol like IRC, but that would require the web server also to be an IRC server and the web client to also be an IRC client, because the server starts speaking the new protocol immediately, over the same TCP connection.

Request headers: The client sets Upgrade to a list of protocols it'd rather be using than HTTP.

Response headers: If the server wants to upgrade, it sends back an Upgrade header saying which protocol it's switching to, and then a blank line. Instead of closing the TCP connection, the server begins speaking the new protocol, and continues speaking the new protocol until the connection is closed.

2xx: Successful

The 2xx status codes indicate that whatever state transition the client asked for has happened.

200 (OK)

Importance: Very high.

In most cases, this is the code the client hopes to see. It indicates that the state transition is complete, and that no more specific code in the 2xx series is appropriate.

Entity-body: For a GET request, a representation of the resource that was the target of the GET. (This will cause a change in application state.) For other requests, a description of the change in resource state: a representation of the current state of the selected resource, or a description of the state transition itself.

201 (Created)

Importance: High.

The server sends this status code when it creates a new resource at the client's request.

Response headers: The `Location` header should contain the canonical URL to the new resource.

Entity-body: Should describe and link to the newly created resource. A representation of that resource is acceptable, if you use the `Location` header to tell the client where the resource actually lives.

202 (Accepted)

Importance: Medium.

The client's request can't or won't be handled in real time. It will be processed later. The request looks valid, but it might turn out to have problems when the server actually gets to it.

This is an appropriate response when a request triggers an asynchronous action, an action in the real world, or a state transition that would take so long that there's no point making the client wait around for a response.

Request headers: The `Prefer` header (see Appendix B) lets the client tell the server how long it's willing to wait around to get a real response instead of a 202.

Response headers: The pending request should be exposed as some kind of resource so the client can check up on it later. The `Location` header can contain the URL to this resource.

Entity-body: If there's no way for the client to check up on the request later, at least give an estimate of when the request will be processed. A problem detail document may be appropriate here, even though this isn't technically a "problem."

Retry-After: The `Retry-After` header can be used to indicate the server's estimate of when the full response will be ready. This header was designed for use with the 5xx and 3xx response codes, but can also be used safely for 202 responses.

203 (Non-Authoritative Information)

Importance: Very low.

This status code is the same as 200 (`OK`), but the server wants the client to know that some of the response headers do not come from the server. They may be mirrored from a previous request of the client's, or obtained from a third party.

Response Headers: The client should know that some headers may not be accurate, and others may be passed along without the server knowing what they mean.

204 (No Content)

Importance: High.

This status code is usually sent out in response to an unsafe request such as a PUT request. It means that the server has carried out the state transition, but that it declines to send back any representation or description of the state transition.

The server may also send 204 in response to a GET request. This means that the resource requested exists, but has an empty representation. Compare 304 (`Not Modified`).

204 is often in-browser JavaScript applications. It lets the server tell the client that its input was accepted, but that the client shouldn't change any UI elements.

Entity-body: Not allowed.

205 (Reset Content)

Importance: Low.

This is just like 204 (`No Content`), but it implies that the client should reset the view or data structure that was the source of the data. If you submit an HTML form in your web browser and the response is 204 ("No Content"), your data stays in the form and you can change it. If you get a 205, the form fields reset to their original values. In data entry terms: 204 is good for making a series of edits to a single record; 205 is good for entering a series of records in succession.

Entity-body: Not allowed.

206 (Partial Content)

Importance: Very high for APIs that support partial GET, low otherwise.

This is just like 200 (OK), but it designates a response to a partial GET request: i.e., one that uses the Content-Range request header. A client usually makes a partial GET request to resume an interrupted download of a large binary representation. I cover partial GET in Chapter 11.

Request headers: The client sends a value for the Content-Range header.

Response headers: The Date header is required. The ETag and Content-Location headers should be set to the same values that would have been sent along with the representation as a whole.

If the entity-body is a single byte range from the representation, the response as a whole must have a Content-Range header explaining which bytes of the representation are being served. If the body is a multipart entity (that is, multiple byte ranges of the representation are being served), the overall media type is multipart/byteranges, and each part must have its own Content-Range header.

Entity-body: Will not contain a full representation, just one or more sequences of bytes from the representation.

3xx: Redirection

The state transition the client asked for has not happened. But if the client is willing to make a slightly different HTTP request, *that* request should do what the client is asking for. In general, the client needs to repeat its request to a different resource.

This is the trickiest set of response codes, because 301 (Moved Permanently), 302 (Found), 303 (See Other), and 307 (Temporary Redirect), are all very similar. Many applications use these status codes indiscriminately as a way of bouncing the client like a ball through a hypermedia pinball machine, with little regard for what this means in terms of application semantics. My main goal in this section is to clear up the confusion.

300 (Multiple Choices)

Importance: Low.

The server can send this status code when it has multiple representations of a requested resource, and it doesn't know which representation the client wants. Either the client didn't use the `Accept-*` headers to specify a representation, or it asked for a representation that doesn't exist.

In this situation, the server can just pick its preferred representation, and send it along with a 200 (`OK`) status code. But it may decide instead to send a 300 along with a list of possible URIs to different representations.

Response headers: If the server has a preferred representation, it can put the URI to that representation in `Location`. As with most other 3xx status codes, the client may automatically follow the URI in `Location`.

Entity-body: A list of hypermedia links, along with the necessary application semantics to let the user make a choice between them.

301 (Moved Permanently)

Importance: Medium.

The server knows which resource the client is trying to access, but the client doesn't care for the URL it used to request the resource. It wants the client to take note of the new URL and use it in future requests.

You can use this status code to keep old URLs from breaking when your API changes its URL structure.

Response headers: The server should put the canonical URL in `Location`.

Entity-body: The server should send a hypermedia document that links to the new location.

302 (Found)

Importance: Very important to *know about*, especially when writing clients. I don't recommend *using* it.

This status code is the ultimate source of most redirection-related confusion. It's *supposed* to be handled just like 307 (`Temporary Redirect`). In fact, in HTTP 1.0 its name was `Moved Temporarily`. Unfortunately, in real life most clients handle 302 just like 303 (`See Other`). The difference hinges on what the client is supposed to do when it gets a 302 in response to a PUT, POST, or DELETE request. See the entries for 307 and 308 (`Permanent Redirect`) if you're interested in the details.

To resolve this ambiguity, in HTTP 1.1 this response code was renamed to `Found`, and response code 307 was created. This response code is still in wide use, but it's ambiguous, and I recommend that your servers send 303, 307, and 308 instead.

Response headers: The `Location` header contains the URL to which the client should resubmit the request.

Entity-body: Should contain a hypermedia link to the new URL, as with 301.

303 (See Other)

Importance: High.

The request has been processed, but instead of the server sending a response document, it's sending the client the URL of a response document. This may be the URL of a static status message, or of some more interesting resource. In the latter case, a 303 is a way for the server to send a representation of a resource without forcing the client to download all that data. The client is expected to follow up with a GET request to the URL mentioned in `Location`, but it doesn't have to.

The 303 status code is a good way to canonicalize your resources. You can make them available through many URLs, but only have one "real" URL per representation. All the other URLs use a 303 to point to the canonical URL for that representation. For instance, a 303 might redirect a request for *http://www.example.com/software/current.tar.gz* to the URL *http://www.example.com/software/1.0.2.tar.gz*.

Compare to 307 (`Temporary Redirect`).

Response headers: The `Location` header contains the URL of the representation.

Entity-body: Should contain a hypermedia link to the new URL, as with 301.

304 (Not Modified)

Importance: High.

This status code is similar to 204 (`No Content`) in that the response body must be empty. But 204 is used when there is no body data to send, and 304 is used when there is data but the client already has it. There's no point in sending it again.

This status code is used in conjunction with conditional HTTP requests. If the client sends an `If-Modified-Since` header with a date of Sunday, and the representation hasn't changed since Sunday, then a 304 is appropriate. A 200 (`OK`) would also be appropriate, but sending the representation again would waste bandwidth, since the client already has it.

Response headers: The `Date` header is required. The `ETag` and `Content-Location` headers should be set to the same values that would have been sent if the response code were 200 (`OK`).

The caching headers `Expires`, `Cache-Control`, and `Vary` are required if they've changed from those sent previously.

There are complicated caching rules about this that I won't cover here, but the server can send updated headers without sending a new body. This is useful when a representation's metadata has changed, but the entity-body hasn't.

Entity-body: Not allowed.

305 (Use Proxy)

Importance: Low.

This status code is used to tell the client that it should repeat its request, but go through an HTTP proxy instead of going to the server directly. This code is rarely used because it's very rare for a server to care that the client used a specific proxy.

This code would be used more frequently if there were proxy-based mirror sites. Today, a mirror site for *http://www.example.com/* provides the same content but at a different URL, say *http://www.example.com.mysite.com/*. The original site might use the 307 (`Temporary Redirect`) status code to send clients to an appropriate mirror site.

If there were proxy-based mirror sites, then you would access the mirror with the same URL as the original (*http://www.example.com/*), but set *http://proxy.mysite.com/* as your proxy. Here, the original *example.com* might use the 305 status code to route clients to a mirror proxy that's geographically close to them.

Web browsers typically don't handle this status code correctly: another reason for its lack of popularity.

Response headers: The `Location` header contains the URL to the proxy.

306: Unused

Importance: None.

The 306 status code never made it into an RFC. It was described in the Internet-Draft "draft-cohen-http-305-306-responses" as `Switch Proxy`, a status code sent by a proxy server to get the client to start using a different proxy. That Internet-Draft expired in 1996, so don't worry about it.

307 (Temporary Redirect)

Importance: High.

The request has not been processed, because the requested resource is not home: it's located at some other URL. The client should resubmit the request to another URL.

For GET requests, where the only thing being requested is that the server send a representation, this status code is identical to 303 (`See Other`). A typical case where 307 is a good response to a GET is when the server wants to send a client to a mirror site. But for POST, PUT, and DELETE requests, where the server is expected to take some action in response to the request, this status code is significantly different from 303.

A 303 in response to a POST, PUT, or DELETE means that the operation has succeeded but that the response entity-body is not being sent along with this request. If the client wants the response entity-body, it needs to make a GET request to another URL.

A 307 in response to a POST, PUT, or DELETE means that the server has not even tried to perform the operation. The client needs to resubmit the entire request to the URL in the Location header.

An analogy may help. You go to a pharmacy with a prescription to be filled. A 303 is the pharmacist saying "We've filled your prescription. Go to the next window to pick up your medicine." A 307 is the pharmacist saying "We've run out of that medicine. Go to the pharmacy next door."

Response headers: The Location header contains the URL to which the client should resubmit the request.

Entity-body: Should contain a hypermedia link to the new URL, as with 301.

308 (Permanent Redirect)

Importance: Medium.

Defined in: Internet-Draft "draft-reschke-http-status-308"

A 308 in response to a GET request is the same as a 301 (Moved Permanently). But a 308 in response to an unsafe request works like 307 (Temporary Redirect): the client should resubmit the request to the URL given in the Location header. The difference is that the client should also use the URL given in the Location header for any *future* requests it was thinking about making.

To continue the pharmacy analogy from my discussion of 307 (Temporary Redirect), a 308 response code is a pharmacy that's gone out of business. Coming back later won't help. You'll have to take your prescription, and all future business, to the pharmacy next door.

This status code is defined in an extension to HTTP which is still in Internet-Draft form. Even after it does become an RFC, it will probably be safer to use 307 even for permanent redirects. Clients may not undertand what a 308 response code means.

4xx: Client-Side Error

These status codes indicate that something is wrong on the client side. There's a problem with authentication, with the format of the representation, with the timing of the request, or with the HTTP client itself. The client needs to fix something on its end.

Problem details (see Chapter 10) are most useful for the 4xx series of codes. For most of these error codes I say that the entity-body may contain a "document." Unless you're using a representation format with a built-in error reporting mechanism, I suggest you make that document a problem detail.

400 (Bad Request)

Importance: Very high.

This is the generic client-side error status, used when no other 4xx error code is appropriate. It's commonly used when the client submits a representation along with a PUT or POST request, and the representation is in the right format, but it doesn't make any sense.

Entity-body: May contain a document explaining the server's view of the client-side problem.

401 (Unauthorized)

Importance: High.

The client sent a request to a protected resource without providing the proper authentication credentials. It may have provided the wrong credentials, or none at all. The credentials may be a username and password, an API key, or an authentication token —whatever the API in question is expecting. It's common for a client to make a request for a URL and accept a 401 just so it knows what kind of credentials to send and in what format. In fact, the HTTP Digest mode of authentication depends on this behavior.

If the server doesn't want to acknowledge the existence of the resource to unauthorized users, it may lie and send a 404 (Not Found) instead of a 401. The downside of this is that clients need to know, in advance, what kind of authentication the server expects for that resource. Protocols like HTTP Digest won't work.

Response headers: The WWW-Authenticate header describes what kind of authentication the server *will* accept.

Entity-body: A document describing the failure; why the credentials (if any were provided) were rejected, and what credentials would be accepted. If a human end-user can get credentials by signing up on a website, or creating a "user account" resource, a hypermedia link to the sign-up resource is also useful.

402 (Payment Required)

Importance: None.

Apart from its name, this status code is not defined in the HTTP standard: it's "reserved for future use." This is because there's no micropayment system for HTTP. That said, if there ever *is* a micropayment system for HTTP, APIs are among the first places that system will start showing up. If you want to charge your users by the HTTP request, and your relationship with them makes that possible, you might have a use for this status code.

But there are already a lot of APIs that charge by the request, and I don't know of any that use this status code. It will probably stay "reserved" forever.

403 (Forbidden)

Importance: Medium.

The client's request is formed correctly, but the server just doesn't want to carry it out. This is not merely a case of insufficient credentials: that would be 401 (Unauthorized). This is more like a resource that is only accessible at certain times, or from certain IP addresses.

A response of 403 implies that the client send a request to a resource that really exists. As with 401 (Unauthorized), if the server doesn't want to give out even this information, it can lie and send a 404 (Not Found) instead.

If the client's request is well formed, why is this status code in the 4xx series (client-side error) instead of the 5xx series (server-side error)? Because the server made its decision based on some aspect of the request other than its form: say, the time of day the request was made.

Entity-body: An optional document explaining why the request was denied.

404 (Not Found)

Importance: High.

Probably the most famous HTTP status code. 404 indicates that the server can't map the client's URL to a resource. Compare 410 (Gone), which is slightly more helpful.

Remember that a 404 may be a lie to cover up a 403 or 401. It might be that the resource exists, but the server doesn't want to let the client know about it.

Entity-body: An optional document explaining the error. The document may contain a hypermedia control for creating a resource in this spot (probably using HTTP PUT).

405 (Method Not Allowed)

Importance: Medium.

The client tried to use an HTTP method that this resource doesn't support. For instance, a read-only resource may support only GET and HEAD. Collection resources (as defined by the collection pattern) generally allow GET and POST, but not PUT or DELETE.

Response headers: The `Allow` header lists the HTTP methods that this resource does support. The following is a sample header:

```
Allow: GET, POST
```

406 (Not Acceptable)

Importance: Medium.

The server may send this response code when the client places so many restrictions on what it considers an acceptable representation (probably using the `Accept-*` request headers) that the server can't send any representation at all. The server may instead choose to ignore the client's pickiness, and simply send its preferred representation along with a response code of 200 (`OK`). This is usually what happens on the human web.

Entity-body: A hypermedia document that links to acceptable representations, in a format similar to that described in 300 (`Multiple Choices`).

407 (Proxy Authentication Required)

Importance: Low.

You'll only see this status code from an HTTP proxy. It's just like 401 (`Unauthorized`), except the problem is not that you can't use the API without credentials; it's that you can't use the *proxy* without credentials. As with 401, the problem may be that the client provided no credentials, or that the credentials provided are bad or insufficient.

Request headers: To send credentials to the proxy, the client uses the `Proxy-Authorization` header instead of the `Authorization` header. The format is identical to that of `Authorization`.

Response headers: Instead of the `Authenticate` header, the proxy fills the `Proxy-Authenticate` header with information about what kind of authentication it expects. The format is identical to that of `Authenticate`.

Note that both the proxy and the API may require credentials, so the client may clear up a 407 only to be hit with a 401 (`Unauthorized`).

Entity-body: A document describing the failure, like the one I described for status code 401.

408 (Request Timeout)

Importance: Low.

If an HTTP client opens a connection to the server, but never sends a request (or never sends the blank line that signals the end of the request), the server should eventually send a 408 response code and close the connection.

409 (Conflict)

Importance: Very high.

The client tried to create an impossible or inconsistent resource state on the server. What is "impossible" or "inconsistent" depends on the API's application semantics. A collection-based API may allow a client to DELETE an empty collection, but send 409 when the client tries to DELETE a collection that still contains members.

Response headers: If the conflict is caused by the existence of some other resource (e.g., the client tries to create a special resource that already exists), the Location header should link to the URL of that resource: that is, the source of the conflict.

Entity-body: Should contain a document that describes the conflicts, so that the client can resolve them if possible.

410 (Gone)

Importance: Medium.

This response code is like 404 (Not Found), but it provides a little more information. It's used when the server knows that the requested URL used to refer to a resource, but no longer does. The server doesn't know any new URL for the resource; if it did, it would send a 301 (Permanent Redirect).

Like the permanent redirect, a 410 response code has the implication that the client should remove the current URL from its vocabulary, and stop making requests for it. Unlike the permanent redirect, the 410 offers no replacement for the bad URL: it's just gone. RFC 2616 suggests using a 410 response code "for limited-time, promotional services and for resources belonging to individuals no longer working at the server's site."

You might be tempted to send this response code in response to a successful DELETE request, but that's a little too cute. The client wouldn't know whether it deleted the resource or whether it was gone before it made their request. The correct response to a successful DELETE request is 200 (OK).

411 (Length Required)

Importance: Low to medium.

An HTTP request that includes a representation should set the Content-Length request header to the length (in bytes) of the entity-body. Sometimes this is inconvenient for the client: for instance, when the representation is being streamed from some other source. So HTTP doesn't require a client to send the Content-Length header with each request. However, the HTTP server is within its rights to require it for any given request. The server is allowed to *interrupt* any request that starts sending a representation without having provided a Content-Length, and demand that the client resubmit the request with a Content-Length header. This is the response code that goes along with the interruption.

If the client lies about the length, or otherwise sends too large a representation, the server may interrupt it and close the connection, but in that case, the response code is 413 (Request Entity Too Large).

412 (Precondition Failed)

Importance: Medium.

The client specified one or more preconditions in its request headers, effectively telling the server to carry out its request only if certain conditions were met. Those conditions were in fact not met, so instead of carrying out the request the server sends this status code.

A common precondition is If-Unmodified-Since. (I covered this in Chapter 11.) The client may PUT a request to modify a resource, but ask that the changes take effect only if no one else has modified the resource since the client last fetched it. Without the precondition, the client might overwrite someone else's changes without realizing it, or might cause a 409 (Conflict).

Request headers: The client might get this response code by using any of the If-Match, If-None-Match, If-Modified-Since, or If-Unmodified-Since headers.

If-None-Match is a bit special. If the client specifies If-None-Match when making a GET or HEAD request, and the precondition fails, then the response code is not 412 but 304 (Not Modified). This is the basis of conditional HTTP GET (also covered in Chapter 11). If a PUT, POST, or DELETE request uses If-None-Match, and the precondition fails, then the response code is 412. The response code is also 412 when a precondition uses the If-Match or If-Unmodified-Since headers, no matter what the HTTP method is.

413 (Request Entity Too Large)

Importance: Low to medium.

This is similar to 411 (Length Required) in that the server can interrupt the client's request with this status code, and close the connection without waiting for the request to complete. The 411 status code was for requests that didn't specify the length of their representation. This status code is for requests that send a representation that's too large for the server to handle.

A look-before-you-leap request (see Chapter 11) is the best way for a client to avoid being interrupted with this error. If the LBYL request gets a response code of 100 (Continue), the client can go ahead and submit the full representation.

Response headers: The problem may be temporary and on the server side (a lack of resources) rather than on the client side (the representation is too damn big). If so, the server may set the Retry-After header to a date or a number of seconds, and the client can retry its request later.

414 (Request-URL Too Long)

Importance: Low.

The HTTP standard imposes no official limit on the length of a URL (and, in my opinion, there shouldn't be any). However, most existing web servers impose an upper limit on the length of a URL, and an API may do the same. The most common cause is a client that puts resource state in the URL, when it should be in the entity-body. Deeply nested data structures can also cause very long URLs. If this is a problem for you, give your resources opaque URLs generated using random numbers, rather than let the URLs get longer than, say, a kilobyte.

If a client connects to a server and starts sending an infinitely long URL, even a server that imposes no predefined maximum URL length may eventually interrupt the request with a 414 response, to free up the TCP connection. The server may also simply drop the connection.

415 (Unsupported Media Type)

Importance: Medium.

The server sends this status code when the client sends a representation in a media type it doesn't understand. The server might have been expecting application/vnd.collec tion+json and the client sent application/json.

If the client sends a document that's got the right media type but the wrong format (such as an XML document written in the wrong vocabulary, or a Collection+JSON document that uses the wrong ALPS profile), a better response is the more generic 400 (Bad Re quest).

416 (Requested Range Not Satisfiable)

Importance: Low.

The server sends this status code when the client asks for a series of byte-ranges from a representation, but the representation is actually too small for any of the byte-ranges to apply. In other words, if you ask for byte 100 of a 99-byte representation, you'll get this status code.

Request headers: This status code will only be sent when the original request included the Range header request field. It will not be sent if the original request included the If-Range header request field;

Response headers: The server should send a Content-Range field that tells the client the actual size of the representation.

417 (Expectation Failed)

Importance: Low to medium.

This response code is the flip side of 100 (Continue). If you make a look-before-you-leap request to see whether the server will accept your representation, and the server decides it will, you get a response code 100 and you can go ahead. If the server decides it won't accept your representation, you get a response code 417, and you shouldn't bother sending your representation.

428 (Precondition Required)

Importance: Medium.

Defined in: RFC 6585.

In Chapter 11, I recommend that API implementations require that clients make their PUT and PATCH requests conditional, as a way of avoiding the lost update problem. Web servers enforce that rule with this status code, which says that the client's request is being rejected because it wasn't made conditional.

Entity-body: Should contain a document explaining which conditional headers (probably If-Match or If-Unmodified-Since) the server will accept.

429 (Too Many Requests)

Importance: Medium.

Defined in: RFC 6585.

This status code enforces a server's rate limiting policy. The client has been sending too many requests lately, and needs to back off.

A server is allowed to simply ignore requests that violate the rate limiting policy, rather than respond to each of them with a 429.

Response headers: The Retry-After header should give a hint as to when the server will accept requests from this client again.

Entity-body: Should contain a document explaining the rate limiting policy.

431 (Request Header Fields Too Large)

Importance: Low.

Defined in: RFC 6585

This is like 413 (`Request Entity Too Large`) or 414 (`Request-URL Too Long`), but here the problem is that there is too much data in the request header fields.

It's legal for a server to put predefined limits on the size of the request headers but I don't think it's a good idea. The `Link` header, in particular, can legitimately get pretty big. If a client connects to a server and starts sending a request with infinitely long headers, the server can just interrupt the request with a 431 response. (The server may also simply drop the connection.)

Entity-body: If there's one particular header that's too large (as opposed to the headers collectively being too large), the entity-body should mention which header is the problem.

451 (Unavailable For Legal Reasons)

Importance: Ideally very low.

Defined in: Internet-Draft "draft-tbray-http-legally-restricted-status"

The client's request is well formed, but the server is legally required to reject it. Usually this is because the server is prohibited from serving a representation through some kind of censorship. The server may also use this status code when refusing to carry out a resource state transition.

This is considered a client-side error even though the request is well formed and the legal requirement exists on the server side. After all, that representation was censored for a reason. There must be something wrong with you, citizen.

5xx: Server-Side Error

The 5xx series of status codes is for representing problems on the server side. These codes usually mean the server is not in a state to carry out the client's request or even see whether it's correct, and that the client should retry its request later. Sometimes the server can estimate *when* the client should retry its request, and put that information into the `Retry-After` response header.

There are fewer 5xx status codes than 4xx status codes, not because fewer things might go wrong on the server, but because there's not much point in being specific. The client can't do anything to fix a problem on the server.

Responses that use these status codes can all include an explanatory document (perhaps a problem detail!) in the entity-body.

500 (Internal Server Error)

Importance: High.

This is the generic server error response. Most web frameworks send this status code if they run request handler code that raises an exception.

501 (Not Implemented)

Importance: Low.

The client tried to use a feature of HTTP (possibly an extended feature) that the server doesn't support.

The most common case is when a client tries to make a request that uses an extension HTTP method like PATCH, which a plain web server doesn't support. This is similar to the response code 405 (`Method Not Allowed`), but 405 implies that the client is using a recognized method on a resource that doesn't support it. A response code of 501 means that the server doesn't recognize the method at all.

502 (Bad Gateway)

Importance: Low.

You'll only get this response code from an HTTP proxy. It indicates that there was a problem with the proxy, or between the proxy and the upstream server, rather than a problem on the upstream server.

If the proxy can't reach the upstream server at all, the response code will be 504 (`Gateway Timeout`) instead.

503 (Service Unavailable)

Importance: Medium to high.

This status code means that the HTTP server is up, but the application underlying the API isn't working properly. The most likely cause is resource starvation: too many requests are coming in at once for the API to handle them all.

Since repeated client requests are probably what's causing the problem, the HTTP server always has the option of refusing to accept a client request, rather than accepting it only to send a 503 response code.

Response headers: The server may send a `Retry-After` header telling the client when to submit the request again.

504 (Gateway Timeout)

Importance: Low.

Like 502 (Bad Gateway), you'll only see this from an HTTP proxy. This status code signals that the proxy couldn't connect to the upstream server.

505 (HTTP Version Not Supported)

Importance: Very low.

The server doesn't support the version of HTTP the client is trying to use. You probably won't see this status code until HTTP 2.0 is announced. Even then, you'll probably only see it when trying to use HTTP 2.0 features on an HTTP 1.1 server.

Entity-body: Should contain a document describing which versions of HTTP the server does support.

511 (Network Authentication Required)

Importance: Medium.

Defined in: RFC 6585

The 511 status code is an attempt to make captive portals less annoying. A captive portal is the website that takes over your web browser when you try to use the wireless network in a coffee shop or hotel room. No matter what web page you request, the captive portal serves the status code 200 (OK) along with a page telling you how to pay for your Internet access. Sometimes the portal serves the status code 302 (Found) and *redirects* the browser to a page telling you how to pay for Internet access.

When this happens in your web browser, it's annoying, but you're a human being. You can read the web page and figure out how to get on the Web proper. When this happens to your API client, it's dangerous. As far as an automated client is concerned, it looks as if the API has shut down and been replaced with an illegible HTML document that probably says "sorry, we're closed." This will crash the client, potentially leaving its data in an inconsistent state.

The 511 status code doesn't make it any easier for an API client to get past the captive portal, but it does give the client a chance to figure out what's going on and exit gracefully, instead of panicking and crashing.

Serving the 511 status code requires that the developer of a captive portal give a damn about user experience, so I don't anticipate it coming into wide use anytime soon. But anticipating a 511 status code on the client side might let you avoid the worst case if someone fires up your API client in a coffee shop.

The Header Codex

HTTP headers are bits of metadata that describe the protocol semantics of an HTTP request or response. Some headers, like If-None-Match, are used only in requests. They're the client's way of telling the server how to handle the request. Some, like ETag, are used only in responses. They're the server's way of conveying information about how the request was processed, or information about the underlying resource that's not present in the representation. Some headers can be used either in a request or response, like the all-important Content-Type, which contains the media type of the entity-body.

There are two excellent guides to the standard HTTP headers. One's in RFC 2616, the HTTP standard itself, and the other's in print, in Appendix C of *HTTP: The Definitive Guide* by David Gourley and Brian Totty (O'Reilly). In this appendix, I'm giving a somewhat perfunctory description of the standard HTTP headers, with an eye toward their use in RESTful APIs, as opposed to other HTTP-based applications like websites and HTTP proxies.

Custom HTTP Headers

Creating a new HTTP method or status code is a very big deal. It basically requires writing an RFC. But anyone who runs an HTTP server is allowed to define their own HTTP headers. AtomPub defines an HTTP header called Slug (covered in an upcoming section). Amazon defines headers like X-amz-acl and X-amz-date for its S3 API.

In *RESTful Web Services*, I gave some advice for when to define a custom HTTP header and what to name it. Over the past few years, I've changed my mind about both of these things. You probably shouldn't create a new HTTP header at all.

A new HTTP header is an extension to HTTP, just like a new HTTP method or status code. If you create a new header, you must document it the way the existing HTTP headers are documented: with a big chunk of precisely worded human-readable documentation. The difference is that when your users put in the work to learn about your custom HTTP header, they can't apply that knowledge to other HTTP servers. Your custom header is a fiat standard, specific to your API.

The good news is that a lot of the use cases for new HTTP headers no longer apply. Hypermedia data formats are more numerous and more flexible than they were just a few years ago. Information that used to go into custom headers can now go directly into a representation. If you need to add new application semantics to an existing media type, you can put that information in a machine-readable profile instead of in a new HTTP header.

You should only create a new HTTP header if you find there's something missing *from the HTTP protocol itself.* Would the world be a better place if your header became a standard extension to HTTP? In that case, go ahead and define a new header. Maybe it *will* become a standard extension, the way the Link header was.

As for naming: I used to advise that custom header names start with the string X- for "extension." If you wanted to call your custom header My-Header, I'd suggest you call it X-My-Header instead. RFC 6648 changed my mind. You shouldn't do this. Just go with My-Header.

The hard-learned lesson from other protocols (as described in RFC 6646) is that the X-prefix is more trouble than it's worth. If your custom HTTP header ever *is* standardized, you won't be able to remove the X- because that would break all the existing clients. This means the X- prefix doesn't reliably indicate the presence of an extension. Since X-doesn't serve the purpose it was designed for, there's no reason to use it. Just pick a good, unique name to start out with.

The Headers

These are the 46 headers listed in RFC 2616, as well as eight headers defined in extension RFCs and Internet-Drafts. I'll present a short section for each header, saying whether it's found in HTTP requests, responses, or both. I'll give my opinion as to how useful the header is for APIs. I'll give a short description of the header, which will get a little longer for tricky or especially important headers. I won't go into detail on what the header values should look like. I figure you're smart and you can look up more detailed information as needed.

Unless otherwise noted, the formal definition of a header can be found in RFC 2616.

Accept

Type: Request header.

Importance: Medium.

The client sends an `Accept` header to tell the server what media types it would prefer the server use for its representations. This is the "content negotiation" technique I covered in Chapter 11. One client might want a HAL document in XML format (`Accept: application/hal+xml`); another might want the HAL+JSON representation of the same HAL document (`Accept: application/hal+json`).

If you implement a parser for this header (or any of the other `Accept-*` headers), see RFC 2616 for the details. The format is a lot more complicated than you might think.

Accept-Charset

Type: Request header.

Importance: Low.

The client sends an `Accept-Charset` header to tell the server what character encoding it would like the server to use in its representations. One client might want the representation of a resource containing Japanese text to be encoded in UTF-8; another might want a Shift-JIS encoding of the same data.

Personally, I think everyone should use UTF-8 or UTF-16 for everything.

Accept-Encoding

Type: Request header.

Importance: Medium to high.

The client sends an `Accept-Encoding` header to tell the server that it can save some bandwidth by compressing the response entity-body with a well-known algorithm like gzip. Despite the name, this has nothing to do with character encodings; that's `Accept-Charset`.

The value of `Accept-Encoding` is called a "content-coding." The IANA keeps a registry of acceptable content-codings at *http://www.iana.org/assignments/http-parameters/http-parameters.xml*. In general, content-codings are only used to compress data as it goes over the wire.

Accept-Language

Type: Request header.

Importance: Low.

The client sends an `Accept-Language` header to tell the server what human language it would like the server to use in its representations. This doesn't affect the format, of course, but it can affect the data.

A value for `Accept-Language` is called a *language tag*. You're probably familiar with a few language tags: English is `en` and American English specifically is `en-us`. RFC 5646 sets out the format for language tags, and the IANA keeps a registry of languages (`en`) and regions (`us`) in machine-readable form at this IANA page (*http://www.iana.org/ assignments/language-subtag-registry*).

Accept-Ranges

Type: Response header.

Importance: Low to medium.

The server sends this header to indicate that it supports partial HTTP GET (see Chapter 11) for a resource. The value of the header must be the literal string `bytes`.

```
Accept-Ranges: bytes
```

This should only come up when the client's download of a representation is interrupted. If the server set the `Accept-Ranges` header in the original response, the client knows it can make a second request to the same URL, providing an appropriate `Range` header. The client can then then restart the download at the point of interruption, and not have to download the entire representation again.

Age

Type: Response header.

Importance: Low.

If the response entity-body does not come fresh from the server, the `Age` header is a measure of how long ago, in seconds, the entity-body left the server. This header is usually set by HTTP caches, so that the client knows it might be getting an old copy of a representation.

Allow

Type: Response header.

Importance: Low to medium.

I briefly discuss this header in Chapter 3. It's sent in response to an OPTIONS request and tells the client a bit about the resource's protocol semantics: specifically, which HTTP methods this resource will respond to.

This header isn't very important, because hypermedia makes a much better discovery mechanism than the OPTIONS method. But some APIs do implement support for OPTIONS.

Authorization

Type: Request header.

Importance: Very high.

This request header contains authorization credentials, such as a username and password, which the client has encoded according to some agreed-upon scheme. The server decodes the credentials and decides whether or not to carry out the request.

This is the only authorization header you should ever need (except for `Proxy-Authorization`, which works on a different level), because it's extensible. The most common schemes are OAuth and HTTP Basic, but the scheme can be anything, so long as both client and server understand it.

There are some other authentication headers that work on top of `Authentication`, notably `X-WSSE`, but those standards are pretty much dead, so I don't cover them in this book.

Cache-Control

Type: Request and response header.

Importance: High.

This header contains a directive to any caches between the client and the server (including local caches on the client or server machines themselves). It spells out the rules for how the data should be cached and when it should be dumped from the cache. This is a very complicated header, but I cover the most basic caching directives ("cache" and "don't cache") in Chapter 11.

Connection

Type: Response header.

Importance: Low.

Most of an HTTP response is a communication from the server to the client. Intermediaries like proxies can look at the response, but nothing in there is aimed at them. But a server can insert extra headers that are aimed at a proxy, and one proxy can insert headers that are aimed at the next proxy in a chain. When this happens, the special headers are named in the `Connection` header. These headers apply to the TCP connection between one machine and another, not to the HTTP connection between server and client. Before passing on the response, the proxy is supposed to remove the special headers and the `Connection` header itself. Of course, it may add its own special communications, and a new `Connection` header, if it wants.

Here's a quick example, since this isn't terribly relevant to this book. The server might send these three HTTP headers in a response that goes through a proxy:

```
Content-Type: text/plain
Proxy-Directive: Deliver this as fast as you can!
Connection: Proxy-Directive
```

`Proxy-Directive` is a custom HTTP header. The server and the proxy understand it, but the client might not. The proxy would remove `Proxy-Directive` and `Connection`, and send the one remaining header to the client:

```
Content-Type: text/plain
```

If you're writing a client and not using proxies, the only value you're likely to see for `Connection` is `close`. That just says that the server will close the TCP connection after completing this request.

Content-Disposition

Type: Response header.

Importance: Medium.

Defined in: RFC 6266.

The `Content-Disposition` header is generally used to indicate that the client should save the entity-body as a file, rather than processing it as a representation. When used, it looks something like this:

```
Content-Disposition: attachment; filename="bug-1234-attachment-1"
```

Any API that can store uploaded files should use `Content-Disposition` to distinguish the uploaded files from documents generated by the API. If an API serves a malformed document, that means there's a bug in the API—unless the malformed document was uploaded by a client and the API is just accurately representing what was uploaded.

In this example, the value `attachment` says that this entity-body is an attachment, and the `filename` parameter suggests which filename to save the document as. That parameter opens up a can of worms, security-wise, which is why the `Content-Disposition` header was explicitly excluded from the HTTP standard. When writing a client that respects `Content-Disposition`, or when allowing API clients to name the files they upload, see the advice in RFC 6266, and please be careful.

Content-Encoding

Type: Response header.

Importance: Medium to high.

This response header is the counterpart to the request header `Accept-Encoding`. The request header asks the server to compress the entity-body using a certain algorithm. This header tells the client which algorithm, if any, the server actually used.

As with `Accept-Encoding`, the value of this header is called a "content-coding", and the IANA keeps a registry of acceptable content-codings at *http://www.iana.org/assignments/http-parameters/http-parameters.xml*. In theory, the content-coding could be any sort of reversible data transformation, but all the registered content-codings are ways of compressing data.

Content-Language

Type: Response header.

Importance: Medium.

This response header is the counterpart to the `Accept-Language` request header, or to a corresponding variable set in a resource's URI. It specifies the natural language a human must understand to get meaning out of the entity-body.

Like all the `Accept-*` headers and their response equivalents, this header may contain multiple values. If the entity-body is a movie in Mandarin with Japanese subtitles, the value for `Content-Language` might be `zh-guoyu,jp`. If one English phrase shows up in the movie, en would probably *not* show up in the `Content-Language` header.

Content-Length

Type: Response header.

Importance: High.

This response header gives the size of the entity-body in bytes. This is important for two reasons: first, a client can read this ahead of time and prepare for a small entity-body or a large one. Second, a client can make a HEAD request to find out how large the entity-body is, without actually requesting it. The value of `Content-Length` might affect the client's decision to fetch the entire entity-body, fetch part of it with `Range`, or not fetch it at all.

Content-Location

Type: Response header.

Importance: Low.

This header tells the client the canonical URL of the resource it requested. Unlike with the value of the `Location` header, this is purely informative. The client is not expected to start using the new URL.

This is mainly useful for APIs that assign different URLs to different representations of a single resource. If the client wants to link to the specific representation obtained through content negotiation, it can use the URI given in `Content-Location`. So if you request */documents/104*, and use the `Accept` and `Accept-Language` headers to specify an HTML representation written in English, you might get back a response that specifies `/documents/104.html.en` as the value for `Content-Location`. That's the link to one specific representation of the resource.

Note that this header is a simple hypermedia control. It works the same way as a link with the IANA-registered link relation `canonical`.

Content-MD5

Type: Response header.

Importance: Low to medium.

This is a cryptographic checksum of the entity-body. The client can use this to check whether or not the entity-body was corrupted in transit. An attacker (such as a man-in-the-middle) can change the entity-body and change the `Content-MD5` header to match, so it's no good for security, just error detection.

Content-Range

Type: Response header.

Importance: Low to medium.

When the client makes a partial GET request with the `Range` request header, this response header says what part of the representation the client is getting.

Content-Type

Type: Request and response header.

Importance: Very high.

The most famous HTTP header, and probably the most important, `Content-Type` gives the media type of the entity-body. The media type serves three purposes:

- It determines which parser the recipient should use to parse the entity-body.

- It often determines the representation's protocol semantics—which parts of the representation are hypermedia controls, and what HTTP requests can be triggered by activating those controls.
- It may also determine the representation's application semantics—what the representation means in terms of real-world concepts and this specific API.

There are other ways of conveying application and protocol semantics, such as links to profiles, but `Content-Type` is the main one. This is why it's such a bad idea to serve `application/json` as your media type. You're passing up a big opportunity.

When serving a document that's described by a media type and a profile, you should serve a `Link` header with a link to the profile.

Cookie

Type: Request header.

Importance: High on the human web, low in the world of APIs.

Defined in: RFC 2109.

This is probably the second-most-famous HTTP header, after `Content-Type`, but it's not in the HTTP standard; it's a Netscape extension.

A cookie is an agreement between the client and the server where the server gets to store some semipersistent state on the client side using the `Set-Cookie` header (more on this in an upcoming section). Once the client gets a cookie, it's expected to return it with every subsequent HTTP request to that server, by setting the `Cookie` header once for each of its cookies. Since the data is sent invisibly in the HTTP headers with every request, it looks like the client and server are sharing state.

Cookies have a bad reputation in REST circles for two reasons. First, the "state" they contain is often just a session ID: a short alphanumeric key that ties into a much larger data structure on the server. This destroys the principle of statelessness, since application state is being kept on the server.

More subtly, once a client accepts a cookie, it's supposed to submit it with all subsequent requests for a certain time. The server is telling the client that it can no longer make the requests it made precookie. This also violates the principle of statelessness.

If you must use cookies, make sure you store *all* the state on the client side. Otherwise, you'll lose a lot of the scalability benefits of REST.

Date

Type: Request and response header.

Importance: High for request, *required* for response.

As a request header, this represents the time on the client at the time the request was sent. As a response header, it represents the time on the server at the time the request was fulfilled. The response-header version of Date is used by caches when calculating whether a cached document is still fresh.

ETag

Type: Response header.

Importance: Very high.

The value of ETag is an opaque string designating a specific version of a representation. Whenever the representation changes, the ETag should also change.

Servers should send ETag in response to GET requests whenever possible. As I show in Chapter 11, clients can make a conditional GET request by sending a previous value of ETag as the value of the If-None-Match request header. If the representation hasn't changed, the ETag hasn't changed either, and the server can save time and bandwidth by not sending the representation again.

The main driver of conditional GET requests is the simpler Last-Modified response header, and its request counterpart If-Modified-Since. The main purpose of ETag is to provide a second line of defense. If a representation changes twice in one second, it will take on only one value for Last-Modified-Since, but two different values for ETag.

If there's an intermediary between your server and the client that modifies your representations (such as Apache's mod_compress module, which transparently compresses representations), that intermediary will also change the value of ETag, in ways that may break conditional requests.

Expect

Type: Request header.

Importance: Medium, but rarely used.

This header is used to signal a look-before-you-leap request (covered in Chapter 11). The server will send the response code 100 (Continue) if the client should "leap" ahead and make the real request. It will send the response code 417 (Expectation Failed) if the client should not "leap."

Expires

Type: Response header.

Importance: Medium.

This header tells the client, or a proxy between the server and client, that it may cache the HTTP response (not just the entity-body!) until a certain time. This is useful because even a conditional HTTP GET that ends up doing nothing has the overhead of an HTTP request. By paying attention to `Expires`, a client can avoid the need to make any HTTP requests at all—at least for a while.

It's usually easier to use the `max-age` caching directive of the `Cache-Control` header. (That's the one I covered back in Chapter 11.) That is, it's easier to say "this representation should be good for about an hour" than to calculate the exact time an hour from now. But if the server knows exactly when a representation will change (because it changes at the same time every hour, every day, or every week), `Expires` is better.

The client should take the value of `Expires` as a rough guide, not as a promise that the entity-body won't change until that time.

From

Type: Request header.

Importance: Very low.

This header works just like the `From` header in an email message. It gives an email address associated with the person making the request. This is never used on the World Wide Web because of privacy concerns, and it's never used in the world of APIs, where we have other ways of identifying clients, like OAuth tokens.

Host

Type: Request header.

Importance: Required.

This header contains the domain name part of the request URL. If a client makes a GET request for *http://www.example.com/page.html*, then the URL that actually gets requested is */page.html* and the value of the `Host` header is `www.example.com` or `www.example.com:80`.

From the client's point of view, this may seem like a strange header to require. It's required because an HTTP server can host any number of domains on a single IP address. This feature is called "name-based virtual hosting," and it saves someone who owns multiple domain names from having to buy a separate computer and/or network card for each one.

The problem with name-based virtual hosting is that when the client opens up a TCP connection, it connects to a server based on its IP address, not its domain name. Without the Host header to contain the domain name, an HTTP server would have no idea which of its virtual hosts was the target of the client's request.

If-Match

Type: Request header.

Importance: High.

This header is best described in terms of other headers. It's used like If-Unmodified-Since (described later), to make HTTP actions other than GET conditional—generally to avoid the lost update problem I mentioned in Chapter 11. But where If-Unmodified-Since takes a time as its value, this header takes an ETag as its value.

Tersely, this header is to If-None-Match and ETag as If-Unmodified-Since is to If-Modified-Since and Last-Modified.

If-Modified-Since

Type: Request header.

Importance: Very high.

This request header is the backbone of conditional HTTP GET. Its value is a value the client found in the Last-Modified response header when it made a previous GET request to this resource. When the client sends that value as If-Modified-Since, it's asking to get a representation only if the representation has changed since the last request.

If the representation has in fact changed since that last request, its new Last-Modified date is more recent than the previous one. That means that the condition If-Modified-Since is met, and the server sends the new representation. If the resource has not changed, the Last-Modified date is the same as it was, and the condition If-Modified-Since fails. The server sends a response code of 304 (Not Modified) and no entity-body. That is, conditional HTTP GET succeeds if this condition fails.

Since Last-Modified is only accurate to within one second, conditional HTTP GET can occasionally give the wrong result if it relies only on If-Modified-Since. This is the main reason why we also use ETag and If-None-Match.

If-None-Match

Type: Request header.

Importance: Very high.

This header is also used in conditional HTTP GET. Its value is taken from the `ETag` response header sent with a previous GET request.

If the representation's `ETag` has changed since that last request, the condition `If-None-Match` succeeds and the server sends the new representation. If the `ETag` is the same as before, the condition fails, and the server sends a response code of 304 ("Not Modified") with no entity-body.

If-Range

Type: Request header.

Importance: Low.

This header is used to make a *conditional* partial GET request. The value of the header comes from the `ETag` or `Last-Modified` response header from a previous range request. The server sends the new range only if *that part* of the entity-body has changed. Otherwise the server sends a 304 (`Not Modified`), even if something changed elsewhere in the entity-body.

Conditional partial GET is not used very often, because it's very unlikely that a client will fetch a few bytes from a larger representation, and *then* try to fetch only those same bytes later.

If-Unmodified-Since

Type: Request header.

Importance: Medium.

Normally a client uses the value of the response header `Last-Modified` as the value of the request header `If-Modified-Since` to perform a conditional GET request. This header also takes the value of `Last-Modified`, but it's usually used for making HTTP actions other than GET into conditional actions. The goal is usually to avoid the lost update problem I discussed in Chapter 11.

If you make your PUT or PATCH request conditional on `If-Unmodified-Since`, then if someone else has changed the resource without your knowledge, your request will always get a response code of 412 (`Precondition Failed`). You can refetch the representation and decide what to do with the new version that someone else modified.

This header can be used with GET, too. See my discussion of the `Range` header for an example.

Last-Modified

Type: Response header.

Importance: Very high.

This header makes conditional HTTP GET possible. It tells the client the last time the representation changed. The client can keep track of this date and use it in the `If-Modified-Since` header of a future request.

In web applications, `Last-Modified` is usually the current time, which makes conditional HTTP GET useless. APIs should try to do better, since API clients often bombard their servers with requests for the same URLs (especially the billboard URL) over and over again.

Link

Type: Request and response header.

Defined in: RFC 5988.

This header serves as a general-purpose hypermedia link. I cover this header many times in the book, notably in Chapter 4 and Chapter 11. Its value is a URL, in angle brackets, and then some parameters (like `rel`) that give context to the URL. For example:

```
Link: <http://www.example.com/story/part2>; rel="next"
```

Although `rel` is the most important parameter associated with this header, RFC 5988 defines a number of others: `hreflang`, `media`, `title`, `title*`, and `type`. The `hreflang` and `type` parameters designate the human language and media type of the target link, just like in HTML's `<a>` tag. The `title` and `title*` parameters are different ways of providing a human-readable title for the link.

The `media` parameter works like the `media` attribute of an HTML `<style>` tag: it explains which display media can be used to display the representation at the other end of the link (`screen`, `print`, `braille`, and so on).

Although `Link` is usually a response header, there are situations where the client needs to send it with a request. If a document requires a profile to make sense of its application semantics, the client that POSTs, PUTs, or PATCHes that document should send a `Link` header along with the document. The value of `Link` should point to the profile document and have `rel="profile"`. The same logic applies to a document that only makes sense when combined with a JSON-LD context.

It's legal to give the `Link` header more than one value:

```
Link: </story/part3>; rel="next", </story/part1>; rel="previous"
```

Or to send the header itself more than once:

```
Link: </story/part3>; rel="next"
Link: </story/part1>; rel="previous"
```

This is true of some other HTTP headers as well, but `Link` and `Link-Template` are the headers where you're most likely to need this feature.

Link-Template

Type: Response header.

Defined in: Expired Internet-Draft "draft-nottingham-link-template".

I covered this header in in Chapter 11. It works just like `Link`, except that its value is a URI Template (RFC 5988). This gives it hypermedia capabilities comparable to an HTML form with `action="GET"`. That's a lot more flexible than `Link`, which is comparable to an HTML <a> tag.

The `Link-Template` header supports all of `Link`'s parameters, plus one more, "var-base," which I covered in Chapter 11.

Location

Type: Response header.

Importance: Very high.

This is one of two HTTP headers defined in RFC 2616 that act as hypermedia links. The other one, `Content-Location`, has a simple, consistent meaning, but the meaning of a `Location` link depends on the status code.

This header is strongly associated with the 3xx (`Redirection`) family of status codes, and much of the confusion surrounding HTTP redirects has to do with the fact that `Location` has a slightly different meaning for each type of redirect:

- When the client's request creates a brand new resource, the response code is 201 (`Created`), and the `Location` header is a link to the newly created resource.

- When the server can't decide which representation to serve, and each representation has its own URL, the status code is 300 (+Multiple Choices+), and the +Location+ header links to the representation the server prefers:

    This is different from the more common situation where there are multiple representations, each with its own URL, and the client uses content negotiation to choose between them. In that case, the status code is 200 (+OK+), +Location+ is not provided, and +Content-Location+ points to the canonical URL of the representation that the client negotiated.

- When the client's request causes a resource to change its URL, the response code is 301 (`Moved Permanently`) and the `Location` header is a link to the original resource at its new location.

- When the client makes a request to the "wrong" URL, but the server can still figure out which resource the client is referring to, the `Location` header is a link to the "right" URL. The response code might be 301, 302 (`Found`), 307 (`Temporary Redirect`), or 308 (`Permanent Redirect`), depending on why exactly this URL is the "wrong" one.

- When the response code is 303 (`See Other`), the resource at the other end of `Location` is not a representation of the requested resource; it's a message explaining how the request was processed. This is usually used by resources that respond to POST requests but that don't have representations of their own.

Max-Forwards

Type: Request header.

Importance: Very low.

This header is mainly used with the TRACE method, which is used to track the proxies that handle a client's HTTP request. I don't cover TRACE in this book, but as part of a TRACE request, `Max-Forwards` is used to limit how many proxies the request can be sent through.

Pragma

Type: Request or response.

Importance: Very low.

The `Pragma` header is a slot for special directives between the client, server, and intermediaries such as proxies. The only official pragma is `no-cache`, which is obsolete in HTTP 1.1; it's the same as sending a value of `no-cache` for the `Cache-Control` header.

You may define your own HTTP pragmas, but it's better to define your own HTTP headers instead. See, (Not that you should do that, either.)

Prefer

Type: Request header.

Importance: Currently low, potentially high.

Defined in: Internet-Draft "draft-snell-http-prefer."

The `Prefer` header lets the client communicate its preferences to the server on various minor issues that aren't covered by the HTTP standard or by the rules associated with a media type. The Internet-Draft that defines `Prefer` proposes an IANA registry of preferences that other web standards can add to, but it also defines six preferences for dealing with three issues that show up frequently in APIs:

- The `handling=lenient` preference tells the server to try to process the request even if there are minor problems with the syntax or semantics. The `handling=strict` preference is the opposite: it tells the server to send an error condition as soon as it finds even the slightest problem.

- The `respond-async` preference lets the server know that if fulfilling the request is going to take a really long time, the client wants the server to send a response code 202 (`Accepted`) instead of making the client wait around for a response. The `wait` preference can be set to a number of seconds (e.g., `wait=10`), which represents how long the client is willing to wait for a real response.

- The `return=minimal` preference is sent along with a request that creates or modifies a resource (PUT, POST, or PATCH). It's the client's way of telling the server that it doesn't want a full representation of the new or modified resource resource. The `return=representation` preference is the opposite. It means the client does want a full representation, even if the server wouldn't normally send one.

If you define your own preferences, keep in mind that they have the same problems as custom HTTP headers. A new preference is an extension to HTTP. You must document it very precisely, the way the other preferences are documented. Your new preference will be a fiat standard, so most clients won't support it. All in all, it's usually easier to create a new hypermedia control than to define a new preference.

Preference-Applied

Type: Response header.

Importance: A little less important than `Prefer`.

Defined in: Internet-Draft "draft-snell-http-prefer."

When a server receives a request that uses `Prefer`, and decides to accommodate some of the client's preferences, it can mention which preferences it accommodated in the `Preference-Applied` header. Sometimes it's not clear if an error was because of `handling=strict`, or if the error would have happened anyway; or whether an entity-body is small because of `return=minimal` or because the representation is just small. The `Preference-Applied` header makes it clear.

Proxy-Authenticate

Type: Response header.

Importance: Low to medium.

Some clients (especially in corporate environments) can only get HTTP access through a proxy server. Some proxy servers require authentication. This header is a proxy's way of demanding authentication. It's sent along with a response code of 407 (Proxy Authentication Required), and it works just like WWW-Authenticate, except it tells the client how to authenticate with the proxy, not with the web server on the other end.

While the response to a WWW-Authenticate challenge goes into Authorization, the response to a Proxy-Authenticate challenge goes into Proxy-Authorization (see the next section). A single request may need to include both Authorization and Proxy-Authorization headers: one to authenticate with the API, the other to authenticate with the proxy.

Since most APIs don't include visible proxies in their architecture, this header is not terribly relevant to the topics covered in this book. But it may be relevant to a client, if there's a proxy between the client and the rest of the Web.

Proxy-Authorization

Type: Request header.

Importance: Low to medium.

This header is an attempt to get a request through a proxy that demands authentication. It works similarly to Authorization. Its format depends on the scheme defined in Proxy-Authenticate, just as the format of Authorization depends on the scheme defined in WWW-Authenticate.

Range

Type: Request.

Importance: Medium.

This header signifies the client's attempt to request only part of a resource's representation (see Chapter 11). A client typically sends this header because it tried earlier to download a large representation and got cut off. Now it's back for the rest of the representation. Because of this, this header is usually coupled with Unless-Modified-Since. If the representation has changed since your last request, you'll need to GET it from the beginning.

Referer

Type: Request header.

Importance: High on the World Wide Web, low for APIs.

When you click a link in your web browser, the browser sends an HTTP request in which the value of the `Referer` header is the URL of the page you were just on. That's the URL that "refered" your client to the URI you're now requesting. Yes, it's misspelled.

Though common on the human web, this header is rarely used in APIs. It can be used to convey a bit of application state (the client's recent path through the API) to the server.

I don't consider the `Referer` header a hypermedia link, even though its value is always a URL, because the header is sent from the client to the server. Hypermedia links flow from the server to the client.

Retry-After

Type: Response header.

Importance: Low to medium.

This header usually comes with a response code that denotes failure: either 413 (`Request Entity Too Large`), 429 (`Too Many Requests`), or one of the 5xx series (`Server-side error`). These codes tell a client that while the server couldn't fulfill the request right now, it might be able to fulfill the same request at a later time. The value of the `Retry-After` header is the time when the client should try again, or the number of seconds it should wait.

If the problem is that the server is overloaded, and the server chooses every client's `Retry-After` value using the same rules, that just guarantees the same clients will make the same requests in the same order a little later, overloading the server again. The server should use some randomization technique to vary `Retry-After`, similar to Ethernet's backoff period.

Set-Cookie

Type: Response header.

Importance: High on the World Wide Web, low for APIs.

Defined in: RFC 2106.

This is an attempt on the server's part to set some semipersistent state in a cookie on the client side. The client is supposed to send an appropriate `Cookie` header with all future requests, until the cookie's expiration date. The client may ignore this header (and that's often a good idea), but there's no guarantee that future requests will get a good response unless they provide the Cookie header. This violates the principle of stateless-ness, which is why I don't recommend using cookies in APIs.

Slug

Type: Request header.

Importance: Fairly high, but only in AtomPub APIs.

Defined in: RFC 5023.

When an AtomPub client POSTs a binary document (like a picture) to a feed, it may put a title for that document in the Slug header. This makes the upload a one-step process instead of a two-step process (upload the file with POST, then edit its metadata with PUT).

TE

Type: Request header.

Importance: Low.

This is another Accept-type header, one that lets the client specify which transfer en-codings it will accept (see the Transfer-Encoding section for an explanation of transfer encodings). *HTTP: The Definitive Guide* points out that a better name would have been Accept-Transfer-Encoding.

A value for TE is called a "transfer-coding", and the IANA keeps a registry of acceptable transfer-codings (*http://www.iana.org/assignments/http-parameters/http-parameters.xml*).

Trailer

Type: Response header.

Importance: Low.

When a server sends an entity-body using chunked transfer encoding, it may choose to put certain HTTP headers at the end of the entity-body rather than before it (see below for details). This turns them from headers into trailers. The server signals that it's going to send a header as a trailer by putting its name as the value of the header called Trail er. Here's one possible value for Trailer:

```
Trailer: Content-Length
```

The server will be providing a value for Content-Length once it's served the entity-body and it knows how many bytes it served.

Transfer-Encoding

Type: Response.

Importance: Low.

Transfer-Encoding has the same purpose as Content-Encoding: to apply some temporary transform to the entity-body (usually compression) that will be transparently undone on the other end. The difference is that "the other end" may be a lot closer to the server with Transfer-Encoding than with Content-Encoding.

Consider a setup in which an HTTP client communicates with a server through a proxy. As far as Content-Encoding is concerned, the two ends of the conversation are the server and the client. But as far as Transfer-Encoding is concerned, there are two conversations happening: one between the client and the proxy, and one between the proxy and the server.

If the server compresses the entity-body and sets Content-Encoding: gzip, the proxy will (probably) leave the entity-body alone and pass it along, still compressed, to the client. But if the server sets Transfer-Encoding: gzip, it's the *proxy's* job to decompress the entity-body and pass it along, uncompressed, to the client.

As with TE, the value of this header is called a "transfer-coding", and the IANA keeps a registry of acceptable transfer-codings at *http://www.iana.org/assignments/http-parameters/http-parameters.xml*. Most of the transfer-codings refer to compression algorithms, and can also be used as values for Content-Encoding, but there's one value that's unique to Transfer-Encoding: chunked.

Sometimes a server needs to send an entity-body without knowing important facts like how large it is. Rather than omitting HTTP headers like Content-Length and Content-MD5 which rely on this information, the server may decide to send the entity-body in chunks, and put Content-Length and the like *after* the entity-body rather than before. Sending Transfer-Encoding: "chunked" is the server's way of announcing it's going to do this. By the time all the chunks have been sent, the server knows the things it didn't know before, and it can send Content-Length and Content-MD5 as "trailers" instead of "headers."

It's an HTTP 1.1 requirement that clients support chunked transfer-encoding, but a lot of programmable clients don't have this support.

Upgrade

Type: Request header.

Importance: Low, potentially high in the future.

If you'd rather be using some protocol other than HTTP, you can tell the server that by sending a `Upgrade` header. If the server happens to speak the protocol you'd rather be using, it will send back a response code of 101 (`Switching Protocols`) and immediately begin speaking the new protocol.

RFC 2817 sets up yet another IANA registry (*http://www.iana.org/assignments/http-upgrade-tokens/*) containing the possible values of the `Upgrade` header. Right now there are only three values in the registry: `HTTP`, `TLS/1.0` (that is, HTTPS) and `WebSocket`.

Apart from WebSocket (a protocol defined for use by web browsers but that doesn't fit the REST paradigm), the `Upgrade` header isn't used very often right now. A client that wants to use HTTPS can just start off using HTTPS. But there will come a time when the HTTP 2.0 standard has been finalized, but before clients can assume that any given server supports HTTP 2.0. During that time, the `Upgrade` header could become quite popular.

User-Agent

Type: Request header.

Importance: High.

This header lets the server know what kind of software is making the HTTP request. On the human web, this is a string that identifies the brand of web browser. In the world of APIs, it usually identifies the HTTP library or client library that was used to write the client. It may identify a specific client program instead.

Soon after the Web became popular, servers started sniffing `User-Agent` to determine what kind of browser was on the other end. They then sent different representations based on the value of `User-Agent`. *This is a terrible idea*. Not only does `User-Agent` sniffing perpetuate incompatibilities between web browsers, it's led to an arms race inside the `User-Agent` header itself.

Almost every browser these days pretends to be Mozilla, because that was the internal code name of the first web browser to become popular (Netscape Navigator). A browser that doesn't pretend to be Mozilla may not get the representation it needs. Some pretend to be both Mozilla and Internet Explorer, so they can trigger code originally intended only to be run on Internet Explorer. A few browsers even allow the user to select the `User-Agent` for every request, to trick servers into sending the right representations. It's a huge mess.

Don't let history repeat itself. An API should only use `User-Agent` to gather statistics and to deny access to poorly programmed clients. It should not use `User-Agent` to tailor its representations to specific clients. The same goes for other ways of identifying a particular software agent, such as OAuth client credentials.

Vary

Type: Response header.

Importance: Low to medium.

The `Vary` header tells the client which request headers it can vary to get different representations of a resource. Here's a sample value:

```
Vary: Accept Accept-Language
```

That value tells the client that it can ask for the representation in a different data format, by setting or changing the `Accept` header. It can ask for the representation in a different language, by setting or changing `Accept-Language`.

That value also tells a cache to cache (say) the Japanese representation of the resource separately from the English representation, even if the two representations have the same URL. The Japanese representation isn't a brand new byte stream that invalidates the cached English version. The two requests sent different values for a header that varies (`Accept-Language`), so the responses should be cached separately.

If the value of `Vary` is `*`, that means that the response should not be cached at all.

Via

Type: Request and response header.

Importance: Low.

When an HTTP request goes directly from the client to the server, or a response goes directly from server to client, there is no `Via` header. When there are intermediaries (like proxies) in the way, each one slaps on a `Via` header on the request or response message. The recipient of the message can look at the `Via` headers to see the path the HTTP message took through the intermediaries.

Warning

Type: Response header (can technically be used with requests).

Importance: Low.

The `Warning` header is a supplement to the HTTP response code. It's usually inserted by an intermediary like a caching proxy, to tell the user about possible problems that aren't obvious from looking at the response.

Like response codes, each HTTP warning has a three-digit numeric value: a "warn-code." Most warnings have to do with cache behavior. This `Warning` says that the caching proxy at `localhost:9090` sent a cached response even though it knew the response to be stale:

```
Warning: 110 localhost:9090 Response is stale
```

The warn-code 110 means "Response is stale" as surely as the HTTP response code 404 means "Not Found." The HTTP standard defines seven warn-codes, which I won't go into here.

WWW-Authenticate

Type: Response header.

Importance: Very high.

This header accompanies a response code of 401 (Unauthorized). It's the server's demand that the client send some authentication next time it requests the URI. It also tells the client what kind of authentication the server expects. This will probably be HTTP Basic Auth, or some version of OAuth.

An API Designer's Guide to the Fielding Dissertation

Throughout this book, I use the term "Fielding constraints" as a conceptual shorthand for the principles that a RESTful system should obey. I talk about "statelessness," "the hypermedia constraint," and so on. This appendix is my attempt to explain in a slightly more formal way what I mean by these terms and how they interact with each other.

The Fielding constraints are the "architectural properties" of the Web defined in Roy Fielding's Ph.D dissertation.[1] It's a difficult work for the average developer to understand, a dense piece of reasoning written in an academic style and operating at a higher level of abstraction than, say, an RFC. So let me start off by showing you the practical benefits that came out of Fielding's work.

Roy Fielding spent most of the 1990s formalizing version 1.0 of the HTTP protocol (in RFC 1945), and developing version 1.1 (which became the famous RFC 2616). The Web was already a huge success, but its very success revealed design problems that would have prevented it from scaling further, to the level we enjoy today.

The Fielding dissertation lays out a number of properties that web-like systems might have, and then picks out the properties that make the Web successful. Then it selects constraints—the Fielding constraints—which will make a generic network system look like the Web. These constraints are REST: a formal architectural definition that captures the essence of the Web.

At first glance, this is pie-in-the-sky thinking. The real Web didn't come from an architectural definition. It was cobbled together by physicists and hackers. There's no reason it should fit into a computer scientist's theoretical framework. And guess what:

---

1. Fielding, Roy Thomas. *Architectural Styles and the Design of Network-based Software Architectures*. Doctoral dissertation, University of California, Irvine, 2000.

it didn't fit! There were lots of disconnects between the idealized web described by the Fielding constraints, and the real-life Web of the mid-1990s. The original definition of "resource" was too focused on static documents. The popular "cookies" extension to HTTP (originally defined in RFC 2109) was causing huge problems. Servers sometimes got valid HTTP requests that they just couldn't figure out how to handle.

This is where Fielding's theorizing paid off. The disconnects between the Fielding constraints and the real-life Web don't mean his model is useless. Those disconnects point out where the problems are! Fixing them will make the real Web more like the idealized web described by REST: a Web without the scalability problems.

HTTP 1.1 (RFC 2616) and the URI standard (RFC 2396) fixed most of the disconnects between theory and practice. The Web was repaired, using the Fielding constraints as a blueprint. The disconnects that couldn't be fixed, such as HTTP cookies, still cause problems today.

I think the ideas behind "REST" are important because web APIs are in roughly the same position as the Web was in the mid-1990s. We have a bunch of cobbled-together systems designed for expedience rather than scalability and long-term maintainability. The Fielding constraints point the way to a better world. Comparing the web APIs we have to an idealized set of principles can show us what needs to be fixed.

So let's take a look at the architectural properties of the Web; the thing the Fielding constraints are trying to capture.

All quotes in this appendix come from the Fielding dissertation. I also recommend reading Fielding's 2008 blog post, "REST APIs must be hypertext-driven" (*http://roy.gbiv.com/untangled/2008/rest-apis-must-be-hypertext-driven*).

Architectural Properties of the Web

Chapter 2 of the Fielding dissertation lays out a bunch of "architectural properties" that a networked system might have: performance, simplicity, reliability, and so on. It's all motherhood-and-apple-pie stuff. No one's going to speak out against "simplicity" or "reliability."

In Chapter 4, Fielding makes the tough choices. That chapter identifies four key architectural properties of the World Wide Web. These are the properties that made the web a success, and Fielding is willing to sacrifice other properties for their sake.

Low Entry-Barrier

> Since participation in the creation and structuring of information was voluntary, a low entry-barrier was necessary to enable sufficient adoption.

The Web took off because it was easy to use. Learning how to use FTP or Telnet required memorizing a lot of arcane commands. But when you started up a web browser, you

---

saw human-readable text, and scattered throughout the text, you saw links to adjacent web pages. Each link included a little bit of context, which helped you decide which link to click on. You'd click on a link and the process would repeat.

Compared to pre-web hypertext systems, it's also very easy to put up a website. You don't need to use a special authoring program to write an HTML page; you can use a text editor.

Extensibility

> While simplicity makes it possible to deploy an initial implementation of a distributed system, extensibility allows us to avoid getting stuck forever with the limitations of what was deployed. Even if it were possible to build a software system that perfectly matches the requirements of its users, those requirements will change over time just as society changes over time. A system intending to be as long-lived as the Web must be prepared for change.

Without extensibility, a system can be deployed only once. So long as its users are happy (and they will be happy at first!), everything is fine. When the users' requirements change, they'll switch to a different system.

The Web has been keeping its users happy for 20 years. Billion-dollar empires have risen and fallen and been replaced by new empires, all based on the same four technologies: HTTP, URI, HTML, and JavaScript.

Distributed Hypermedia

> Distributed hypermedia allows the presentation and control information to be stored at remote locations.

In any client-server system, the server has authority over the dataset. It's "stored at remote locations." A client can try to change the dataset, but its changes are always subject to the server's approval.

The principle of distributed hypermedia takes the instructions about what you can do with the data ("presentation and control information"), and treats it the same way as the data itself. The server is in charge of all of it.

A web server uses HTML documents to convey resource state, to announce the links between resources (safe transitions), and to announce the allowable mechanisms for modifying resource state (unsafe transitions). The client reads all of this information out of hypermedia documents it receives from the server, documents which can change as the system changes.

Where else might the "presentation and control information" go? It can be programmed into the client, or it can be kept outside the system completely, in human-readable documentation. That's how most of today's APIs do it. Both of those techniques make it very difficult to change the way the server works, without breaking the client. And if you can't change the server, you don't have extensibility.

Internet-Scale

"Internet-scale" sounds like a buzzword meaning "really big," but Fielding has two specific things in mind. The first, "anarchic scalability," rejects the idea of long-term relationships or coordination between different parts of the system.

> Clients cannot be expected to maintain knowledge of all servers. Servers cannot be expected to retain knowledge of state across requests. Hypermedia data elements cannot retain "back-pointers," an identifier for each data element that references them, since the number of references to a resource is proportional to the number of people interested in that information.

The second, "independent deployment," says that since there are no long-term relationships, different parts of the system will change at different rates.

> Multiple organizational boundaries also means that the system must be prepared for gradual and fragmented change, where old and new implementations co-exist without preventing the new implementations from making use of their extended capabilities… The architecture as a whole must be designed to ease the deployment of architectural elements in a partial, iterative fashion, since it is not possible to force deployment in an orderly manner.

APIs Are Not (Quite) the Web

Those are the four key architectural properties of the Web, as Fielding sees them. It's clear that some of these properties apply to web APIs as well. All else being equal, we'd prefer an extensible system to one that can't change over time. Even a small API is "Internet-scale" if it's on the public Internet, because it faces the problems that come with anarchic scalability and independent deployment.

But it would be a mistake to assume that these principles can be transferred directly to the world of web APIs. There's one big, defining difference between the Web and a web API: the semantic gap. This one difference destabilizes the relationships between the architectural properties of the Web and forces us to choose between the four desirable properties.

When a human being is making all the decisions, "distributed hypermedia" is the easiest way to lower the "entry-barrier." A human sees all the possible state transitions and gets to choose one, in the moment. But without a human in the decision-making loop, a programmer must create a software program capable of filling in for the missing human. In that situation, "distributed hypermedia" *raises* the "entry-barrier." Hypermedia documents divide an individual problem into tiny chunks, and creating a decision-making robot requires an understanding of the problem space as a whole.

The easiest way to lower the "entry-barrier" for a web API is to get rid of the "distributed hypermedia" property, and describe a system ahead of time, in human-readable prose.

The problem with that is, the "distributed hypermedia" property is the only thing holding up the "extensibility" property. Changing some human-readable text won't change the client's view of the system to match. Without "distributed hypermedia," *nothing* is guaranteed to change a client's view of the system. "Internet scale" says there are too many clients to track, and that un-upgraded clients might stick around for a long time.

When those clients contain hardcoded information that could have gone into "distributed hypermedia" instead, you lose "extensibility." Your API starts off looking like the answer to your users' prayers, but as their requirements change, they drift away, and you can't change to keep them.

On the Web, the four architectural principles reinforce each other. In the world of web APIs, they're in tension. There are three ways of resolving the tension:

- If you have some way of forcing all your clients to upgrade in lockstep, you can give up "Internet-scale." Then you can have a "low entry-barrier" and "extensibility" without needing to use "distributed hypermedia." This is a common choice for an API deployed within a company.

- If you need "Internet scale," you can give up "extensibility" and "distributed hypermedia" for the sake of a "low entry-barrier." Most of today's public web APIs do this.

- Or you can embrace "distributed hypermedia," and get "extensibility" and "Internet scale" at the cost of a higher "entry-barrier." That's the approach I take in this book. My work on ALPS, and on profiles in general, is an attempt to lower the "entry-barrier" for hypermedia APIs.

Interface Constraints

Now let's take a look at the Fielding constraints, the rules that give the World Wide Web its desirable architectural properties. The four most famous Fielding constraints are found in a single remark in Chapter 5 of the dissertation:

> REST is defined by four interface constraints: identification of resources; manipulation of resources through representations; self-descriptive messages; and, hypermedia as the engine of application state. These constraints will be discussed in Section 5.2.

These constraints make up REST's "uniform interface." They are indeed discussed in Section 5.2, but not in the convenient list format you might have expected. In this section, I'll discuss them individually.

Identification of Resources

> Traditional hypertext systems… use unique node or document identifiers that change every time the information changes, relying on link servers to maintain references separately from the content. Since centralized link servers are an anathema to the immense scale and multi-organizational domain requirements of the Web, REST relies instead on the author choosing a resource identifier that best fits the nature of the concept being identified.

"Identification of resources" is Fielding's name for what I call "addressability." A URI identifies a resource. The resource's state may change, but its URI stays the same. If a resource's URI does change, the server uses hypermedia (the `Location` header) to direct clients to the new URI.

The Web is so dominant today that it's now hard to imagine those "traditional hypertext systems" that changed their identifiers all the time. But it's not hard to imagine another problem: websites and APIs that assign too much resource state to a single URL, like the restaurant websites I complained about in Chapter 1.

Manipulation of Resources Through Representations

> REST components perform actions on a resource by using a representation to capture the current or intended state of that resource and transferring that representation between components. A representation is a sequence of bytes, plus representation metadata to describe those bytes.

The Web takes an expansive view of the concept of "resource." A resource can be anything. This means there are resources—physical objects and abstract concepts—that can't be sent over the Internet. Nonetheless, we can talk about these resources, using representations.

A representation is a "sequence of bytes," so it can be transferred over the network. It "capture[s] the current or intended state of the resource," so clients can use it as a stand-in for the real thing. And a representation is not tied to the server-side code that generated it, which means it doesn't have to change when the server implementation changes.

On the Web, clients and servers manipulate resources by sending representations back and forth using a small set of standardized HTTP methods (GET and POST). A web API may add a few more methods (PUT, DELETE, and so on), but it's still a small set that requires community consensus to extend. The richness of the interactions between clients and servers is almost entirely found in the representations they send each other.

Self-Descriptive Messages

> REST enables intermediate processing by constraining messages to be self-descriptive: interaction is stateless between requests, standard methods and media types are used to

---

indicate semantics and exchange information, and responses explicitly indicate cacheability.

An HTTP message contains all the information necessary for the recipient to understand it. There's no free-floating documentation nearby that clients are also expected to understand. If understanding a message requires comprehending some other document, like a media type definition or a profile, then the message ought to contain a reference to that document, in the `Content-Type` or `Link` header.

Let's take Fielding's examples one at a time:

1. "Interaction is stateless between requests." The statelessness constraint (covered below) is just a special case of the self-descriptive message constraint. In a stateless system, a server can handle a client's request without having to remember how it handled all that client's previous requests. Each request stands alone.

2. "Standard methods and media types are used to indicate semantics and exchange information." Pretty straightforward. If an HTTP response doesn't include the `Content-Type` header, the client doesn't know how to parse the entity-body. If an HTTP request didn't mention the HTTP method to use, or made up its own methods, the server wouldn't know how to handle it.

3. "Responses explicitly indicate cacheability." A client just got an HTTP response from a web server. Does it make sense for the client to cache the response? If so, for how long? For a minute, or for a year?

   The client shouldn't have to make this decision. The server is in a much better position to know how long the response can be safely cached. Therefore, it's the server's job to give that information to the client.

   Now, here's where self-describing messages come in. In HTTP, the server conveys caching information by adding a header to *the very HTTP response that might be cached*. There's no out-of-band communication where the server explains how to cache the message it just sent. The caching instructions are part of the message, and they're cached along with the message. When it's time to retrieve the message from cache and check whether it's still fresh, the client can make that decision based on information that's right there in the message.

Earlier versions of HTTP fell short of the "self-descriptive messages" ideal. Section 6.3.2 of Fielding discusses some problems that this caused. Most notably, without the `Host` header, there was no way for the server to know which domain name should handle an incoming HTTP request. This made it very difficult to host multiple domains on one server.

Even in HTTP 1.1, a response message doesn't contain any information tying it to the original request. This is a failure to live up to the self-descriptive message constraint.

Compare this to the CoAP protocol, which ties responses to requests using tokens and message IDs. HTTP 2.0 will probably do something similar.

The Hypermedia Constraint

The Fielding dissertation never explicitly defines the notorious phrase "hypermedia as the engine of application state," but if you understand the individual concepts, it should make sense:

1. All application state is kept on the client side. Changes to application state are the client's responsibility.
2. The client can only change its application state by making an HTTP request and processing the response.
3. How does the client know which requests it can make next? By looking at the hypermedia controls in the representations it's received so far.
4. Therefore, hypermedia controls are the driving force behind changes in application state.

The hypermedia constraint is not a chore you must perform to be "RESTful." It's the payoff for obeying the other constraints. It gives you extensibility. The hypermedia constraint allows a smart client to automatically adapt to changes on the server side. It allows a server to change its underlying implementation without breaking all of its clients.

> Hypermedia was chosen as the user interface because of its simplicity and generality: the same interface can be used regardless of the information source, the flexibility of hypermedia relationships (links) allows for unlimited structuring, and the direct manipulation of links allows the complex relationships within the information to guide the reader through an application.

Architectural Constraints

Chapter 3 of Fielding takes a lot of different possible network architectures and decomposes them into their "architectural properties": atomic, interchangeable constraints on a generic "null style." Chapter 3 shows that these primitive constraints can be combined to describe common architectures like distributed object systems.

Fielding's famous Chapter 5, "Representational State Transfer," applies this deconstructive approach to the World Wide Web. It turns out the Web is composed of five of the properties from Fielding's Chapter 3 ("Client-Server," "Stateless," "Cache," "Layered System," and "Code on Demand"). There's also a sixth property ("Uniform Interface"), which is made up of the four interface constraints I covered earlier. The uniform interface constraint covers most of the things that make the Web unique.

In general, web APIs care a lot about "Client-Server," "Stateless," "Cache," and "Uniform Interface." "Layered System" is more important to the deployment of web APIs than to their design. Web APIs don't really use "Code on Demand" at all. That said, here's a detailed look at all of the Web's architectural constraints.

Client-Server

> A client component, desiring that a service be performed, sends a request to the server via a connector. The server either rejects or performs the request and sends a response back to the client.

This one should be familiar, because client-server is the dominant network architecture on the Internet. It shows up even in places you might not have expected it. Many peer-to-peer architectures are client-server architectures; it's just that a given peer sometimes acts as a "client" and sometimes as a "server."

The main competitor to the client-server architecture is the event-based integration architecture, in which components continually broadcast events over the network, while listening for events they're interested in. There's no one-to-one communication between parts of the system, in which one party could be considered the "client" and another the "server." There's only broadcasting and eavesdropping.

Statelessness

> The goal is to improve server scalability by eliminating any need for the server to maintain an awareness of the client state beyond the current request.

As far as an HTTP server is concerned, when a client is not currently making a request, the client doesn't exist. All application state—information about a particular client's path through the application—belongs to the client. The server doesn't care.

If some piece of application state is so important that the server needs to care, it should become resource state. It should be made a resource, with its own URL. That way the server has control over the state, but the client can manipulate it the way it manipulates other resources.

In particular, this means you should not store session IDs on the server. To quote Fielding:

> One form of abuse is to include information that identifies the current user within all of the URI referenced by a hypermedia response representation. Such embedded user-ids can be used to maintain session state on the server, track user behavior by logging their actions, or carry user preferences across multiple actions... by violating REST's constraints, these systems also cause shared caching to become ineffective, reduce server scalability, and result in undesirable effects when a user shares those references with others.

Caching

> This form of replication is most often found in cases where the potential data set far exceeds the capacity of any one client, as in the WWW[.]

Thanks to the self-descriptive message constraint, all the information necessary to understand a response is contained in the response itself. Thanks to the statelessness constraint, an HTTP request can be considered on its own, independent of any other requests. These two constraints make caching possible. An HTTP client can automatically match its requests to previous responses it received, possibly saving a round trip over the network. As Fielding says, "the best application performance is obtained by not using the network."

Uniform Interface

> Implementations are decoupled from the services they provide, which encourages independent evolvability. The trade-off, though, is that a uniform interface degrades efficiency, since information is transferred in a standardized form rather than one which is specific to an application's needs. The REST interface is designed to be efficient for large-grain hypermedia data transfer, optimizing for the common case of the Web, but resulting in an interface that is not optimal for other forms of architectural interaction.

I already covered the uniform interface. It's made up of the four interface constraints I covered earlier: addressability, manipulation of resources through representations, self-descriptive messages, and the hypermedia constraint.

Fielding points out that these constraints are biased toward "large-grain hypermedia data transfer." A typical Web browser starts its day by sending a GET request to a URL (addressability) and retrieving a big HTML representation full of links (use of representations). Its human user reads the document and follows one of the links (the hypermedia constraint). This makes the browser send another GET request and retrieve another HTML representation full of links.

The majority of HTTP requests are GET requests that carry out safe state transitions. This is why so many of HTTP's performance optimizations—caching, conditional requests, partial requests—focus on reducing the cost of GET requests.

If API designs were heavily oriented around unsafe state transitions, there'd be a big disconnect between the Web's uniform interface and the interface that would best meet the needs of API clients. But it turns out API clients also spend most of their time doing large-grain data transfer (if not hypermedia transfer). That's why a so-called "RESTful" API can be very successful even without obeying the hypermedia constraint. It's giving its users the benefit of the other three interface constraints.

Some hypermedia-aware APIs ignore the "large-grain" part of "large-grain hypermedia transfer." Instead of serving a big document that conveys a lot of resource state (such as an hCard document describing a person), they split up the information across several

---

resources (giving separate URLs to the person's given name, family name, and date of birth). The client must make several GET requests to get the information it needs. The result is a "chatty" API with very high latency.

This isn't technically wrong, but it is bad for performance. HTTP 2.0 should make it practical to write this kind of API: one based on *small-grain* hypermedia transfer.

Layered System

> Layered-client-server adds proxy and gateway components to the client-server style…
> These additional mediator components can be added in multiple layers to add features
> like load balancing and security checking to the system.

Throughout this book I talk about HTTP clients—bits of software that originate HTTP requests—and HTTP servers—bits of software that originate HTTP responses. But the HTTP spec defines two other bits of software that can go between client and server: proxies and gateways. All of these things are *components* in an HTTP system.

A proxy receives HTTP requests from components (clients, proxies, and gateways), just like a web server. Unlike a web server, a proxy doesn't handle the request itself. Instead, it passes the request on to another component (a server, a proxy, or a gateway) and waits for a response. When it receives a response, the proxy passes it back to the component that sent the request. A proxy may modify requests and responses in transit; to compress data, to eliminate identifying information, or to perform censorship.

A gateway is a proxy that translates between HTTP and some other protocol. A gateway might take an HTTP request, turn it into a series of commands to download a file from an FTP server, and then serve the downloaded file as the entity-body of an HTTP response. As far as the client is concerned, it's making normal HTTP requests and getting representations of HTTP resources.

The "layered system" constraint is less about proxies and gateways, and more about the fact that adding one between client and server is a nearly transparent operation. A client doesn't know whether it's talking directly to a server, or whether it's talking to a proxy that talks to a proxy that talks to a gateway.

Clients, servers, proxies and gateways all have the same interface. There's no special "proxy protocol." Proxies receive HTTP requests and send HTTP responses. There are some special proxy-related status codes (which I mention in Appendix A); a few HTTP headers for controlling proxies (Appendix B); and two HTTP methods, CONNECT and TRACE, for using and debugging proxies. But to a client, a proxy looks just like an HTTP server. To a server, a proxy looks just like an HTTP client.

HTTP does define a lot of complicated rules for how the "layered system" architectural element interacts with the "caching" element, but that drama plays out entirely within a proxy component. Clients and servers don't have to deal with it.

Proxies are very useful in real-world API deployments. A proxy can perform load balancing by sending different requests off to different servers. A proxy can cache frequently accessed representations so that client requests don't always make it to the server. But I don't cover proxies and gateways in this book, because the whole premise of a layered system is that they're invisible. The other Fielding constraints, especially statelessness, make it possible to add and remove huge chains of intermediaries between client and server, without either client or server noticing.

For a detailed treatment of proxies and gateways, I recommend Chapters 6 and 8 of HTTP: The Definitive Guide.

Code on Demand

> [A] client component has access to a set of resources, but not the know-how on how to process them. It sends a request to a remote server for the code representing that know-how, receives that code, and executes it locally.... [T]he most significant limitation is the lack of visibility due to the server sending code instead of simple data. Lack of visibility leads to obvious deployment problems if the client cannot trust the servers.

Code on demand does for software what hypermedia does for data. The World Wide Web works on code on demand, but I don't cover it in this book, because I don't have good advice for using it in the context of a web API. Of the dozens of hypermedia formats I've covered, the only one with support for code on demand is HTML.

HTML's secret is the `<script>` tag, which automatically fetches a representation of a resource and then executes that representation as (JavaScript) code. Thanks to the `<script>` tag, a user who visits your website can download and run a complex software application. When the application changes, the human user "reinstalls" the code by reloading the web page and downloading everything again.

The dominant deployment strategy for API client code is to write libraries in various programming languages (APIs for APIs, if you will), and offer them for download by individual developers. This is a bad idea, for the same reason hypermedia-ignorant APIs are a bad idea. It destroys extensibility. Eventually the client changes, but nobody tells the existing installed base. The old version of the client starts up and runs the same code it always ran, but now it's the wrong code.

Code on demand can solve this problem. With code on demand, client libraries could download new versions of themselves as they were released. As long as the client's programming-language API stayed the same, code based on the client library would continue to work as the underlying implementation changed.

The problem is, nobody really likes the idea of automatically downloading and running code from someone else's server. If a server that serves hypermedia documents is compromised, its clients might get bogus data. That's bad, but it could be a lot worse. If a server that serves code on demand is compromised, its clients might also become compromised!

Code on demand works on the Web because a web browser runs downloaded JavaScript code in a sandbox. Even so, code on demand leads to browser security problems like cross-site scripting attacks. Automated clients typically don't typically run in a sandbox. They need access to local filesystems, databases, and other system resources. Bad code-on-demand can do a lot of damage to a system.

In an environment where all parties trust each other (such as within a company), it may make sense to deploy using code on demand. But that's the environment where the case for a RESTful architecture is weakest, and there are other well-established ways for a trusted server to deploy software to clients.

For all these reasons, I don't anticipate code on demand replacing downloadable clients anytime soon. A downloadable client for a hypermedia-aware API is a lot less likely to break when the API changes, making it possible to live without code-on-demand.

Summary

The Web's success comes from these four architectural properties:

Low entry-barrier
> It's easy to learn how to use the Web, and it's easy to build a website.

Extensibility
> Individual websites can change overnight, without breaking their clients. Over the course of decades, the Web as a whole changes drastically, but the underlying technologies don't change all that much.

Distributed hypermedia
> Information about what a client might do with a server's data is kept in the same place as the data, and sent to the client in the same documents.

Internet-scale
> There are no long-term relationships between parts of the system, and different parts can change at different rates.

These architectural properties are realized on the Web by the six architectural constraints:

Client-server
> All communication on the Web is one-to-one.

Stateless
> When a client is not currently making a request, the server doesn't know it exists.

Cache
  A client can save trips over the network by reusing previous responses from a cache.

Layered system
  Intermediaries such as proxies can be invisibly inserted between client and server.

Code on demand
  The server can send executable code in addition to data. This code is automatically deployed when the client requests it, and will be automatically redeployed if it changes.

The uniform interface
  This is an umbrella term for the four interface constraints:

Identification of resources
  Each resource is identified by a stable URI.

Manipulation of resources through representations
  The server describes resource state by sending representations to the client. The client manipulates resource state by sending representations to the server.

Self-descriptive messages
  All the information necessary to understand a request or response message is contained in (or at least linked to from) the message itself.

The hypermedia constraint
  The server manipulates the client's state by sending a hypermedia "menu" containing options from which the client is free to choose.

These nine (or ten, depending on how you count) constraints are the Fielding constraints.

Conclusion

If the semantic gap didn't exist, designing a web API would be exactly the same as designing a website. We could slavishly copy the Web without really understanding how it worked. We wouldn't need the Fielding dissertation, and we wouldn't need to judge our APIs against the Fielding constraints, because we'd already have a successful practical example of the system we wanted to create.

The Web is *almost* good enough for our purposes, but not quite. We'd like to build on its success, but we can't use the exact same principles. The solution is in the often-ignored first half of the Fielding dissertation, which shows where the Fielding constraints came from in the first place. They came from a procedure that went something like this:

1. Write down all the architectural properties it would be nice for your system to have.

2. Figure out which of those properties you really need, and which ones you're willing to sacrifice.

3. Come up with a set of architectural constraints that will give your system the properties you really need.

4. Design a set of protocols and other standards that work together to embody the constraints (HTTP, URI, HTML, JavaScript).

5. Over the course of decades, as problems become apparent, iterate steps 2—4 (HTTP 0.9, HTTP 1.0, HTTP 1.1, and the forthcoming HTTP 2.0).

Web APIs introduce a new constraint: the semantic gap. We've been arguing around the semantic gap for over a decade, and although we've reached consensus that a few of the Fielding constraints are still relevant, a solution is nowhere in sight. To see which side of the argument you're on, you must decide which of the Web's architectural properties are most important to you.

Is it low entry-barrier, the property that allows people to use a website with no site-specific training? Is it extensibility, the property that allows a website to undergo a complete redesign without breaking its clients? Or is it Internet scale, the property that allows everyone to use the web browser of their choice and upgrade at their own pace?

I've chosen extensibility and Internet scale, at the expense of low entry-barrier. That's because the semantic gap raises the entry-barrier all on its own. Any API is more difficult to use than an equivalent website. A hypermedia-based design raises the entry-barrier higher, but it gives you extensibility and Internet scale, which are essential for the long term.

And this is a long-term project. We can get the entry-barrier back down with smarter client libraries, with agreements to use common hypermedia types and common sets of application semantics. But if we give up extensibility and Internet scale, we'll never get them back.

Glossary

application semantics

A representation's application semantics explain the underlying resource in terms of real-world concepts. Two HTML documents may use exactly the same tags but have completely different application semantics—one of them describes a person, and the other describes a medical procedure.

If a document format is designed to represent real-world concepts, we can say the format itself has application semantics. The Maze+XML format has the application semantics necessary to represent maze games. The HTML format has the application semantics of a human-readable document. The HAL format has no application semantics to speak of: each user must supply their own.

The term "application semantics" was invented for this book. It's not a standardized term.

application state

Information about the client's path through an API is application state. Most clients start in the same state, at an API's "home page." As they make different choices, they trigger different hypermedia controls, they end up in different places, and their application states diverge.

cache

A repository of HTTP responses, used to improve client performance. A client can sometimes reuse a cached response instead of sending a request over the network.

code on demand

One of the Fielding constraints. This one says that the server may send executable code in addition to data. This code is automatically deployed on the client and can change along with the rest of the server implementation. APIs rarely implement this constraint due to security concerns.

connectedness

My term for the hypermedia constraint (q.v.). I prefer this term because it focuses on what I find important: that resources are "connected" to each other by safe state transitions..

dereferencing

A computerized process that turns a URL into a representation. For *http:* URLs, dereferencing means sending an HTTP GET request to the URL.

embedded link

A link that, when triggered, adds to the client's application state instead of replacing it. Embedded links are often triggered automatically, as with HTML's `<img>` and

`<script>` tags. Contrast *outbound link*, and see also *transclusion*.

entity-body

The document associated with an HTTP request or response. Typically, this document is a representation of some resource.

header

A key-value pair associated with an HTTP request or response.

HATEOAS

Acronym for "hypermedia as the engine of application state" (q.v.).

hypermedia

Hypermedia is data, sent from the server to the client, which explains what the client can do next. HTML links and forms are hypermedia. The defining feature of a RESTful API is that it obeys the hypermedia constraint: its representations contain hypermedia controls which describe possible state transitions.

hypermedia as the engine of application state

One of the Fielding constraints. I call it the "hypermedia constraint" for short. The server manipulates the client's state by sending a hypermedia "menu" containing options from which the client is free to choose.

hypermedia control

A hypermedia control describes a state transition. In a web API, a hypermedia control usually has two parts. The most important part is the description of an HTTP request (or a family of requests) that the client might make. Less important is the link relation, which explains the state transition that will happen if the client makes that HTTP request.

Some hypermedia controls are supposed to be triggered automatically (like HTML's `<img>` tag). Others will only be triggered if the client decides to trigger them (like HTML's `<a>` tag).

HTTP method

Also called "HTTP verb." That part of an HTTP request that tells the server, on a very basic level, what the client wants to do to a resource.

idempotent

An idempotent state transition has the same effect whether it is triggered once, or more than once. The HTTP methods PUT, DELETE, LINK, and UNLINK are supposed to be idempotent. A client can retry these methods over an unreliable network until they go through.

Any safe state transition (q.v.) is also idempotent.

information resource

A resource whose native form is a stream of bits, as opposed to a physical object or an abstract concept. An information resource can serve as its own representation.

link relation

A string associated with a hypermedia control. The link relation explains which state transition will happen if the client triggers the control. A link relation may describe a change in application state (such as `next` and `previous`), or a change in resource state (such as `edit`).

RFC 5988 defines two kinds of link relations: *extension* relations, which are URIs; and *registered* relations, short strings that must be "registered" somewhere to avoid collisions.

media type

A media type (also called a *content type* or *MIME type*) is a short string identifying the format of a document. Once you know a document's media type, you can parse it. You may also be able to understand of its application and protocol semantics.

outbound link

A hypermedia control that replaces the client's application state with a brand new state when triggered. An HTML `<a>` tag contains an outbound link. Contrast *embedded link*.

overloaded POST

Using the HTTP POST method to trigger a state transition that can do anything at all. Contrast *POST-to-append*.

POST-to-append

Using the HTTP POST method to create a new resource "beneath" another one. Contrast *overloaded POST*.

profile

A profile explains bits of a document's semantics that aren't covered by its media type. A profile is like a pair of magic glasses that reveals previously unseen aspects of a document's meaning.

For example, the hCard profile can turn an ordinary HTML document into a description of a human being. There's nothing in the HTML standard about describing human beings. The profile does the extra work.

A client that doesn't understand a profile can still parse a document and get information out of it, based on its understanding of the document's media type. But it'll be missing an extra layer of semantics.

protocol semantics

A hypermedia control talks about an HTTP request (or a family of requests) that a client might make. These are its protocol semantics. They tell you which subset of the HTTP protocol is useful in this situation.

A hypermedia control may also have application semantics. The application semantics explain in real-world terms what information needs to be provided to the server along with the HTTP request, what will happen in response to the request, or how the client should incorporate the response into its workflow.

When a document contains hypermedia controls, we say the document itself has protocol semantics. The document allows all of the HTTP requests defined by its hypermedia controls.

When a document format allows for hypermedia controls, we say the format itself has protocol semantics. For example, we can say that the protocol semantics of HTML allow for GET and POST requests, but not PUT requests.

The term "protocol semantics" was invented for this book. It's not a standard term.

representation

A representation is a piece of data that describes the state of a resource. Typically, a representation is a document used as the entity-body of an HTTP request or response. In some cases, it may help to think of the entire request or response message as a "representation."

When a server sends a representation to a client, it's describing the current state of a resource. When a client sends a representation to a server, it's trying to modify the state of a resource.

resource

A resource can be anything: a web page, a person, that person's name, a measurement of his weight on a given day, his relationship to another person... anything at all. The only restriction is that a resource must have its own URI. Without a URI, there's nothing to talk about.

A client will never directly interact with a resource. It only sees descriptions of a resource's state, written down in representations.

resource state

Representations are full of resource state. A representation conveys information about the current state of the resource (when a server sends a representation to a client), or about the desired new state of the resource (when a client sends a representation to a server).

In the world of web APIs, resource state is typically divided up into discrete chunks (such as a person's name), with each piece described by a semantic descriptor. But this is more a fact about the way we write computer programs than a fact about REST. The World Wide Web doesn't work this way.

resource type

When you want to talk about the real-world thing or concept behind a resource (as opposed to the data in its representations), you can use a resource type. A resource type is a URI that classifies a resource under an abstract category like person (or, to be more precise, `http://schema.org/Person` or `http://xmlns.com/foaf/0.1/Person`).

safe

Triggering a safe state transition should has the same effect on resource state as doing nothing at all. The HTTP methods GET, HEAD, and OPTIONS are supposed to be safe.

self-descriptive messages

One of the Fielding constraints. It says that all the information necessary to understand a request or response message is contained in (or at least linked to from) the message itself.

semantic descriptor

A short string that names a discrete piece of resource state. A semantic descriptor is usually given a human-readable description by a nearby profile, and different profiles may give different names to the same information: consider "given-name" (hCard), "givenName" (schema.org), and "firstName" (FOAF).

The term "semantic descriptor" was invented for this book. It's not a standard term.

semantic gap

The gap between the structure of a document and its real-world meaning—its application semantics. Media types, machine-readable profiles, and human-readable documentation bridge the semantic gap in different ways, but bridging the gap always requires the intervention of a human being at some point.

The term "semantic gap" was invented for this book. It's not a standard term. We call the challenge of bridging the semantic gap the *semantic challenge*.

statelessness

One of the Fielding constraints. The upshot of the statelessness constraint is that the client is in charge of all application state, and the server is in charge of all resource state.

state transition

A change in application or resource state. A link relation is the name of a state transition. A hypermedia control explains which HTTP request will trigger a particular state transition.

transclusion

Embedded links (q.v.) transclude one representation into another. When a web browser encounters an `<img>` tag in an HTML document, it makes an HTTP request for a binary image and dynamically inserts a rendering of that image into the rendering of the HTML document. There's no need to keep the image and the HTML document in sync; they might even be on different servers.

uniform interface

One of the Fielding constraints. An umbrella term for the four "interface constraints" that describe the workings of the Web: identification of resources, manipulation of resources through representations, self-descriptive messages, and hypermedia as the engine of application state.

The uniform interface constraint covers most of what people think about when they think about "REST."

URI

A string that uniquely identifies a resource.

URL

A URI that can be dereferenced to get a representation. Not every URI is a URL. There's no way to dereference the URI *urn:isbn:9781449358063*, so it's not a URL.

Index

We'd like to hear your suggestions for improving our indexes. Send email to index@oreilly.com.

extension link relations, 64

F

Fiat standards, xxiii, 56, 157
Fielding constraints
    definition of, 29, 343
    development of, 356
    for uniform interfaces, 347
    hypermedia and, 350
    Representational State Transfer, 350
    resource identification, 348
    resource manipulation through representa-
        tions, 348
    self-descriptive messages, 349
Fielding, Roy, 29, 343
filesystems, 259
fn class, 114
FOAF, 285
<form> tags, 48, 111
From headers, 329
FTP (file transfer protocol), 14

G

GeoJSON, 225–230
GET method, 6
    as a safe method, 18, 25
    conditional GET, 242, 248
    details of, 34
    function of, 33
    in collection-based design, 100
    partial GET, 246
    pipelining, 247
    with <form> tag, 48, 111
Gopher protocol, 14
gzip, 245

H

HAL (Hypertext Application Language)
    basics of, 125, 216
HAL+JSON documents, 126
HAL+XML documents, 126
HATEOAS (hypermedia as the engine of appli-
    cation state)
    definition of, 360
    example of, 14
hCard format, 113

HEAD method
    details of, 40
    function of, 33
header-based content negotiation, 241
headers
    definition of, 360
    number available, 238
        (see also HTTP headers)
hMaze microformat, 114
home pages, in design process, 163, 170
Host headers, 329
HTML (HyperText Markup Language)
    adding application semantics to forms, 119
    as hypermedia format, 46, 109, 216
    benefits of, 110
    changing resource state with, 117
    class attribute, 112
    data structure in, 110
    hMaze microformat, 114
    HTML4 limitations, 124
    HTML5 advantages, 124
    hypermedia controls in, 110
    id attribute, 112
    microdata in, 116
    microformats for, 113
    plug-in application semantics for, 111
    rel attribute, 111
HTTP extensions
    LINK method, 258
    PATCH method, 257
    UNLINK method, 258
    WebDAV, 259
HTTP headers
    Accept, 239, 321
    Accept-Charset, 321
    Accept-Encoding, 245, 321
    Accept-Language, 239, 322
    Accept-Ranges, 246, 322
    Age, 322
    Allow, 322
    Authorization, 323
    Cache-Control, 242, 323
    Connection, 324
    Content-Disposition, 324
    Content-Encoding, 246, 325
    Content-Language, 325
    Content-Length, 325
    Content-Location, 218, 326
    Content-MD5, 326

About the Authors

Leonard Richardson (*http://www.crummy.com/*) is the coauthor of the *Ruby Cookbook* (O'Reilly) and of several open source libraries, including Beautiful Soup. A California native, he currently lives in New York.

An internationally known author and lecturer, **Mike Amundsen** travels throughout the United States and Europe consulting and speaking on a wide range of topics including distributed network architecture, web application development, and cloud computing. His recent work focuses on the role hypermedia plays in creating and maintaining applications that can successfully evolve over time. His 2011 book, *Building Hypermedia APIs with HTML5 and Node* (O'Reilly), is an oft-cited reference on building adaptable distributed systems. When he is not working, Mike enjoys spending time with his family in Kentucky.

Sam Ruby (*http://intertwingly.net/*) is a prominent software developer who is a cochair of the W3C HTML Working Group and has made significant contributions to many of the Apache Software Foundation's open source software projects. He is a senior technical staff member in the Emerging Technologies Group of IBM.

Colophon

The animal on the cover of *RESTful Web APIs* is Hoffmann's two-toed sloth (*Choloepus hoffmanni*). Hoffmann's two-toed sloth, named after German naturalist, Karl Hoffmann, is found in rainforests in Central and South America. Hoffmann's two-toed sloth is named for its two curved forefeet, which it uses to hang upside down on tree limbs.

Adult two-toed sloths typically grow up to 21 to 28 inches in length and weigh around 4.6 to 20 pounds. The large difference in weight is due to the fact that it typically takes up to a month for its three stomachs to digest its food content. Female two-toed sloths tend to be larger than their male counterparts. Both male and female two-toed sloths have tan or light brown fur with a slight greenish color due to algae. The diet of the two-toed sloth consists of fruit, flowers, and mostly tree leaves.

The two-toed sloth is a primarily nocturnal creature that spends most of its time in trees. Like many sloths, the two-toed sloth is a notoriously slow animal, but this slowness is due to its low-energy diet. Like many other species of sloth, they have bad eyesight and hearing, making them an easy target for predators.

The cover image is from Cassell's *Natural History*. The cover font is Adobe ITC Garamond. The text font is Adobe Minion Pro; the heading font is Adobe Myriad Condensed; and the code font is Dalton Maag's Ubuntu Mono.

Get even more for your money.

Join the O'Reilly Community, and register the O'Reilly books you own. It's free, and you'll get:

- $4.99 ebook upgrade offer
- 40% upgrade offer on O'Reilly print books
- Membership discounts on books and events
- Free lifetime updates to ebooks and videos
- Multiple ebook formats, DRM FREE
- Participation in the O'Reilly community
- Newsletters
- Account management
- 100% Satisfaction Guarantee

Signing up is easy:

1. Go to: oreilly.com/go/register
2. Create an O'Reilly login.
3. Provide your address.
4. Register your books.

Note: English-language books only

To order books online:
oreilly.com/store

For questions about products or an order:
orders@oreilly.com

To sign up to get topic-specific email announcements and/or news about upcoming books, conferences, special offers, and new technologies:
elists@oreilly.com

For technical questions about book content:
booktech@oreilly.com

To submit new book proposals to our editors:
proposals@oreilly.com

O'Reilly books are available in multiple DRM-free ebook formats. For more information:
oreilly.com/ebooks

O'REILLY®

9 781449 358068